Through Frosted Glass

by

Robin Blick

Published by New Generation Publishing in 2020

Copyright © Robin Blick 2018

Third and Revised Edition

The author asserts the moral right under the Copyright, Designs and Patents Act 1988 to be identified as the author of this work.

All Rights reserved. No part of this publication may be reproduced, stored in a retrieval system or transmitted, in any form or by any means without the prior consent of the author, nor be otherwise circulated in any form of binding or cover other than that in which it is published and without a similar condition being imposed on the subsequent purchaser.

Paperback ISBN: 978-1-80031-572-3
Hardback ISBN: 978-1-80031-571-6

www.newgeneration-publishing.com

New Generation Publishing

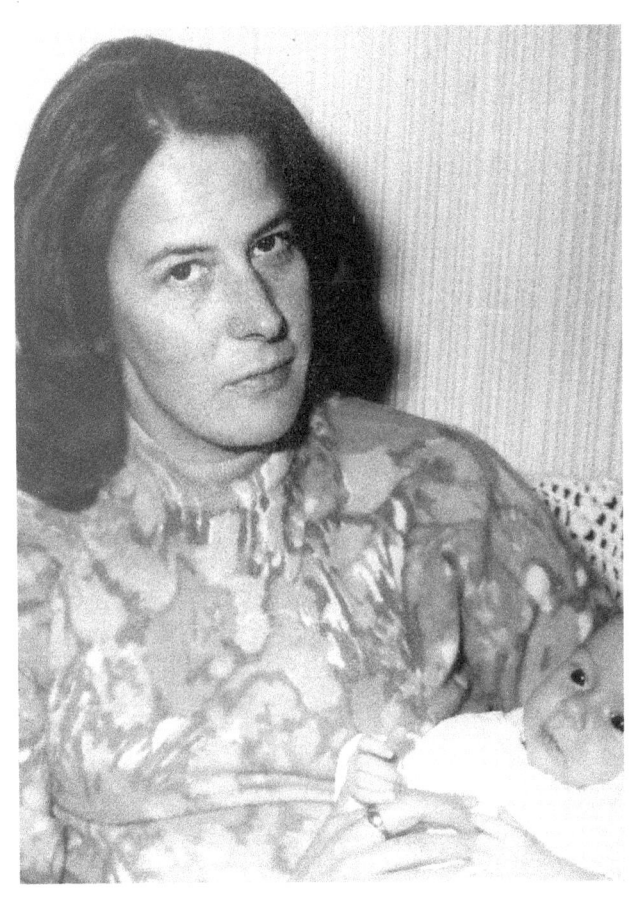

My Maureen

Not on fables of a time to come,
But this life's rock we built our love,
And were there found to be a god,
Still would I worship you alone.

Foreword

We *homo sapiens* are not only endowed more than any other species with the faculty of rational thought. We are also all born with an unequalled capacity for love, and no less with the need to be loved. And as we journey through our lives, we learn, all too often painfully, that reason and love, and indeed all that makes us no less *homo affectum* than *sapiens,* are not comfortable partners, and indeed can find themselves at war, tearing us apart, seated as they are in entirely separate locations of the brain. In conventional terms, we understand it as the difference between thinking and feeling. Did we but know it, for much of our lives, and in any number of situations, the cerebral cortex is at odds, and even at times at war, with the hypothalamus. That is why when depicted by art in all its forms, it is not comedy that moves us most, but, as the ancient Greeks understood, tragedy, which reveals humankind in all its frailties, while comedy, if we are lucky, only makes us laugh. Perhaps Aeschylus, Sophocles and Euripides have something to teach Hollywood, with its convention that every story must have a happy ending. Tragedy cuts its way to the very core of who and what we are, *homo divisa,* torn apart by forces intrinsic to our being that cannot be reconciled. Such is the stuff of my story.

What is true for the individual is multiplied a millionfold and more in the collective affairs of our species. History is replete with examples of what calamities will ensue if we allow feeling to intrude where only reason should rule. It is partly a matter of numbers, or as the German philosopher Hegel once said, the moment when changes in quantity produce a change in quality. The same people will behave differently when they are alone, at work, or amongst their families and intimate friends, than in a crowd, for example at a mass meeting or sporting contest. In the first, reason and social norms will tend to prevail, in the second, emotion. Depending upon circumstance, the reverse is also true. Two people (or even more) will do in bed what the law does not permit in public. A saying has it that there is a time and a place everything. Everything? In the 1930s, at enormous rallies, the Nazis demanded that Germans should cast reason aside and instead, 'think with their blood'. The result was the Second World War and the Holocaust.

Today, only now on the left, we witness a no less pernicious politics of 'identity', in which the feelings of those with certain genetic characteristics, be they of skin or gender, override considerations based on reason and evidence. This is indeed ironic, because for two centuries, as the debate raged over whether nature or nurture is the primary determinant of human behaviour, it was always the left, beginning with the Enlightenment and the French revolution's advocacy of the equality and brotherhood of mankind no less than its liberty, that favoured nurture, and the right, culminating in the Nazi theory and practice of racial inequality, that stressed nature and heredity.

Liberty, the right to speak what is in one's mind, to contest, to ridicule, if needs be to offend, has also gone the same way, complementing a battery of so-called 'hate speech' laws primarily designed to criminalise criticism of a certain religion imported to our shores. The new mantras for political discourse are, before you speak, 'check you privilege', (meaning one's genes or sexual preferences) do not offend, and 'always punch upwards', the target being the 'white patriarchy'. Those who do not conform are 'no platformed', heckled, slandered as racists, Islamophobes or transphobes, or physically intimidated into silence. These tactics, designed to supress the public discussion and advocacy of certain unpalatable truths and ideas, have contributed to the creating of a world of alterative facts, post truths and fake news, where subjectivity rules, where those whose brains have pickled by post-modernism tell us in all seriousness that what science regards as reality is merely a 'social construct' (not only gender, but even gravity), a world where every opinion, no matter how absurd, has to be 'respected', especially if it is religious, and even more so, of one religion in particular. Thanks to the betrayal of reason perpetrated by leftist academics, we in the west no longer inhabit a world that values objective, evidence-based scholarship. It is one in which its 'experts' are derided and ridiculed by demagogic populists of both left and right. Traditional polarities of the political spectrum no longer apply, as conspiracy theories, once the monopoly of the far right, migrate to the left. 9/11? An 'inside job'. By whom? Take your pick...George Bush? The Jews? Elvis? Anybody, just so long they are not the 19 Muslims who actually did it. Refutations of these and other conspiracies are dismissed as 'cover ups' by an 'establishment' which is always assumed to have something to hide.

It is not only conspiracy theories which have found a new home on the left. There was a time...it seems so long ago now...when it subscribed to Martin Luther King's maxim that a person should be judged not by the colour of their skin, but the quality of their character. It has now been supplanted on the left by Hitler's belief that the 'value of a man is determined by his inner racial virtues'. As a result, 'identity' politics, be it of gender, sexual orientation or race, now infests the left, where it can be a sin to be born white, male and heterosexual, but not considered 'hate speech' to post on-line messages with the hash tag 'kill all men', for a Toronto Black Lives Matter activist to describe all white people, women as well as men, as 'sub human', possessing 'recessive genetic defects' or Sasha Johnson, the Black Panther-attired leader of Oxford Black Lives Matter, to call a black man who disagreed with her a 'coon', and, as an advocate of 'Black Power', to tweet that 'the white man will not be our equal, he will be our slave'.

In apartheid South Africa, the whites, who constituted 20% of its population, after decades of unrelenting, ruthless repression, found themselves unable to sustain their ascendency over an unarmed, largely black non-white majority of 80%, a ratio of 1 to 4. Johnson's black power, if enforced in the UK, would require 3% of its population, its blacks, ruling over its (enslaved) whites, who, at the 2011 census, comprised 87% of the UK population, a ratio of 1 to 30. If indeed she is an Oxford University student, one suspects her chosen subject is not maths, history or demography.

Let those who are tempted to take again the path of genetic politics ponder the words of a white, very privileged heterosexual Victorian male, John Stuart Mill: 'Of all the vulgar modes of escaping from consideration of social and moral influences on the mind, the most vulgar is that of attributing the diversities of conduct and character to inherent natural differences.'

It would have been beyond the comprehension of both Mill and King, as fervent believers in the intellectual and moral progress of mankind, that in the second decade of the twenty-first century, self-defining liberals and leftists, many of whose parents would have rallied to the cause of racial integration in the days of Jim Crow, would be endorsing the demand for racially segregated 'safe spaces', dining facilities and even dormitories on university campuses. (This and other aspects of left-wing capitulations to the politics of identity are examined in more detail in my *Socialism of Fools: The Rise and Fall of Comrade* Corbyn, New Generation Publishing, 2020)

In these times when for so many, reality and truth are what we want them to be, we are in danger of betraying a legacy that reaches back to the ancient Greeks, and is the life-blood of modern civilisation in all its endeavours; the knowledge that there is only one reality, only one truth about it, and that these truths are, by their nature, discoverable.

I said at the beginning '*homo sapiens*', literally, not *thinking*, as often assumed, but *wise* person, the classification first coined in 1758 by Carl Linnaeus to distinguish modern man from his more primitive predecessors. But Linnaeus was being too kind to his own species. We are not born with wisdom, as the examples above demonstrate, but only the mental capacity to acquire it. And the history of mankind furnishes more than sufficient proofs that unlike knowledge, for example in science and technology, which is inherited, transmitted and accumulated socially, wisdom comes only through personal experience, often at great cost and is not, once acquired, as Lamarck and Lysenko, Stalin's quack agronomist, would have us believe, biologically inherited It is as if each of us, both individually and collectively as members of society, has to start from square one. Everyone agrees that we must learn the lessons of history, for example that appeasement encourages the aggressor to demand more. But the lessons continue to be unlearned. If it were otherwise, humanity would not have repeated over the last century, and what is more, on an unprecedented scale, the stupidities and barbarities of its infancy. Hegel, that often-obscure titan of German philosophy, for once spoke clearly when he coined his famous epigram, 'the owl of Minerva spreads its wings only with the falling of the dusk,' meaning that only at history's end will true wisdom come.

Consider just this. The same technology that in the year 2003, enabled images to be transmitted to earth from a space craft orbiting Jupiter, was later used by religious zealots to disseminate across our planet videos of decapacitations as a means of recruitment to their cause. *And it worked.* And why not? After all, they were simply obeying a command in their thirteen-hundred-year-old holy book, which in Chapter 8, Verse 12, instructed them to 'cast terror into the hearts of those who disbelieved and 'smite them above the neck'. Even more hard to comprehend is that the prospect of slicing off the heads of fellow human sufficed to persuade thousands of well-educated hereditary Muslims, like the notorious 'Jihadi John', to turn their backs on friends, family, and in some cases, a successful professional career (some as doctors would you believe) and take a one-way trip to Syria. Wielding the executioner's knife proved no less seductive even for western adult converts who hitherto had no knowledge of or contact with the religion of peace. Such an extraordinary phenomenon seems to defy any rational explanation. But there must be one, and if we could find it, it would surely help to explain why millions of apparently civilised Germans either acquiesced or willingly participated in the murder of six million Jews.

In citing the lunacies and barbarities committed in the name of Islam, we have far from fully plumbed the depths of contemporary human stupidity, moral depravity, credulity and seemingly wilful blindness. Of all whom the *Koran* describes as 'those who disbelieve' we must surely give pride of place to the current Pope, Francis II, spiritual and moral guide of the world's 1.2 billion infidel Roman Catholics, whom together with the Jews, the prophet Mohammed commanded his followers to 'take not friends'. Yet after reading the book in which is to be found (unless his was an expurgated edition) the instruction to behead the unbelievers, that is, along with the rest of the world's five billion infidels, himself, the Pope announced to the world that Islam and the *Koran* 'were opposed to *every form of violence*'. (My emphasis)

One can only assume from such a categorical statement that the Pope does not regard amputating a head simply because its owner has a different religion, or a hand or foot for theft, as acts of violence. Even so, what must he have made of the passage in the *Koran*, Chapter 5, Verse 33, which warns that 'those who wage war against God and His Messenger' should be 'punished by death, crucifixion' and the 'amputation of an alternate hand and foot'? Jesus also died on the cross, for our sins, so we are told. But surely crucifying him was a sin, indeed, there is no greater crime for the Roman church than that of deicide, because according to the doctrine of the Trinity, Jesus was both the son of God and God. Yet when the *Koran* authorises the crucifying of unbelievers, the Pope, as with decapitation, finds in this no evidence of Islamic violence. If decapitation, amputation and crucifixion do not qualify in the Pope's reckoning as religiously-inspired acts of violence, what does? Certainly not hi-jacking and then flying a passenger jet into a skyscraper.

What is it with Popes? Is this the best God can do with

his appointed representatives on planet earth? Pius XII heard and saw no evil as the Nazis murdered six million Jews, and afterwards helped some of their murderers escape the justice they so richly deserved, while Francis II's predecessor, former Hitler Youth Benedict XVI, seemed to spend most of his time protecting his paedophile clergy from prosecution. Then back in the sixties, we had Paul VI, the patron saint of back-street abortionists, who banned the use of the contraceptive pill. This did not inhibit the Vatican from investing, in addition to the pornography, arms and tobacco industries, a firm which manufactures... yes...*the pill*. Popes have even banned the use of condoms to prevent, not conception, as with the pill, but the spread of aids.

One cannot but wonder... if it is true, as cardinals say, that they seek and are given God's guidance in the election of a new Pope, why is it that they invariably vote for different candidates, and when the final choice is made, often after days or even weeks of very worldly horse-trading (while beyond the confines of St Peters, bookies shout the odds on the front-runners) why does the winner so often turn out to be such a bad lot?

But this is nothing new. In earlier times, one might expect that occupants of the chair of St Peter would embody the piety of their age. Yet two Popes were randy teenagers, while another two were murdered by cuckholded husbands. Others worshipped the devil, ran brothels (superseded today by 'massage parlours' for gay Vatican clergy) and begat children whom they passed off as nephews and nieces, and then, if they were boys, appointed to high office in the church. One Pope, John XXIII, was deposed after being found guilty of 54 crimes, of which only five, the mildest, were made public, namely piracy, murder, rape, sodomy and incest. Another struck a blow for his faith by anticipating by eight centuries the Nazi regulation that Jews had to wear a distinguishing mark on their clothing, and by ruling, again in relation to the Jews, that 'whoever is led to Christianity by violence, by fear and torture receives the imprint of Christianity and can be forced to observe the

Christian faith.'

Extracting confessions of heresy by torture as we all know was a routine matter for the Catholic Church. But here we have conversion by the same method. Can this be the Church founded by the sermoniser on the Mount? For good measure, the same Pope decreed that Magna Carta, despite its being drafted by Stephen Langton, Archbishop of Canterbury, and its first article declaring that 'the church shall be free', was heretical, since it made kings subject to temporal laws, and not those of God. In the light of the Holocaust, of far greater enduring import was his declaration that the only reason 'the Christian must not exterminate the Jews' was that they were needed to serve as 'the living witnesses to the truth of Christianity'. All this, and more, and yet, according to the website *Catholicism.org*, the Pope in question was 'one of the greatest in history', the first to proclaim himself 'Vicar of Christ', the stand-in for Jesus no less. His chosen name? Innocent III. Who says the devout don't have a sense of humour?

Like my father's vicar, there have also been atheist Popes. One, Leo X, a scion of the Florentine banking house of Medici, on being elected by the customary methods, jubilantly proclaimed, 'Since God has given us the Papacy, now let us enjoy it'. And enjoy it he did. At a lavish Vatican Easter banquet, in the company of seven booncompanions, two of whom recorded the event for posterity, he raised his chalice and proposed a toast: 'How well we know what a profitable superstition this fable of Christ has been for us and our predecessors.' But finding out by how much is another matter entirely. The Vatican bank, whose carefully massaged accounts were only published for the first time in 2013, had its criminal associations with the Mafia and the shady P2 Masonic lodge exposed after 'God's Banker', Roberto Calvi was found hanging from London's Blackfriars Bridge in 1982, weighed down with bricks in his pockets and £15,000 in three different currencies in his wallet. (The inquest conveniently returned a verdict of suicide, even though this has since been proved to have been technically impossible.)

After they were published, a scrutiny of the Vatican accounts revealed a large number of at the very least dubious deposits and withdrawals, with some suspected of being related either to money-laundering or, in the case of holdings by Islamic regimes, to do with funding terrorism. What was that the Pope said about Islam not being violent, and the Bible about not serving mammon?

Yes, I digress, as I will again when the occasion requires it, because life does not move in a single straight line. We are buffeted from all sides by events over which we have little, if any control, while far fewer are of our own making and more often not than not lead to consequences that we neither anticipated not wanted. Either through choice or necessity, we take to many byways on our journey, and my fascination with, no less than my enmity towards organised religion, re-kindled by an event over which I can assure the reader I had no control whatsoever, namely 9/11. But for now, enough of the God squad, and to return to *la condition humaine* of mere mortals.

As it is with every generation, so with every individual, each has to begin anew to learn by their experiences the inescapable lessons taught by life and death, of which the hardest and cruellest of all is that while nature and evolution have given us more liberally than any other living creature the power of reason and the wonderful gift of love, they have not endowed us so generously with the capacity to cope with the loss of those we love. Like no other emotion, love can enrich life, of those who feel and give it, and those who receive it. But grief? Whatever grief councillors may say, I do not see how the loss of a loved one can be shared anyone more than can the loss of an arm or a leg.

Living – and dying – as we do in a bread and circuses culture that panders to and feeds on a craving for instant gratification, and in which anything considered worth doing has to be described as fun (even studying the history of Nazi Germany, if we are to believe one of its leading exponents...Now boys and girls, let's have some fun...the Holocaust) one of its direst consequences has been the utter debasement of the act and meaning of love. Instead of love as the spontaneous desire to give all and share all with the one that one loves, an act of giving that asks for nothing in return, the word now serves to describe the desire to want, to take, to have, to buy, to consume. Likewise, with grief. Since the funeral of Princess Diana, it has become the norm, following the example set by politicians and celebrities, to 'emote', to advertise to the world on the latest electronic gadget a simulated despair and desolation at the death of total strangers.

This is not grief, since it evaporates as quickly and as painlessly as it comes. And neither is it compassion. Compassion is what we feel for the living, for the bereaved, for the grieving, not for the dead. Grief, like its twin, love, is spontaneous, all-consuming, overwhelming, enduring. The death of a loved one marks us for the rest of our lives, because our memories of them never leave us. Grief no more than love can be turned on and off like a tap, as its ersatz version now is in response to the latest news headlines. How can we grieve the death of someone of whom we have no memories and whom we have never loved?

Grief is the terrible price we pay for the enduring memory of the joys and glories of our lost loves and, as I have discovered, we pay it in a measure equal to each. Though we can in time perhaps learn to live with our grief, it will never leave us unless, that is, we lose our memories. But this impossible, because we are our memories, the sum total of all that has gone before and what makes us who we are.

The now prevalent abuse of such emotionally laden words as love and grief is part of a more general misuse of language, one of whose manifestations is born of an almost pathological fear of being seen as in any way 'privileged'. In these politically correct times, not being a 'victim' can invalidate anything one has to say on an ever-expanding range of subjects, irrespective of their intrinsic merit, the logical fallacy known as '*ad hominem*', the dishonest attempt to refute a proposition by attempting to discredit who says it, and ignoring what is being said. If one cannot pass oneself off as victim - and how the categories multiply - one can at least pretend to be 'humble'. Here the Queen, as befits her exalted station, has set the example. Whenever her faithful subjects assemble outside one of her five palaces to celebrate one of her several anniversaries, she invariably declares that she has been 'humbled' by their devotion. Likewise, film stars when awarded Oscars, Olympic athletes who win gold medals, politicians who win elections and in fact almost anyone who has either inherited or achieved public acclaim. How different from Dicken's day, when letters to the rich and powerful would be signed with the obsequious 'your most humble and obedient servant'. Only in the world of sporting journalism does its true meaning survive, where to be humbled means to have been administered a well-deserved thrashing. Assuming the guise of humility is now so much the accept norm, the 'done thing', that it can occur even at quite modest levels. My local paper ran a story on its sports page with the oxymoronic headline, 'Humbled to get Honour'. Surely, he meant to say, honoured, proud or even privileged. But instead of saying privileged, he checked it, and said, without meaning it, the exact opposite. If I genuinely felt humbled by an award, I would refuse it. *Chambers Dictionary* has evidently yet to catch up with the new, politically correct function of 'humbled', because it defines the word as 'to be abused, mortified, degraded', and is cognate with 'humiliated', in effect to feel oneself to be at the bottom of the pile, a loser, not, like our 'humbled' Queen, in her capacities as God's anointed Head of State, of the Commonwealth, the Church of England and the Armed Forces, by birth a winner, at the very top. How true the saying, 'humility is the worst form of conceit'.

Humble and its cognates are far from being the only words to have metamorphosed into their opposites, in so doing, emulating 1984 Newspeak, in which 'war is peace, and freedom is slavery'. On campuses, where the employment of highly paid 'diversity' and 'inclusivity' officers is standard practice, the remit is not, as one might naively assume, to promote these objectives in the realm of ideas, but to cater for the presumed special needs of students who are not white, male and heterosexual, as if they are some way incapable of looking after themselves and require a *loco parentis*. This mollycoddling in turn requires that such students need 'safe spaces', 'trigger warnings' and bans on controversial guest speakers that protect them from exposure to ideas they will find disturbing and physically threatening. So, diversity of identity necessitates uniformity of approved thought, and inclusion, the exclusion of those with the wrong thoughts. As they saying goes, if you treat grown-ups like children, some will behave like children. And that is exactly what has happened in the USA, where safe space infantilization of black students has led to the granting of a return to the very same practices of the Jim Crow era to which many attribute the problems experienced by black people today

In this book, I write of many things...politics, history, philosophy, ethics, music, psychology, theology. etymology, all matters which at different times in my life, I have evinced more than a passing interest, and in some instances, commanded my active, indeed passionate involvement. A story of the times and deeds of a single life, it is above a memorial to its most all-consuming passion, the woman I loved for nigh on sixty years, and who in the last seventeen years of her life, brought me unqualified joy and a contentment and fulfilment that I had never previously known. The story of our love is in many ways not a conventional one, and I have been assured by those that know it that it is a story worth the telling. But I tell it not for that reason alone. I have learned a truth that comes to all who suffer the loss of their lover. It is that grief, like love, cannot be conjured away by reason, because like love it comes from the very core of our being and indeed is the inescapable consequence of having loved and then lost one's love by death. And I have also learned that the grief we have to endure on the death of the one we love, and here I speak only of the love of lovers, is commensurate with the intensity and vintage of that same love.

In one of his wittiest epigrams, George Bernard Shaw said that youth is wasted on the young. And so, he could have added, are love and lovemaking. Making and sharing love has not only been the source and subject of some of our most sublime artistic creations. They are themselves akin to an art form, and require for their fulfilment not only passion but skill. There is no reason why age should diminish the first, and experience can only enhance the second.

What can the young truly know of love and grief? The young understand little of either because the passage of time binds like no other force. The longer and deeper the love, the more the intensity of the trauma of its loss of those with whom we have shared it. And so it has to be. For those who survive and have to endure the death of their beloved, love necessarily comes at the price of grief. We cannot escape paying it. However, we can, I believe, prepare ourselves for it, and by so doing, render it more bearable and even, as I am attempting to do now, by confronting it and transform grief into an enduring memorial to the loved one we have lost.

What has sustained me in the worst moments that have followed my Maureen's death is the certain knowledge that I was the love of her life, and that she knew no less surely, she was mine. As lovers do, we often spoke such words. But now that I am alone, I still have the testimonies to our love, because in what we wrote to each other, we said with a passion and conviction that brooks no doubt. Maureen has gone, but her letter declaring her love for me, which I reproduce in this book together with mine, remains. It is both my most precious possession and, in my grief, my main source of strength. So I say to the reader, who one day, may well find themselves in similar straights, do as we did.

I

I begin as I end, with Maureen, the love and the light of my life. My enduring passion for Maureen was set ablaze sixty three years ago, one November day in 1957, when I glimpsed this gorgeous black-haired beauty as she sauntered, without being aware of it, seductively, up a flight of stairs of a cosmetic factory situated in what was then the London Borough of Tottenham...the sublime amidst the mundane. Her white overall was smeared down the front with what I took to be lipstick, and Puritan though I then was, my loins throbbed at the sight of her perfectly contoured legs. So unforgettable was this moment – I can see her just as clearly now – that I was able to relate this vision in every detail (save that is for the legs) in a love poem I sent Maureen when I found her again forty-two years later. Perhaps it was not what romantics like to call love at first sight, but lust at first sight it certainly was. Love is not static, it either grows or withers. One thing is certain: that first encounter sowed the seeds of what was to become the ruling passion, and no less obsession, of my life. I know now that from that instant, I was in her thrall for ever.

Maureen Joyce Griggs, as she was then, began life, as I did a little more than two years previously, in North Middlesex Hospital in the London Borough of Edmonton, on the 4 January 1939. And another co-incidence, one of several, involved another hospital, Chase Farm, a few miles to the north in Enfield, where my mother, Elsie, worked as a nurse before she married my father, Bill, and where she died of breast cancer a mere twenty or so years later. This was same hospital where Maureen, still only a baby, nearly died after an operation for acute peritonitis and where, some thirty years later, her only child, Andrea was born, who, again co-incidentally, shares with me the same birthday, 19 October. Both Maureen and I have unusual surnames. Griggs, which gave Maureen her school nickname, Griggo, is Scottish, to be more precise, Pictish in origin and related to the much more common Scottish Greig. Both are derived from the diminutive of Gregory. The Norwegian composer Edward Grieg's father was of Scottish descent. As for the even rarer Blick, it is probably Teutonic in origin, since in German, it means 'look' 'view' or 'glance'. There have been several attempts by amateur genealogists to trace its origin. It could be Jewish, (Yiddish is akin to German) Huguenot or Flemish, from Bliq, a village in Belgium. A family tree in the possession of my younger brother Gerald traces my father's paternal ancestors back to the mid-18th century, to one William Daniel Blick, a cooper by trade, who hailed from Newington in the plebeian heart of old London. All his male descendants down to my dad's father pursued similar artisan occupations and were born, married and worked in the same small area of London. All bore the same Teutonic name, William, down to the middle name of my elder brother Peter.

The pre-industrial London craftsmen were the backbone of the radical movements of their day, free-thinking in matter religious and always agitating for political and social reform, the precursors, and in later years pioneers of Chartism and the skilled workers' trade unions of the mid-nineteenth century. I cannot prove it, but I have good reasons to suppose that the radical politics of my father were an inheritance of William Daniel Blick, cooper.

While both my parents were of cockney stock, Elsie from Stepney and Bill from nearby Shoreditch, Maureen's beloved dad Freddy, one of a brood of eleven, hailed from what was at the turn of the century a still largely rural Enfield. Swansea-born Alice, Maureen's mother, had a truly Celtic pedigree, part Welsh, and part Irish. In the thirties, like millions of others from similar backgrounds, both Maureen's father and mine fell on hard times. Freddy signed up for a term in the army that took him to what is now modern Iraq, while Bill, a gifted multilinguist, came home after losing his job at a German shipping company in Bremerhaven, only to spend the next few years tramping the streets of London in futile pursuit of employment. It was this dispiriting experience – one he once told me haunted him in his dreams – that more than any other convinced him to become involved in far-left politics, a legacy that I inherited in full measure.

Those who specialise in such things assure us that the imprint of the family marks us for life. If true, and it probably is, it may well have contributed to Maureen as an only child being more self-reliant that most, and in later life, when she first knew and in time came to care for me, stubborn to the point of being reluctant to yield up any of her independence for the sake of love. It was a decision, or rather a lack of one, she later much regretted no less than myself. 'I was stupid,' she told me when, after parting, we met again thirty-three years on. But as we shall see, no more so than I was at the time. In fact, probably less.

I was the middle one of three boys, Peter, the elder, and Gerald. Peter was more Asperger's (an inheritance of mixed blessing from our father I came to recognise only after his death) than me by some distance, being totally immersed in sound reproduction. His obsession stood him in good stead in later years, when with several patented inventions to his name, he became a much sought-after sound engineer, travelling round the UK and the continent installing sound systems at elite cinemas, including Warner Brothers in Leicester Square. Shy and introverted in the extreme, he never married and through self-neglect that often goes with being a recluse, died well before his time. Gerald was the most 'normal' of the three. When his dream of becoming, a novelist came to nothing he settled for a successful career as a librarian. His life has been marked by two tragedies, first losing his mother while a child, and then his son Daniel, a high-flying banker, who after nearly succumbing to an overdose, hanged himself at the age of thirty. Unlike Peter, who had no interest in sport whatsoever, except to wind up me, a Spurs supporter like my dad, by saying under his breath but audibly, 'up the Arsenal' every time the radio football results announced a Gunners victory. Gerald was and still is a keen, one might say fanatical tennis player, competing in national veterans' tournaments and, as result, again unlike Peter, remains for his age remarkably fit.

When after a long illness with breast cancer, our mother died in September 1953, we three brothers, with me now in my middle teens, were augmented by the arrival of stepbrother Chris, the only child of Gwen, a widow who had remained the best friend of my mother from their nursing days at Chase Farm. Within a matter of weeks, my father had married Gwen, a decent sort, more out of dire necessity than love. But they rubbed along quite well, which is more than I can say for myself. I must have deep down resented her supplanting my mother, even though Gwen had shown great courage in taking on the care of four grown boys. When I related this phase of my life to Maureen some years later, she rightly berated me for my lack of gratitude. Looking back, my only justified grudge against Gwen was her failing to consult my father's three sons over the arrangements for his funeral. Had we been asked, and knowing our father's views about religion, we would have insisted on a humanist ceremony. Instead, we were confronted with the *fait accomplis* of a Christian one. Outraged, I quietly slipped out of the chapel. As for my dad, he loved and missed Elsie so profoundly that he even confided to me shortly after her death that but for us boys, he would have 'done away' with himself. It was about then that I noticed he had removed my mum's photo from his wallet. His heart had been broken. How could I, a teenage schoolboy who knew next to nothing of life and nothing at all of the love of lovers, begin to comprehend his anguish? I cannot explain why, but I only properly grieved for my mother when a full ten years after her death, my dad showed me a photograph of my mum in her pre-war nurse's uniform. It was then that I shed tears for her for the first time, but not the last.

But I run ahead. Within a year of the outbreak of war in September 1939, Maureen and I (again co-incidentally) had become not so distant neighbours in the rural backwaters of Buckinghamshire. About a year after the outbreak of the war, Maureen had been sent there by her parents to stay on a smallholding with family friends, a childless couple, to recuperate from a near-fatal operation for peritonitis, while the same year, I was one of thousands of London evacuees fleeing the blitz. Whereas Maureen's guardian was strict, and not averse to dealing out the occasional hefty slap, I was initially billeted with Aunt Lilly, one of my mum's two sisters, a fat, rumbustious, easy-going, jolly woman who dwarfed her quietly spoken and rather fastidious husband Tom, a technician with the Pye radio firm. They had two boys, John, about my age, and David, a bit younger, whom they had adopted. When after our re-union, Maureen and I compared notes on our war-time experiences, we found that we had been living but a few miles apart, she in Buckingham, I just a few miles down the road in Hardwick, a small village outside Aylesbury. In the summer of 2000, we revisited each of our country retreats, and discovered, much to our pleasure and surprise, that they were both as we remembered them.

While Maureen spent most the war in her Buckingham idyll, after a no less blissful two years with Lilly and Tom, I was shunted off to my mum's other sister, Gladys, who lived in Upminster, Essex, with her husband Bert and their sexually precocious daughter Valery, who was a little older than me. She seemed to know all there was to know about what she called, quite accurately on reflection, 'baby making'. And it was not only talk, because one night in our shared bedroom, she attempted with my assistance to give a practical demonstration of what was involved in this undertaking. Seeing that I was only seven years old at the time, it was only to be expected that for all her encouragement, I failed miserably to rise to the occasion. Perhaps together with my mild Asperger's, this experience accounts for my later inhibitions when it came to acting on my amorous feelings.

There was also in residence a rather mysterious and youthful 'Uncle Claude', whose relationship to the rest of the family I at first could not quite work out. I learned in time that he was the over-indulged baby of my mum's family, never lasting in a job more than a few weeks, sponging off his sister Gladys, and full of talk about what job he was going to do next but never did.

Unlike Maureen, who for the duration of the war was totally unaware of the epic battles being fought out around the globe, my memories are very different. There was an anti-aircraft gun battery situated just down the road from my home in Edmonton, North London, where on most nights, the air raid siren would begin to wail, and the guns open up on the Nazi bombers above. On the way to school the next morning (this was just before my evacuation), I and other boys would pick up shrapnel and swap unwanted items as we would in peace time exchange cigarette picture cards.

My next encounter with the realities of war came when I was transferred from Aunt Lilly's cottage in what seemed me at the time to be sleepy Buckinghamshire to Upminster in Essex. In fact, Buckinghamshire was anything but a backwater, being host to two US Army Force bases, a military hospital, prisoner-of-war camps, a training school for Commonwealth pilots and the residence of the Czechoslovak government-in-exile and the exile King Zog of Albania. It was also witness to epoch-shaping events of a related kind when in the mid-seventeenth century, under the Cromwell Commonwealth, the Levellers, heirs to the radical seeds first sown by Magna Carta and the peasant rebels of 1381, enunciated as never before the principles of the liberty and democracy being defended by US airmen stationed, just a few miles away from Maureen and I, at Bovingdon and Cheddington. Only one in five US bomber crewmen (all volunteers be it noted) survived to complete their 35-mission tour of duty in in the first two years of operations, when day raids rendered them easy targets for German fighters and flak guns. Night bombing, adopted in 1943, reduced losses, but even so, the survival rate overall was barely 50%. How right then that looking down on the very field at Runneymede where Magna Carta was enacted on June 16, 1215, there should be the memorial to the

55,000 airmen who gave their lives defending one of the foundation stones of western civilisation, that all, no matter what their station, should have both access and be subject to the same laws. Try telling that to Rowan Williams, the previous Archbishop of Canterbury, who believes the United Kingdom should incorporate elements of Islamic law, the *Sharia*, into its legal system to accommodate what he believed, correctly for more than 50% of them, were the wishes of its Muslims.

Upminster lay near to the flight path of *Luftwaffe* bombers making for London up the Thames estuary, and Allied bombers heading the other way to Germany. It so happened that to get to and from my new school at Upminster Bridge, I had to travel eastwards one stop on the Essex branch of the District Line. One day after school, instead of catching the usual electric train home, I climbed aboard one powered by a much more inviting steam locomotive. Packed to bursting with servicemen in full uniform, it roared past my stop heading full speed for London. Seeing my obvious state of distress as my train whizzed by station after station, some kindly soldiers put me off at Barking, the final stop before London, and helped to set me on my way back home via the less glamorous District line. I can recall quite clearly that I was aware that travelling with me on that train were men who were headed for some distant battlefront, some of them for sure never to return.

Then there was Uncle Claude's map. It was pinned up on a wall in the living room. Again, I can clearly remember Claude triumphantly tracing the movements on the Eastern front – this must have after the battle of Stalingrad – as the Red Army began to drive the Nazis back to Berlin. But clearest of all in my memory, and I can still picture and hear it now, was the evening of 30 May 1942. Double British Summer-Time operated then, and being a sunny day, it was still very light. Uncle Bert was, like his brother-in-law Tom, a very reserved man. His hobby was making model war-planes, bombers mostly as I recall, out of scraps of metal and the like...there were no kits to buy in those times. And he was very good at it. I can still remember the acrid smell of the glue and paint he used.

That evening, Bert was out in the garden, and I was indoors, in the back room that looked out to where Bert was standing, looking up at the sky. Then I heard a rumbling sound that had become louder and louder. It was real bombers, hundreds in strict formation, part of the first thousand bomber raid on Germany (1,047 to be precise) as, weighed down with their bomb loads, their engines roared flat out, struggling to gain more altitude. As I have said, Bert was a reserved man. But there he was, brandishing his fist, and bellowing above the din, 'Give it to them, give it to them.' And give it them they did. One of the few buildings left standing the next morning in Cologne city centre was the magnificent twin-towered Cathedral, which Maureen and I admired and photographed from across the Rhine more than sixty decades later. After more than year of England being blitzed by Hitler's *Luftwaffe,* and just as Bomber Harris had promised, the Nazis were reaping what they had sown.

Once back at home at the war's end, I closely followed news of the arrest and then trial of the top Nazi leaders at Nuremberg. I remember reading accounts of the court proceedings in the Communist Party's *Daily Worker* (now *Morning Star*) and seeing their newsreel coverage at our local cinema. Ten went to the gallows, nearly all of them unrepentant, while hundreds more escaped the noose via the Vatican's 'rate line' to South America and the Middle East.

While I have always been opposed to capital punishment for what might be best described as 'civilian' crimes, I feel compelled to make an exception in the unique case of those responsible for the calculated extermination of six million human beings purely on account of their ethnic origins. No prison term, however long or harsh, can possibly atone for a crime of such monstrous proportions. That is of course if one believes in retribution which, as it happens, I do.

And what, as the question used to go, did our fathers do in the war? As I was indulging the boyish pursuits of shrapnel-swapping and bomber spotting, and Maureen serving her time as an apprentice farm-hand, my dad, by now too old for the armed forces, was drafted into the fire brigade and despatched to the London docks to dowse the infernos of the Blitz, while Maureen's Freddy was helping to build bombers to dish out the same treatment to German port cities like Hamburg, as was the father of my future wife, Karen..

By another quirk of fate, it was again the war, only this time its conclusion, that brought Maureen and I with our parents to Trafalgar Square to celebrate VE Day on 8 May 1945. Maureen was by now six years old, I was eight. With the peace that followed began what some would say was my political mis-education. And since it was my political commitments that were in large part one of the causes of my parting from Maureen after five years of an ever-deepening friendship, their story needs to be told.

Perhaps I should begin by pointing out that the year of my birth, 1936, was one punctuated by a series of momentous political events, all them heralding the war that was to come three years later, events which I was to write about decades hence in the course of my twin careers as academic and political activist. In the March of that year, Hitler called the bluff of Britain and France by marching his army into the Rhineland in defiance of the Versailles Treaty. In May, rioting Arabs foreshadowed the current Middle East conflict between Israel and its Muslim enemies by staging a pogrom of Jews in the Palestinian British Mandate. In the same month, defying a toothless League of Nations, Mussolini proclaimed the creation of his Fascist empire in Abyssinia. In July, General Franco, with the backing of landowners, wealthy businessmen, reactionary army officers, the Catholic church, Hitler and Mussolini, launched his civil war against the Spanish republic. In August, Stalin staged the first of his infamous show trials of Lenin's old comrades. Finally, in October, Mosely's black-shirted fascists and leftists clashed in the East End 'Battle of Cable Street'. What a year! And there was much worse to come.

My father was like me one of three sons, the others being Eddie and Bert. Eddie became a fireman and a communist, and Bert a white-collar worker and closet Tory. There was also a sister, Flo, who had, as they say, ambitions above her station, and fulfilled them by marrying the brother of the radio comedian Sam Costa. By the time I knew her, she was talking posh, wearing black netting around her face, and painting her fingernails a bright red, which revolted me (as artificially coloured fingernails still do). Their dad, also William, was a compositor in the print trade, and as an active trade unionist, held the highly responsible post of Father of his chapel. Born at the turn of the century, William junior grew up not only in a family where political matters were an everyday topic of conversation, but in a world torn apart by war and its ensuing political and social upheavals

In Britain, the Labour Party, founded in 1900, was beginning to supplant the Liberals as the main opposition to the Conservatives. Industrial militancy surged, climaxing in the General Strike of 1926. Abroad, even greater changes were in train. There was the 'Great War', and in its wake, radical political change, much of it violent, right across Europe. Monarchies fell, to be replaced by democratic republics in Germany and Austria, and by a totalitarian version of communism in Russia. In Italy, the far right won out as fascism beat back the leftist challenge. Not surprisingly, all these historic events left their mark on my father. Just before the war, he had won a free scholarship to the elite fee-paying Enfield Grammar School, five years later matriculating in all seven compulsory subjects. Finding himself in a class composed almost entirely of boys from wealthy homes and opinions to match, he rather naively set about trying to convert Tory toffs to a rather leftish version of socialism. They replied by squeezing him between two classroom benches.

Nothing daunted, my dad joined the Labour Party in his late teens, and was instrumental in founding the party's first youth section, which in later years served chiefly as a battleground between any number of leftist factions. On his return from Germany after losing his job in Bremerhaven, he, like many others of his generation across Europe, became convinced that the only answer to the failings of capitalism and the menace of fascism was communism. I am not sure when exactly he joined the Communist Party, but he told me that he took part in a bid to disrupt Sir Oswald Mosely's black shirt rally at the London Olympia stadium in 1934, and but for his family obligations, would have volunteered to fight in Spain against General Franco's fascists in 1936. Both were primarily communist initiatives. Certainly, by the end of the war, my dad must have become a highly-trusted party member, because, posing as loyal Labourite, he was one of a select few trusted to participate in a typical clandestine leftist infiltration of the Labour Party.

In my father's case, this did not go entirely to plan. Bill was anything but a yes-man, and he did not take kindly to the Communist Party's advocacy of continuing the war-time coalition under Churchill. I recall him proudly showing me the copy of a letter he wrote to the then leader of the communist party, Harry Pollitt, in which he argued cogently, and as it proved, correctly, that Labour would win the upcoming General Election and so be able to form a government on its own. Again, I do not know precisely when or why my dad left the Communist Party (Gerald tells me it was after the suppression of the Hungarian revolution by the Kremlin in 1956) but I do remember that when, in my later teens, I was considering following in his footsteps, he, without overtly trying to dissuade me, stated with some vehemence that the Communist Party was run by a gang of crooks, something he had obviously learned by his own experiences as a member. How right he was, even though it would take me a good few more years before I found it out, as is usually the case, as I have already said, the hard way, by experience. And I should here make it clear that at no time did my dad try to impose on me his own political views. Rather I absorbed them by osmosis. After all, I grew up in a home where my parents and the occasional guest discussed politics and current events as a matter of course, as one might the weather, so naturally, it was from quite an early age that I used to listen with increasing fascination to what they had to say about them.

Understandably then, there are several political events from my childhood that I can still recall quite clearly. The earliest occurred at what proved to be one of the great turning point in British history. On the day the results of the 1945 General Election were being announced over the radio, my mother for some reason had to go out, so she left me with pencil and paper, and strict instructions to write them down, though without explaining to me why they were so important. I don't remember how I coped with this task, but I do recall being aware that something of great significance was happening. And indeed, it was. Labour won by a landslide, with a majority of one hundred and forty-six, and went on to lay the foundations of our welfare state. Five years later, on the eve of the next General Election, my dad took me to a Tory election meeting at the local town hall. Edmonton, where we lived, was a safe Labour seat, so a squad of Labour supporters, no doubt augmented by communists, decided to have some fun at the doomed Tories' expense by occupying the un-reserved places in the balcony, there to unleash salvoes of barracking and heckling that at times rendered the speakers inaudible. I loved it, as by now I was fully aware of which side we, that is our family, were on, and why. But on the way home, my dad offered words of caution. 'Don't be impressed by who makes the most noise, but by what they say.' And again, he was right.

I can also remember my dad having a letter published in the local paper during the time of the Korean War. Without saying it in so many words, the purpose of my dad's letter was to defend Stalin's foreign policy, being one which, unlike that of the United States, was supposedly entirely devoted to the cause of world peace. Looking back, I can now see that he must still have been operating inside the

Labour Party as an under-cover communist, a tactic that later become known as entryism when deployed by the Communist Party's deadly rivals, the Trotskyists. Little did I know that ten or so years later, I would be joining one of their many fractious grouplets, all of whom were at that time engaged in exactly the same duplicitous undertaking, my first step along a path that would tear me away from my beloved Maureen.

Then of course there was – and still is, I regret to say – religion. Like many parents in those days, devout or not, mine, who belonged to the latter category, packed me off to Sunday School so they could indulge in one of the seven deadly sins. As for me, all I can recall is a room above a shop at the end of our road where a lady related what I am sure would have been morally edifying stories from the Bible. Another contact with religion, apart from school assemblies, was compulsory monthly attendance at church parades when I was briefly a member of the boy scouts. Briefly, because I found the services so mind-numbingly boring and a total waste of time that I started to dodge them, which led rapidly to my expulsion. This of course was a time when membership of the boy scouts required the taking of a religious oath. However, my heathen tendencies did not prove an obstacle to my continued selection, after my expulsion, for the troop football team. My only really serious encounter with organised religion occurred in my third year at grammar school, when a friend died of a sudden brain haemorrhage. The presiding clergyman at his funeral intoned that it was not his place to explain why one so young had been taken from those who loved him. I remember thinking to myself, 'But it is. That is precisely your job'.

At home, I can recall only three occasions on which religion ever became a subject for comment by my parents, and one was at my own instigation. I must have been around sixteen years old at the time when I asked my dad if he believed in God. Instead of giving me a direct answer, he told me a story. When he was about my age, but unlike me, a church goer (he had a good tenor voice, and sang in the choir) he confessed to his vicar that he was wrestling with this very same question. The vicar replied that he had no doubts whatsoever. God did not exist. The conclusion I, like my Dad, was left to draw was that if there were clergymen who did not believe in God, why should anyone else.

On another occasion, apropos what I cannot now remember, my dad cited Karl Marx's dictum that 'religion is the opiate of the people'. By way of an example, he recited to me the nowadays rarely sung and theologically incorrect third verse of the hymn 'All things bright and beautiful': 'The rich man in his castle, the poor man at his gate, God made them high and lowly, He ordered their estate'. (In the same passage quoted by my father, Marx makes the trenchant observation, now out of fashion on the left when applied to Islam, that 'the criticism of religion is the beginning of all criticism.') The only comment I can recall my mum making about religion was to condemn, with such feeling as befits a former nurse, the Roman Catholic teaching that faced with a choice between saving a mother in labour and her baby, the doctor or midwife must save the child and let the mother die. So, although over time I got the drift of what my parents felt about religion and politics, I was never aware of any attempt to make me conform to their opinions, and this liberal attitude I and my wife attempted to emulate in the upbringing of our own two children. If they asked what we thought about this or that, we would tell them, since they had a right to know. But what they might think or believe was up to them.

The only occasion on which I found this difficult was when both of my children came home just after starting school for the first time. They each asked me the same question…who or what is God? Andrew was four, Katharine five, yet here they were, asking a question that down the ages, theologians have been saying is beyond human comprehension. This absurd situation had only arisen because here in the UK, unlike nearly all other countries in the civilised world, all state schools must by law require pupils to participate in, not just attend, a daily act of worship. Because of this law, (which most parents today, including many religious ones, oppose) I was put in a situation that no parent, whether believer or not, should have to cope with. Should I say, some people believe that someone called God made everything, while others say he (God was still male then) does not exist and leave it at that? But children want to know what their parents think, at least mine did, just as I did. But if I tell them what I believe to be the truth, that there is no proof whatsoever for the existence of a god or gods, then they will wonder why their school is telling them the opposite.

I can't remember exactly how I dealt with it, (though Katherine insists that I told her there was no god) but my point is, the situation should never have arisen. Why not do as they do in France and the USA, where churches are for religion, and schools for education? Learn *about* religion and its many versions by all means. But compelling children from the age of four to pray to an entity they cannot possibly comprehend is both a waste of valuable school time and, more to the point, a violation of a child's right to make up its mind in its own good time about the big questions of life and death. So much for religion, at least until it thrust itself back into my life, just like everyone else's, after 9/11. Meantime, there was politics.

Though it was in my last two years at grammar school when I was studying for my A levels that I really began to take a serious interest in politics, I had become fascinated by history at a much earlier age. I waded through all ten bulky volumes of Arthur Mee's *Children's Encyclopaedia*, and was awestruck – as I still am – by the account and depiction by Jacques-Louis David of the heroism of Leonidas and his doomed Three Hundred at the battle of Thermopylae, and only a little less enthralled, so I must confess, by the exploits of British colonists in Africa. (A sad comment our times, the film 300 has been criticised for being anti-Islam, even though it depicts events that occurred nine centuries before the birth of Mohammed. Four members of Iran's puppet parliament called on all Muslim countries to ban the film, re-acting the response of a number of Islamic governments to Schindler's *List*, which they banned for being unsympathetic to the Nazis.)

Although it must be all of seventy years ago now, I still have a vivid memory of the time when my dad took me with him on a visit to two elderly blue stockings in a large house in Hammersmith. They could have been distant relatives, but more likely, looking back, old party comrades. One room was lined with bookshelves, and I was invited to take home with me any one volume I took a fancy to. In the end, I chose, quite why I don't remember, Prescott's classic *History of the Conquest of Mexico*. Over the next few days I devoured its highly non-PC chronicle of plunder and rapine visited on the Aztecs by Hernando Cortes and his *Conquistadores*. Evidently, I was not yet 'on message' as they say now, when it came to anti-imperialism. But then I was not yet in my teens, and as I said, my parents quite rightly left me to my own devices when it came to forming opinions.

Like my dad, I only began to take a more active interest in politics when I passed the scholarship, or 11 plus as it later became known (more often than not pejoratively) and began my secondary education at Edmonton County Grammar School, situated just five minutes from home on the Cambridge Road, now the A10. And thereby hangs a tale. We three Blick brothers, like our dad, all suffered from asthma, so our parents, decided it would improve our health if we were transferred at the appropriate age – around nine – from our nearby elementary school to what was known as the Open-Air School some distance further away. (Most pupils, including the Blicks, consequently had to be collected and returned home by coach.)

And so, one by one, the Blick brothers were fed into a school which for sure lived up to the first part of its name. First Peter, two years my senior, then me, and then six years later, Gerald, a late war baby, underwent a regime of seemingly non-stop outdoor activities. Come rain, hail, gale, shine or snow, the huge classroom windows remained open. An hour each day was devoted to what was, officially at least, compulsory sleep in a large barn-like structure that on one of its longest sides, was entirely open to the elements. The few who actually did manage to doze off after dinner were allowed to sleep on when the hour was up. What with games, whole mornings or afternoons of gardening, extended playtimes and the rest, there was scant time left for academic instruction. Inevitably, the scholarship pass rate at this English prototype of a boot-camp was abysmally low. In fact, to the best of my knowledge (there is a website devoted to the history and reminiscences of the school) only three pupils passed the exam in the years when the Blick brothers were in attendance: Peter Blick, Robin Blick and Gerald Blick. Some years on, I discovered the probable reason why we had all been despatched to an institution that condemned nearly all its inmates to academic failure when I learned, once again, quite how I can't now remember, that the head master, a Mr Ripley, was a communist.

Once established in the intellectually stimulating and academically demanding environment of my grammar school, I made friends, few in number it is true, who to one extent or another shared my political interests and burgeoning leftist convictions. And by the time I had begun to study for my A Levels, I felt confident enough to defend my beliefs in the forum of the sixth form debating society, where I spoke for, and of course lost, by eight votes to more than twice that number, a motion in support of communism. Not that I cared that much. More importantly, I had discovered that I could speak to a largely unsympathetic audience (bear in mind this was at the height of the cold war) without stage fright or losing the thread of the argument. This facility was to stand me in good stead in my later life as a political campaigner. Thirty years on, and I would be addressing a far more sympathetic audience of twenty thousand in Hyde Park. It was a rally called by the movement I with two others of like mind had helped to found, the Polish Solidarity Campaign, to protest against the suppression of the Polish trade union *Solidarnosc*, ironically, by a communist regime. And alongside me on the platform were, amongst other speakers, the celebrated Labour historian Edward Thompson and two nationally known MPs, Shirley Williams, one of the 'Gang of Four' who broke from the Labour Party to found the Social Democratic Alliance (later to merge with the Liberal Party) and Peter Shaw, like Williams a former high-ranking Labour cabinet minister.

Even when I was at school, it was not all just talk, though there was plenty of that. Convictions should, I have always believed, lead to action. And so in the spring term of my first year in the sixth form, perhaps, looking back, also providing a distraction from the loss of my mother the previous September, I launched a pupil's union, open to all those above the third year. Officials were duly elected at a mass meeting in the art room, and I edited a monthly newsletter, my first foray in the world of political journalism. Nobody who knew seemed to care that I was a communist, even though this was the fifties, as I said, at the height of the cold war. Perhaps this was because the sole activity undertaken by the union was not a Grange Hill-style pupil strike or demonstration, but to take a coach load of members to the West End to see a production of the US imperialist musical Guys and Dolls. Membership swelled to well over a hundred, only to fade away over the summer holidays, which was just as well, because there were exams that needed passing in the second year.

Academically, I had always struggled a bit with maths and science, but once I reached the sixth form I could concentrate on the subjects that really interested me, above all, history, but also English and French. Latin was a grind, but in those days, without it, it was impossible to go on to a degree course in any arts subject. My history teacher throughout my seven years at Edmonton County was Joan Henderson, a lovely lady to whom I owe so much of my undiminished fascination, indeed obsession, with the past. She was a regular blue stocking, totally dedicated to her subject, and, quite normally for female teachers in those days, unmarried. She specialised in the later Tudors, and was a leading authority on the Elizabethan Parliaments.

By the time I reached the sixth form, I had become one of a series of always male pupils chosen to be students of special interest and promise. Looking back, it is obvious that hers was more than an academic involvement, though that was always her prime concern. Living with her mum as she was then, there were no men in her life, or children, so it is not unreasonable, given her circumstances, to assume that pupils like me (and I think that from the way she sometimes behaved towards me she may well have found out that I had lost my mother) served as substitutes for the second. But why only boys? Well, by the time we chosen ones reached the six forms, we had long grown out of short trousers, and were approaching fully-grown young men, 17 and 18 years old. Need I say more?

Two years above me, Joan's *protege* happened to be a good friend of mine, whom I had got to know really well through playing with him in the school football and cricket first teams. One year below me, there was another friend of mine who I got to know in the same way. And one year above me, the chosen one was none other than Roy, later Sir Roy Strong, who became in later years something of an establishment celebrity as Director of both the National Portrait Gallery and the Albert and Victoria Museum, and subsequently TV broadcaster and author. When his and my mentor died in 2003, Strong payed tribute to Joan's inspirational teaching in the *Daily Telegraph*, recalling that 'she was such a giving person not only to me, but also to many other pupils.', Being one of them, that I can vouch for.

After I left school, Joan asked to come and visit her at her home in Queens Park. On my arrival, I was taken into the living, room and rather like a new boyfriend, was introduced to her mother, saying, with something like a blush, 'this is Blick' Blick indeed. I went to see her once more, and then, I am sorry to say, lost touch with her, because. as Strong says in his tribute I too 'owed a great debt to a remarkable teacher',

Not that I was a swot. I was as sport-mad as my dad, who had been a very successful club cricketer in his pre-war days (that is how he first met my mum, who used to watch him play at the Enfield club ground). I won my football and cricket colours, and like my dad before me, cheered on Tottenham Hotspur from behind the goal at the Paxton Road end of the ground, the very same vantage point where Maureen, by this time a no less sporty tom boy, told me she also stood with her school friends. Another near encounter. And they may well have been yet one more. After we got together again she recalled playing hockey for her school in an away game at Edmonton County in the same year I would have quite possibly been playing for my school's football first eleven only yards away from her on the hockey pitch.

Together with history, my other great passion has been music. In that regard too, I was fortunate, in that I grew up in a home that valued classical music. Although neither of my parents played an instrument, the record cabinet was chock a bloc with 78s of the masters, later to be progressively replaced by LPs, while the radio was nearly always tuned either to what was then the Home Service or the Third programme. One of my first recollections of hearing classical music in the live so to speak was at what must have almost certainly been a Promenade concert at the Albert Hall. My clearest memory of that event is being exited by the timpanis thundering away in the climaxes of Dvorak's New World Symphony. As I have said, my dad sang in his church choir, and he would often when at home render arias and choruses from Handel's Messiah in a very tuneful light tenor voice.

My dad's great loves were Beethoven and especially Schubert, not only their popular orchestral works, but their more complex and demanding chamber music, which I am to this day grateful he particularly encouraged me to listen to. Once I later in life became acquainted with the story of Schubert's short life, sometimes, depending on the composition, I could not listen to his music without it bringing floods of tears to my eyes. Every note, no matter how joyful the passage, to my ears, and I know I am not alone in this, seems laden with sadness, the technical term for which is 'major key pathos'. Like his idol Beethoven, there is much of the heroic in Schubert's life story. While cursed with deafness, at least Beethoven had the compensation of seeing if not hearing all his works not only performed, but receiving in his lifetime the acclaim they deserved. Schubert's audiences were almost exclusively composed of a small circle of equally impecuniary bohemian admirers. Consequently some of his finest major compositions had to await their first performances years, in some cases decades, after his death, because unlike Beethoven and Mozart, his lowly social status prevented him from gaining access to aristocratic patronage essential for public performance and acclaim.

Class was also a barrier to a happy love life. Lacking the means to legally entitle him to marry, frequent visits to local brothels resulted, as it did for so many young men in his situation, in syphilis, and it was this that killed him at the age of 31, to his last days composing works of searing beauty. The *Oxford Companion to Music* pays its tribute to not only music's but one of mankind's true heroes. Unable to support himself as a musician, Schubert had to work full-time as a teacher at his father's school Even so, 'there followed a period of sustained creativity which strains credulity. In the space of three years his compositions included five [yes, *five*] symphonies, four masses [even though he was a free-thinker] three string quartets, three piano sonatas, six [yes, *six*] operas and some 300 or more songs'. And meanwhile, there was the day job.

Over the following years, having begun with Beethoven and Schubert, and then Mozart, my greatest passion became, and has remained, the incomparable Johann Sebastian Bach, for me not only the most sublimely gifted, inventive and inspired of all composers, but also the great human being that has ever lived or will live. In the first judgement at least, I am in good company. In the *Oxford Companion*, the entry for all other composers begins in the same matter of fact way, with the birth and death dates and then listing their major works etc. With Bach, it begins, 'Bach, the supreme genius...'.

My second claim rests partly at least on what I believe is the entirely reasonable proposition that whereas the great discoveries of science would, sooner or later, have been made even if Newton, Einstein and Darwin had not been born, the same is not true of the music of Bach or, for that matter, of any other composer or creative artist. The progress of science is not wilful but incremental, advancing with a certain inner logic, while art, although influenced by what has gone before, both positively and negatively, is creative, driven by inspiration. Proving my point, Gottfried Leibniz discovered calculus entirely independently of Newton, as did Alfred Russel Wallace the principle of natural selection from Darwin. Excluding cases of plagiarism, there is no equivalent to this phenomenon in the world of artistic creation. No two composers have independently composed remotely similar, let alone identical symphonies.

Yes, mathematicians see beauty in equations, and astronomers in the constellations, while music, like the plastic and pictorial arts, is subject to the same laws of physics and number, specifically acoustics, that govern the material universe. But that does alter the fact that while science discovers what is already there, and has been for billions of years, art creates something original. For these reasons I submit that the music of Bach is unique in a way that even the discoveries of the greatest of scientists are not. Finally, and here I grant my argument rests on a subjective element, Bach is supreme not only as a composer, but as a human being, because I believe, but cannot prove, that music is mankind's most sublime creation, being the artistic medium that has the capacity to move us more profoundly than any other, and that by its very nature, is, or at the very least, has the capacity to become the universal language of all mankind. Words describe. Music simply is.

My first encounter with Bach was my dad's 78 of Leopold Stokowski's orchestration of the Toccata and Fugue in D Minor, which featured in the Disney film *Fantasia*. It sounded like no other music I had ever heard...not surprisingly really, since none of the other records in my dad's collection were of the baroque era, which effectively ended with Bach's death in 1750. My real epiphany came one evening - I was just turned 18 at the time - when quite by accident I heard on what was then the Third programme what is generally accepted to be Bach's greatest work, his B Minor Mass. I was overwhelmed by its splendour, its dance-like rhythms, the complexity but also the clarity of its fugues, and above all, the trumpets as they seemed to soar up the very heaven that Bach so fervently believed in. Next day at school, still on a high, I buttonholed our music teacher. I had to tell him about my revelation, for such it was.

Twenty-two years later, when the Voyager spacecraft began its odyssey beyond our solar system, it carried on board the Golden Disc, on which was recorded music representative of our species. There were six items in the classical mode: the Queen of the Night's aria from Mozart's opera, The Magic Flute; the first movement of Beethoven's Fifth Symphony and the Cavatina from his String Quartet Number 13; and *three* by Bach, the first movement of his Brandenburg Concerto Number Two, the Gavotte from Partita Number 3 for violin and the Prelude and Fugue in C Major from Book Two of the Well-Tempered Clavier. I have no quarrel with order of priority; Bach 3, Beethoven 2, Mozart 1. My only regret is that space could not have be found for Schubert and Wagner, and that instead of one of the chosen Bach items, his most sublime creation, the *Cum Sancto Spirito* from his B Minor Mass should have been included. But the concept was a noble one.

After my discovery of Bach there came another... Wagner. (We had a portrait of Wagner on our living room wall, but none of his records, which looking back, I now find strange Was it because of his politics? But then, why the portrait?) Again, I had the Third programme on, and again found myself listening to music like no other...*Tristan and Isolde*. I did not understand the words, or know the plot...it was all totally new to me...but its power, profundity and intensity were of an order that I have only found in the music of Bach.

The impact of hearing the opera for the first time was truly immense, but evidently, and thankfully, not as traumatic as that experienced by the Austrian symphonist Anton Bruckner, who worshipped Wagner only a little less than his Catholic God. After attending for the first time a performance of *Tristan and Isolde*, he had a nervous breakdown that lasted a full three months. His reaction, though extreme, was shared by many of his contemporariesin the world of the arts and indeed beyond. One biographer of Wagner argues that the opera not only 'gave to Western culture a new concept of musical language, expression and tonality' but extended to 'the powerful spell it exerted on literature and the visual arts, even upon human thought and behaviour, of an order achieved by few other single works in the history of art'. As I said, I had no comprehension of the plot, but the searing, overpowering nature of the music alone, culminating in the palpable anguish of the final third Act, was sufficient to leave me in little doubt that Wagner was seeking to plumb and express through the medium of music something too profound, too immediate, too dreadful, too tragic but also too ecstatic than could be conveyed in even the most poetic of language. Words describe. Music is.

Only when later in life I became familiar with the opera's text and its creator's philosophy did I fully comprehend that above all, *Tristan* is about the impossibility of fully consummating passionate, erotic love this side of the grave. This is why like youth, and I have suggested, also sensual, sexual love, although it makes for wonderful listening, Wagner's *Tristan* is wasted on the young, in the sense that it treats of torments that only afflict mature adults when confronted with making a choice between two imperatives, as the theme song of that controversial masterpiece of a movie, *High Noon* has it, between love and duty, when it is one between killing a gang of hoodlums and his pacifist bride-to-be, or in the opera, between the world of the night, of passion, and of the day, of conventional morals and affairs of state. In the film, true to the Hollywood tradition, love and duty are at the end reconciled when the Quaker lady picks up a gun. But with Wagner, here at his most pessimistic as a result of the influence of the philosophy of Schopenhauer, there is only redemption through death. Apart from opening up a whole new world of music for me, I cannot say that like it did for some, *Tristan and Isolde* changed my life. But it with doubt helps me to understand why I spent the best part of it with Maureen and at her death, wished I could end it by dying with her.

Bach, the devout Lutheran and solid family man, composer of hundreds of cantatas but not a single opera, and Wagner the libertine, sybarite, profligate, sponger and shameless political turncoat, and with four of his operas, his *Ring* cycle, wholly derived from pagan myths…an unlikely couple to be sure. Yet I later discovered that Wagner, who was not given to showering compliments on other members of his profession, especially Jews, described Bach as 'the greatest miracle in all music'. As they say, it takes one to recognise one, even though Bach would have without doubt dismissed Wagner's unapparelled accolade as absurd. When asked to account for his success as a musician, he simply replied, without any false modesty, 'I worked hard', whereas Wagner would have and probably did say, 'because I am a genius'. Another musician who was both a genius and worked hard was Charlie Parker, who revolutionised jazz no less than Wagner did opera. Born into the direst poverty and unlike Bach, a family that had no musical tradition, he mastered his instrument, the alto sax, and all he need to know about music theory by practising ten hours a day, every day, for three years. The rest, as they say, is history.

Like many devotees of classical music, for some years my feelings about Wagner's abilities as a composer were clouded by his frequently vented disgusting prejudices against the Jews in general and musical ones in particular, most notably Mendelssohn and Giacomo Meyerbeer, who both rendered him invaluable and unsolicited services when as a young unknown in a Saxon cultural backwater, he embarked on his career as a composer. Wagner loathed the Jews, but recognising his incomparable artistic genius, they worshiped him. In addition to Mendelssohn and Meyerbeer, I have identified a dozen or more Jews who without their unstinting services none of Wagner's epoch-making triumphs would have been possible, which included not only re-casting the entire nature and production of opera, but with his revolutionary design for his theatre at Bayreuth, creating the prototype of the modern opera house, as well as inventing new instruments, devising a system for training of singers, and not least, being what his biographer describes the 'father of the modern art of conducting'. All this and more out of one human brain. What those Jews received in return for their selfless devotion to the realisation of its stupendous energy and vision were vile diatribes of the likes of *Judaism in Music*. Yet even at his funeral, *three of his pall-bearers were Jews*. As if to complicate still further his tortured schizophrenic relationship with a race he affected to despise, we have the identity of the two pianists Wagner chose to live with him as residential *repetiteurs*, Karl Tausig and Joseph Rubinstein. *They too were Jews*. Bereft after his idol's death in 1883, Rubinstein committed suicide. One can hardly imagine any Jew paying Hitler the same compliment.

Over time, I learned, not to overlook or excuse, but to separate the dark side of Wagner the Jew-baiter, the user, the manipulator, from the music, to the extent that I now believe that Wagner, though in ways very different from those of either Schubert or Beethoven, lived a life that for all its many sordid episodes, was truly heroic. When passing judgment on Wagner's readiness to sacrifice not only himself, but all those around him, to his art, it should never be forgotten that those who were so used were also in every sense both knowing and consenting adults. Even his harshest critics cannot deny that he sought neither fame nor fortune for their own sake but in the single-minded pursuit of an art form that as he intended, has changed the nature of music and indeed of all culture for ever, and at that, in the broadest sense of the term. To put it crudely, a decent nine to five family man could never have created *Tristan and Isolde*.

Understandably, for decades, there was an informal ban on Wagner being performed in Israel, until in 2001, Daniel Barenboim decided the time had come to see beyond the anti-Semite revered by Hitler to the creator of some of the world's most sublime music, operas in which not one Jew is portrayed nor the remotest allusion made to his racial bigotry. At the end of a concert programme performed in Jerusalem by his Berliner StaatsKapelle, Barenboim announced that he would like to conduct the Prelude to *Tristan and Isolde*. Being the kind of man, he is, he did not beat about the bush: 'There are people sitting in the audience for whom Wagner does not spark Nazi associations. I appreciate those for whom the associations are oppressive. It will be democratic to play a Wagner encore for those who wish to hear it. I am turning to you now and asking whether I can play Wagner.' Those who did not want to listen were invited to leave. After a 30-minute debate, in which Barenboim was called a fascist, a small number left, leaving the vast majority to savour music which is least of all about hate, but exalts passionate if forbidden love How much more human and universal can art be?

II

Growing up in what was, thanks to my father, a highbrow environment, it is hardly surprising that what is now called pop music was beneath my contempt. This was also the case, at least until my later teens with jazz, especially of the modern school exemplified by Stan Kenton's big band, which was all the vogue with some of my sixth form contemporaries at Edmonton County, and which in my first literary effort, I denounced in an article for the school magazine. My Damascus moment came when I was persuaded by a friend to visit the Wood Green Jazz Club, which held its sessions at the Fishmongers Arms in Wood Green High Street, just a short bus ride from my home.

The band that night was Chris Barber's, which had only recently been formed after a bust-up with its previous leader, trumpeter Ken Colyer, whom the rest of the band had considered obsessively purist in his approach to the New Orleans style. It took only a few notes from his replacement, Pat Halcox, to convince of me of two things; firstly that, I had been utterly, totally wrong in my dismissal of jazz, and secondly, that I wanted to be a jazz trumpeter. (My elder brother Peter's tastes never underwent any change whatsoever, being confined totally to the baroque and the Viennese classics, stopping in 1828 with the death of Schubert. A musical acquaintance of his once told me that Peter regarded even Brahms, the most classical of all the romantics, as a 'dangerous modernist'. After learning the rudiments of music on the recorder, Peter graduated to the clarinet, in his later years playing in small chamber ensembles to a quite high level of competence.)

My first step to becoming a jazz musician required getting myself a trumpet. In my last year at school, my weekly income was five shillings a week pocket money, while the cost of even the cheapest trumpet, as I soon found out, was around twenty pounds. Nothing deterred, I paid a visit to Charing Cross Road, which in those long-gone days, could boast of at least four musical instrument shops. I found one that displayed in its window a trumpet for a little more than the sum already mentioned. There was also in the window a sign to the effect that hire purchase terms were available for potential customers, and no initial deposit required. That did it. Desperate to get my hands on a trumpet come what may, I banished from my mind any thought as to the possible, indeed certain consequences of signing a hire purchase agreement far in excess of anything that my modest income could support. In I went.

To my amazement, after taking my details, all that the salesman required to complete the purchase was the name and address of a guarantor. I gave my father's name and address, and that was that. I walked out the shop with a gleaming brand-new trumpet without having paid a penny for it. It occurred to me later that I could have just as easily given two totally false names and addresses, and the salesman would have been none the wiser. When I got home, I succeeded in smuggling my prized purchase into my bedroom, and with a sock stuffed into its bell for a mute, blew my first notes. A few days later, what I had been dreading inevitably came to pass. My father confronted me with the letter confirming his status as guarantor for my hire purchase agreement. Faced with what amounted to a *fait accomplis*, he told me he would clear the debt with a single payment. My gamble, for such it was, had worked. He could quite easily, and reasonably, have insisted that I return an instrument which I had obtained under false pretences. But he did not and for that, because of what followed, I have been ever grateful.

My next step was to buy 'a teach yourself' trumpet tutor, and set about mastering the instrument and the rudiments of musical theory, about which I knew next to nothing. As to the trumpet, at first glance, it looks a far more straightforward task to learn than most other wind instruments, having only three valves rather than the eight or so finger holes and nearly as many keys of for example a clarinet. However, unlike a clarinet or a saxophone, there is no obvious logic as to which valve or valves to press to produce a certain note, or when not to press any, but play what are called open notes. In all, not counting open notes, there are six different fingering positions. The notes they produce are all down to what is called the harmonic series, the technical term for how a note is generated by creating a column of vibrating air of a certain length. This is done on a trumpet, or any other brass instrument, by a combination of lip tension and pressure on the mouthpiece and varying the length of tubing by depressing and releasing the appropriate valves. After a while, with repetition, just like driving a car or any other mechanical operation, this becomes instinctive, and the player is able to focus on mastering other aspects of playing the instrument, such as volume, tone, style etc.

Having got to this stage after a few months of if not blood, sweat and tears, then plenty of spittle, I bought a book of Louis Armstrong solos from his classic 1925 Hot Five ensemble. Talk about going in the deep end...Cornet Chop Suey, Strutting with Some Barbecue, Potato Head Blues. Learning to read the parts was hard enough, let alone trying to play them. At least having the LP, and hearing what they were supposed to sound like was as helpful as it was discouraging. I also bought a book of studies, called *Trumpet Velocity* (still in print) which sets the player tasks of increasing difficulty in all twelve keys, and through the trumpet's range from top to bottom, about three octaves. Learning to play in five or six sharps, which most trumpeters never do, stood me in good stead when many years later I played in guitar-led bands, which, because of the tuning of the strings, inviably use only sharp keys. Within about a year, I thought I had made enough technical progress, knew enough jazz standards, and grasped the basics of improvisation, namely that it is based on following a chord progression, to go public as it were. I had already formed my own New Orleans band, comprised largely of old school friends, and after some months of rehearsals, thought myself competent enough to try sitting in with one of the semi-pro bands then gigging around north London.

This was the heyday of what was known as 'trad', before rock and roll usurped jazz and folk as the prime vehicle for aspiring musical novices to find fame and fortune, or at the very least, which was more likely, learn the basics of music and to play an instrument tolerably well.

At the top of the pecking order there was a handful of full time, big name bands led by the likes of Chris Barber, Ken Colyer, Alex Welsh and Humphrey Lyttleton. Below them were other full-time bands with a smaller fan base, but just about scraping a living...Cy Lawrie, Eric Silk and Terry Lightfoot come to mind. But there were more. Further down again, there were the part-timers with a day job. Sandy Brown and Bill Brunskill were as good as the full timers, while for others, far more numerous, who did the odd local pub gig here or there for a few quid, it was more of a hobby. These together comprised the London trad scene, though there were not only widely varying levels of competence, but variety of styles, from Colyer's obsessive New Orleans orthodoxy to Lyttleton's more catholic mainstream approach. He outraged the purists by hiring Bruce Turner, a fine alto sax player.

I made my public debut in the summer in 1956 with a band in the former category called the Bourbon Street Ramblers who did a regular Sunday lunchtime slot at a pub on Tottenham High Road not far from the Spurs ground. 'Sitting in' was quite common at such gigs, the only proviso being that you could play well enough not to make a fool of yourself or, more to the point, the rest of the band. After a couple of visits to the venue with a couple of friends, and having taken the measure of the band in question, I decided that the time had come. The next Sunday, I asked the band leader, the pianist, if I could sit in for a number. He said of course, and the cornetist (I can still remember his name...Dave Gillard) took a break. I chose an old New Orleans standard, 'The Girls go Crazy about the Way I Walk', *double entendre* for something a little more intimate. Another coincidence: My debut on the Swansea music scene 44 years later, with Maureen in the audience hearing me play for the first time, was at the local Jazz Club, sitting in on cornet with a New Orleans band playing ... yes... the Girls go Crazy. It's a simple number, and with only an eight-bar sequence of three chords, easy to improvise to. Anyway, back in 1956, even though I was then not nearly as proficient, I survived, and my two friends gave me the thumbs-up after my solo.

My debut had a strange sequel. Some weeks later, I sat in with another band (I forget its name) at a gig a couple of miles up the same road, only across the border in my home town of Edmonton. This was a more formal evening affair, in a hall, and the band was up on a stage. Funnily enough, although the number I played on was called 'My bucket's got a hole in it', (another New Orleans standard) the chords were exactly the same as the Girls go Crazy, the only difference being (apart of course from the tune) that it was played much slower. When I got down from the stage at the end of the number, I was approached by a chap who introduced himself as the manager of the Bourbon Street Ramblers, who asked me if I would like to come to a band rehearsal. Given they already had a cornet player, Dave Gillard, I thought it was a bit odd, but I said yes. At the rehearsal in the pianist's front room, all seemed to go well, as we ran through numbers we each knew. That was last I heard of them, except that I found out, I can't remember how, that Dave Gillard had been spending too much time with his girlfriend and not enough with the band, and my appearance at the rehearsal was intended to serve as warning that he was not indispensable, a bit like a substitute warming up on the touchline.

But that was not the end of the story. A few years ago, I came across a website devoted to the jazz scene in Enfield back in the hey-day of the trad era. I sent an item relating, amongst other reminiscences of those times, my strange encounter with the Ramblers. The editor of the website got back to me, thanking me for my contribution, but adding that he would have to edit out the funny business with Dave Gillard, as the editor knew him personally and feared he would take umbrage if the story got out...and this was after more than fifty years... And so when my item duly appeared (it is still up there) all traces of information pertaining to my debut on the London jazz scene had disappeared down the memory hole.

By this time, jazz, and trying to play it, had become one of my great passions, but I continued to explore the world of the classical genres, and my expanding record collection reflected both interests. And here I must relate another musical encounter that occurred, this time not at a gig, but in the most unlikely of locations. The summer of 1956, after completing my second year at university, I took a holiday job at a bakery in Enfield, loading vans on permanent nights. We worked in teams of two to a van, and my partner was a personable young man called Tod Handley. I soon discovered that like me, he was a student, in his case, of music at Oxford. For two months, as we loaded our vans, we talked music, all night, every night.

Tod's great ambition was to become a conductor and, in that capacity, to promote the works of home-grown composers whom he believed had been unjustly neglected. I discovered this when I began enthusing over the fugal complexity of the final movement of Mozart's last symphony, number 41, the Jupiter. 'Ah...Jupiter...Holst at his very best' Todd interjected. He was thinking of the Planets Suite by the quintessentially English (despite his name) Gustave Holst. I could not but respect then, as I do now, his single-minded resolve to devote his future career as a conductor almost exclusively to the promotion of British classical music of the last hundred and fifty or so years, but I could not then, and do not now, share his enthusiasm for composers who, but for a few exceptions, most notably Elgar, Vaughn Williams and Britain, I have always regarded as at best in the third rank in comparison with their continental contemporaries, because they are competing with the likes of Brahms, Sibelius, Greig, Debussy, Ravel, Bartok, Stravinsky, Shostakovich, Tchaikovsky, Wagner, Webern, Puccini and Dvorak, to mention only a few. Delius? Bax? Parry? Arnold? Walton? It is simply no contest.

When a radio announcer, a conductor or performer refers to a work as being 'neglected', as they all too frequently do, I always ask myself, could this be because it deserves to be? Music, like all culture, exists in a competitive environment. Resources, time, audiences and performers are not infinite. Inevitably therefore, the popularity or 'neglect' of a composition is at least partially subject to the same laws of selection that operate in the natural world. Granted, the fickleness of taste, vested interest and the like play a part, but not I believe the decisive one. Quality, however defined, wins out. Tod clearly believed otherwise, that factors other than merit were at play, and devoted his life to proving it, as. his Wikipedia entry reveals:

'Vernon George "Todd" Handley CBE was a British conductor known in particular for his support for British composers. He was born of a Welsh father and an Irish mother into a musical family in Enfield London...Awards: Classic Brit Lifetime Achievement Award, Brit Award for Best Classic Recording.'

I greatly admire Tod for achieving the goal he set himself and the depth if not the breadth of his musical knowledge, though there was one bone of contention we could never resolve. I was incredulous when he dismissed Beethoven as glib (or was it suave?), attempting to prove his point by humming a descending three-note chromatic passage from the finale of his seventh symphony. My near-outrage was augmented by this not only my being my favourite Beethoven symphony at the time, but also my favourite movement, with its' relentlessly demonic rhythm (Wagner called it the 'apotheosis of the dance') and heroic French horns, soaring to what I discovered was the uppermost limit of the instrument's range when, many years later, I eventually mastered what is, along with the piccolo trumpet (which I also play), the most demanding of brass instruments.

In addition to working with someone who shared my enthusiasm for music, the job had another bonus, also a musical one. In the slack periods between the arrival of vans for loading, I could practice my trumpet in a disused part of the building. Wanting a challenge to improve my technique, I bought a book of Louis Armstrong solos, and was soon getting my chops and fingers round some of the harder numbers. From my first encounter with Chris Barber at the Fishmongers Arms, much would follow, not all of its musical, and not only for myself, but also for Maureen, because it was our shared interest in jazz that provided me with the opportunity to make her acquaintance.

I never got to form a viable gigging New Orleans band. The people I played with were mainly friends from my school days who were either not up to it, or moved away from London when they went to university or to do their National Service, which ended in 1963. The only serious playing I did was freelancing at London university gigs put on by student unions at the various colleges, including a couple with the saxophonist George Khan, who went on to make it big time ('a living legend' is how one jazz magazine describes him) and the occasional sitting in with pro bands who played in the lunch breaks. One such was with the rhythm section of the Humphrey Lyttleton band. By this time, I had been introduced to modern jazz by a very talented pianist I had got know, and after weekly sessions at his home running through the basic repertoire of what was a much more challenging idiom than the very basic New Orleans fare I had cut my teeth on, I took the plunge guesting with a number of modern-style student combos gigging round the London circuit.

Meanwhile, my personal circumstances had undergone a significant change shortly after leaving school. Instead of trying to get on with my step-mother Gwen, I took the easy, selfish way out and moved into lodgings. I had a small room on the first floor at the front of the house, equipped with a single gas ring, which proved to be the cause of the first of a series of evictions. I had been there for a few weeks when one day, after lighting the ring, I dropped the match into a plastic rubbish bin, which promptly caught alight. In no time, smoking was billowing out of the window, and I was looking for new digs. I saw an advert in a shop window which directed me to a small pre-first-world war terraced house in Bush Hill Park, situated, not far from my parental home, between Edmonton and Enfield. The house was owned by a working-class elderly couple, and there was another lodger *in situ*, or rather two, an unmarried mother and her small boy, the product, as I later gathered, of a brief liaison with a wealthy married man.

I soon discovered I shared an interest with the landlord, because he played the cornet in the local Salvation Army band, whose citadel was just over the road. His wife, who definitely wore the trousers, told me she had been expelled from the Aunt Sally after she had been spotted in pub, not selling the *War Cry*, but enjoying a pint. The experience had turned her rather sour so far as organised religion was concerned, and she would sound off with a vehemence that led me to assume that she was an atheist. This she may well have been, because on one occasion, she likened belief in God to a child's in Father Christmas. My mistake, which led to my second eviction, was failing to appreciate that such comments were intended only for domestic ears. When I made a heretical remark in the presence of a visitor from the Aunt Sally, she gave me my marching orders the next morning.

Needing a bed for the night, and too proud to go back home, I asked an old school friend if he could put me up for a few days until I found myself new digs. His parents, whom I knew, were quite amenable to the idea, so I moved in. Very quickly, things started to go seriously wrong. My friend, as he was up till then, was an only child, and he began to resent what he obviously regarded as the undue attention I was getting from his mother. His mounting jealousy boiled over at a meal time, when his mother served me a larger portion of meat than she had put on his plate. Enraged, he lashed out at me, and as I fended him off, his father called out to his mother, 'you'd better go and make the bed up for you two'. Minutes later, I was on the street again, this time the victim not of my stupidity but of somebody else's. But it was still eviction number three.

My next, and for a while, my last port of call, took me to Brimsdown, an industrial area located in east Enfield close to the River Lea and as it happened, only a mile or so from where Maureen lived in what was called Enfield Highway. Here too there were two other lodgers, both single men. From one of them, a decent north country chap, I bought for a couple of quid a set of golf clubs. The landlady was nearly stone deaf, and thereby hangs a tale of great import that will be told in due course. All went well here for several months. I was well fed and there were no complications with religion or jealous offspring (and husbands). And, conveniently as it turned out, just down the road was a large industrial estate. So, when needing an income after completing my degree course, I easily found a job (this was the era of full, indeed over-full employment) as a foundry man with the firm of Johnsons, who specialised in smelting and processing metals. In no hurry to embark on 'a career' (in fact the prospect horrified me) I had decided to take what is now called a 'gap year', not by back-packing around Australia or the Andes, but, as befitted an impecuniary as well as rather romantic leftist, by joining, if only briefly, the ranks of the industrial proletariat. And this was when my education in the ways of the real world began. Intent on merging with my fellow workers, I rather naively adopted my middle name, Arthur, as Robin sounded too effete for my new surroundings. My concern was to be accepted as one of us, and not seen as one of them.

After a couple of weeks on day-time general duties, I was inducted as a grade one furnaceman (the highest was grade four) into the world of twelve-hour shifts, ever-hungry furnaces, glowing ores and huge ladles of molten metal. I was assigned to a large, long shed, which housed a blast furnace at one end, loaded from a platform on a higher level, and a long line of furnaces which were loaded with ore by shovel from ground level through doors raised and lowered by chains on a pully. The constant roar of the oil burners was deafening. the air full of smoke and fumes, and the heat when the furnaces were going full blast, well over a 100 degrees Fahrenheit. The process was of necessity a continuous one, day and night, week on week, and went through a fixed routine, which involved loading (the technical term was charging) the furnace with ore, which sometimes had to be broken up with huge hammers, then smelting, which, depending on the metal, could take anything up to eight hours or so, and when ready, poured or ladled into moulds. Ladling copper, which had a very high melting point, required the wearing of an asbestos suit and a helmet with a glass visor, giving the wearer the appearance of a sci-fic spaceman. In no time, I developed Popeye-sized biceps wielding a ladle that full loaded, weighed well over a hundred pounds.

The pattern of work was highly irregular, because the cycle did not coincide with shift times. Some days or nights, it would be loading, on others tapping or ladling, and others doing nothing at all. The night shift, when there was no management brass around, was very relaxed, People would kip in a wheel barrow, play cards or read. Once I got the measure of the set up, I found a corner to practice my trumpet. What with the din, I didn't need a mute. The work force was organised into three teams that on paper, were supposed to rotate in eight-hour shifts, 6.00 AM to 2.00 PM, 2.00 PM to 10.00 PM and so on back round to 6.00 AM. At the week-end, the shifts moved round one, so everyone took turns at each of three shifts, morning, afternoons and nights.

Frequently however, when the work load increased, there were two shifts, both of 12 hours, 6.00 AM to 6.00 PM, and 6.00 PM to 6.00 AM, with each shift staying on or coming in early for another four hours. Nobody complained, because it meant higher overtime rates, which on a Sunday night, were double. One week I netted around £16.00, a huge sum for those days for someone of my age.

My pay packed contained something I had never seen before...a five-pound note. I also had another novel experience...joining a trade union, the Amalgamated Union of Foundry Workers, which in 1967 was absorbed by the much larger Amalgamated Engineering Workers Union.

I soon settled into the rhythm of shift work, and in fact found as a single young man, it had several advantages over a normal day job, one being that unless I was on a twelve-hour shift, after finishing nights at 6.00 AM, I would collect my golf clubs from my digs and cycle to the not too distant municipal golf course at Whitewebbs long before any staff arrived to collect the fee for the round. Another was that it gave me ample time to practice my trumpet or do the rounds of the second-hand record shops that in those days proliferated in the Soho area.

As was the time-honoured custom with heavy manual work, and believe me, it was heavy, I was not accepted as a fellow worker until I had proved I was pulling my weight, literally. Passengers were not look on kindly in a job that was both physically demanding and potentially life threatening. (I learned in due course than not so long before I started, ore exploding in one of the furnaces had torn the door off its chains with such force it that sliced clean through a stoker's neck.) For two or three weeks, nobody spoke to me except in connection with the work, until one day, as if some collective decision had been made, I was one us. It was then that my shift charge hand, aptly named Charlie Charge, took me to one side and told me some home truths about a certain Arthur Tew, generally known as Tewie, who worked on days. Nobody seemed to like him, and Charlie explained why. Before the war, he worked as a black-leg during a strike. That, and his generally garrulous disposition - he always had what looked like a leer on his face - had rendered him what amounted to a pariah. Charlie put me on my guard, warning me that. he would approach me with some sob story about his unpalatable past.

And sure, enough he did. Unprompted by me, he claimed that he was unaware a strike was in progress - a likely tale, I thought, but as I did not want to get into an argument with him, I said nothing. But from my reaction, he could see I didn't believe him. Then, a few days later, he approached me, and in his sneering way, said, with an air of mystery and triumph, 'I know your story'. 'My story', such as it was, had been gleaned from his daughter, who was 'going out' out with someone in the cricket team I was playing for. And so the wind-ups continued, until one day, I stupidly gave him a taste of his own medicine. I forget now exactly what I said to him but whatever it was, it was sufficiently below the belt to provoke him into swinging a punch at me. Luckily, Charlie Charge was able to break it up before it got out of hand. As we were both clearly guilty of industrial misconduct, we had to appear before the site manager. Naively, I assumed that my shift shop steward would take my side, firstly because of Tew's general unpopularity and the reason for it, and secondly, more crucially, because Tew had landed the first blow. Not a bit of it. The union man, who spoke first, described what happened, and quite rightly blamed me for deliberately provoking Tew. The manager then gave Tew a mild ticking off, made it clear no further action was called for and then, as Tew and the steward left the office, told me to stay behind. At once, it became clear from what he said that my cover had been blown, that my naive though well-intentioned attempt to pass myself off as 'one of us' had been seen through, perhaps by none other than Tewie himself, with his claim that he 'knew my story'. 'They call you the college boy' said the manager...'why is that?' I told him it was became I was. 'They also tell me you have a lot to say for yourself... politics and suchlike'. That was also true. 'The time for that is when you've seen a something of life...it's obvious by the way you've behaved that the cradle marks aren't off your arse yet. You had no business provoking Arthur like that. He's a sad old man. Leave him alone like everybody else does.' That was it...a mild reprimand, and back to work. I have referred on several occasions to occasions when the paths of the lives of Maureen and myself approached without converging.

Reminiscing to Maureen more than forty years later about my time at Johnsons, in the course of which I mentioned my dealings with Arthur Tew, she recalled that she was at that very same time friendly with his daughter, and knew his morose character only too well from the frequent visits she paid to her friend's home. This co-incidence, I submit, is truly uncanny. Another series of seemingly (because nothing happens by pure chance) chance events would bring us together.

III

How did I come to see Maureen for the first time on the stairs of a cosmetic factory in north London? Maureen had returned from her rural exile to her parents' home in Enfield at the end of the war. She too passed her scholarship, and with such high marks that she was offered a place at the elite Tottenham High school for girls. There she was truly in her element, both as a scholar and in the many sports that the school competed in. After passing six O Levels as they were called then, in the sixth form she specialised in science subjects, but never took her A levels, leaving after completing her first year. I never asked Maureen why she made this choice, but I can hazard a guess, based on comments she used to make, that she was not enamoured with the prospect of becoming a school teacher, which in those days, was a common destination awaiting a grammar school pupil of her background. Maureen the school girl must have already revealed the non-conformist, individualist side that I came to know only too well, because her leaving testimonial, while acknowledging her academic abilities, described her as 'arrogant and self-centred', She conceded to me that the first was true, but regarded the second as most unfair, an objection born out in full measure by her entire adult life, which on two occasions, over a period of many years, saw Maureen putting the needs of first, as single parent, those of her daughter, and then, as the sole carer for her Alzheimers mother, before her own.

Maureen's school days were indeed, as the saying goes, among the happiest of her life, and she often used to tell about them with deeply-felt nostalgia. Not long after we got together again, driving down Tottenham High Road on a visit to London to see her daughter then living in Ponders End, we pulled up outside her old school's gates. (It had long been closed by the local Labour council as being too elitist. Its aim was evidently to level down, rather than to raise up.)

She looked down the path that led to the school entrance,

and then turned to me and said, wistfully: 'I wish I was back at school.' And yes, for all her sophistication and worldly wisdom, there was always something of the school girl in Maureen, not childish, but childlike, with her vast collection of vintage kitschy figurines and ornaments, and her menagerie of woolly and stuffed animals. Not long after I moved in with Maureen, she attended a Tottenham High former pupil's reunion in London, where she met up with old school friends she had not seen for something like 45 years. On her return, she said to me, with maybe just the slightest hint of *schadenfreude*, that she looked the youngest of the lot. When she played me the video that had been made of the event (which I have had transferred to DVD), I saw for myself that she was right….and by some good few years

Unlike me, Maureen excelled at science subjects, and would for sure have collected a batch of A levels in them had she not left after only one year in the sixth form to begin her career as a cosmetic chemist with Lentheric, The firm, originally a Paris-based company founded in 1875, later merged with Yardley. The proof, if any were needed, of her academic prowess came when after no more two years of part-time study at evening classes, Maureen received the following letter:

'SOCIETY OF COSMETIC CHEMISTS
OF GREAT BRITAIN

August 17, 1959
Miss M. J. Griggs,
42, Eastfield Road,
Enfield,
MIDDX.

Dear Miss Griggs,

I have pleasure in informing you that you have successfully passed the examination which entitles to receive the Diploma of the Society. I understand from the report of the examiners that the candidates who sat this year have reached the highest standards yet in any of the examinations. Your success in being one of the seven people who qualified is, therefore, all the more to be commended.

[After inviting Maureen to the presentation ceremony, the letter concludes]

With best wishes for your future in the cosmetic industry,

Yours sincerely,
Robert H Marriott, D. Sc, F.R.I.C President.'

It was so typical of Maureen that she never so much as mentioned to me this achievement either then or later, let alone show me the letter, which I only discovered in her desk shortly after she died. And I also only learned from her daughter after Maureen's death that again attending only evening classes at Brunel University, she was awarded a degree in the highly exacting discipline of micro-biology. Though Maureen pursued a scientific career, she had from a very early age a love of literature, especially poetry. And while possessed of a razor-sharp intellect, just like her incomparable beauty, she never flaunted it, reserving her forensic skills for private mental jousts, at which she excelled and greatly savoured, as I can testify.

After leaving school in 1956 at the age of seventeen, Maureen's employment, with Lentheric continued until the birth of her daughter and only child Andrea in 1971. The factory was situated only a short walk from Tottenham High, so her journey by bus to and from work remained unchanged from her school days. There, as she acquired a succession of formidable qualifications, she rose to become supervisor of her department. It was also at Lentheric where I, an aspiring academic, would-be revolutionary, apprentice jazz trumpeter and total failure with the opposite sex, met the woman who would become in time my first lover and I hers, and then, nearly forty years later, with Maureen now more than ever the supreme passion of my life, also each other's last.

The story of how our paths first crossed is the usual one for such encounters, as I have already said, one of a series of seemingly chance occurrences that at the time had no particular, let alone life-shaping significance. I was not, as it happens, an employee of Lentheric. I was a humble yard man for the pharmacists Savory and Moore, a company that fortunately for me, shared the building and its yard with Maureen's This is how I came to be there. In the Summer of that year, 1957, I was living in my Brimsdown digs conveniently close to where I worked at Johnson's. And as I have said, the landlady was partially deaf. Quite reasonably, her husband made it very clear from the beginning that he couldn't stand my tuneless trumpet exercises, so lacking a practice mute, I stuffed a sock in the bell. When he was out at work, I blasted way, knowing that his wife, downstairs in the kitchen, could not hear me. This routine worked quite well until one day, the landlord came home early and hearing the din upstairs, gave me my marching orders. Eviction number four. Quite frankly, being independent was getting too much like hard work. Seeing that I was now on much better terms with my stepmother, I asked my dad if I could come back home. Permission was given, but with the proviso that out of consideration for Gwen, I found a job that did not entail shift work. This was fair enough, seeing the needless grief I had given her in the past.

Having moved back in, I asked at work if there was any possibility of reverting to the day shift. The answer was no. If it had been yes, I would never have met Maureen. Redundant, through no real fault of my own, I now needed employment of some sort to see out my 'gap year'. At the local labour exchange (now job centre) I was given a card and directed to a chemical factory in Tottenham. Overpowered by the acidic stench of the place, I said no thank you. I returned to the exchange the next day, and was this time presented, sometime in October 1957, with a card that directed me to the tall building in Lawrence Road, South Tottenham, that housed the two companies, Lentheric and Savory and Moore, and where Maureen had been employed at the first for a little more than a year. And it so happened, as Maureen once related to me, that Lentheric was not her first choice either, but like Savory and Moore for me, her second. Because my landlord came home early, a sequence of events and circumstances, some beyond my control, delivered me to the scene of the most magical moment and encounter of my life, one that would shape my destiny and Maureen's like no other.

Unlike Maureen, whose truly ravishing beauty had ensured that she would never want for admirers, at the time of my first glimpse of her on the stairs at Lentheric, my success rate with the girls amounted to a tiny fraction more than zero, even though I had enjoyed the theoretical advantage of attending a mixed grammar school. There had of course been my abysmal failure with Pamela, one year below me in the lower sixth form. Idealist Puritan that I then was, with my mind always reaching for noble and uplifting goals, and moreover brought up in a family of boys, I looked upon girls in the same idealistic way, holding them in awe, and consequently never entertaining, or least, repressing, the notion that the kind of girl who might be interested in me would want anything other than the cerebral. So in my futile efforts to attract their interest, I invariably played to what I believed was my *forte*, namely talk, chiefly about things that I hoped would interest and impress, because they were, to me at any rate, important. Some indeed were impressed, but only with me as a curiosity, because all I seemed capable of was just that, talk and at that, usually about politics. Over time I acquired the reputation, one I must admit that was not entirely undeserved, of being a bit of a freak, albeit a clever one. So, understandably, girls always looked elsewhere for action. Then my luck changed. Or at least, so I thought.

Pam, a slender, pretty, but not beautiful girl, with a more than a hint of a north country accent, was a highly talented pianist, and was duly impressed, not by my advocacy of communism to be sure, but by my knowledge and love of classical music, the inheritance from my dad that has proved the most enduring and rewarding, and my burgeoning skill on the trumpet. But this time, there was something more, because with hindsight, for what that is worth, I think she actually found me physically attractive. And yet after a few dates, the first of which was arranged by a go-between because I was too shy to ask her out directly, I was given the heave-ho. I quickly discovered why. I talked the talk as they say, but precious little else. I well remember using a musical angle to convince her of my atheism…some hopes…this was the 1950s, when all decent young women were supposed to be, and many were, pious Christians. How come, I asked her, that your beneficent and all-powerful God decided Mozart had to die at 35, and Schubert at 31, while allowing swine like Hitler to live long enough to do their evil deeds? I can see her now, in her front room by her piano (we had been playing a duet), giving me a slightly embarrassed smile…but no answer. Not surprising really, when you consider that theologians can't agree on one, preferring instead simply to call it 'theodicy' (idiocy would be more appropriate), this being the name for the mystery, for reasons that are beyond our ken, of why a benevolent, loving God repeatedly allows (or even makes, as with the Flood so the Bible says) terrible things to happen to his creatures, and the worst to his chosen people, while having the power to prevent them. Here we have one of many vindications of my definition of theology, one which Maureen, being unbeliever like me, was rather taken with: 'Theology says much about nothing, and explains nothing about anything'. My favourite on the subject is Mark Twain's 'faith is believing what you know ain't so.' Talking of mysteries, to paraphrase Samuel Johnson's famous quip about patriotism, they all too often serve as the last refuge of the devout, as was demonstrated when the then Archbishop of Canterbury Robert Runcie was asked by his *Guardian* interviewer, 'what is God, exactly?'. After a long pause, England's number authority on the subject replied: 'God is...a mystery.' Only conventionally religious, Pam was an intelligent girl, but she wanted something more tactile than purely cerebral stimulation. We went to a couple of concerts, one at the Festival Hall with Beecham conducting Beethoven's Eroica symphony, boating on a lake, once to the pictures... four or five dates in all. Only on the third or fourth did I pluck up the courage to kiss her goodnight, and even then, it was just a timid pick, in case she took offence. She probably felt insulted. Finding me woefully wanting in the basics, after a couple of months she gave me up as a bad job, and teamed up with a friend of mine at the local cricket and tennis club where the three of were members Realising too late why I had been dumped, I was not unduly surprised when she moved on to someone whom I knew was a seasoned operator with the ladies. Pam would go down in history as not only my first girl friend, technically defined as such, but my last.

Common sense and experience should have told me that my prospects of making any headway with the gorgeous black-haired young woman who ambled so voluptuously up and down the factory stairs were nil. I was so obviously out of my league. But since when did common sense dictate to the kind of passion and yearning that Maureen had aroused in me? At the very least, I could feast my eyes upon her. It did not take me long to work out the times I could spy on her as she came down from her own department to the canteen on a lower floor for a tea break. I positioned myself behind a door in a corridor leading on to the stairs, and waited to catch a glimpse of her. This voyeuristic routine continued for several weeks and on into the New Year. Then one day, she glanced towards me and caught my eye, and we exchanged fleeting looks. Many years later she told me she knew exactly what I was up to, because, obviously not by coincidence, I was always there when she was. What next, I wondered.

Again, the possibility of using the services of an intermediary occurred to me. I rather artfully struck up an acquaintance with a young lad who worked in her section. He was able to tell me her name, and, as an added bonus amongst other information about her, that she liked jazz. A day or so later, I lent him an LP of Humphrey Lyttleton's jazz band, and asked him to pass it on to Maureen, which he duly did. A few more days went by and then, wonder of wonders, meeting me on the stairs, Maureen spoke to me for the first time, to thank me for the loan. From then on, we exchanged a few occasional pleasantries. How I was able to summon up the nerve for my next move, I shall never know. Perhaps it was simply a triumph, by far not for the only time in my life, of passion over reason, because by now, I was madly if albeit as I thought, hopelessly in love. This was the beginning of a devotion so powerful, so all-consuming that sixty years and more on, it endures undiminished after her death, as I know it will until mine.

    I asked my go-between if he knew Maureen's address. Yes, he did, or least he thought he did. It was in fact 42 Eastfield Road, Enfield Wash, though he gave me the wrong number, a house nearly opposite hers on the other side of the road. So, one April evening in 1958, sixty two years ago as I write these lines, I took a trolley bus from Edmonton to the top of her street and after ringing at the wrong door and asking for Maureen, was directed over the road to number 42. As I stood at her door, summoning up the courage to ring on the bell, I heard coming from inside the joyous sounds of Humphrey Lyttleton playing Panama Rag. Heart pounding, I rang the bell. The door opened, and there she stood, not only the most gloriously beautiful woman but the most wondrous sight I have beheld in my entire life. The memory of that moment will remain with me, clear as ever, to my dying day. When, forty-two years later, I began my desperate second wooing of Maureen, I dedicated and sent to her a poem that recalled the beginnings of my first:

    Some dingy stairs winding up Long ago
    It was November.

Young fool. I thought I knew so much Until I saw your eyes that burned within, Haughty crooked nose
Pitiless black hair.

I remember
That gloomy morning
Red smears on your crumpled white coat As you slowly climbed
And with a saucy swagger sauntered by.

I remember Gazing in wonder For
Until that moment I thought I knew
That truth and beauty
Were Marx and Bach.
Till then I thought I knew so much Till then.

I still remember This longing
Being branded in my brain With wondrous pain
And though you will not allow Strangely in my soul
Humbled by your mystery Knowing now I knew so little.

I will remember being Fixed by this holy moment I could not comprehend And never will.

I remember Knowing
I loved you Not later Then.
Not caring (though I cared) Where this led.
I used to scoff And still do At fate
But more wisely, For this chance
Strangely, with you not knowing, Became my destiny and
Fuel of my fire, Then,
Not later.

I remember As in a trance
I vowed Not later Then
Out loud – I was an earnest fool – To seek you out.
I had no hopes you understand And never did

But something more Flaming darkly as your eyes.
All this I remember
One glowing, gloomy day In November
Long ago.

I remember
One April day so long ago
When on a trolley bus to Waltham Cross 679 I will swear
With fearful tread and pounding heart I first came to you.
By devious means I knew your house Or nearly so.
And once corrected, number 42, walked up Your tiny path, garden to left
To stand quaking at your door.

Trembling there, I heard familiar sounds – Humphrey Lyttleton playing Panama Rag. You must be in I thought
And rang the bell.

I remember that April day just dark Framed by the now open door Your startled look
Thinking what I do not know But asking me in
You foolish thing.
I remember that now dark April day A cosy room
Doors to right Fire to the left
Two armchairs facing And sofa to right
And far corner from the front door Record player and cabinet.

I will remember This room until I die
Where we first sat so long ago Facing
Talking.

What you thought I still cannot say But I remember
Now so close
Gazing helpless at you dark beauty Sensing your fire within

And knowing what seemed mere chance Was now my destiny.

August, 1999

Why did she invite me in? Quite honestly, I was never really able to find out. When we were together again, she was always more than a little reluctant to talk about those distant times, objecting that my insatiable curiosity concerning what exactly she was up to was more than a little 'maudlin'. She also explained, and this was nearer the truth as she understood it, that her reluctance to talk about the subject was because as she put it, 'I treated you very badly,' to which I would reply, perfectly truthfully, that there could have been no better treat for me then than to be able to share an evening with her once a week, as became the rule, for five whole years. Putting aside false modesty, I can only assume that she found me interesting in ways that set me apart from the kind of male company she told me was used to. I was given evidence this was so when I visited her forty-two years later, once again uninvited, in her Swansea home, one that less than five months later would also be mine. At the very outset of that first encounter, unprompted, she assured me that she had kept the promise she made to me at what we both believed was our final and tearful parting thirty-four years before, when she made a sobbing pledge 'never never never' to forget me.

From the outset, and for some time after, it was made clear to me, without it ever being stated, that our friendship was to be strictly Platonic. And so it was, for two years or more, apart from a token goodnight touching of the lips. But I had my foot in the door, and my bum on one her armchairs, and that for me was beyond my wildest dreams. I had performed well enough that first evening to be invited around the following Monday, talking about jazz, which by now I knew Maureen had a special liking for, and any other subject that helped keep the ball rolling. She knew I played the trumpet, because one morning as she came in to work, I had serenaded her with a fanfare from the roof of her work place. Set on impressing her with the breadth and depth my musical tastes, that first Monday I had arrived with my cherished box set of Bach's B Minor Mass, paid for by the sweat of my brow during my stint as furnaceman. If she was impressed, she certainly didn't show it, a response, or rather lack of one, to which there would be only rare exceptions. I can see her now so clearly that first magical evening, in a red skirt and a white blouse, as she coolly leafed her way through the accompanying booklet, and then after some reflection, chose and played one of the three LPs. Looking at Maureen as she sat there opposite me, I remember thinking, there can be nothing in the world so enticing, so fascinating, so exiting, so erotic, as a woman who is both beautiful and intelligent.

Although rarely one to outwardly enthuse, she must already have had a special liking for Bach, because some months later, we met up quite by chance on the bus going home from an all-Bach concert at the Proms where she had been with some friends from work. (In those pre-populist times, when the Proms, were not diluted by an ever-increasing number of evenings devoted to 'world music', Jazz, film music, rock, pop, and even sport, under the inane rubric of 'something for everybody', to the exclusion one year of any performance of a work by Schubert, each Wednesday was a Bach evening, while Fridays were reserved for Beethoven.)

Nearly half a century on from that first of what would be more than 200 such visits, Maureen and I were sitting, not as on that first evening, in facing armchairs, but side by side in Swansea's Brangwyn Hall, overcome by the majesty of that same sublime work, who's *Cum Sancto Spirito,* with its soaring trumpets, thundering percussion, passages of searing pathos and joyous jazz-like syncopation, and throughout, a pulsating 6/8 dance rhythm, is in my admittedly subjective judgment the greatest artistic creation of the human race. Afterwards, as we made our way to the car, Maureen exclaimed, most uncharacteristically, 'that was glorious', a word I had never heard her say before, and only once since, when one glowing sunny morning, as we drove down the Brenner pass between the snow-capped peaks of the Austrian Alps, she cried: 'This is glorious; who needs paradise?' Not Maureen. Her passions were of this world, above of all for nature and music and, I have reason to believe, for me.

The front room of Maureen's home, like the terraced house, was quite small, but very cosy. That first Monday we sat, as we did for the next two years and more, on two facing armchairs, three yards or may be a little more apart. I found hard to believe that here I was, at last, at the age of twenty-one, for the first time alone with a woman whom I had the most profound love for, whom I desired to possess sexually without any feeling of guilt, and yet I was at totally at ease with in her company, as I felt reasonably sure she was in mine. After all, why else had she asked to come? Or to ask me to come again the next Monday? I so clearly remember thinking, over and over again, *this is the woman, the only woman, I want to spend the rest of my life with.* Her or nobody. But I also believed, and in this I now know I was mistaken, that such a hope was absurd, that the best, the very best I could expect, was what already seemed within my reach, a friendship, a meeting of minds, but never of bodies. Looking back, what was most extraordinary, though I did not think so at the time, was that nothing about Maureen in those first encounters surprised me, that she was just as I not only had hoped but expected her to be; articulate, cultured, inquisitive, self-contained, serious, above all, possessed of a dignity rarely encountered in one so young.

And so the pattern of music and talk was set, save for three exceptions. A few weeks after my first official visit, I pushed my luck and asked Maureen if she would like to come with me to Ken Colyer's club just off Charing Cross Road in Little Newport Street. To my amazement as well as delight, she said yes…a date, my first for three years! It was now May 1958, the time of a protracted London bus strike, so instead of catching the bus to a tube station, we had to go by (steam) train from Brimsdown to Liverpool Street, and from there take the tube to Leicester Square. *En route* to the venue in a surface section of the Metropolitan Line, I drew Maureen's attention to the bright red sign that spelt out the name of the Communist Party's *Daily Worker* at the top of the tall building in Farringdon Road where the paper was produced. Need I say that she was not impressed. Three years later I was, more fool me.

For the first time, we sat side by side, on chairs near the front of the venue, while dancers jived at the back. Maureen must have taken rather fancy to the drummer, because she said to me, 'He's not wearing a ring.' *Is she a flirt?* I wondered. Surely not. Then later on, she turned and suddenly brought her face close to mine, as if to kiss me, and then withdrew just as suddenly. *Is she teasing me?* Back on her doorstep afterwards, with my entire body trembling, I kissed Maureen for the first time, very lightly. Her lips did not respond. This also set a pattern, for the next two years. Some nights as I took my leave she would close the front garden gate between as if to say, nothing doing, not even a peck. We made one more excursion to the Colyer club a few weeks later, and that was it. When I bought tickets for another jazz gig, she was really cross, refused to come, and told me never to do it again. I realised then that I had to settle for the role of an all-purpose entertainer, and felt glad and indeed honoured and privileged to be such. But although with a bit of stretch I could be classified as a friend, I was most definitely not her boyfriend.

This was, though I can't recall thinking so at the time, the exact reverse of my brief liaison with Pam. I frankly confess, though it is no sin in my secular book, that I was consumed not only by my love for Maureen, but from the outset, lusted after her no less madly. And who could blame me? Without ever flaunting her many charms, and in fact because of it, she exuded a slow-burning but deep sexuality that at times, before we began to become physically intimate, drove me to near distraction, since I knew that any attempt, however tentative, to give expression to my desires would put at risk the friendship that I so treasured. But gazing in barely disguised wonder at her beauty aroused in me not only the most intense erotic yearnings, but an equally overwhelming sense of the sacred. I readily admit without any embarrassment that I *worshipped* Maureen.

Although my idea of the sacred is entirely secular and earthbound, and I am as much an atheist now as I was then, my interest in religion has led me to the conclusion that while primitive man's fear of death and ignorance of the workings of the world have nourished its growth, there resides at the heart of the human psyche an unquenchable thirst for the transcendent, for meaning and purpose, a reaching out beyond one's self, and above all to love and be loved as the only means whereby we can escape from the loneliness which is otherwise our earthly lot. Unlike Catholic theology, which is saturated and obsessed with guilt about matters sexual, (hence the cult of the virgin and the supposed moral superiority of clerical celibacy) in the Lutheran version, the two kinds of love, the sacred and the profane, become one, with Jesus portrayed as the bridegroom and the bride the believing Christian, as in Bach's Cantata *Wachet Auf, ruft uns die stimme* ('Wake up, cries the watchman's voice'), adapted from the erotic Old Testament's *Song of Songs*. There, the soprano sings 'My beloved is mine', and is answered by the bass, 'And I am yours'. They then sing together, 'Love shall naught be sundered'. (After his break with Rome, Luther, an Augustinian monk, set the example for his fellow clergy by marrying Katharina von Bara, a nun, declaring to doubters that it would 'rile the Pope, cause the angels to laugh, and the devil to weep.')

All of this entered into to my love for Maureen save for this difference. Religion teaches that if we obey and love God above all worldly things, He will love us back. I struck and expected no such deal with Maureen. Yes, I loved her above all other worldly things, but unconditionally, whether she loved me or not, and after I had been visiting her for a little more than a year, somehow summoned up the courage to tell her, making it clear as I did so, to save her any embarrassment, that I did not except her to say anything in reply. Even so, she was still a little upset. But I had to tell her. However, I could see she quite liked it when, on another occasion, I told her, as we said goodnight, that she was 'bloody attractive'. But then what woman in those politically incorrect times wouldn't have? I never expected Maureen to have anything more than friendly feelings towards me. All I dared hope for was that she should continue to let me into her life for a few precious hours a week.

I was so lacking in confidence that I could win her affections that at the beginning, each time we parted, I feared it would be for the last time. I can see now that it was precisely because, so far as Maureen was concerned, there was no romantic dimension to our friendship, that my terrors would prove groundless. But I clearly recall very early on that since my undefinable status was somewhat precarious, and that one day, my services, such as they were, could be therefore easily dispensed with, deciding to adopt a tactic that might at least postpone the dreaded moment. I would nearly always bring a record I had just bought, or sometimes a book, and leave it with her, thereby, like Scheherazade, hopefully keeping at bay the day of my demise. I not experienced, more's the pity, the joy of 1001 nights with Maureen – I had to wait forty years for that privilege – but at the time, I was overjoyed to settle for what proved to be more than 200 evenings. As weeks and then months passed, my fears gradually melted away. I had become something of fixture in her weekly schedule, one that she evidently quite enjoyed and possibly even looked forward to. It was evident even to me, with my oversize inferiority complex where women were concerned, that Maureen found me interesting, even stimulating company, if not, as I assumed then, physically attractive. At least I thought, she liked my brain, if not my body.

Over the next two years or so, our friendship gradually deepened as we discovered, as from the beginning I had not only hoped but firmly believed we would, that we had so much in common. There was always music, classical, and jazz. We soon found there was large overlap between our tastes, with Maureen also into the up-market end of the more popular genres. While I quickly came to appreciate the jazz infused range and richness of Ella Fitzgerald, Maureen was left a little cold by my LP of a late Beethoven string quartet, saying said she'd rather listen to Dave Brubeck's, one comprised of piano, bass, drums, and alto sax.

I suppose everyone's musical tastes are at least partly influenced by their own personality. This was certainly true in Maureen's case, to a remarkable degree. Today, girls and young women, especially when they have been murdered, are expected to be 'bubbly', while their male counterparts must be 'good for a laugh'. If there is a word to describe their opposite, then it would fit Maureen exactly. In all the years I have spent in her company, she never bubbled, and unlike me, rarely cried. Devoid of emotions? Never. She just contained them. The composer she loved most, she told me, was Sibelius, because she felt at one with his austere darkness. If she had been acquainted with the songs of the Elizabethan lutenist and composer John Dowland, I am sure she would have recognised herself in his soulful melancholy. And yes, I can truthfully say that in the twenty-two years that I have known her, five as a young woman and the last seventeen that she spent with me, I hardly ever saw or heard Maureen laugh. The most one could expect was an occasional wry smile, one more of irony than amusement. One of my most enduring memories of the young Maureen occurred when we were listening to a Sibelius LP I had brought round. She was, as usual, sitting opposite me, wearing a dress of blue shot silk (sixty years on, I can I still remember every item in her wardrobe) that she had made herself. With first strains of *Valse Triste,* she sprang to her feet, and began to dance to the sudden alternating moods of the music, from joy to despair, but with the latter always in the ascendant. This was not an act. This was, as over time I learned, the real Maureen. That is why I chose it to be played at her funeral. And she was right. When it comes to it, our lives both as individuals and as members of a species are, for all their moments of joy, essentially tragic, doomed, along with all our works, however sublime, to extinction. Over 90% of life forms that ever existed on our planet are now extinct. Why should we be the one exception? Our turn will and must come. There will come a time when, as with all other species, the last human being will die alone on this, or possibly another planet, in an environment that is no longer able to provide the essentials for our continued existence. The same process that 13.7 billion years set in motion the chain of events that created on planet Earth and, for all we know, elsewhere, the conditions necessary for life, will culminate in the death of the universe some 100 trillion years from now.

Often in our years together, we talked of such things late into the night. Maureen's favourite TV viewing was programmes and series devoted to astronomy, science and wild life. Being of what some might regard as an overly serious disposition, like myself, though less extremely so, Maureen neither sought nor found pleasure in human company beyond that of a select few. Beyond that, she preferred the company of animals, most of all, her ever-fluctuating brood of stray cats.. 'Small talk', as it is for me, was for her too an alien art form. Maureen was never more fulfilled (I would not say 'happy') than amidst nature, and in her deep appreciation of high culture, be it art, music or literature. Given our similar psyches, it was only to be expected we would always talk about what we, and I believe rightly, regarded as important things. Temperamentally, we had much in common, but we were in no sense two peas in the proverbial pod. For a start, out backgrounds differed in many ways. I was one of three brothers, brought up, as I have already related, in an intensely political environment, and with a father who had his circumstances and the times been more favourable, would have been either been a poet or an academic. Maureen was an only child, born to an atheist father whose political involvement went little further than voting Labour, and a mother who voted Tory and was born, raised, and stayed a Roman Catholic, to be sure of lukewarm convictions, but sufficient to insist that her daughter be baptised into the same faith. Maureen had a particular aversion for the religion of her birth, so I used to rib her from time to time that she was stuck with it for life, because while under Cannon Law, there are no fewer than 12 grounds for ex-communication. (these do not include complicity in the Holocaust or that matter any number of other heinous crimes, just so long as you confess them, not to the police, but a priest.) Like Islam, the Roman church makes no provision for resignations.

In my five years of visiting Maureen at her home, I met her dad, Freddie, only a few times, since being the shy person that I was then, and still am, I rarely ventured into the Griggs's living room at the rear of the house, though on my arrival, Maureen's mum often used to come into the front room with a cup of tea and a chat.. On the first occasion that I met Maureen's dad, so as to avoid putting my foot in it by sounding off about politics, I steered our conversation towards football and his memories of the Spurs team of his younger days, a subject about which I was well-informed, since my dad, being of the same generation, was also a Spurs fan, and had in fact been among the crowd at Stamford Bridge that saw the Spurs beat Wolverhampton Wanderers one nil to win the FA cup in 1921. I think Freddie was quite impressed when I was able to not only rattle off the names of the Spurs team, but also of the player who scored the only goal of the game, Jimmy Dimmock.

I saw a lot more of Maureen's mum, Alice, who struck me as a warm-hearted, vital lady, still very attractive for her age. As I said, she used to bring me in a cup of tea while I was waiting for Maureen to make her always solemn and silent entrance. From what Maureen told me, her mother rather took a fancy to me, saying I had 'a lovely face when I smiled'. She must have seen me as possible mate for her daughter, because, as Maureen related to me shortly after we got together, when she announced her engagement to her future husband, Terry, (this would have been some four years after we had parted) instead of congratulating her, he mum said, 'pity about Robin'! Alice and Freddie were very unlike in some ways. She had an adventurous, even flighty streak (far less commonly than is the case now, Maureen had been conceived out of wedlock).

Before she was married, and this was again unusual for the time, as Maureen told it, she would go nude bathing by night in Swansea Bay, in male company. And while Freddie would be quite content to spend his annual holidays at home, just taking it easy, or with his wife's relatives in Swansea, Alice would make for the continent, seeing some of the sights Maureen and I would visit as much as half a century later. So much for Maureen's parents, in some ways, an odd couple. But anyway, they rubbed along.

From the very beginning, our evenings would follow a set routine. As I have said, she would make this silent, impassive, almost forbidding entrance, sit down in the armchair opposite me, and either put on a record, or wait for me to the make an opening conversational gambit. After the first few visits, and having tumbled to what was expected of me, rather like the lecturer I would eventually become, I would prepare one or two topics that I could dilate upon with some authority and no less crucially, of a nature that would arouse her interest…music…current events, football (we were both Spurs fans), books I had been reading. One of my special interests at the time was the then fashionable existentialism of Jean Paul Sartre, as expounded not only in his voluminous and at times almost opaque philosophical writings, but more accessibly in his celebrated trilogy, *Roads to Freedom*. I lent all three volumes to Maureen, and when we parted, I asked her to keep them. They are still on her bookshelf, along with all the others I bequeathed to her. Some of the books I either lent or gave to Maureen she passed on to her mum, who was also an avid reader. One volume in particular proved to be such strong sexual meat that even shocked her broad-minded and far from devout mum: Henry Miller's *Tropic of Cancer*. And Maureen was certainly no prude either. I can so clearly remember her triumphantly displaying to me her copy of *Lady Chatterley's Lover* days after the jury in the famous obscenity trial of Penguin Books had unanimously legalised its publication, proving that nothing guarantees literary success more than notoriety, and as with Eve, the irresistible urge to taste forbidden fruit. Just as with the Papal list of forbidden books abolished only in 1966, the *Index Librorum Prohibitorum*, Ayatollah Khomeini's still operative *fatwah* death sentence passed on Salman Rushdie for his *Satanic Verses*, the Obscene Publications Act, which outlawed until 1936 the printing and sale in the UK of that masterwork of modernism, James Joyce's *Ulysses*, and the ban on the sale in England and Wales (but not Scotland) of Peter Wright's *Spycatcher*, censorship had again achieved the opposite effect to the one intended, with millions buying a book they would otherwise have never heard of, let alone read. As a First Amendment free speecher (this being one of several bones of contention with Maureen's daughter, though not with her mother), I rejoice at these triumphs of our natural inquisitiveness over what will always, in the long run, prove to be the futile attempts of those in power to repress it. *Vive la liberte de la presse*!

IV

From the very beginning, an almost desperate anticipation of our next evening together began to intrude ever more persistently into my everyday life. I would count the days to our next meeting, and then on the day, the hours and even the minutes. It made no difference that my passion for Maureen was one that I dared not reveal, and that I knew was not requited. Just to be alone in the same room with her when once she had seemed so impossibly out of reach was enough. It was not long before Maureen established a certain rather odd routine. On my arrival, usually between 7.30 and 8.00pm, she would always let me in, and then, more often than not, without a word of greeting, leave me sitting in her front room in the armchair with its back to the front door. (The old terraced house had no hallway, the front door opening directly onto the right-hand side of the front room.) Maureen would then disappear into the kitchen-cum living room at the back, to do what I never inquired, to then reappear about an hour or so later, again usually without saying a word. The silence was normally broken by Maureen putting on a record. At other times, she would just sit there, never smiling, but gloriously beautiful, as if challenging me to say something either interesting or to cheer her up. Maureen was not acting. She was by her nature melancholy to a degree, a temperament reflected, as I have said, in her empathy with the dark tones of her favourite composer's hauntingly sombre *Valse Triste*, which for this reason I chose to bid farewell to Maureen at her funeral.

It was the shared love of music that more than anything else, over the next few months and then years, gradually drew us closer, aided by a constant supply of new LPs that I brought each week for Maureen to listen to. Her interest was sustained by the fact that my tastes in jazz were rapidly broadening. By the time I met Maureen, I was already a skilled enough trumpeter to be able to hold my own in a New Orleans style jazz band. But having been introduced by my pianist friend to the far more challenging but also exhilarating complexities of modern jazz in the bebop style of Charlie Parker, dead at 35 through drug abuse, and my idol, the superlatively gifted trumpeter Clifford Brown, killed in a car crash at 25, I felt it was time to move on. Round at my friend's place, we would work our way through the basic modern repertoire, plus some numbers he had composed himself, until we reached a level of proficiency that suggested it was time to form a proper band and do some gigging. Augmented by a drummer and double bass player, (this was long before electric bases nearly put the acoustic upright version out of business) we made our debut by playing in the interval at a local Saturday night dance. It was at this gig that I received my first payment as a musician...£1.00.

Around this it time, it occurred to me to me that my burgeoning skills as a trumpeter provided me with an opportunity, putting it bluntly, to show off to Maureen. Here, I thought, I could impress her in a field other than mere talk. Unlike New Orleans style, playing modern jazz on the trumpet demanded the ability to play at the very top register of the instrument, which fortunately I was able to do with some facility. (I am pleased to say I still can, though to make it easier, for many years now, I have used a piccolo trumpet, (as pictured at the end of this book) which plays an octave up from the conventional B flat version.) So one evening, I arrived with my trumpet-cornet, a hybrid instrument much favoured by trad jazzers of that era. Imagine my (suppressed) elation when after successfully negotiating a tricky passage in the top register, she gave me a look of astonished admiration, and patted me affectionately on the top of my head. Perhaps, I thought, this is the way to her heart, and, again I freely confess, to her gorgeous body. After all, music is the food of lust no less than of love.

Around this time, I had begun to indulge a predilection, so far as my then meagre resources would allow, for acquiring musical instruments and teaching myself to play them to varying levels of proficiency, an obsession that today, has culminated in a collection of around twenty, nearly all of them of the reed and brass families. After my trumpet recital came a few weeks later another on my newly acquired alto saxophone, a near-faultless rendition of one her jazz favourites, *Take the A Train*, a Duke Ellington number. Now on a roll (or at least, so I thought), I sustained the momentum by playing Men of Harlech on my keyless flute to her Welsh mother, who by this time, as Maureen later told me, had taken quite a liking to me, though much good did it do me. Finally, there was my cheap Spanish guitar, on which I attempted a very crude imitation of flamenco. Though she never said so until about forty years later, I could see from her reactions that Maureen was greatly impressed with my versatility.

Until my arrival on the scene, Maureen had never owned a musical instrument, though she did tell many years later than during her stay in Buckingham, she had played the trumpet in a school band, though at her age then, it could only have been a toy one. But she did have a very accurate and pure singing voice, which she often demonstrated to me by her ability to reproduce exactly the demanding vocal lines sung by the incomparable Ella Fitzgerald. She learned musical theory and sight reading at Tottenham High, and had sung in Bach's St Mathew Passion with her school choir. All that was lacking was an instrument. Here at least, fortune smiled upon me. Maureen had a particular fondness for the Mozart clarinet quintet and concerto, no doubt chiefly for the melancholy and wistful beauty of the clarinet passages in their slow movements (for the same reason as the Sibelius, the concerto movement was played at her funeral). It so happened that at the time, an old school friend who played in the same football team as myself (the Joan Henderson history protege in the year below me) who in turn knew a student at his college who had a clarinet for sale. Was I interested? Was I! When I told her what was on offer, so was Maureen. The asking price was a little under forty pounds, a bit steep for those days for a second-hand clarinet, but it was in very good condition…and amazingly still is. So keen was I to generate another reason for her to continue seeing me (I now pictured myself as her clarinet tutor) that to make sure she bought it, I told Maureen it would cost her only thirty. She said yes. I gladly paid the difference. As she could read music, she made quite rapid progress, to the point where she could play well enough for me to accompany her on my guitar. I even composed a few simple pieces we could play together. This was for me, if not for Maureen, sheer bliss.

The only substantial change in our routine over the first three years or so was the day, or rather evening, on which it took place. Partly I think because the hour of my departure became ever later – this I took to be a positive indicator of the value placed on my services – after some months, my slot was shifted to Friday, an upgrade of sorts maybe, but leaving with me the thought that I was now serving as an *hors d'oeuvres* for what I naturally assumed were Maureen's Saturday night frolics with other, how shall I put it… more normal male company.

This was an entirely reasonable assumption, since I have a clear recollection of her telling me round about that time, rather hesitantly, as we set opposite each other in her front room's two armchairs (it would be some time yet before we get around to sharing the sofa, of which more anon) that she had 'a friend'. Given the context, I was clearly intended to understand that he was not just a friend (of sorts) like me, but Maureen's boyfriend. But that did not inhibit me from telling her, as I have already related, that as we said goodnight one Friday, that I loved her. When I saw how much distress this had caused her, I quickly added, 'You don't have to say anything.' Neither did she, then or later. Next Friday, it was as if it had never happened. But now she knew for sure what must have been pretty obvious to her from the very beginning.

Despite being warned off making any serious advances or entertaining any false hopes in the kindest possible manner by her allusion to what must surely have been her boyfriend, things were not so straightforward as I was led to believe, though what I took to be the existing set up hardly merited that description either.

Not long before her death, Maureen said to me that from the very beginning, 'I liked your profile,' her way of saying she found me interesting and stimulating company. My, let us say, unorthodox situation arose partly at least from the fact that so far as I was able to ascertain, the mysterious 'friend', whom I later learned was called Neil, was already *in situ* when I arrived on the scene or had arrived on it pretty soon after, and one boyfriend at a time was evidently quite enough even for the flighty Maureen. Hence my allotted role as entertainer and, to a limited degree, for want of a more apt description, enlightener, at least in certain matters. But in the early autumn of 1960, despite Neil's continued presence on the scene, that was about to change in a manner and with repercussions that I could not possibly have anticipated. I had been back on the academic treadmill for the best part of two years, punctuated by less cerebral graft in the summer and Christmas holidays to help pay for the unsolicited Griggs Geld that I continued to bestow upon her most Fridays.

One balmy late September night, in accordance with the now long-established routine, I said goodnight just inside the slightly ajar door and kissed her gently on the lips, expecting the customary *pro-forma* peck. But not this time! In a surge of what I can now only assume must have been a long pent up desire, she pressed her body against mine and kissed me, almost desperately. With my head swimming, I responded as best I knew how. As passion fed off passion, she became more aroused, her tongue reaching into my mouth. After how long, given my state of mind, I cannot say, our lips parted as if by mutual agreement and we bid each other goodnight. I realised at that moment – and I am sure I was meant to – that much, if not everything, had changed, and that whatever the future might hold for us, there would be no going back to my former station. True, I was still not Maureen's boyfriend, nor would I ever be. But

I was no longer just her entertainer. There was now a physical dimension to our friendship that she had quite deliberately chosen to initiate. And though I could not then have possibly anticipated it, that kiss set in train a series of events that would culminate in us becoming lovers. When, more than forty years later, I reminisced, as I was want to do, about that wonderful moment, and how I could remember almost to the day when it happened, Maureen was very embarrassed and apologetic, saying how wrong she had been to wait all that time before giving me a proper kiss…further evidence that not all was as I was led to believe or had assumed in those first two years.

As I hoped, and indeed expected, that ecstatic goodnight kiss was not a special treat. And for that reason, as I have indicated, it marked a turning point in our friendship. But before that got properly underway, shortly afterwards, we went out on our third, and as it turned out, last date to see the stage production of *West Side Story*, her (and my) favourite musical. How could we have known then that forty years later, almost to the day, we would see the same production at Swansea's Grand Theatre? Who said history doesn't repeat itself? Well not exactly. Within minutes of returning home, with both of us much moved by the memories of times past, and myself thoroughly aroused by how enticing she looked sitting on her settee in her quite short yellow dress, displaying her still gloriously voluptuous legs, I found myself saying, and this was quite out of character for me, 'Do you want to be screwed?' to which she replied, even more out character: 'You bet I do.' But I digress. By this time, Maureen's attachments were becoming rather complicated, because, as she recently related to me with some amusement, when she told Neil about our date (why, she never said, but knowing Maureen, I can guess) in a fit of jealousy, he insisted that he take her to the same show the very next week. Naturally, I was never told at the time of this rather peculiar development. Yes, Neil was evidently still officially at least the boyfriend. But her affections were not his unique property, In fact, as I learned from her daughter shortly after her mother died, sometime after Maureen and I parted in the Summer of 1963, she and Neil became engaged to be married, only for Maureen to break it off. Looking back on those times, I can see now how my arrival on the scene had greatly complicated Maureen's emotional life, though she compounded the complications by not only telling me about Neil, but telling Neil, her official boyfriend and prospective fiancé, about me. What *was* she playing at? I can only assume that Neil had put his foot down and had insisted that there could be no more dates with me. But what did I care, because in Maureen's front room, things were becoming slowly but steadily more intimate, a development that only deepens the mystery surrounding her relationship with both myself and my unseen rival Neil.

Luckily for me, Maureen liked doing crossword puzzles and quizzes. Her dad used to bring home the London *Evening News*, long now defunct, which always had a crossword puzzle. To do them together, we needed to sit on the sofa, another departure from the old routine. There was no kissing or cuddling, at least not for a good time yet. To sit close to her was enough. Another bonus for me was the opportunity to display my general knowledge. One question required the name of the Spaniard who led the conquest of Mexico. If the reader will recall, I had, of course, read the book as a child, and was able to supply not only his name, but the correct dates of the conquest. Maureen was truly impressed, as she was with my providing the correct answer to a question which required the most goals scored by a First Division team in a single season: 128 by Aston Villa in 1930-31. More correct answers led to quizzes and crosswords become a feature of the evening's itinerary I was discovering that having a good memory was not only an academic asset. It could also serve as means to more intimacy. And there was the added bonus that Neil while might be Maureen's boyfriend, I was proving myself to be her Renaissance Man. And now it was becoming evident even to me that this beautiful woman actually found me sexually attractive. The weekly goodnight kisses become more protracted. I could feel her body trembling as she pressed it against mine. This was surely something like love.

Unlike Maureen, politics were in my DNA. At the time I met her, I would have described myself as being on the far left, a communist of sorts, but very far from uncritical of the Soviet variety. For example, I donated a pound, a fair sum for an impecuniary student, to a fund for refugees fleeing the Soviet repression of the Hungarian Revolution in November 1956. More interested in causes than joining any party, in 1959 I was one of the five thousand supporters of the Campaign for Nuclear Disarmament who took to the road to march to London from the nuclear weapons centre at Aldermaston in Berkshire.

Maureen was interested in politics, and far more knowledgeable about them than most young woman. But unlike me, her interests did not lead to action. She was far too busy anyway with her studies. And being under twenty-one, she could not even vote. Had she been able to, it would have almost certainly like Freddy who took the pro-Labour *Daily Herald* and voted accordingly. It was her attitude to religion that really puzzled me. Most Sundays, she would attend the local Plymouth Brethren with her friend Joyce, whose parents were both devoted members of the congregation, and had their daughter on what they mistakenly believed was a was a very tight leash. Many years later, Maureen explained to me that she was acting as a chaperon for her wayward friend, who with her connivance, would engage in pursuits that were strictly forbidden by the ultra-strict code of the Brethren. As to Maureen's own beliefs at that time, it is hard for me to say, became although she knew where I stood, I never really pressed her on the subject. Unlike her dad, she would certainly not have described herself as an atheist, more like a sceptic or doubter who was shopping around and had not yet found the answer.

Alice Griggs, from how Maureen described her, was

vaguely Tory. It was much the same in matters religious, Catholic, though like many, more by habit (being part Irish) than conviction, as was evident from her skinny dipping on Swansea beaches and her pre-marital adventures (but at least minus a condom) with Maureen's father to be. With evident pride, since she loved her Freddy dearly, Maureen told me (in the wake of 9/11) that based on his pre-war experiences in the Middle East, her dad had predicted, long before it became a reality, that the next world conflict would fought out between Islam and the West. How fitting then that my most recently published work, provisionally entitled *Allah's Useful Idiots* but for tactical reasons, since in the current political climate, no book-seller would risk stocking it, changed to *The Socialism of Fools: The Rise and Fall of Comrade Corbyn,* should be devoted to this very same subject and that I should have dedicated it, after her death, to Freddy's beloved daughter.

We are now in the spring of 1961. By this time, I was sharing digs with a student friend in a cramped room just off Great Portland Street, not far from the West End. It just so happened that he shared my political views, and agreed that the time had come to commit ourselves to the cause. And what was this cause? Pretty much the same as my father's at a similar age; to rid the world of poverty, war, oppression, ignorance, disease...the list could go on. The means? The abolition of capitalism and its replacement by socialism. It seemed so obvious, and no less simple. As the saying goes, 'if you're not a communist at twenty, where's your heart? If you're still a communist at forty, where's your brain?' And, sure enough, by about that age, my heart had indeed started to function properly.

The Labour Party, my flat-mate and I agreed, was hopelessly comprised by its reformism. So far as we knew at that time, that left only the Communist Party, flawed though it was by its uncritical deference to its Soviet masters. We entertained the illusion that by joining the party, we, with others of a like mind, could put it to rights. And so one April day, perhaps in my case, influenced in my decision by Yuri Gagarin's spectacular pioneering circumnavigation of the earth a few days previously, we made tracks to the party headquarters in King Street, Covent Garden, and were duly signed up. We were allocated to the Central London Students branch, which organised university students in the London area. Thus began my career as an aspiring revolutionary. It never occurred to me then or indeed for at least another two years, that this step could lead to my separation from the woman I loved so deeply, and cared for more than anything else in the world, including my dreams of revolution. Yet it proved to be a decision that was fated to leave an indelible imprint not only on my life, but also Maureen's. Her dad said when he learned from her of my new political commitment, 'One day he'll learn.' I did, but far too late.

The movement I had just joined had, from its foundation in 1920, always been one of the smallest communist parties in the western world, both in absolute terms and even more so in relation to the British population. Born at time when the Labour Party was getting into its stride, forming its first government four years later under Ramsay MacDonald, the party was never able to win a significant following amongst its target constituency, the industrial working class. The party membership peaked at around 50,000 during the Second World War, when it bathed in the reflected glory of the Red Army. With the onset of the Cold War and the Soviet repressions in Hungary in 1956, membership declined catastrophically, and stood at around 30,000 when I joined in 1961. The party was, however, successful at either recruiting or at least influencing a large number of prominent trade union leaders, intellectuals and cultural figures, some of whom were household names, many in the latter two categories being ideally qualified for fronting the campaigns the party launched from time to time. These, more often than not, either had the aim of promoting the achievements and describing the happy life of the Soviet people, or defending the Kremlin's foreign policy, which was invariable depicted as one of peace. (The daughter of one such celebrity, the actor Michael Redgrave, was destined to perform, literally, a similar promotional role for the Trotskyist Workers Revolutionary Party of one Gerry Healy, of whom more anon.)

Aside from the predominance of the Labour Party, one of the main impediments to its growth was the Communist Party's notorious subservience to Moscow. Until the Soviet invasion of Czechoslovakia in August 1968, the party had never publicly voiced any criticism of Soviet policies and actions, for example the Moscow show trials and purges of the 1930s, when Stalin framed-up and executed nearly of Lenin's closest comrade and the general staff of the Red Army, an act of self-abasement only equalled by the party's endorsement of Stalin's pact with Hitler in August 1939 and the Kremlin's bloody suppression of workers uprisings in East Germany in 1953 and Hungary in 1956. This was the party that, with a little help from those of a like mind, we thought we could set to rights. In truth, as we both soon discovered, it was not a matter of rejuvenating an essentially healthy organism partly disfigured by a few Cromwellian warts, but lancing and draining a poisonous outgrowth on the British Labour and trade union movement. Over the next few months, a series of momentous political events led me to realise why Trotsky described Stalinism as the cancer of the workers' movement.

Meanwhile, my three-year friendship with Maureen was deepening into something approaching romance, albeit of an undefinable kind. I began to write poems for (and some about) her, some of which, if they took her fancy, she would later read out to me. Imagine my feelings when some forty years later, scrabbling around in her desk for something or other, I discovered she had carefully preserved every single one in a plastic folder. Some, predictably, were overtly political and others, rather laboured attempts at satire and the like. Nevertheless, Maureen must have been quite taken with my efforts at the time, because she told me when we met up again that she had looked upon me as another Browning in the making. Praise indeed, but reading them again now, I think largely undeserved, except possibly for the two that were not very heavily disguised love poems. It was these that Maureen, obviously not by chance, had chosen to copy out on a typewriter. Since the passion and devotion, they conveyed had evidently moved her to do so, I reproduce the better of the two, which when I first gave it to her, she, uncharacteristically clearly touched, read out to me:

AFFIRMATION

I ask no bargain save rejection
Of the mirrored wish of vanity's reflected self, For what prisoned obligations gifts ensnare
I absolve.
I crave no favour more than truth's homage, That this incidental ray has through love's prism Cast the spectrum of my mortality.
Time's harsh eclipse, though full, shall leave This precious gleam imaged still,
That by its shadowed pledge I shall, Affirming, divine the globe
Of each man's sun.

Come the summer of 1961, in the wake of my enlistment, as I fondly imagined, in the ranks of the revolutionary army, there occurred another no less radical change in my life, at the time completely unconnected to the first, but destined in time to collide with it, and with consequences that were certainly tragic for me, and I now believe for Maureen also. The student friend I shared my room with returned in the summer vacation to his family home in the Midlands, leaving me as the sole occupant. I cannot now remember whose idea it was, but the upshot was that for the first time, I became the host, and Maureen the guest. One Friday I met Maureen from work at Great Portland Street tube station, and we walked the short distance down to my room. It was so small, there was only space to squeeze in two beds against each wall, leaving a narrow gap in between. As there was no room for armchairs, let alone a sofa, we set side by side on my bed. I dutifully followed the routine long-established at 42 Eastfield Road, putting on a couple of records. Then sensing that perhaps this time, in this different setting, something more was wanted of me, I turned to Maureen and kissed her. Her response told me I was right. And so it continued for the rest of that evening. And not just that evening. Back at number 42 on Maureen's sofa, like the first proper kiss on her doorstep a year previously, this new level of intimacy became the norm. If I can use an admittedly distinctly unromantic image, it was like a ratchet, with each forward movement registering a greater intimacy from which there was no regression. Where was this leading? What did I mean to Maureen? And where did this leave the 'friend'? Whatever the answers to these questions might have been, I knew I dare not ask. We never once talked about our feelings for each other. Me because I was afraid it would break the spell by in some way putting her on the spot about our relationship; Maureen, I sensed, I think rightly, because of her other commitment. So, to put it rather crudely I admit, but also accurately, we 'got on with it'. As they say, actions speak louder than words. What I do realise now is that step by step, Maureen's growing feelings for me were drawing her ever deeper into a predicament that at the outset, she had felt able to avoid.

At this same time, towards then end of 1961, my political involvements underwent a no less dramatic evolution, caused by great events far removed from the sofa at 42, Eastfield Road. In August of that year, to stem the accelerating flow of Germans emigrating to the West, the Soviet authorities ordered their East German satraps to construct a wall separating off East Berlin from its Western sector. As the remaining gaps in the wall closed, so East German border guards began shooting those who made a last desperate dash for freedom. This greatly troubled me. First Hungary in 1956, and now this. Why were so many Germans ready to risk their lives in a near suicidal attempt to escape from what I been assured was a communist paradise? A matter of weeks later, the USSR initiated a series of hydrogen bomb tests in the atmosphere, exactly what I had marched against two years previously. Finally, at the 22nd Congress of the Soviet Communist Party, Khrushchev made a speech, on this occasion in public, denouncing the crimes of Stalin. My head span. Was communism a fraud, or just its Soviet version?

But the event which more than any other pushed me over the brink into the ranks of the Trotskyist Socialist Labour League, and by the same token, set me on a path towards my parting from Maureen, was the day, 16 October 1961, when Paris riot police under the command of the former Nazi collaborator, Maurice Papon, were set loose on a peaceful demonstration of 30,000 Algerians demanding independence from French rule. Even now, it is not known how many Algerians were killed, many of them beaten up and drowned in the River Seine, but the total is well in excess of a hundred. Worst of all, given my membership of the Communist Party, was that its far more influential French counterpart (it regularly recorded around 25% of the vote in elections) had some years previously voted in the National Assembly to give emergency powers to the army stationed in Algeria to crush the country's independence movement, the FLN. The result was massacres and torture on an ever-expanding scale, later graphically chronicled in the film *The Battle of Algiers*. By the war's end in 1962 something like a million Algerian Arabs had been killed, and countless more displaced from their homes.

A manifesto against the war, signed by 121 prominent intellectuals and cultural figures, including the philosopher Jean-Paul Satre, the feminist writer Simone de Beauvoir, the conductor Pierre Boulez, the novelist, Alain Robbe-Grillet, the actress Simone Signoret and Francois Truffaut, the film maker. *But not* a *single member of the French Communist Party*. When, in Clermont Ferrand, parents lay on the railway lines to prevent the departure of the troop train taking their conscripted sons to be trained as murderers and torturers, the communist mayor of the city persuaded them to abandon their protest. Continuing the same policy, the French communists mounted no protests against the Paris massacre, the reason being, as it was quite correctly explained to me later by my new Trotskyist comrades, that Soviet interests required that nothing be done to embarrass or alienate the government of President De Gaulle, who at that time, was very friendly with the Kremlin, while far less so with the United States.

It was at this precise time, when I had so many questions but no answers, that I met Mark Jenkins, a mature student of economics, who was to prove a firm friend and comrade over the next fifty and more years. We got talking about politics, and having aired my doubts as to the wisdom of certain Soviet policies, he revealed to me that he was associated with an organisation I had never heard of before, called the Socialist Labour League. (Some twelve years later, in 1973 the SLL changed its name to the Workers Revolutionary Party, now sporting a galaxy of thespians headed by that renowned proletarian warrior, Vanessa Redgrave.) Mark was able to give answers to my doubts that I found totally convincing. It was quite simple really. The Kremlin could not care less about the Algerians. There were much bigger, geopolitical fish to fry. The inveterate anti-American De Gaulle had always been the weakest link in the NATO chain, and Soviet policy was directed towards detaching it altogether. If that meant supporting continued French rule in Algeria, so be it.

Intrigued, to say the least, I agreed to continue our discussions. Our exchanges shifted to other, but clearly related issues that troubled me, the Berlin Wall, the Soviet H-bomb tests, Soviet foreign policy, Khrushchev's revelations about Stalin's crimes Was the USSR even a socialist country when its economy and standards of living clearly lagged so far behind the capitalist west? Mark had answers off pat for all my questions and doubts. What intrigued most of all was that for the first time, I was confronted by an analysis and political line to the left of the Communist Party's. So, who were the Socialist Labour

League exactly? Obviously not anarchists...But what then? When Mark gave me a pamphlet to read...it was about the rise of the Nazis...the answer was on the front cover. It was by Leon Trotsky.

Of course, I knew who Trotsky was, but little or nothing about his political legacy. He was one of the leaders of the Russian Revolution of 1917 who when Lenin died in 1924, fell out with Stalin, though over what I had no clear idea. He ended up in exile in Mexico and was assassinated by an agent of Stalin in 1940. That was about the extent of my knowledge of Trotsky. To my shame, I did not even know he was head of the Red Army in the civil war that followed the revolution. Over the next few months I set about remedying this deficiency, beginning a serious study of the writings of Trotsky, while continuing my discussions with Mark, and in due course, with leading members of the SLL. This is the substance of what I gleaned from my reading, and my conversations. To summarise, and unavoidably, to simplify matters, the SLL saw itself as continuing in the tradition of the Bolshevik Revolution of November 1917, a revolution which had been betrayed by Stalin and his usurping clique, whose main concern was to preserve the newly-won privileges of the party elite at the expense of the Soviet masses and Lenin's original goal of world revolution. Rule by terror and the maintenance of vast social and economic inequalities at home, and abroad, compromise with world capitalism: this for Trotsky summed up the essence of Stalin's policy. After being exiled in 1929, Trotsky initially hoped to win support for his polices in the western communist parties, but met with very little success. After seeking to merge, largely unsuccessfully, with other small anti-Stalin groups, in 1938, Trotsky founded his own movement, the Fourth International, to challenge the Third, which had been founded by the Bolsheviks in 1919 with a view to spreading their revolution to the west, but like the parent Bolshevik

Party had, by the late 1920s, succumbed to the total domination of Stalin and his placemen. (The First International had been founded by Marx and Engels in 1864, but went into terminal decline after the suppression of the Paris Commune in 1871. It was eventually replaced by the Second in 1889, which is still in business today as the Socialist International, representing all the social democratic and labour parties of the civilised world.)

Only in, of places, the USA, did Trotskyism gain a significant foothold in the labour movement. In 1934, its working-class militants led and won a general strike in Minneapolis for the recognition of the Teamsters union, a victory gained in the teeth of state and vigilante violence and even murder (two dead, 67 wounded just in one day). A small but resourceful and determined group of Trotskyists had helped to inspire the spectacular rise of the CIO, the Congress of Industrial Organisations, to become the largest trade union federation in the world. Despite the many differences I would now have with them were they still alive, these honest and courageous class warriors I nevertheless regard as my comrades.

Purist political movements, like their religious counterparts, with whom they ironically share many features, are vulnerable to bitter, if often obscure doctrinal disputes and splits, and the Fourth International, being one such movement, has proved to be no exception to this tendency. Struggling to recover from the ravages of the second world war, and since his murder in 1940, lacking the authority of a figure equal in stature to Trotsky, the comrades fell out over how to rebuild and expand a movement that by comparison with its Stalinist and social democratic rivals, was miniscule. One faction proposed secretly joining the larger western communist parties, notably in France and Italy, hoping thereby to push them to the left. This tactic, known as 'deep entry', was opposed by the other faction, horrified at the prospect of the kind of compromises this would entail in order to be accepted as loyal Stalinists. The resulting split produced two movements, each claiming the title Fourth International. The SLL belonged to the later grouping, along with its co-thinkers in France and the USA. All this I learned only sometime after I became a member, in December 1961.

For the two years that I then operated as a largely clandestine oppositionist inside the Communist Party, there was a great deal concerning the SLL's past that remained a closed book to me, mainly because my main focus had been on the history of Stalinism and the ideas of the man to whom the League owed its allegiance. What little I did learn was gleaned from obscure allusions to past factional conflicts, which, though at the time the irony escaped me, just like the Communist Party's, invariably ended in expulsions. I also became aware of the existence of rival Trotskyist grouplets, each ironically being the product of a purge by Gerry Healy, who occupied the same post of General Secretary that enabled Stalin to eliminate, physically in his case, his political opponents. Re-enforcing the similarity with religious movements, the expellees from the SLL were invariably referred in tones more suited to the Catholic Inquisition's persecution of heretics than a secular movement based on rational principles…'revisionist', 'opportunist' and 'renegade' being the most favoured.

In fact, had I known it, the movement I had joined, with a fanatical hatred of all its rivals far more venomous than any directed against the Tories, was already exhibiting some of the classic symptoms of a sect, and having eliminated all threats to his total dominance, under Healy's sole leadership was well on the way to the final stage of the progression to a cult, one accompanied as always by the leader's sexual exploitation of its younger female members. As I learned many years later, Healy was already 'at it', when I joined, though on much more modest scale than the herculean performance he subsequently sustained, when his maintenance of a harem of more than twenty female comrades led to a spectacular public exposure and downfall in 1985.

When the Fourth International divided in the early 1950s over the strategy of 'deep entry' into mass Stalinist parties, it was understood by the opponents of this policy that the same objections did not apply to entry into social democratic parties, where, unlike the SLL, differences of opinion were regarded as normal and indeed, productive. In this more liberal environment, it was entirely possible, unlike in the monolithic communist parties, to advance policies which were at odds the with leadership, while taking care to conceal a higher allegiance to the Fourth International. (Trotsky had in fact proposed this tactic, known as 'entryism', in the middle 1930s.) With its federal structure, the Labour Party was ideally suited to such an operation, comprising as it did a broad coalition of the trades unions and individual members in constituency branches, together with a large number and variety of affiliated bodies such as the Fabián Society and the Co-operative movement, and groupings which campaigned for their own distinctive polices. Normally, the only restriction placed on their activity was that they and their individual members could not stand against or support rival candidates in elections.

Up until 1959, Healy and his supporters, known, but only to themselves, as 'The Club', and comprised largely, like Healy, of ex-members of the Communist Party, also operated on this basis in the Labour Party, exploiting a laxity granted to party critics that, ironically, Lenin had outlawed in 1921 with his ban on oppositional groupings in what was already the only legal party in Soviet Russia. Possessed by the messianic delusion that he was destined to lead not only the British, but the world communist revolution - and the conviction that British capitalism was approaching its death throes, in 1959, the same year the Tories won a general election with a majority of 100 seats (the biggest since Baldwin's in 1924 until Thatcher's in 1983) Healy publicly launched the Socialist Labour League, effectively, if not in name, as a party within a party.

Inevitably, and I believe as Healy intended, once League members identified themselves as supporters of the SLL, it was proscribed by and its members expelled from the Labour Party. The accusations of witch-hunting that ensued were ironic, bearing in mind Healy's own ruthless suppression of even the mildest dissent within his own movement. The last foothold of the SLL in the Labour Party was the party's youth movement, the Young Socialists, which served purely as a battle ground between three Trotskyist factions; Healy's, the 'deep entrists', who later achieved notoriety in Liverpool as the 'Militant Tendency' after its brief but disastrous capture of the city's Labour council, and the International Socialists, later the Socialist Workers Party, whose founder, Tony Cliff, had been expelled by Healy for adopting a neutralist position on the Koran war. The I.S. were always referred to by the SLL as 'state capitalists', because this was the definition the group gave to the USSR and its east European colonies, contrary to the 'orthodox' position, inherited from Trotsky, that they were neither capitalist nor, as the Communist Party claimed, socialist, but 'deformed workers' states'.

Healy lost his last foothold in the Labour Party when his faction was expelled from the Young Socialists in 1964. Using the same name, the expellees became the youth section of the SLL, several of whose more attractive and compliant female members were inducted into Healy's ever-expanding harem. The League was now set on the course that would lead in 1969 to the launching of his own daily paper, the *Workers Press* (with me as its Foreign Editor) and then, in 1973, the formation of the Workers Revolutionary Party, by which I had departed two years previously. Yet despite the nomenclature, like nearly all far left groups, what existed in reality was a party for the workers, but not of them. When I joined, in 1961, the membership could have been no more than 200, many, if not most of middle class provenance, and the proportion increased as students like myself joined and disillusioned older working-class members, habituated to life in the Labour Party, dropped out. By the time of my departure in 1971, nearly all the full-time staff at the head office were (female) ex-students, with most of them employed with an eye to their suitability as the leader's concubines. With the advent of the WRP, the middle-class ascendency became even more pronounced, dramatised, literally, by an influx of well-heeled thespians. Meantime, a revolt against the party's unrealistic policies by car workers at the Oxford Leyland plant, largely instigated, I am proud to say, by Mark and myself, led to their expulsion *en masse,* so completing the bourgeoisification of Healy's party.

It will legitimately be asked, and in all probability with a degree of justified incredulity - why, having seen through the fraudulent claims and experienced at first hand the machinations of the bureaucratic regime of the Communist Party, did I remain in a movement which not only replicated, but complemented them with the thuggery and debauchery of its leader? I had even been a victim of the first, whereas concerning the second, because of its nature, I knew nothing until some years after I left, though there were fleeting moments when I had my suspicions, only then to dismisses them as equivalent to *lèse majesté*. Not to excuse my gullibility, but to understand an experience I shared with others in a similar predicament, I offer a parallel.

As I have already related, down the ages Popes have been guilty of the most appalling crimes, on a scale infinitely greater than any perpetrated by comrade Healy. In recent years, Catholic parents have discovered that their children are being raped by their priest, sometimes even with the knowledge of and protection from criminal charges by their superiors, yet in almost every case, the faithful have retained their faith, and even their loyalty to the institutions and persons who have abused their trust, to the extent that they have been persuaded to become complicit in protecting the guilty from prosecution. For some, faith has no limits. Just as Roman Catholic doctrine has it that 'outside the church there is no salvation', so Healy used to repeat *ad infinitum* that without revolutionary leadership, this being his own, there could be no revolution, and hence, no deliverance from the evils of capitalism.. Under Stalin, and also Healy, this doctrine was further distilled until the success of the entire revolutionary enterprise became dependent on the genius of its single leader…a total negation of the two most fundamental axioms of Karl Marx, that all history is the history of class struggle, and that the working class can only be emancipated by its own efforts.

In addition to subscribing to the core principles of Leninism, what also kept me in the SLL for ten years, and many others faced with the same dilemma, was my separation of the ideas from those who were perverting them, just as Catholics do. And there was much about these ideas that were, and I believe still are to be respected. Though Mark and I long ago…it must more than forty years now…became disenchanted with the kind of politics Trotsky's epigones practised, we still agreed that he without doubt possessed far and away the most brilliant and penetrating political intellect of the 20th century. In the space of only ten years, he uniquely predicted no fewer than five momentous historic events. In 1931, he warned that if the Stalinists persisted in their suicidal policy in Germany of refusing to formed an anti-fascist united front with the socialists (the Stalinists called them 'social fascists') Hitler would come to power and crush them both. He would of course be proved right. Nearly a year before the conclusion of the Nazi-Soviet Pact on August 23, 1939, Trotsky forecast that Stalin would make a deal with Hitler. He also foresaw that no more than two years after the signing of the pact, Hitler would invade the Soviet Union., which he did on June 22, 1941.

Finally, there was the Second World War and the Holocaust. This is what he wrote in December 1938: 'The number of countries that expel the Jews grows without cease. The number of countries able |[and one can say, willing] to accept them decreases. It is possible to imagine without difficulty what awaits the Jews at the mere outbreak of the future world war. But even without war, the next development of the reaction signifies with certainty the physical extermatoin of the Jews.' Five out of five. Not bad, especially when you compare it to Chamberlain's 'peace for our time'. Pity no-one was listening. Unrivalled as a Cassandra, his unshakable belief that the revolution which began in Russia in November 1917 would eventually conquer the entire world has been totally refuted by the history of the next hundred years. In a speech heralding what he believed was the onset of world communist revolution, made one year after the Bolshevik seizure of power, Trotsky announced with total conviction that 'the last fight, the fight to the death, has begun', that 'complete success' would take at most 'a few more years' and possibly, 'if things go well', 'a few more months'. How wrong can you be?

All but the most purblind of his followers would have to admit that the last century has witnessed, not the world-wide triumph of communism, but, for all its many sins, the global conquest of the world by its mortal enemy, capitalism, and its restoration, even in the land that saw the birth of the first communist state, and, crowning irony, also in China, by the successors to Mao Tse Tung. Where Trotsky erred, and spectacularly was in his inability to draw the necessary conclusions from the failure of communism to spread to the western world, to the very countries where Marx believed it would begin. Neither Trotsky nor Lenin took into account the huge gulf that separated the traditions, political cultures and institutions of the civilised West and the still semi-barbaric East. The brutal, essentially Asiatic methods adopted by first Lenin and then Stalin, at enormous human cost, and with at best, meagre benefits for the mass of the population, could never hope to command sufficient popular support in those two strongholds of liberal democratic capitalism, western Europe and north America, where centuries of struggle for democracy and individual freedom had created a liberal political culture totally alien to the Russian form of communism. As a result, nowhere in the western world has a communist party, unlike its social democratic rivals, remotely approached winning a majority in a democratically elected parliament.

Even Trotsky, the most internationalist of all the Bolshevik leaders, was unable to transcend the conditions of his time and place, of a Russia that was more Asiatic than European, of the barbaric legacy, frequently acknowdged by both himself and Lenin, of the 'Tartar yoke', of the centuries of plunder and ravaging by the Golden Horde of Genghis Khan and his successors, a Russia that under the despotism of the tsars, was so isolated from the rest of Europe that it was left untouched by the Reformation and the Renaissance. The final result was a tsarist empire so stunted in its development that it could not but help in its turn, shape the political and moral culture of the regime that replaced it. Even today, the legacy remains. Though Putin's authoritarian Russia possesses the world's largest nuclear arsenal, critical journalists and politicians are assassinated, even abroad, like Trotsky, while the expectation of life for its men, 66 and falling is far closer to 'third world' countries such as Pakistan, at 65, than it is to those of the first, like Germany, at 78.

The highly centralised, and some would argue, as I do in my *Seeds of Evil*, elitist methods of organisation and political mobilisation that proved effective for a small minority seizing and holding to power in a semi-Asiatic, semi-feudal Russia have, for these same reasons, proved themselves utterly alien to, and therefore lacking in popular appeal, in countries that stand on a far higher level of all-round development. Their continued advocacy by the far left has, as one would expect, resulted in decades of fragmentation and marginalisation... until, that is, an unpredictable and unprecedented combination of events led to their capture and near-ruination of the Labour Party by the eastern-oriented Corbynistas, with their Bolshevik associations, obsessional hatred of Israel and endorsement of Jihadi movements dedicated to its destruction.

This is of course all wisdom long after the event. At the time, in the autumn of 1961, Trotsky, in the midst of my progressive disenchantment with the Soviet government and its British apologists, seemed to have all the answers as to why the communism of Marx and Lenin (at the time, I mistakenly saw no principled distinction between the two) had failed to live up to their expectations. The explanation I had arrived at, and it was pretty close to the truth, was that under Stalin and his successors, Soviet policy had totally subordinated their policies to the preservation of the power and privileges of the ruling elite, and not the goal of world socialism. What I could not see then, and it would be another twenty or so years before I did, was that the seeds of Stalin's evil were sown by Lenin (hence the title of my book on the subject). and that the goal of a world communist revolution on the Bolshevik model was sheer fantasy. Contrary to the Trotskyist legend, it was not under Stalin's but Lenin's leadership that the progression began from a fleeting multi-party soviet democracy to a one-party and then one faction party, only then to culminate in the rule of single despot under Stalin. But that realisation had to wait the best part of twenty years.

Greatly relieved that I did not have to throw the communist baby out with the Stalinist bath water, after meeting the SLL's chief in a pub and attending a couple of education classes at the League's offices in Clapham, I decided to join. About this time, I participated in a demonstration held by the League outside the French Embassy to protest against the detention without trial of the leader of the FLN and future first President of independent Algeria, Ahmed Ben Bella. A few months previously, I might have asked myself, *where is the Communist Party?* Now, I knew the answer.

Having joined the SLL, I found myself in a situation very similar to that of my dad, when he operated inside the Labour Party on behalf of the Communist Party. My allotted task, which I must say I quickly warmed to, was to remain in the Communist Party, posing as a loyal if occasional critical member (as my dad did in the Labour Party) with the aim of winning over more recruits to the League. Unlike the Militant tactic of 'deep entry' already referred to, I no longer entertained the illusion that the Communist Party could be pushed to the left. My aim was the exact opposite, to win recruits to the SLL by demonstrating that the more we criticised current party policies, the more likely it was that the party leadership would respond by silencing and then, if that failed, expelling us. And this is indeed exactly what happened.

The opportunity to create a clandestine opposition among the party's London student membership arose when two other communist parties, the Chinese and the Italian, began to publicly criticise the polices of the then Soviet leader, Nikita Khrushchev, though doing so from totally opposed standpoints. While the Chinese took him to task for his pursuit of what was called 'peaceful coexistence' with the West, the reformist policies being pursued, with Soviet approval, by western parties like the British and the Italian, and not, least, the public dethronement of Stalin by Khrushchev at the Soviet party congress in 1961, the Italians demanded the right to follow more moderate policies better suited to Italian conditions, whether the Kremlin approved of them or not, and to criticise those of the Soviet Union they disagreed with, a stance that later became known as 'Euro-communism'. There were also allusions to Khrushchev's own far from minor role in the years of the Stalin terror, and the demand for the exoneration of its victims. There was even an unprecedented call for the rehabilitation of Stalin's arch-enemy, Trotsky, which produced an outraged public rebuke from the ultra-loyalist and still Stalinist French Communist Party.

These almost unprecedented open divergencies in the international communist movement (the only party previously to have broken ranks had been that of Yugoslavia under Tito back in 1948) provided me with the perfect pretext to set my plan in motion. Already, the Central London Students' branch was becoming polarised between entrenched, mainly 'second generation' party loyalists and a larger group of rank and file members who wanted to discuss amongst a number of questions the issues raised by the Chinese and Italian parties. It did not take me long to identify who might be most responsive to my subversive tactics and what was no less essential, to be trusted to treat anything critical I might say as strictly confidential. It was even easier to identify who my opponents would be. The student branch was dominated, as I have already said, by a clique of second-generation Stalinists, all them from upper middle class, professional families, and a number of equally prosperous Asian post-graduate students, one of whom, a real hard-line Stalinist as I recall, was Dipak Nandy, the father of Labour Shadow

Foreign Secretary Lisa Nandy. For all their leftist posturing, they were on the way up, and they let you know it. I used to think, what do your smug lot need communism for? You've already got it made.

Among them were some who would later achieve pre-eminence in their chosen fields of study. One, a somewhat arrogant hard-core Stalinist, who spotted me quite early on as a dissenter, was John Williamson, son of Bob, a high ranking American communist. He became one of the UK's leading embryologists. (He featured in TV science programme I saw many years later.) Socially part of the ruling clique, but sharing none of their arrogance or their almost pathological fear of controversy, was an amiable and irreverent law student, Stephen, now Sir Stephen Sedley. The son of a Jewish immigrant and life-long communist, he became Britain's leading authority on human rights legalisation. Called to the bar in 1964, and a QC in 1981, he was appointed a High Court Judge in 1992, serving in the Queen's Bench Division.

His ascent continued when in 1999 he was appointed to the Court of Appeal as a Lord Justice of Appeal, and then both a Judge ad *hoc* of the European Court of Justice and a Member ad *hoc* of the Judicial Committee of the Privy Council. Following his retirement, in 2011 he became a visiting Professor at Oxford University. Despite his belonging to what might best be called the party student inner circle, even then, he revealed the libertarian sympathies that became so evident in his later career, palpably enjoying the sometimes-heated exchanges that I provoked when challenging party orthodoxies. Unlike myself and those who became my supporters, in these debates, Stephen positioned himself on the extreme reformist wing of the party. What he objected to, and here we made common cause, was the bureaucratic party regime, whose automatic reflex was the attempt to stifle even the mildest criticism of party policy. As befitted an advocate, Stephen savoured a good argument, and always used to greet my arrival at a branch meeting with a friendly anticipatory comment. Like his daughter, Dipak Nandy also made it big time, after a brief but successful career in academe, in 1968 founding and becoming Director of the Runnymede Trust, before moving on in 1973 to serve as an adviser to various government agencies on race relations issues. These and similar tales of riches to even more riches would make an interesting study if it answered the question, of the communist student cohort of the 1960s, 'where are they now, and how did they get there?

The petty bureaucrats of the Communist Party that I crossed swords with are long gone, In their place, we have what can only described as a neo-Stalinist thought policing, imposed by any number of public agencies, whether in the form of political correctness, which requires one to not say what one thinks, but to think what one ought to say; by so-called 'hate speech' laws, calibrated to protect religion, and one in particular, from critical scrutiny; and on university campuses, where one would have expected that here at least, free debate is sacrosanct, by 'no platforming', 'safe spaces' and to protect delicate, 'snow flake' students from ideas that distress them, 'trigger warnings'. (These are issues that I discuss in some detail in my *Socialism of Fools*.) Contrast this incipient totalitarianism - for that is what it is - with Stephen's definition and robust defence of freedom of expression which, as a First Amendmenteer, I endorse one hundred per cent: 'Free speech not only includes the inoffensive [the definition favoured by leading Muslims and the politically correct] but the irritating, the contentious, the eccentric, the heretical [yes, especially the heretical], the unwelcome and the provocative provided it does not tend to provoke violence. Freedom only to speak inoffensively is not worth having.' Perhaps knowingly, Stephen was echoing the same principle, couched in almost identical terms, advocated by two libertarian leftists, Rosa Luxemburg's 'freedom is always for the one who thinks differently,' and George Orwell's 'freedom is the right to tell people what they do not want to hear.' Today, in Politically Correct Britain where, according to a survey,

30% of the population are afraid to express their opinions in public about a certain religion, doing what Orwell defends could land you in court and possibly in prison serving a sentence of up to seven years.

Stephen could always be relied on to defend my right to criticise party policy, but found my proposed alternative, a return to the revolutionary strategy of Lenin (for obvious tactical reasons, Trotsky was never so much as mentioned let alone praised) ludicrously extreme. (He was of course right, but it took me another twenty years before I came to the same conclusion.) Consequently, I never saw him as potential recruit to my opposition. (In the course of pursuing their respective callings, the paths of Stephen and my son, a leading authority on British constitutional history, have crossed on a number of occasions. As they say, it's a small world.)

I found the ideal partner in subversion in David Longley, a free-thinking Oxford graduate who had moved back to London to study for a Post Graduate Certificate of Education. David's parents worked for UNESCO, and from the way he talked about them, they had been either members of or close to the Communist Party in their younger days.

The peripatetic nature of his parent's work meant that David had been brought up mainly in Europe, and as a result, had become fluent in a number of languages, including Italian, something that was to prove to be an asset when I hit upon the ruse of having the controversial Italian documents published. This was only feasible because as fortune would have it, I had a few months previously been elected editor of an official party publication, *Communist Student*, so I suggested to David that we bring out a special edition just containing the Italian and French polemics, while protecting ourselves from accusations of partiality by making no editorial comments. In the normal run of things, the magazine editor would commission articles which, after being vetted by the party's full-time student organiser to ensure their orthodoxy, would be printed and then dispatched to be sold to university students around the country. I knew that the nature of edition I was envisaging - the spectacle of the two largest communist parties in the western world slugging it out over the merits of Stalin and Trotsky – would never be sanctioned by the powers that be. The only alternative was to conduct the entire operation in total secrecy, from translation to printing and distribution.

Non-conformist and exuding self-confidence (during his national service he had risen to the rank of lieutenant) it was easy enough to induct David into this, the phase one of my agenda, the formation of a critical but loyal opposition that had its ostensible (but as I knew, unrealisable) aim of ridding the party of its Stalinist legacy and ending the blind acceptance of all things Soviet. Of course, the chances of this happening were zero. Since Lenin's ban on factions in 1921, oppositions had never since been looked kindly upon in communist parties, as hundreds of British party members learned when they were expelled for protesting against the crushing of the Hungarian Revolution by the Red Army in 1956. My opposition was therefore doomed to suffer the same fate, as by now having got the measure of the regime I was up against, I knew it would. Although publishing the unauthorised edition of *Communist Student* would make myself and David marked men so far as the party leadership was concerned, it would also, by the same token, make us the focus of any incipient opposition. And so it proved.

There is absolutely no doubt that the production of *Communist Student* would have been impossible without David's several invaluable contributions. First there was the translation of the Italian material. (The French was translated by another dissident party member.) But how to get it printed? Here David really came up trumps. His parents were on very friendly terms with another old lefty, Gordon Frazer, a publisher and literary editor who also marketed arty greetings cords. A lovely, warm-hearted and erudite man, he died well before his time in a car accident in 1981. During the war, he served in British intelligence, and was parachuted into Yugoslavia to liaise with Tito's partisans. After the war, he worked as head of Radio for

UNESCO, which is how he met David's parents. In 1954, he left UNESCO to return to his publishing business.

When David explained to him what we were up to, and asked if he help in any way, Gordon offered us not only the free use of the facilities of his Primrose Hill office, but even the *gratis* services of his secretary, which included her ending up in bed with David. Once the translations were finished, she typed them up on stencils to be printed on the Gestetner. By this time, early 1962 if my memory serves me aright, I was able call on the services of a couple of fellow dissidents, one of whom, my flat mate, helped with the printing, collating, stapling etc, while the other, who was bilingual, did the French translation. David and I worked non-stop for at least a day and night until the job was completed. We then circulated the magazine around the London membership and waited to see the reaction. We did not have to wait long. It caused a sensation amongst its eager readers, and outrage among the party top brass.

A day or so after its appearance, the student organiser, Walter Patterson, convened an emergency meeting at the party headquarters, where the riot act was read to myself and David. Why had we not gone through the approved channels? As if he didn't know. Then there was the matter of the highly controversial contents. Publishing them, he argued, could be seen as the British party taking sides in a dispute between two fraternal parties, and that could lead to no end of trouble. In that case, replied David, which side has *Communist Student* taken? Of course, he couldn't say.

A few more days later, there was another emergency meeting, this time of the Central London Students' branch. The Stalinists were out in force, their well-tuned antennae correctly sensing that something was up. Another riot act was read by the chairperson, a real hard case married to a party *apparatchik*. Her lecture, directed chiefly at me, was replete with quotations from Stalin on party discipline, a subject he was undeniably an authority on. David wondered why I did not defend myself more forcefully than I did. The reason was, the Stalinists were out in force, and we were as yet heavily outnumbered. Over the next year or so, that changed as David and I won more recruits to our secret faction, all the time insisting (untruthfully on my part, but I genuinely believed necessarily) the object was nothing but the reform of the party. One by one, by the end of 1962, David and I won the confidence of half a dozen or so members who, as they gained in conviction and confidence, joined in our criticism of the party's policies, which we attacked as reformist, and its subservience to the Soviet Union. From time to time, I would visit the SLL head office in Clapham to report to the League's General Secretary Gerry Healy on the progress of my factional work in the Communist Party. Otherwise, as I was not attached to a specific branch, I saw very little of the SLL except at what were called aggregate meetings, attended by the entire London membership, either for an educational class, or to be addressed by Healy on current political issues. Unusually for such highly centralised movement (ironically, far more so even than the Communist Party) I was effectively allowed to function as a virtual free agent.

I had also by then made my debut as a writer, albeit anonymously, in an article that enabled me to combine three of my four great passions, music, history and politics. And when it appeared, I proudly showed it to the greatest of them all, Maureen. Why anonymous? Because it was published in the SLL's weekly journal, *The Newsletter*, whose attacks on the policies of the Communist Party ensured that its contents were closely monitored by the party leadership. Therefore, to protect my identity, I was given the by-line, 'A member of the Communist Party'.

The incident that occasioned the article was the cancellation in Moscow of a performance of the thirteenth symphony of the Soviet Union's premier composer Dimitri Shostakovich, sub-titled *Babi Yar*. It featured a choral setting of a poem of the same title by the contemporary non-conformist poet, Yevgeni Yevtushenko, and its subject matter was the massacre by the Nazis of 33,000 Soviet Jews in the Babi Yar ravine outside Kiev in September 1941. The poem not only expressed outrage at the crime, but no less at the fact that there was no memorial commemorating the massacre, and that in official Soviet accounts of Nazi atrocities, there was no reference to the Jewish identity of their victims. This practice continued until the break-up of the USSR in 1991. Shostakovich shared the poet's revulsion at not only the toleration, but exploitation of anti-Semitism by the Soviet authorities, and it was this that led to their collaboration on the symphony.

Once the project became public knowledge in the Summer of 1962, its creators became the target of abuse by the media and party leaders, with Khrushchev (like his predecessor, Stalin, an inveterate anti-Semite) threatening to ban its performance. Fearful for the future of their careers, conductors refused to conduct the work, musicians to perform in it. Attempts to prevent its performance continued right up to the premiere in Moscow on December 18, 1962 A singer cancelled his appearance at the last minute, saying he had been instructed to fill in for a singer at the Bolshoi who had allegedly been taken ill. The conductor was instructed to drop the first movement, it being the most controversial. He refused. The choir, who obviously had also been 'got at', threatened to walk out, and only agreed to perform after pleading by Yevtushenko. During the actual performance, TV equipment was noisily dismantled...but all to no avail. The symphony was greeted with rapturous applause by a packed audience. Nothing succeeds like notoriety.

The Moscow correspondent of the British Communist Party journal, the *Daily Worker* (now the *Morning Star*) may well have been unaware of the full extent of the back-stage machinations, because his enthusiasm for the work, and endorsement of its political message, was no less than that of its Russian audience. As a regular and studious follower of the party's press, and in view of the subject of the symphony, I read the review with some interest. Then, some weeks later, I learned, though not in the *Daily Worker*, that a third performance of the symphony had been cancelled. This imposition of censorship on two of the Soviet Union's most illustrious and internationally famed artists raised a number of political and historical questions that needed exploring. The result was my article in the *Newsletter* warning that the Soviet Union could well be faced with a return to the total regimentation of culture of the Stalin era. Hence the title, *Is it a return to the Dark Age?* (In addition to the Corbynista variety, Stalinist anti-Semitism is a subject I explore in some detail in my *Socialism of Fools*) By this time, early in 1963, I had moved, or rather, yet again been evicted (I can't recall why) from my small room off Regent Street to a ground floor flat in Hampstead, where now, earning a fair living as a part-time lecturer, I was able to afford the rent for a large room, which I shared with David, who had moved in several months previously. (To transport what was by now my sizable collection of books on various erudite and esoteric subjects, David had borrowed Gordon Frazer's Rolls Royce, which caused something of a sensation when it pulled up in a rather dingy and narrow side street.) As there was only one bed in our room, David as the sitting tenant pulled rank and consigned me to a large sofa. We shared the ground floor kitchen and bathroom and a huge communal living room with three other male tenants, also all graduates.

A few weeks after I had moved in, late one evening, as we were chatting about party matters, I decided the charade had gone on long enough. I felt it was time to come clean and tell him whom and what I was working for. David was at first not so much shocked as intrigued. By the early hours of the next morning, and a couple of breaks for refreshments, I had won him over. Within a few days he became the first of a succession of converts who made the pilgrimage to Clapham. David and I could now work as team for the same goal, and to such good effect that before we were finally exposed a year later (my expulsion was even reported in the national press) we must have added at least a dozen or so new members to Comrade Healy's miniscule organisation.

As well as for an easy lay, Healy also had a nose for big money, whether it was from Gaddafi's oil, heiresses to Fyffes bananas and South African diamonds or an heir to Arkell's beer. When I told him how Gordon Frazer had helped with the production of *Communist Student*, he could hardly contain himself. He reached for a book on his bookshelf. It was Trotsky's *Problems of the Chinese Revolution*, which judging by the look of it, was long out of print. 'See if you can get him to finance a new edition', said Healy, handing me the volume. 'China is in the news'. He was of course referring to the public row that had just broken out between Peking and Moscow. David arranged to meet Gordon to pass on the book and make the best case we could for Healy's request. We met, in of all places, the members' tea terrace at Regents Park Zoo. Gordon was, of course, a member of the Zoological Society. Sitting at the table next to us was an old acquaintance of Gordon's, Aldous Huxley whose novels I used to devour in my late teens.

After we explained at some length what the SLL was, and the relevance of the book, Gordon agreed to read it and let us know his decision. We met up again at out Hampstead flat a week or so later, where we laid on a meal, not very well prepared I must admit. Gordon was very nice about it, but having the read the book, he couldn't really see himself financing a book that was not sufficiently relevant to the current situation in China. Of course, he was right, because Trotsky only dealt with events up to the early 1930s.

From time to time I related to Maureen the details of my cloak and dagger activities in the Communist Party, which amused her no end. She was especially intrigued by my encounters with Gordon Frazer, as she knew all about his greeting cards, being the very tasteful young woman that she was. Judging from her reaction, she must have seen these escapades as my latest obsession, rather like Toad. If only it had been that and nothing more. Quite possibly things would have turned out differently between us if like Labour Party, and the Communist Party for that matter, the

SLL had not demanded total commitment from its members, or as the Bible succinctly puts it, insisted thou canst not serve two masters.

Until this point, early 1963, my involvements in politics and, for want of a better word, my relationship with Maureen, had never been in conflict. But now the time was approaching when I would be compelled to choose between them, precisely the dilemma with which I began this book...the choice between love and civil duty, the conflict between passion and reason, or as Wagner depicts it in *Tristan*, between the worlds and claims of night and day. Both were now bearing down upon me, demanding resolution. There was on the one hand, my increasing commitment to the Socialist Labour League, and specifically, my role in the Communist Party, which was now coming to fruition, and on the other, there was the change in my friendship with Maureen, one that had been physically warm but not intimately so, to one that had become, initially implicitly, sexual.

One evening back in the summer of 1962, sitting side by side on the sofa, with my right arm around her, Maureen let me ease my hand inside her invitingly low-cut bright yellow dress and first cup and then gently caress her breast. That was only the beginning. Over the next few months our physical relationship became ever more intimate, to the point that she not only allowed but so clearly wanted me to explore and pay homage to every part of her beautiful body. So far as Maureen was concerned, this was never intended to happen. She was never the kind of woman who would cheapen herself. But happen it did, because I think by this time, despite herself, and what her intentions towards Neil, she had come to love me. She confessed to me not long before we parted, 'I tried to stop myself, but I couldn't.'

What exactly were her feelings towards me in those final months before, in the most tragic of circumstances, we became lovers, I will never know for certain, because it was a subject that understandably, she was extremely reluctant to talk about.. What I do know is that she harboured a profound sense of guilt, and also, I believe of regret, for, as she put it more than once many years later, having treated me so badly. She would never expand on what she meant by this and I think I know why. It was, I believe, because she felt she had selfishly and perhaps unkindly taken advantage of my love and loyalty towards her, and of the sensual pleasure and even excitement which despite my total lack of any previous experience, I somehow had managed to arouse in her, while at the same continuing a more committed relationship with her 'friend', the safe, 'normal,' 9 to 5 Neil.

Be that as it may, the complexity of our situations had reached the point where we both now faced decisions that would affect the rest of our lives. Totally out of her normal character, which was that of an exceptionally honest and moral person, Maureen was now leading a double emotional life, and for all I knew then, a sexual one. though in this I was mistaken. I too had divided loyalties, for a woman I loved with all my being, and with whom I wanted to spend the rest of my life, and for a cause that I then fervently believed would make possible the betterment of mankind. But there was no doubt in my mind that faced with that dilemma, the choice would always have been Maureen. If only I had told her. I was afraid to, while she, I am sure, just blotted it out. But never once did we talk about our futures. It was as if we were both in a limbo.

Since I sensed, and I now believe correctly, that Maureen's preferred solution would have been, were it possible, to let things continue they were, I felt it was left to me to force the issue. After five years of being ever more deeply, indeed desperately in love with Maureen, I was now in emotional turmoil. I believed I had no other option than to find out what her choice would be. Afraid that a direct question, in effect amounting to what in those times would have been a proposal of marriage would frighten her, and quite probably imperil our now deep friendship, I chose a more indirect approach. I knew, because she had told me, that she had taken at least one holiday in Jersey as part of a small group of men and women of around the same age as herself. And I assumed, rightly or wrongly, that among the party would have been Neil. Foolishly, I decided to make this a test case. Would she, I asked, come on holiday just with me? Maureen's answer was an instant, almost aggressive, no. It was the same response that in later years would become a reflex reaction to anything that threatened to disturb the established pattern of her life. How I persuaded her to say yes to becoming my lover either then, or again thirty-seven years later, I shall never quite understand. But this was an emphatic no. I felt crushed, though I tried not to show it. The legacy of that one word, uttered without a moment's reflection, would remain with both of us for the rest of our lives.

V

I am sure Maureen did not realise the implications of her reply to my invitation. But now I felt I was left with no alternative than to find a way to part from the woman I loved, and in my heart, I knew I would never stop loving, without, if that were possible, hurting her feelings in any way. If only there had been no 'friend', no Neil, who of course in the end she never married, but just myself and Maureen, I would then gladly have continued as we were, hoping that in time, she would love me deeply enough to marry me. That is what I wanted so desperately, perhaps too much so, but now I was convinced it could not be. Sooner or later, she would have to choose, and I was sure it would be Neil.

A week or so later, I told her that I had been instructed by my comrades to move to Liverpool to assume responsibilities for political activities in the city. It was of course a lie, though such directives were indeed issued from time to time. Maureen showed little if any reaction, which helped to convince me that I had made the right decision. But that was so typical of Maureen. Inwardly, she was, as she told me many years later, 'devastated'. She even confessed to me a week or so after I broke the news of my fictitious departure to Liverpool that her mother had found her in some distress, and when asked why, said I was I going away. The gist of her mother's reply was that it was her own fault. Yes, that was partly true, but far from the whole story. I should have somehow found the resolve to persist, and left it to Maureen to make the choice for herself instead of trying to force it upon her. If only…if only...

I could not contemplate parting from Maureen, almost certainly as I thought then for ever, without asking her if she would allow me to make love to her. I cannot now recall precisely the words I used, but whatever they were, this time she did not say no. Perhaps she found it easy to say yes because by this time, we had become so intimate that making love would have been but a small step from what had gone before, in each case, not only with her consent but also encouragement. Maureen had taken some days off work to revise for an examination, so she suggested that she would once again visit me. By this time, David had moved in with his girlfriend in a rather plush flat in Lambeth, leaving me as the sole occupant of the room we had shared. Without having to say so, each of us knew that this would be our first experience of making love, and yet it felt so natural to at last be naked together. And we were not ashamed.

Even though that first fumbling attempt did not go so well, Maureen wanted us to continue as much as I did. A new routine was again established. She would visit me, or more often, we would make love at her home. On one of these occasions, something very strange happened which, because it was one of several taboo subjects for Maureen from those times, I still puzzle over to this day. Late one evening (after we had made love, properly, in her front room), Maureen said to me, in her typical matter of fact way, 'Neil would go mad if he knew about this,' and then added: 'He is as tall as you, but you have a much better physique.' What was I to make of that? That she found me sexually more attractive, and preferred me to be her lover, but for Neil to be her boyfriend? Surely not. It left me with the only possible conclusion that for all its passion, her love making was Maureen's way of saying goodbye.

It was as this time, June 1963, that I had not only had my first experiences of making love, but also of a Socialist Labour League Conference, an exotic coupling (sic) to be sure and one that could not have focused more starkly the import of the decision I had just made. Always an annual event, usually, as on this occasion, at Whitsun, the conference operated under conditions of secrecy more appropriate for an underground party in a police state. The location of the venue was kept secret until the last possible moment, those attending being conducted to it after meeting a member of the League's office staff at a prearranged location. That year, the conference was held in a large hall to the rear of the Cora Hotel just off Tottenham Court Road. Guards were placed at the entrance to the hall, and no one except a select few could enter or leave without showing their credentials card. All those attending were instructed not to talk politics amongst themselves outside the hall, especially in cafes and restaurants. In Healy's mind, if nobody else's, these measures were necessary because his movement, being the only viable threat to the British ruling class, was subject to the most intense scrutiny and even penetration by the intelligence agencies. While it was in all likelihood the case that the SLL, like all other far left movements, was subject to such measures, they were undoubtedly exaggerated to convince the membership of what was in reality a grossly inflated picture of the League's importance, and at the same time, to justify and sustain a Stalinist-style policing of their activities, private lives, such as were permitted, and even thoughts. In other words, what Healy was creating was a cult, not a conventional political movement. In accordance with this objective, which required creating the atmosphere and regime of a movement under a state of permanent siege, (both Lenin and Stalin used this tactic to the same end), without revealing the source of his information, shortly after the conference ended, Healy announced that its entire proceedings had been tape recorded by MI5. Perhaps Healy, by this time already subject to the messianic delusions that were to precipitate his downfall, really did believe that his every movement and utterance was being monitored. Some years later, I was at a top-level meeting in Healy's office when suddenly, he ordered that a coat be placed over a phone to prevent Special Branch, who as always, were listening in, from recording our voices. On another occasion, Healy announced to a similar gathering that come the revolution, not the police or the army, but the thrice-cursed Pabloites would be, and I quote, 'picking us off with machine guns equipped with telescopic sights'. Again, I think it was possible he actually believed it, just as the leaders of religious cults down the ages have their message that the end days and the Rapture are neigh. After their expulsion by Healy for sundry heinous heresies, his leftist rivals became in his eyes so many secular anti-Christs, capable of any infamy after having sold their souls to the satanic bourgeoisie. The method Healy employed to prevent any future such defections and betrayals was to stage hours-long sessions of breast-beating confessions of multiple sins. This ritual, called 'self-criticism', was initially devised (but never practised himself) by Stalin as a device to identify, discredit and weed out his political opponents. It culminated in the abject confessions of monstrous (fictitious) crimes at the trials of these same opponents in the three Moscow trials of 1936-7-8. (Some years after my joining the ranks of the damned, I penned an article for the *New Statesman* that likened the Healy cult to its thirteenth counterpart, the sect known as the Flagellants, which went one step further, self 'mortifying the flesh' with whips.)

As to the conference itself, had my critical faculties been in working order, I would have recognised at once that all its proceedings replicated, only in a far in more extreme form, those of the party I had rebelled against. For example, all motions were carried unanimously. When the time came at the end of the conference to elect its leading body, the central committee, the procedure followed replicated exactly the one adopted by the Stalinists in the late 1920s. Instead of delegates nominating and voting on individual candidates to serve on the new committee, the outgoing committee would prepare an approved panel of candidates, consisting almost entirely of its existing members, which would then be voted on *en bloc*. This was the method by which the SLL elected its central committee, or rather, how the committee re-elected itself.

The so-called discussions on the reports followed the same pattern. Only on one occasion in my ten years of membership did I hear a dissenting voice coming from the speaker's platform. In 1967, a highly respected economic historian, Tom Kemp of Hull University, challenged

Healy's insistence that British capitalism was in terminal. decline. This was akin to a Christian denying the divinity of Christ, and it was treated as such by the assembled faithful. In the session devoted to a discussion of Healy's main report, to evade a scolding from the Dear Leader, a speaker might begin with the phrase, 'as comrade Healy has said', only to be cut short with the interjection by Healy, 'I didn't say that'. Wisely, I made my debut in the discussion on the international report, delivered, not by Healy, but Cliff Slaughter, a sociology lecturer at Leeds University. By now *au fait* with the substance of the split with the 'deep entrists', who were labelled, after the name of their most prominent leader, Michel Pablo, 'Pabloites', I launched into an attack on their policies, and was duly rewarded when my speech was reproduced in the SLL's theoretical journal, *Labour Review*. This time, again to protect my identity from Communist Party scrutiny (there was ample evidence that like its Soviet comrades, the party closely monitored all Trotskyist publications) I was given the by-line Robert Black, a *nom de plume* that would stay with me for the next twelve years. I did not know it at the time, but not only had my speech been recorded but my photo taken. I discovered this when many years later it appeared in one of Healy's broadsides against 'Blick- Jenkins' for having the audacity to doubt the correctness of his party's polices. Of this too, more anon.

It was a month or so after the conference, possibly as a result of my competent performance there and the success of my undercover work in the Communist Party, that Healy decided it was time for me to step up and take on new responsibilities of a strictly party nature. I was to relocate to Scotland for a year, and assist the full-time organiser in extending the scope of the League's activities. The fiction that I had invented to explain my parting from Maureen had become a reality, only that Glasgow was my destination, not Liverpool. And anyway, there could now be no turning back, because already I had made a decision which was both at the time and in its consequences morally indefensible, and one which ironically, placed me in a situation similar, if not virtually identical, to Maureen's with Neil. The only substantial difference was that whereas I knew something of hers, she knew nothing of mine. It came about like this. The thought of being totally alone after becoming Maureen's lover, only then to lose her, led me to seek a new companionship, if not the same love, with a woman who, unlike Maureen, was committed to the same political cause as myself.

Our families had much in common. Karen's father, a shop steward in a large Cardiff factory, was also a communist, the only difference being that unlike my dad, he remained a loyal party member until the very end. Both our families had a great respect for culture and learning, above all for a love of classical music. Karen was herself an accomplished pianist and like Maureen, had won a scholarship to an elite girls' school, the largely fee paying and no less prestigious Howell's in Llandaff, north Cardiff. There the similarities ended. Maureen took the route of the sciences, while Karen's great passion was history, which she went on to study for a degree at Bedford College, London. It was then that I first met Karen when we were both members of the London student branch of the Communist Party, she with the doubts that would rapidly lead to her conversion to Trotskyism, and myself then operating as an under-cover recruiting agent for Gerry Healy's Socialist Labour League.

It was not a marriage of political convenience, but neither was it founded for my part on the passion I felt for Maureen and which, at the end, she felt for me. Just before we both left for Glasgow, and while I was still seeing and making love to Maureen, we married and, in time, she became the mother of our two children. For their sakes and not to save myself from any well-merited shame or embarrassment, I will say no more concerning my family than is necessary to describe the chain of events that led to my re- union with Maureen thirty-six years later. But I must say here firstly, that after I deserted Karen for Maureen, she in time found a new partner in Eric, and that when Maureen died, as the compassionate person that she is, Karen sent me a note expressing her sympathy for my loss.

A matter of weeks before my departure for Glasgow, my operation inside the Communist Party took an extraordinary turn. Until January 1963, the rumbling dispute between the Chinese and Soviet Communist Parties had been conducted by attacks on surrogates, with the Albanians, who supported Peking, being accused by the Kremlin of an adventurist foreign policy that engendered world peace (Albania's population then stood at a little under 2 million) while Tito's Yugoslavia, its hated Balkan neighbour, serving as a proxy for Moscow, was denounced by Peking for having abandoned the revolutionary principles of Leninism. There was never the least doubt, given its past servility to Moscow, that the British party would take the side of the Soviets, issuing an official statement to this effect on January 12, 1963.

What particularly riled, and worried, the British party leadership was not only the criticism the Chinese had made of its programme, which contrary to classic Leninism, (but not Marx) advocated a peaceful parliamentary transition to socialism, but the fact that a dispute had again become public. First the Italians and the French, then the Albanians and the Yugoslavs, now the Chinese and the Soviets. The much-vaunted world communist unity was bursting at its seams. Who might be next? (It proved to be the Czechs, whose attempt in 1968 to create a 'socialism with a human face' was crushed, like the Hungarians before them, by the Red Army, then the Poles, with workers' rebellions in 1970, 1976 and, in 1980, with *Solidarnosc*.) In a vain attempt to keep the lid on a dispute that could easily, and in fact did spread to its own ranks, the party's statement proposed the 'present public polemics should stop' and be replaced by an international conference of communist parties. It never met. Once the gloves were off, it proved impossible to prevent the debate trickling down to party branches where, even if only on a small scale, there was support for the

Chinese line. Eventually, a meeting was convened where the party position would made clear to the London membership. Naturally David and I attended, anticipating a lively evening. We were not disappointed. It was our first experience of a meeting where those present were not just students but a cross section of the party's membership. The large hall was packed and buzzing with expectation. There had been nothing like it since the revolt in the party against the Kremlin's suppression of the Hungarian revolution in November 1956. After a party hack had spelt out the official line, the meeting was thrown open to questions and discussion...a rare privilege. One of the many contributions from the floor came from a vehement supporter of the Chinese positions. His name, which I learned at the end of the meeting when he approached me, was Michael McCreery. He had thanked me for coming to his defence over the matter of what he called his 'blue blood', because I had objected when, to discredit his opinions, snide references were made to his privileged family background (he had been educated at Eton and Oxford) and the fact that his father was General Sir Richard McCreery, who succeeded Montgomery as commander of the British 8th Army in Italy in the later stages of the second world war. I had pointed out that none other than Lenin himself had enjoyed the privileges of being been born into the Russian nobility.

Perhaps assuming (wrongly of course, if that was indeed the case) that I shared his endorsement of the Chinese line, he suggested we meet up some time for an exchange of views. I sensed at once that something was afoot. Was he too involved in a secret faction, not, like mine, Trotskyist, but Maoist? It didn't take long to find out. A few days later, I was visited, not by Michael, but one of his fellow conspirators, who explained to me what was going on. A small group of members, convinced that the party was irrevocably committed to Kremlin-style reformism, had decided to launch a breakaway movement based on what they regarded as the revolutionary polices being advocated by the Chinese Communist Party. McCreery himself had been in opposition to the party leadership since 1961, and had formed a shadowy group of co-thinkers named the Committee to defeat Revisionism for Communist Unity, an odd title to say the least for an organisation that was about to split from its parent party. It was evident from what I was told about his intentions that McCreery was in a desperate hurry to come out openly for Maoism, possibly because he had already been diagnosed with the cancer that was to kill him two years later, but also, just as likely, for fear of being outflanked by other Maoist groups which were already bidding for the Peking franchise. Without committing myself to the enterprise (doing so would have put an abrupt end to my factional activity in the Communist Party) we agreed to keep in touch.

This development placed me in something of a quandary. I was already involved in one clandestine undertaking. Should I now sign up for another? Wheels within wheels...This was too important a decision to make on my own. A meeting was quickly arranged at Clapham, where David and myself outlined to Healy and his second in command, Mike Banda, who McCreery was and what his plans entailed. After a long discussion, it was agreed that David and myself should remain in contact with McCreery's Committee, but purely with the intention of causing it as much disruption as possible. Healy did not want yet another left-wing group queering his pitch.

The opportunity came when McCreery formally launched his breakaway organisation at a meeting in a large upstairs room at a London pub, the Lucas Arms, in November 1963. Admission was by invitation only, and although I was by now in Glasgow, it was agreed that I should attend, together with David. There were around forty or so present, about half of whom were McCreery's core supporters. The rest had come along to see what was on offer. Sensing from various comments that there was widespread unease with McCreery's insistence on an open and immediate split with the Communist Party, David and I exploited it to such effect that when McCreery formally moved that the Committee be officially launched, his motion received only fifteen votes Even some of his supporters had deserted him. The Committee limped on for a year, with McCreery visiting Albania (but not Peking) for a meeting with its ultra-Stalinist dictator Enver Hoxha, only to deposed from the Committee's leadership shortly afterwards. Following a series of acrimonious splits, and with the loss of McCreery's funding after his death in 1965, the Committee to Defeat Revisionism for Communist Unity was no more. We had done what Healy wanted.

Two months earlier, in late September, a matter of days before I and my wife left for Glasgow, Maureen and I made love for what we both believed would be the last time. Afterwards, holding each other at her slightly open door, and both of us near to tears, I told her, because it was true, and still is, she was the best friend I had ever had. Now sobbing, she replied that I was one of the nicest people she had ever known. And then I asked, because I had to know, did she love me? 'Yes,' she said, 'in my own funny way.' That was enough, more than enough. We kissed one last time, and then I took my leave. I turned to catch one last glimpse of her framed in the doorway, watching me as I made my way up Eastfield Road, leaving the woman who was more precious to me than anything in the entire world, who had aroused in me the deepest passion and longing a human being can feel and endure. What fools we both had been. But this was not the end. For we had lit a love in each other that would never die. And as mementos of our time together and token of my love for her, I left with her my Griggs geld, the records and books I had brought with me every time I came to see her. And they there they sit now, 57 years later, on her book shelves and in her record cabinet, mementos of our first times together, and the birth of our love for each other.

There is little that I know about Maureen's first few years after our parting. She became engaged to Neil, precisely when I cannot say, and then broke it off, again, I don't know when, though they remained good friends in times to come. As Maureen's daughter described him to me, Neil, like the man she did marry in 1967, was in every way my direct opposite, conservative not only with a small c, but also, I believe with a large one. Perhaps this is why Maureen had taken an interest in me by way of a contrast. He worked for an insurance company, and either imbibed or was already endowed with the attitudes that are best suited to such a calling, one of which is a pre-occupation with risk. This intruded into his personal life, to the extent Maureen grew tired of his constant procrastinations when it came to arrangements for getting married, with Neil always insisting on saving up for this and that. Whether she broke it off out of sheer frustration, or simply because she became aware that it wouldn't work anyway, I do not know. But the result was that for the first time in many years, Maureen was unattached.

What of me? I arrived with my wife in Glasgow at the end of September 1963. I had no clear idea of what my specific responsibilities would be, other than what Healy had described to me shortly before my departure as the 'fructifying of the youth work', since this had become the main focus of the SLL nationally in the battle to wrest control of the Labour Party's youth movement, the Young Socialists, from two rival Trotskyist factions, the International Socialists (the 'State Capitalists') and the 'deep entryists' of the Militant Tendency. Healy's strategy was to flood the YS branches by recruiting non-political youth literally off the streets, attracting them with dances and discos. Once enrolled on this spurious basis, they could then be used as voting fodder to elect SLL candidates to the YS National Committee. One of my tasks was to ensure the election of the SLL's Scottish Region candidate, a rather dour, humourless chap by the name of John Robertson. At least in this, if precious little else, I was successful. In 1964, with the support of the Scottish delegate, the SLL gained a narrow majority on the YS national Committee, and were then promptly expelled by the senior party for what they were - Healyite entryists.

I had headed for the Clydeside buoyed up with all manner of illusions about my new assignment. I knew that the region had been famed (or feared) as the 'Red Clyde' since the beginning of the century. A hotbed of trade union militancy and political radicalism, it was the backbone in its heyday of the Independent Labour Party, and in later years, one of the strongholds of the Communist Party, electing one of its only two MPs, the former engineering workers' leader Willie Gallacher, (the other was Phil Piratin in Mile End) in 1935 and 1945. Like South Wales, it had produced more than its fair share of labour leaders...James Maxton of the ILP and Manny Shinwell, a minister in the post-war Attlee government being just two of a dozen or more who became national figures on the left. As proof of my naivety (and not mine alone be it said,) I have to confess I genuinely believed that it was now the turn of the Trotskyists to be the masters of the Red Clyde. But then, who would have predicted that fifty years on, it would have turned tartan?

On our arrival in Glasgow we were temporarily put up at the home of the SLL's full-time Scotland organiser, Bob Shaw, and his wife, Mickie, a school teacher, on the understanding that we would find permeant accommodation elsewhere in due course. Before we did, the Shaws were visited for a week-end by their daughter Aileen, who had become engaged to Paul Jennings, who she had met while attending a school for journalism. Aileen would the following year become editor of Healy's youth paper, *Keep Left*, and Paul in 1969 of his daily paper, *Workers Press*, on which I served for two years as Foreign Editor. In that capacity, I came to know them both well, and found them a very pleasant couple, unlike many other of Healy's *apparatchiks*.

When I first met her at the Shaws, Aileen was a very pretty and self-possessed young woman, still only seventeen years of age. Yet tragedy awaited her. After moving to London with Paul, she became the favourite concubine of a Healy well into his fifties. How fitting that twenty-two years later, she would become Healy's nemesis. After being accused by Healy of being a police agent and beaten with a chair, Aileen revealed in a statement to the WRP central committee that not only herself, but at least twenty six other women party members had been effectively reduced to the role of Healy's sex slaves. Two months later, on my forty ninth birthday, October 19, 1985, Healy was ejected from his own party, taking with him, along with other illustrious thespians, Corin and Vanessa Redgrave. We will return to this spectacular episode in due course.

After our brief stay at the Shaws, we found very congenial accommodation with a charming lady, whom we assumed to be divorcee, and her small boy, Kevin, in Drumchapel, a windswept and soulless housing estate located at the western extremity of Glasgow. Once we had settled in, I applied to the Glasgow educational authority for a teaching post, only to be turned down on the grounds that my impeccable academic qualifications had no standing in Scotland. I wrote back, pointing out that according to an item in the *Glasgow Herald*, the city's schools were understaffed by approximately a thousand teachers, adding that perhaps the same paper would be interested to know why someone who was fully qualified to teach in England was being denied the opportunity to help reduce this deficit. A few days later, my request for a post was granted, at what was probably one of the toughest secondary schools in Scotland. Like the city's two major football teams and their Northern Ireland counterparts, Glasgow's schools were divided strictly according to religion, and with similar consequences. Mine, in Springburn, a typically for its time run-down area in the north of Glasgow, was 'proddy', as the vernacular had it. Just a little way down the road, so a pupil told me, was a Catholic school. To avoid after-school sectarian warfare, the two schools staggered their leaving times. The school itself was segregated along gender lines.

It required only few days of attempting to bring enlightenment to my charges to realise that the purpose of my appointment was not to reduce Glasgow's chronic teacher shortage, but to burn me off as quickly as possible. It was all too obvious why the class I had been assigned to had lacked a regular teacher. I had found myself in front of a class of thirty or so boys in their middle teens of whom the kindest that can be said is that except for a tiny minority, they displayed not the remotest interest in improving their minds in ways required by the school's curriculum. Their aspirations lay elsewhere, as I quickly discovered when I took the morning register. Some days, one or more boys would be missing, and replaced by others who were not on the register. The reason for this rotation was explained to me, again in the vernacular. The comings and goings of my pupils were due to their either falling foul of the criminal justice system, or being ejected from it. The school also had its own justice system. On my very first day, every so often I could hear a cracking sound, and then a yell of pain, coming from classrooms adjacent to mine. Again, my class explained to me what was going on. What I could hear was the tawse being administered to the hands of insufficiently docile pupils. The tawse was a long leather belt, issued on demand to all teachers by the school, and presumably with the approval of the Glasgow educational authorities. Its use was only outlawed in 1987.

I quickly discovered that all the school's male staff had equipped themselves with this weapon, and were very free with its use. Asked in the staff room one day why I had not applied for one, I explained that I did not believe in beating children either at school or at home. My reply was generally regarded as being very naïve. It was made clear to me that the kind of boys we had in our charge could only be kept in line by such methods. There the matter was left, at any rate for the time being. Then, a few weeks later, I was approached, discreetly, by one of the oldest teachers, as it so happened, a hardened Stalinist. He said to me in strictest confidence that some of the other teaching staff were concerned that my not using the tawse was undermining the overall standard of discipline in the school. It was necessary for all staff to present a united front, in other words, I too had to start flogging my pupils. He also offered friendly words of advice. The standard issue tawse was useless. 'No teacher uses it here. They even don't feel it.' He offered to give me the address of someone on the Isle of Skye who made to order his own heavy duty tawse, which I was assured would do the job properly.

A few more weeks passed, until one morning, a pupil arrived in my class late. He was holding his wrist with his other hand, and I could see blood dripping from where the veins had been cut open. He told me he had been tawsed by the headmaster for being late. I sent the boy to the medical room to get his wound dressed. Moments later, the boy was back in my class room, this time accompanied by the headmaster. He took me to one side, and told me that the boy could not receive medical treatment because the cause of his injury would have to be included in the record of his case. So there the boy sat, with blood dripping from his open wound onto his desk lid. A few moments later, my class was interrupted for a third time. It was the headmaster again, the sadist who administered what he now evidently feared might prove to be an illegal assault on one of his charges. He took me aside once more to inform me that for no stated reason, I had become 'surplus to requirements', and that I was to finish up that same day.

As Scotland evidently had no use for my pedagogic talents, I lowered my sights somewhat, and at the suggestion of a bus conductor member of the SLL's Glasgow branch, applied for the same job. With no previous experience or qualifications required, I naively assumed this time, all would go well. I passed the simple maths test with flying colours, perhaps too well, because when it was my turn to be interviewed, the official behind the desk looked me up and down, and then said I was unsuited to the job on account of my height, the reason being I would be constantly banging my head on the roof of the upper deck. Yet my bus conductor comrade was barely an inch shorter than my six feet. Was it just another case of anti-English prejudice? Or possibly something more sinister? What I do know is that after I returned to London and applied for a teaching job in Tottenham, the local Labour Party received a letter from the Borough educational authority warning that I would probably be applying for membership of the Tottenham Labour Party, and that as a known Trotskyist, on no account should I be allowed to join.

Throughout my six-month stay in Scotland my wife, who had interrupted her history degree course to be with me, continued her studies privately, while I travelled around Scotland organising and speaking at public meetings, conducting education classes for new members and selling the League's weekly paper, the *Newsletter*, at the crack of very cold dawns outside the gates of factories, shipyards and docks, and generally busying myself with the task of preparing for a revolution on the Clydeside. After being sacked from my teaching job and having then to subsist on the dole, this in fact became a virtually full-time, though unpaid, occupation. And the task I faced was formidable, to say the least.

The SLL membership was no more than thirty, compared to Scotland's population of a little over five million. It was organised into branches in Glasgow, Edinburgh, Ayr and Aberdeen. Apart from a half dozen or so older trade unionists, mainly ex-Communist Party members who, being family men, gave very little time to the League, the rest of the membership was comprised of students, recruits from the Labour Party Young Socialists and drifters picked up at the local labour exchange, known in the vernacular as 'the bru'. And that was about it. The grim reality, which it did not take me long to discover, was that the SLL had virtually no presence in and no influence whatsoever upon the Scottish labour movement. Like the League everywhere else, a futile attempt was being made to colonise from the outside territory that had been fully occupied for the best part of half a century by the Labour and Communist Parties.

I also quickly learned that totally unlike most of

England, the local labour movement was just as deeply riven by religion as on the terraces at the city's two major football clubs. Each Labour Party and trade branch in Glasgow was either controlled by a Protestant or a Catholic clique. Skilled work was for Protestants, unskilled for Catholics...just like Belfast. Also, as in Belfast, Glasgow was geographically divided by religion, the only difference being that the Protestants lived in the west, and the Catholics in the east. All this was totally new to me, not least the discovery that even in the predominately working-class areas of Protestant west Glasgow, at elections, Tories would be returned in seats which anywhere else would be solidly Labour. Enter a working-class home in Glasgow, which I often did, and as likely as not, in the living room there would be a huge picture on the wall of either the Queen, King Billy or the Pope. And this was the Red Clyde?

For all my dedication to the cause, and it was still considerable, my initial idealism was slowly being subverted by what proved to be well-founded doubts that the task I had been set, irrespective of my total local experience in what was an entirely new field of activity, was utterly impossible. We were hammering on and shouting through a door that could only be opened from the inside. Even though the occasional worker would buy the *Newsletter* or take a leaflet at the factory gate, it never led to anything. In the entire seven months of my stay in Glasgow, despite the thousands of hours expended on the attempt, the SLL did not recruit a single adult trade unionist into its ranks. The only success recorded...and in the balance, it counted for nothing...was in the outvoting of rival Trotskyist factions in the battle to secure the election of the Scottish representative on the Young Socialists National Committee.,

My doubts were of a kind that in a movement of zealots, one naturally preferred to keep to oneself. I did not even reveal them to my wife. But for that very reason they nagged away all the more persistently. Without becoming properly aware of it, I was carrying out my allotted tasks more from a sense of duty than conviction, an all too familiar characteristic of not only secular organisations, but those founded on religious principles. But what did not wane was my love and longing for Maureen. Looking back now, I can see that I had totally deluded myself into believing that my changed circumstances...my marriage, and the new political tasks that had taken me far away from my old haunts...would in time, ease the pangs of our parting. I was so wrong.

Unrelentingly, every day, my thoughts, and at night my dreams, were of Maureen, so much did I miss her. Somehow, I just had to see her again, if only for just one more time. After weeks of agonising I wrote to Maureen, using an accommodation address for a reply, asking if I could come to see her one evening over the Christmas holidays, when I would be in London for a meeting. Naturally, I said nothing about my marital status. In her reply, she said I could, which overjoyed me. But there were passages in her letter that made me weep uncontrollably, since they hinted of loneliness and a great sadness.

Just like she did with my poems nearly forty years before, Maureen kept all the letters I wrote to her once I had found her again for the last time and it is to them that I will have recourse to help tell the story of how at last we came to be together. In one I tried to recall as best I could after the passage of thirty-seven years the circumstances and my motives for wanting to meet her once more.

'The misery of life up there, and the emotional turmoil of my life had recently passed through, and was still in, was not the most conducive setting for a happy start to my marriage. Despite my hopes that my time with you, while remaining a wonderful memory with me, would not haunt me as my life became filled with my political activities and my new emotional ties, that was not to be. We, as you might recall, wrote to each other. I should have told you what I had done, that is, married, but did not, even though it would have made you pleased, perhaps, that I had found somebody who was

willing to risk sharing their life with me. I did not tell you because I felt a terrible sense of guilt that I had betrayed you. When I first saw you that day in Lentheric, I fell in love with you and being perhaps naïve, and very romantic, I wanted then to be loyal to you for the rest of my life. I found that very easy, despite not having any real hopes, for the next five years or so. And then, when the real test came, I failed you. Today, and for a long time before, I can see that this was unreal and even absurd. But, obsessed romantic that I was, that is how I felt. Out of fear of loneliness, I had betrayed my love for you. So I told nothing of my new situation. Then, as you will recall, I came to see you in London, at Christmas time 1963. I came, partly, just to see you (I had missed you so) and also, possibly, to make love with you, with feelings I knew I could not share with anyone else. Was this wrong? Yes, of course. Wrong to my wife, whom though I did not love like I did and do you, I owed my loyalty to. And wrong to you, because had you known of my situation, you would never have allowed what took place to happen.'

Karen and I had been staying with her parents in Cardiff over the holiday period. As planned, she then returned to Glasgow on her own, while I travelled to London to attend the meeting at the SLL's headquarters in Clapham and spent the night at an old friend's flat in Pimlico. I had arranged to visit Maureen the next day before catching the train back to Glasgow the following morning. As if in a trance, I repeated the same journey I must have made two hundred times and more over those previous five years. I rang the doorbell. Again, the same routine, as if only a week had lapsed since my previous visit. She let me in and left me to sit in my customary armchair nearest the door. As before, on her return, we talked, but only a little, for what was there to say?, listened to some music, and then, without a word said, made love.

Afterwards, we sat silently, both sensing that this was harming both of us, perhaps her more than me. 'You shouldn't have come,' she said, without resentment, because the decision had been hers no less than mine. And she was right. The past was done, or so I thought, and we had no future. Was it because of Neil? Or perhaps my visit and making love again had rekindled feelings she had tried to put behind her? I do not know, and I think quite rightly, I never asked her when many years later, the opportunity came to do so. The feelings of regret that pervaded our parting, which though unbearably sad, had lacked something of the tenderness and passion of our previous farewell, and I think this was because they were mixed with a sense of guilt on both our parts. Guilt, even though on this occasion nothing had been said of Neil, and certainly not of a wife that Maureen did not know existed. And instead of being allowed to heal, old wounds had been opened again. I am sure we both thought, though neither of us said as much, that it was time they were closed for good. More for her sake than mine, I resolved never to attempt to either contact or see Maureen again. Yet within less than two years, I had broken that resolution not once, but twice.

VI

My wife and I returned to London from Glasgow in the spring of 1964, she to resume later that year her history degree course at Bedford College, and myself to a London SLL that bristled with hostility towards me. This did not come as total surprise, because during the last few weeks in Scotland, Bob Shaw had made it pretty clear to me that I had not lived up to either his or Healy's expectations, and that I was to be called back to London several months earlier than had been planned. After staying with my dad and Gwen at their new home in Ealing while we looked for accommodation, we moved into a single room about a mile away. Next came a very unpleasant encounter with Healy, the first of many. I had let him down in Scotland, quite how and why was never made clear. Instead, what rapidly did become clear was that I was *persona non-grata* not only with Healy, but virtually the entire London membership. Judging from comments made about me at the first London membership meeting I attended, even before my return, the word had gone out that I was arrogant, 'hostile to the youth', (that was true, and with good reason) and needed a long spell in the ranks before I could be again trusted with any important assignments. Members whom I had never met before or had no dealings with seemed to know all about my failings, real and invented, and treated me accordingly.

I was assigned to the Ealing branch of the SLL, and for the first time but far from the last, experienced the dead hand of the female *apparatchiks* who staffed the League's London headquarters. The one in charge of my branch, like all the rest, struggled to utter a coherent sentence. Her knowledge of Marxism and history was effectively zero. Her only talent lay in relaying back to Healy anything untoward that had occurred in a branch meeting. It so happened that I had made contact with a dissident group in the Ealing branch of the Young Communist League though I cannot now recall how this came about. I naturally reported this in the branch. Within a matter of a day or so, I was instructed to cease all contacts with Communist Party members, not by my branch, but by my ex flatmate, David Longley! It was only then that I learned, that while I was in Scotland, he had been taken on as a full-time SLL organiser, with his main responsibility being work in the Communist Party, from which I was now excluded, with no reason given.

I found out why some ten years later, when one of the Ealing YCLers told me of a meeting he had attended at the 1964 SLL Summer camp. The meeting, addressed by Healy, was only for those dozen or so who had joined the SLL from the Communist Party or the YCL through their contact with me. They were warned that what they were about be told was to remain a secret, especially from me, since I was the subject of the meeting. Healy claimed he had evidence that I was creating, or at least intended to create, a secret oppositional faction in the SLL, with the support of those I had recruited into the League from the Communist Party. Healy instructed all those present at the meeting to break any political and personal connections they may have had with me, and to regard me as a potential threat to the SLL. No wonder I was being treated like a pariah, and that David had supplanted my role in the Communist Party.

By calling the meeting, what Healy had in fact done was to execute a classic Stalinist pre-emptive strike. He knew full well I had no plan at that time to form an opposition. But what he also knew better than anyone else was that all the previous oppositions in the SLL had been created by former members of the Communist Party, in each case directed not so much against the policies of the League, but Healy's autocratic leadership of it, which were redolent of the regime that they had each rebelled against in the course of their break from Stalinism. By isolating me from those I had recruited from the Communist Party, he was insuring himself against any such occurrence in the future.

Or so he believed. The problem for Healy was that he needed people like me no less than his bevy of *apparatchiks* and informers. It was exclusively the ex-Communist Party members who were capable not only of factional disloyalty, but of writing for his press, giving lectures on Marxist theory and history, and generally raising the political level of the movement above the frantic mindless activism generated by the fruitless pursuit of 'the youth'. It was for this reason that my ten years of membership in the SLL were a series of oscillations between the two poles of persecution and mistrust on the one hand, and from time to time being needed to perform tasks I both revelled in, and could savour the *schadenfreude* of knowing that I could execute them infinitely better than any of his acolytes. Together with my devotion to the ideas, it is the latter that explains in part why I stayed for as long as I did. My experience was far from unique. Like Stalin, this blowing hot and cold was one of the ways Healy kept a tight leash on his movement, by generating an atmosphere of uncertainty and even at times fear. One could be in favour one moment, and out the next, without really knowing why, or when it would happen. Later that same year, my increasing resentment at my treatment led me take the first tentative steps towards doing what Healy was seeing to prevent…the formation of a clandestine opposition, one that differed from the one I organised in the communist party in that it genuinely aimed at reform. I discreetly contacted a small circle of League members who I had recruited from the communist party and who, like me, I knew recognised in the Healy apparatus the very same blinkered, narrow-minded and domineering ways that led us to rebel against Stalinism. Naive in the extreme, we believed that it was not so much Healy himself that was the problem, or the League's sectarian policies and tactics, but his selection of full-time party workers, who to a woman were political illiterates. Little did we understand that his preference for beddable moronic groupies was no accident, that in Healy's party apparatus of the blind, its one-eyed General Secretary was king. After a couple of furtive gathering at my Tottenham lodgings, we agreed that only way ahead was to supplant Healy's clueless but loyal minions with a staff that could think and if needs be, act critically, though how this was to be done we never got around to discussing, because inevitably Healy, who like Stalin, had a nose that could smell dissent a mile off, rumbled our little operation before it got off the ground. He had somehow got wind of the resentment that had been being brewing in the South London branch over the expensive outfits and hair dos sported by Healy's favourite concubine, the already-mentioned and recently married Aileen Shaw, now Jennings. Aileen just been appointed Editor of *Keep Left*, the monthly journal of the now independent SLL youth movement, the Young Socialists, and Healy saw to it that she had a wardrobe fitting for her new station. A saying went the rounds: 'Who pays for Aileen's outfits?' Answer : 'You do.' Healy struck quickly and, given the special circumstances, brutally. Three of our little faction were stewarding a Young Socialists dance on a Saturday evening when who should arrive in a big car but Mike Banda, who told us to get in. Sensing something was up, we of course complied. In total silence, we were driven to League HQ in Clapham, and marched upstairs to Healy's office on the first floor. As we entered, we saw, sitting at his desk a scowling Healy, and Banda's brother Tony seated in another chair. If I remember rightly, two other leading League members were also present, full-time organiser Reg Perry, all things considered, a decent bloke, and Ted Knight, who had been expelled from the Norwood Labour in 1956 as a Healy entryist, only to be re-admitted in 1970, where he soon teemed up with Ken Livingstone. (More of that anon.) Knight had been in the car with Mike Banda when he came to collet us. As an ultra-loyal member of the same South London branch, he was almost certainly Healy's informant about the Aileen business. Facing Healy, also seated in a chair, was one of our faction, Geoff, also from the South London branch.. His face was covered with tear stains, and his dishevelled clothes with dust. It was obvious he had been beaten up and probably kicked around on the floor.

Healy addressed the three new arrivals. 'This comrade has come clean. He's done the right thing. Now its your turn. Tell me all about you little faction.' Having no particular desire to end up in the same state as his initially reluctant confessor, we did. The upshot was that we four miscreants each signed a declaration admitting that we had formed a secret faction, contrary to the rules of the SLL, and undertaking never to do so again. And that was it…for the time being. But as the moving spirit in the undertaking, I was a marked men, as I was soon to discover.

What happened that night was far from being an isolated event. Both Mark and myself, along with several others I could name, were subjected to physical attacks by Healy. Mine occurred at the 1966 summer camp, held under canvas in the Sussex Downs. In the main marquee one evening, while a social was in progress, I felt a thump between my shoulder blades. I turned, and there was Healy, snarling and breathing whiskey fumes into my face. I was marched off to a smaller nearby tent, where Bob Shaw was seated on a bench. Several other party members were standing to one side, serving as either guards, or witnesses to testify against the accused. One of the guards was Reg Perry, the camp organiser. What he was witnessing must have disgusted him, because after the camp broke up a couple of days later, he vanished, never to be seen again. This is, proclaimed Healy, opening the proceedings, 'a proletarian court in the middle of the Sussex Downs'. First in the dock was Bob Shaw. His crime, as testified to by a YS member from Glasgow, was to have failed to organise a Young Socialists' football league…beyond any doubt, a betrayal of the world proletariat. Healy roared incoherently at the accused, and then punched him in the chest. Poor Bob, a frail middle-aged man, fell backwards on to the grass, picked himself up, replaced the bench, which had fallen over, and re-positioned himself so as to receive more blow to the body and kicks in the shins. This Gestapo-style interrogation went for half an hour or so..

Then it was my turn. My crime, no less deplorable than

Bob's, had been to return a day late from guard duty at the League's Clapham premises. That this had been approved by Healy's second-in-command, Mike Banda, was irrelevant. Like Bob, I was deliberately sabotaging the movement, though quite why or how was never made clear. Testifying against me was Dany, Mark's recently married wife. She was already one of Healy's expanding roster of concubines, suggesting that a prompt cuckholding of party members' new wives lent an extra frisson to the proceedings. Then Healy's fists got to work. One blow caught me very hard on an ear, and for week or so after, it stayed deaf. The reader may well ask, why did I not fight back, or least defend myself? If I had have done, I would have had a far worse beating from the assembled guards. After an hour or so of this insanity, I was conducted by one of the guards back to my tent which I shared with my wife. I told her what had going on, and she was furious. Just as I was dropping off to sleep, a guard, I think it was Reg Perry, called me back to the Healy tent, where Bob was again being interrogated and beaten. He was followed by Jack Gale, like Shaw a long-standing League member, based in Leeds. His case, if we can it that, was a curious one. Either Healy or one of his female *apparatchiks* cum concubines would make it their business to saunter casually on a tour of the tents, where most members would be relaxing after, or rather recovering from an aggregate meeting or educational session in the main marquee. Remarks made in what the more inexperienced members assumed was an informal conversation would then be mangled out of all recognition at an aggregate meeting into a dire deviation from ideological rectitude. In the case of Jack Gale, who was much too long in the tooth to be caught out by this subterfuge, the deviationist remarks in question, which were subsequently construed as being derogatory of Healy, were allegedly made by one of his two young children. One had asked Healy, rather in the manner of the child in the Emperor's New Clothes, 'why have you got the biggest tent'? Which indeed he had. Healy snarled at his father, 'he got it from you'. He then shaped up to thump Gale as he had Shaw, but before the blow landed, Gale exclaimed 'No Gerry, I've got a weak heart', which also happened to be true. The (non-violent) working over of Gale continued for a half hour so. Then it was my turn once more, only this time Healy was a little more coherent., Perhaps he was beginning to sober up. He challenged me to take my story of the night's proceedings to the *Daily Mail,* knowing full well that my loyalty was such that I would never consider doing such a thing. (I should have gone to the police) Then it was back to my tent and then, just as before, back to Healy's for one last session. By this time, it was nearly dawn.

By a somewhat devious route, the proceedings of Healy's 'proletarian court' found their way into a 2014 biography of the distinctly non-proletarian Vanessa Redgrave, *Vanessa: The Life of Vanessa Redgrave.* To get background on his subject's political commitments, specifically the Healy movement, the American author, Dan Callahan, interviewed Tim Wohlforth, the one-time leader of the Workers League, the US branch of the Socialist Labour League and later, Workers Revolutionary Party. This is how Tim, with whom I became very friendly in our post Healy years, describes it:

'Healy had these camps in England, and I used to bring people over to them. There would be sometimes up to a thousand working class kids camping out in these tents. And they had Party people running around trying to keep order, many of whom were intellectuals not necessarily skilled at that kind of thing. Late at night, when everyone was bleary eyed, Healy would have people taken into his tent [actually, it was a tent reserved for leadership meetings] and, in at least two cases I know, he would hold these people and have them beaten up. One of them was Robin Blick, and I know his wife Karen very well, and I know this happened to him. Robin was a brilliant guy [thanks Tim!], and did a lot of work for their paper.'

The next morning, the last day of the camp, an emergency meeting had been called in the main tent. Some of the 200 or so members present had already got wind of the previous night's proceedings, and that I was to be subject of the speech to be delivered by Healy. After he had finished enumerating my many and varied sins, a procession of speakers filed up to the platform to either embellish or add to them. In his zeal, one of them, a certain Paddy O'Regan, a thuggish Healy 'enforcer', and the husband of Sheila Torrance, one of a shrinking number of non-concubine *apparatchiks* at Healy's HQ, demanded my expulsion from the League, not divining that this was far from being Healy's intention. Need I say that I was not afforded the right to reply? Later that day, the camp broke up, and cars and vans began to ferry members back to their home towns. The van I was in was driven by David Longley, who throughout the two-hour journey, said not a word to me. But then neither did anyone else. I had become an unperson.

Once back at our flat (by this time, time, we were living in Chiswick), I told Karen I was leaving. Healy was a thug, and his acolytes were no better. But Healy was an old hand at the game he had been playing with me. A few days later, he called round, sat down and in a soft voice said that it had all been a test, that we have to be tough, and that when he had heard I had left, it took it as a personal blow, so much did he value my services to the movement. In an avuncular way, he said he saw himself in me when he was my age, and that one day I too would a leader of the movement. And of course, mug that I was, I fell for it. Soon, I was back in favour, writing articles for the *Newsletter* and the next year, 1967, 'elected' onto the SLL's highest body, the Central Committee and then, in turn, elevated to the pinnacle of power in the movement, the Political Committee, Healy's equivalent to the Soviet Communist Party's Politburo. Faith in the ideal had triumphed over reason and evidence. In truth, I had become a disciple, albeit a not totally unquestioning one, of a cult, identical in all its essentials save a belief in the supernatural, to its religious counterparts. Some thirty-four years later, to be precise on February 6, 2000, I gave a talk in London to the secularist

South Place Ethical Society on this very theme that was subsequently published in its monthly bulletin. Entitled *Soviet Communism - A Secular Religion*? I drew a series of parallels between communist movements and religion, listing them under eleven headings and giving examples of each, which I summarise below:

Sacred Texts: The Bible and the *Koran*; the writings of the founding fathers of modern communism, Marx and Engels; *Apostolic succession*: Jesus and the Popes; Marx, Lenin and then either Stalin or Trotsky;

Schismatics: Catholics and Protestants; Stalin and Trotsky; *Holy relics and Icons*: The Shroud of Turin (a fake) and the bones of saints (likewise); the mummified corpse of Lenin;

Heresy: Unitarianism; Trotskyism, Pabloism, state capitalism;

Heaven and Hell: Paradise, Hell; Communism, capitalism;

Caesaro-Papism (the fusion of church and state): the Vatican City, Iran, Saudi Arabia and any other Islamic state that enforces Sharia Law; the fusion of (the only) party and state, viz. the USSR, China, North Korea, Cuba:

Censorship: The Papal Index; *Glavlit,* the Soviet censorship body;

Festivals: Saints and Holy days, weeks and months; May Day and anniversaries of leaders and revolutions;

Faith over reason: Papal geocentrism; Lenin's rejection of modern physics, and Stalin's of genetics;

Cults: Moonies; Jonestown; Stalin, Mao, the three North Koran Kims, Ceausescu, Pol Pot, Castro, Healy.

I should have added another:

Eschatology; the End Days, the Last Judgement, the Rapture; the triumph of world communism.

The daily grind, for such it was, of party work was never

to crowd out my only partly submerged longing for Maureen. That first year back in London, I sent her a Christmas card, saying I still loved her, which was of course true, and gave my father's address for a reply if she so wished. But there was none. But I still had this craving to see her, even if it was if it was only to catch a glimpse of her secretly, from a distance, just as I had first done some eight years before when I spied on her as she sauntered up and down the stairs at Lentheric. It so happened that my wife and I were living in Tottenham, not far from Lentheric, where I assumed (correctly as it turned out) she still worked. I described what ensued in one of the letters I wrote to Maureen after I had found and visited her in Swansea.

'Living where I did was so strange, being so close to you and where I had come to know you. In the end, I could resist the pull no longer and sent you a Christmas card to your old address saying that I still loved you, and asking you, if you wished, to write to me at my father's address (wisely you did not). Then, one cold January evening in 1965, I waited outside Lentheric to see if you emerged at your usual time (5.00 pm if I remember correctly). Rather later than that time, you did, wearing a red coat, with a couple of other women, who then went their separate ways. I can still remember vividly my feelings...of longing, of such sadness. Yet I had to do it.'

Some weeks afterwards, the same sensations overpowered me once more when this time, purely by chance, I caught a glimpse of Maureen, again in her red coat, sitting on a side seat at the rear end of a bus on her way home from work. As I write these lines, such is the invincible power of love to command the senses and the brain, I can see as clearly now as I saw her but fleetingly then, her red coat, her divine legs, her glorious jet-black hair, and her face, as it could be so often, a trifle glum, for as I have said, Maureen rarely smiled.

Having located and then paid my first visit to Maureen

in the August of 1999, I subjected her to an almost daily bombardment of letters. Some told of my anguished and undiminished love for her, and my desire, however hopeless, to at last live with her as man and wife. In others,

I treated of times long gone but which were still fresh in both our memories. Since I owed her an explanation, one letter in particular described how it came about that once again, I found myself unable to sustain my resolve not to seek her out:

'In the Autumn of 1965, by now no longer living in Tottenham, but having been directed (by the League) to live in Chiswick (the reasons are too complicated and don't matter anyway) and having just started a lecturing job at what was then the Polytechnic of North East London, I found myself travelling from Liverpool Street Station to Brimsdown, en route to Enfield to address a public meeting. This was the purist impulse. Only when I arrived at Brimsdown, with a view to catching a bus from there to the centre of Enfield (would it be the 135?) did I find myself thinking of you. Brimsdown was the station where we met to go to Ken Colyer's on one of our rare dates, the first in fact (there was a bus strike at the time). Instead of catching the bus, I walked to the bottom of your road. The rest you know. Even then, I never expected what happened. I was quite prepared to find you out, moved, or married. But not to be so warm. As we walked up the road, each to catch our respective buses (you were off out for an evening in Broxbourne) you asked me round again. And as we parted, I kissed you, to which you responded with some warmth. I then said to you, "Did you mind me doing that?" to which you replied, "I'll think about it." I spent the rest of the evening in a daze, performing as best I could at the meeting but with my mind and emotions very far away.

All the judgments one can make about what I did in December 1963 now apply here too, and yet, at the time, I felt no guilt. Though the renewal of our relationship (how I hate that banal word) was never quite the same as before

(how could it be?) it released in me feelings that were infinitely more intense than any I had experienced in my marriage. Of course, it was doomed. You were becoming involved with the man who was to become your husband.

What a strange irony. First there was Neil. And yet we made love. Then Terrence. I knew well of the first. There was only a hint, but enough, of the second. And now again. [This was an allusion to Les, a postman who lived in London with his mother, and with whom Maureen at the time I found and then met her again had a long-standing but not profound emotional attachment.] Has it occurred to you that our situations, though not identical, have been not once, but two or maybe (now) three times, a little alike?'

In inviting me to see her again in November 1965, Maureen must have understood that as on the previous occasion, it could quite easily lead to our making love, which indeed it did, and which I am now sure she wanted. We knew that we were again playing with the fire of a love and lust that time and separation had proved incapable of extinguishing. There was no talk of a future. How could there be? And also, little of the past. It was too painful. But there was the passion of the moment, one so strong that it blotted out all rational and for me and possibly also for Maureen, all moral considerations. My weekly visits, and our love making continued until one evening, early in the New Year, Maureen told me she could not carry on. She did not to tell me why. She did not have to. A few weeks previously, she had described to me a Duke Ellington concert she had attended, I presumed with a male companion. This was the Neil story all over again, only this time, I had no grounds for feeling any jealousy. I already knew then it was the end. She asked me to come just once more to make love to her for the last time. As we parted on that so sad night, choking back my weeping I begged her not to forget me. More moved that I had ever seen her before or rarely since for that matter, Maureen sobbed, 'never never, never .' And to that pledge, I was to discover thirty-three years later, she remained true. I know exactly the day, or rather the night, that we parted for what we both truly believed was the last time. The next day, the news broke that Kwame Nkrumah, the leftist dictator of Ghana, had been overthrown by a military coup. That day was February 24, 1966. We met again, thirty three years later, on the anniversary of a far more momentous coup, only this time, a diplomatic one, being the pact between Hitler and Stalin of August 23, 1939, the deal to carve up Poland that launched the Second World War.

And so we resumed our separate lives, in body if not entirely in spirit; I to five more years of an increasingly disillusioning pursuit of a phantom revolution, and in time, the raising of a family of two children, and Maureen to a doomed marriage and the trials of a single parent mother. I say doomed because, as Maureen told me after we came together, Terry was not the man she first took him to be. 'How could I have been so wrong about him?' she once said to me. Even on her wedding day, she had a premonition that her marriage would not last. And sure enough, Maureen increasingly found that her husband, from an Irish Catholic family, did not want an equal partner, but one who deferred to him all important matters.

Even so, she stood by him when his dream of becoming the owner of a chain of newsagents was shattered when one of his brothers, entrusted to manage one of his shops, embezzled the takings and forced Terry into bankruptcy. The end came when, unable or unwilling to shoulder the responsibilities of fatherhood, Terry took up with a barmaid whilst the family were on holiday by the Blackwater Estuary in Essex, as irony would have it, not far from where Healy used to hold his summer educational camps in the early 1970s. As both Maureen and her daughter have both said to me, Terrence and I were diametric opposites in every sense. Politically to the right and a bit of a racist, his ruling ambition was to be a successful capitalist, while mine was to be a revolutionary and put people like him out of business. To cap it all, he was an Arsenal fan.

In addition to contributing to my separation from Maureen, my political commitment was such that it led to my abandoning my other great love, that of music making, and it would be another twenty years or more before I resumed it. Just before I left for Scotland, I pawned my trumpet. I never claimed it back. But I still had my guitar. My only creative activities, if they warranted that description, were to feature from 1969 to 1971 as the Foreign Editor, under the *sobriquet* of Robert Black, of the League's now daily journal, the *Workers Press,* and to write a book published by the same organisation with the self-explanatory title, *Stalinism in Britain.* Although now almost unobtainable, it has continued to be cited as a source in studies of the British Communist Party.

My short career as a professional revolutionary journalist began one late September day in 1969, when a phone call to the college where I was then working was redirected to my staff room. I picked up the phone to hear a voice in an all-too familiar rough Irish brogue instructing me to immediately hand in my notice and report for duty at the *Workers Press* editorial office in Clapham. A matter of days later, I had been installed in a small room equipped with a desk, chair, typewriter, book case and an Associated Press ticker tape machine. Armed with these technical resources, over the next two years I must have generated thousands upon thousands of column inches on the progress of the global struggle of the oppressed for emancipation, always taking care to remind readers that without the guidance of comrade Healy's movement, they were doomed to defeat.

The staff of the paper was comprised of party stalwarts such as myself and a smaller number of recruits from the world of professional journalism, the most prominent being Alex Mitchell, an Australian who, after moving to London, had worked as a high profile investigative journalist for Murdoch's *Sunday Times* and Granada TV. (Mitchell's years with Healy are related in at times hilarious detail in in his autobiography, *Come the Revolution* where, unlike others of his ilk, considering the damage I did to his party, he speaks quite kindly of me.) At the time, I naively assumed that in accordance with communist ethics, we were all being paid the same salary, as I was receiving a pittance way below the official trade union rate. Many years later, at an ex-Healyite re-union, I met a former colleague on the *Workers Press* who told me that in order to maintain the lifestyle to which they had been accustomed in their previous employments, on pay day, the likes of Alex Mitchell were slipped an envelope containing the sum required to make up the difference. Some comrades were evidently more equal than others. At the time, I knew nothing of this Orwellian arrangement, which in a way was just as well, because together the two years devoted to my clandestine operation in the Communist Party, the last two years as Foreign Editor of *Workers Press* were my best times in SLL, and for the same reason, because I was in my element, the world of inspiring ideas, and reporting and commenting on great world events, even if I had no influence over them.

After two years as an underpaid, overworked, and sometimes unjustly abused journalist, I parted company with my Trotskyist comrades in the summer of 1971, partly because of my disagreement with the League's endorsement of Arab terrorism, though mainly in revulsion against what I had all too belatedly come to see as the movement's corrupt, undemocratic and repressive regime. And a year previously I had become a father, another powerful inducement to re-enter the world of reality. But shortly before I left, I had one assignment that I can still look back on with a certain amount of pride. In the spring of 1971, the Bengali population of what was then still East Pakistan made a bid for independence from their political masters in the western half of the country. I not only covered from afar the course of the often-bloody freedom struggle, I also interviewed in London many of the exiled leaders of the Awami League, the party leading the independence struggle. In recognition of my support for their cause, on August 27, 1971, I was a guest at the inauguration of the

Goring Street Mission of what was soon to become the High Commission of the newly independent state of Bangladesh. The articles I wrote for the *Workers Press* were later published by the SLL in a booklet entitled *The Fight for Bangladesh*, again under my by-line of Robert Black.

Throughout my ten years of membership, I can honestly say there is not much else that gives me the same satisfaction., and a great deal more that I am now ashamed of. The movement I was part of heaped vitriol on Churchill at the time of his state funeral in January 1965, the only commoner to receive such an honour in British history, and rightly so. Without his leadership in the summer of 1940, we could now be speaking German. No less deplorably, I fully supported the Arabs in their war against Israel in June 1967, and said so in an article I wrote for the SLL youth paper, *Keep Left*. True, I did add a caveat to the effect that such support in no way involved the endorsement Arab anti-Semitism, while knowing full well that their goal was to drive the Jews into the sea.

Even when the SLL conducted actions whose stated objectives I can still endorse, at least up to a point, it did so in ways that rendered them counter-productive. Healy always had two pathogical fears; of being involved in an action or campaign he could not control and, related to this, of his movement being contaminated by contact with its Trotskyist rivals, the renegades. This was understandable, because over the years, all the defections, and they were substantial and sometimes spectacular, had been in the same direction, out of the Healy mad house into something that in Trotskyist terms at least, was more sane and sensible. To take one example of many. At the height of the Vietnam war, a coalition of various leftist groups organised a march through central London, which attracted something in the region of 100,000 demonstrators. The SLL's contribution to the proceedings was to hand out a leaflet with the heading 'Why We are Not Marching'. Whatever the reasons given – if I'm not mistaken, it had something to with the participation of the Young Liberals - they were not the real ones. It was a matter of simple arithmetic. 100,000 against the SLL's 300. A few weeks later, Healy's 300 staged his own, purely proletarian march.

The actual circumstances of my departure from the SLL are worth the telling. One of the devices Healy employed to keep his eye on the movement was to plant spies in its constituent branches, chiefly in the London area. In each case, his trusted informant would be one of his concubines, who were invariably employed at the party headquarters for sundry duties, including the horizontal. Supplementing this system of surveillance worthy of a KGB or Gestapo was another that while not officially recognised, was all the more effective because one could never be certain who they were. To gain favour, or simply out of pure spite, members would retail back to Head Office reports of real or invented misdemeanours, doctrinal deviations or derelictions of duty on the party of fellow branch members, especially those who were generally known to be out of favour, as I all too frequently was. These tales would, more often than not, result in either a dressing down, possibly physical, from Healy, or a reprimand at a branch meeting. With my reputation, to my shame and regret, largely undeserved, as an instigator of subversion, I was a sitting target for a system of thought policing that owed nothing to Orwell's Big Brother. The inquisitorial nature of the Healy regime was brought home to me when not long after I had returned to London, I foolishly let slip to a branch member that the previous Sunday I had played a round of pitch and put golf with my dad. This became the pretext for a protracted hectoring session for my bourgeois tendencies at the next branch meeting. Had I known it at the time, I could have objected, true, at the risk of limb if not life, that far from being a pursuit of the leisured classes, golf was banned by a Brussels court in 1360 and the Scottish Parliament in 1457 as subversive of the social order.

Although not yet *au fait* concerning its sexual dimension, over the years of my membership of the SLL, I had become only too aware as to the functioning of the official spy system, and of who were its (always female) operatives. By August 1971, my disgust at Healy's regime had reached the point so many had arrived at before me, and I was looking for a pretext to literally walk out of the movement. Cretin that she was, the spy in question (another of Healy's cuckholding conquests) presented it to me on a plate. I already had intimations that I was due to be hauled over the coals at an upcoming branch meeting on a spurious charge of failing in my local duties, which alone of the paper's staff, I was expected to perform in addition to my full-time job as *Workers Press* Foreign Editor.

As I left home for the meeting, in an upstairs pub room ten minutes' walk away, I said to my wife (she stayed at home babysitting our first child), 'Have my dinner ready, I'll be back soon.' She laughed, knowing full well what I intended. No sooner had the meeting got under way than just as I expected and hoped, the attack on me began, launched by the spy. I demanded the right to reply, knowing full well it would be denied me. When it was, I stood up and to a stunned silence, walked out of the meeting. Ten minutes later, I was back home eating my dinner. It was all over, and it felt marvellous. I was a free man.

About two hours later, just after I had gone to bed, for once quite early, there was a knock at the door of our second-floor flat. It was the spy, together with the same previously mentioned almost uniquely non-concubine female apparatchik from party HQ, who had joined in the charge against me at the earlier meeting. It was a hot night, and so I had left open the bedroom window which faced onto the balcony where the two Healy stooges were standing. When they saw I was in bed, they started to hector me through the open window, at which point my wife came into the bedroom and told them to fuck off. Then, nothing deterred, the non-concubine Healyite attempted to climb into the bedroom through the window, presumably to continue the attempt to save my soul at closer quarters. I, in the buff (as I said, it was hot night), leapt out of bed to close it, in doing so, exposing my naked body full frontal to the would-be intruder. There was a scream, followed by a quick retreat, and then a muffled conversation, to the effect that it was a waste of time continuing, since I wasn't 'a youth', one observation I was happy not to contest. They then made off, no doubt to report to their leader on the defection of the ex-comrade Blick from the ranks of Healy's revolutionary army. Then...nothing...until a few weeks later, the phone rang, and I picked it up. 'Healy speaking.' I put it down with great relish. I was a free man. But I also needed a job.

At my first interview at the local labour exchange I explained my situation. I had been a journalist for a number of years (I was rather vague about who for) but I wanted to get back into the world of academe. I gave my contact details and academic qualifications, and on being registered as unemployed, discovered that my weekly benefit would be substantially higher than the salary paid to me by Comrade Healy. I had no great hopes that an academic post would be forthcoming from an agency that was mainly geared to providing routine manual and clerical employment. But I was wrong, because a few days later, a well-spoken lady rang to tell that there was a vacancy at the London School of Economics for a lecturer in politics. She was confident I would get the job once my previous employer furnished the necessary reference. And therein lay the difficulty, because purely out of spite, when requested to do so, Healy declined to forward any reference to my potential employer, so the offer fell through. I had this confirmed to me in a roundabout way by the friend with whom I had shared the little flat off Great Portland Street. Not long after leaving the SLL, I got back in touch with him. He was now a sociology lecturer at the LSE, and had an interesting story to tell me. He had been approached by a fellow member of staff who, as a long-standing member of the SLL, was obviously fully appraised of my friend's connection with me in the communist party opposition, and with evident delight told him how Healy had sabotaged my prospects of a job at the LSE. He made it very clear that the intention had been to prevent my influencing students in ways detrimental to the cause.

Healy's vendetta against me meant that without a reference from my last employer, my CV would be left with a two-year gap that I would find impossible to explain away. After nearly two years of unemployment, during which I fulfilled the duties of a househusband and child carer for my daughter Katharine while my wife worked as full-time teacher in a local girls' secondary school, with the help of my friend Mark, who had resigned from the SLL some time before me, I found my way back into the teaching profession, one that I had been ill-advised to leave in the first place. My opportunity came when Mark recommended me to stand in for an economics lecturer who had taken extended sick leave at the college where he was then working. Once my foot was in the door, more classes came my way, until some five years later I was promoted to a full-time post without any references being required. I saw it as another victory over Healy. I was now not only a free man, but a properly employed one. But the best was yet to come. Revenge they say is best served cold. So true. It was becoming work colleagues that enabled Mark and myself to join forces to take a sweet revenge on the man who had for a decade exploited our political idealism and dedication to the movement he had corrupted and degraded. We also had other axes to grind of an even more personal nature. We had both been physically assaulted by Healy, he had tried to ruin for life my academic prospects, and Mark had suffered the added humiliation of having his wife, with whom Healy was already having an affair, abducted and added to the roster of the Sultan of Clapham's harem.

VII

The opportunity to level things with Healy arose when in late 1973, the Socialist Labour League transformed itself into the grossly misleadingly titled Workers Revolutionary Party, with the intention no less of displacing the Labour and Communist Parties as the major force on the British left. Such delusions of grandeur rapidly proved to be an accurate guide to the state of mind of the new party's leader. Healy had taken into his head that Britain was heading for a political melt down, specifically a Latin America-style military coup, in which not only certain ministers of the Conservative government of Edward Heath would be complicit, but the leaders of the very trade unions against which the coup was to be principally directed. Armed with back copies of the WRP's daily paper, Mark and I went to work in my kitchen one evening in January 1974, and by the early hours of the next morning, had produced a carefully crafted demolition of Healy's fantasy.

Healy had played right into our hands, because for all his claims to being the custodian of Trotskyist orthodoxy, he had foisted on his new party a policy lifted straight out of Stalin's copy book. It so happened that I was in the final stages of writing my two volume *Fascism in Germany* (like *Stalinism in Britain* out of print, but available on-line as a free download) which examined in some detail the ultra-left policies being pursued by Stalin that contributed greatly to the victory of the Nazis in 1933, which like the WRP's, included denouncing trade union leaders as fascists, the only difference being, and it was purely a semantic one, that to save its blushes, the WRP preferred the term 'corporatism' and its cognates, as they were used by Mussolini's fascists to describe their goal of a society in which independent trade unions had been abolished. The irony was that Stalin's policy was now being replicated by WRP, to be sure not with the same tragic consequences, but nevertheless, providing a siting target for anyone out to prove how far Healy had departed from what might best be called traditional Trotskyism.

The substance of the matter was as follows. Back in the late 1920s, tiring of a series of failed attempts to inveigle social democratic parties and trade unions into a so-called 'united front' with the communists, (a tactic Lenin likened to placing a rope round a man's neck and hanging him) Stalin did one of his many about-turns, and denounced the social democrats as fascists, or rather, 'social fascists', to distinguish them from the other variety represented by the likes of Hitler and Mussolini. Precisely because they were fascists disguised as socialists, they were to be seen and fought as the 'main enemy', far more dangerous than Hitler's Nazis, hell-bent on imposing a fascist dictatorship over the ruins of their own labour movement. Trotsky, now in exile, denounced this policy as suicidal, and instead advocated a united front of all workers' organisations against the real fascists. In duplicating Stalin's strategy, Healy's *Workers Press* even went so far as to accuse the leaders of the British trade unions of conspiring with the Tories, the armed forces and the employers to create a corporate state, a term used by Mussolini to describe the fascist policy of eliminating trade unions and replacing them with 'corporations' which regimented the workers instead of representing them. It never struck me at the time how ironic it was that Trotsky's critique of the very same policy now being pursued by Healy had, more than anything else, convinced me to join the Socialist Labour League.

Combing through a file of recent issues of the *Workers Press*, we culled from them samples of Healy's lunacies and fantasies, and demonstrated just how remote the WRP was both from reality, and the polices and principles of what had hitherto been universally understood as Trotskyism. Mark and I found particularly amusing that after Healy's predictions of doom and disaster, a miner's strike (called by some of the very same trade union leaders who were supposedly involved a military coup against their own members) led not to the tanks on the streets and concentration camps confidently predicted by Healy, but a general election, the ousting of the Tories and a Labour government. In this election (February 1974) the WRP, set on staking its claim as force to be reckoned with on the left, fielded nine candidates, with Vanessa Redgrave standing in East Ham. They lost all their deposits, averaging 466 votes per seat. This proved to be by far their best performance. In 1985, shortly before the party imploded in the wake of the Healy sex scandal, ten candidates averaged 124 votes per seat.

Once duplicated, and using my contact details for responses, our critique of Healyism was posted to as many current or former WRP members for whom we had addresses. As we had hoped, it was not long before we were contacted by members who to one extent or another shared our criticisms of Healy's policies. At the same time, Mark contacted a French Trotskyist group, the Organisation Communiste Internationaliste, who had fallen out with Healy some three years previously, and were now engaged in creating an international organisation to challenge the rump controlled by Healy after the split in 1971. Our relationship with the OCI proved in the long run to be a marriage of convenience, but one that lasted long enough to make Healy fear for his grip on his own movement. Keen to establish a foothold in Britain, the OCI dispatched an English-speaking emissary to find out what our intentions were. Bearing in mind that both Mark and myself had joined and then been disillusioned by first the Stalinists and then the Healyites, we were in no particular hurry to resume the quest for the holy grail of undefiled communism. Our aim had been, and in fact remained, to make life for Healy as unpleasant as possible. And in this we succeeded, judging by his response to it.

In reply to our critique, he launched a series of publications and articles in his press directed against 'Blick-Jenkins', a designation that led some confused WRP members, (of whom there were many) to assume that the target of these diatribes was a single person with a double-barrelled name. Concerned to highlight our French connection, the snappy tittle of the first of these productions, a 112-page book, read: *A Reply* to *the British Agents of the OCI Liquidationists*. (In the Bolshevik lexicon, 'liquidationists' are those who fail to place sufficient emphasis on the importance of party organisation. (Certainly, no one could justly accuse Healy of that particular deviation.)

It was indeed unfortunate for Healy, and what in the long run proved to be his undoing, that the most enthusiastic endorsement Mark and I received of our broadside against the WRP's policies was from the party's only significant industrial base, located at the Leyland car plant in Cowley, Oxford. As seasoned trade unionists, they knew that Healy's accusation that their own union's leaders were involved in the preparations for a military coup against their own members was sheer nonsense. The most prominent of this group of Leyland car workers was Alan Thornett, then a Deputy Senior Convenor at the Cowley works, who had acquired a little while previously national notoriety after a newspaper investigation into industrial relations at Leyland described him as The Mole for his unobtrusive but highly effective style of trade union leadership. Even the *Spectator*, the right of centre weekly review, carried a feature article on him on him entitled *Out of Molehills*.

Later, after I had won his confidence and begun our several months of collaboration in the fight against Healy, Thornett said the impact on himself and his fellow party members at Cowley of our critique of Healy's policies had been 'devastating'. Had Healy known, he would have had good cause to be concerned at such a reaction. As someone whose occupation as an internal truck driver and trade union responsibilities lent at least a modicum of credibility to the WRP's proletarian pretensions, Thornett not only sat on its leading body, the central committee, but was also being groomed as a possible successor to Healy as the party's General Secretary.

When I contacted Thornett through an intermediary, he

was understandably extremely hesitant about meeting someone who had been publicly denounced by the WRP as the 'British agent' of his party's most despised enemies. Thornett therefore at the outset very sensibly, made it a condition that any negotiations concerning the possibility of a coordinated attack on Healy had to be conducted in the utmost secrecy. The result was a midnight rendezvous in Thornett's car on a layby at exit 10 of the M40, at which after several hours of at times rather fraught exchanges concerning our relative positions, we agreed that I would give all the assistance he needed to prepare himself for and to conduct his attack on Healy's policies and authoritarian regime. To this end, it was agreed that on his way from Oxford to leadership meetings at the party headquarters in Clapham, Thornett would call in at my flat in Acton, always entering and leaving via the fire escape in case, and this was not an absurd suspicion, that my flat was under observation. After we discussed tactics for the upcoming confrontation with Healy and company, he would exit the same way as he came. Later that same night, he would usually drop in on his way back to Oxford to let me know how the meeting went. (Once again, it never occurred to me then, but here I was, for the third time, involved in an under-cover operation in an alien political organisation, first the Communist Party, then McCreery's Maoists, and now Healy's WRP only this time, from the outside, working through an intermediary. Perhaps I had missed my true vocation.)

These clandestine rendezvous continued until Thornett and his Leyland comrades, some 200 in all, were expelled *en masse* at the end of 1974, the self-inflicted death knell for the WRP's claim to be more than in name a party of workers. In the Wikipedia entry on Healy, this exodus, which I will with all due lack of modesty, claim the credit for, brought to an end any influence the WRP had in the British trade union movement, with the dubious exception of the actors' union, Equity:

'In 1974, some 200 hundred members around Alan Thornett, then a leading militant in the automobile industry at Cowley, were expelled from the party.... From this point, the WRP lost members and become ever more isolated from the rest of the labour movement.'

Humiliated and enraged by the emergence of an opposition of this unprecedented scale and strategic importance, the WRP General Secretary's response was entirely true to past form in similar situations. Wikipedia relates that 'Healy was known to have punched members of the party central committee while theoretical [sic] discussions were in progress'. One of the beatings took place in one of the flats rented by the party situated across the road from its Clapham HQ, where were also accommodated full-time staff doubling up as concubines.

My collaboration with Thornett had an extraordinary sequel. Once expelled, he and his fellow expellees launched a new group called the Workers Socialist League. From the very beginning its leaders publicly denied they had had any previous dealings with 'Blick-Jenkins', the reason given to inquiring members at the first WSL conference in May 1975 was that in Thornett's own words, 'we didn't want to make our connections with Blick and Jenkins public because it would have isolated us from WRP members.' This was plausible enough at the time, but five years later, when the same considerations no longer applied, they were still denying it, as in a two-page article in the WSL's *Socialist Press* of May 21, 1980. Healy knew they were lying, and devised a clever ruse to prove it. His opportunity came when after years of dissemblement by Thornett's Workers Socialist League, I decided to make a public statement on the affair, which a former member of both the SLL and then the WSL, Adam Westoby, distributed at a WSL public meeting in London. Dated November 4, 1980, it meticulously itemised chronologically each stage in the process of collaboration between myself and Thornett in his fight against the Healy leadership, right up to his expulsion at the end of 1974.

In April 1981 I was contacted, via Adam, by a youngish woman who said she was a member of Thornett's group, (and, as soon proved be the case, also a Healy 'mole'), but after reading my account, had doubts about the truth of its version of the split with Healy. Could she come around to see me, and perhaps obtain from me a true account of the episode? Rather naively, I duly obliged. In fact, she brought with her a lengthy statement signed by herself, and prepared for her no doubt by Healy, based on the account I had given in my leaflet. She asked if I would sign it, which I did after reading it carefully. Only a matter of days later, on April 18, in a three-page spread devoted to what it called 'the Blick connection', both my account and the signed statement were published in Healy's daily paper, *The News Line* (it had changed its name from *Workers Press* in 1976) together with photos of Mark and myself and, would you believe, as further *prima facie* evidence, even one of the fire escape leading up to the kitchen door of my flat. The caption read: 'Blick's West London Flat…Thornett and his clique would scale the fire escape for secret anti-party meetings.' Introducing the two documents, *The News Line*, for once truthfully, claimed that 'they provide complete proof of the identities of those who took part in the party- wrecking and also the back-stabbing tactics they employed. These individuals included Robin Blick and Mark Jenkins, who are notorious anti-communists and rapid anti- Trotskyists. Yet as the documents show, it was Blick who wrote Thornett's so-called 'opposition' documents and prepared his speeches.'

Thornett finally came clean, twenty-four years after the event, in his book, *Inside Cowley*, published in 1998 as the second of his three-volume autobiography, with a Foreword by the one-time Healyite and now Corbynista film director Ken Loach. Although sketchy as to the details and extent of the collaboration, he cites a speech he made to the WRP central committee on October 1974 that had been 'rehearsed' by 'members of the Bulletin Group' (in fact by only myself) and makes the admission, for the first time, that he had been in 'direct discussions with the Bulletin Group, which was helping us to prepare the fight and write the documents.'

Because it precipitated what was by far the largest purge in the entire history of the British and possibly the world Trotskyist movement), accounts of my collaboration with Thornett have been featured in a large number of left wing publications in Britain and abroad, and many of them, more than a dozen, remain posted on the internet this to this day, even including a German translation of the declaration solicited by Healy's spy, in a lengthy critique of Healy's politics entitled *Vom Trotskismus zu Oppportunismus*.

The same article, in the original English, quoted at length from my declaration, dwelling with simulated outrage on the conspiratorial nature of my dealings with Thornett. 'What a wretched and cowardly group: in the dead of night on a deserted service road, it plotted the overthrow of a long-established party leadership which had played an historic role in the world Trotskyist movement.' Mark and I were denounced as 'two cowardly middle-class renegades', 'scoundrels who were to eventually become open anti-communists', whose sole objective 'was to bring about the removal of Healy from the party leadership'. Spot on.

The Wikipedia entry on the affair, as one would hope and indeed expect, tells the same story minus the invective. 'Thornett did have meetings with Blick and Jenkins from the Bulletin Group...the initial document upon which the Thornett opposition was founded was written by Bulletin Group members, essentially Robin Blick, in consultation with Mark Jenkins and John Archer (another former member of the Healy movement).'

Healy, the prime target and eventual victim of the operation launched by 'Blick-Jenkins', later provided his own version of events in an article entitled *The Thornett Conspiracy,* available on-line:

'In 1974, a serious attempt was made by hostile forces to disrupt the internal life of the Workers Revolutionary Party. Ex-WRP members Robin Blick and Mark Jenkins supplied documents to Alan Thornett, WRP CC member and leading shop steward at the British Leyland works at Cowley, Oxford, for presentation to the Central Committee. The documents were intended to subvert the party philosophical and political perspectives onto [sic] erroneous formal opportunist lines.'

The prime mover in this conspiracy was alleged to be Joseph Hansen who, as Trotsky's secretary in Mexico, had been present at the time of the exiled Bolshevik's assassination by a Stalinist agent in August 1940. Hansen had been a long-standing leading member of the American Socialist Workers Party, yet another organisation that fell out with Healy, in 1963. According to Healy, who never did such things by halves, 'Hansen was subsequently exposed [naturally by Healy] as an agent of Soviet and [!] American intelligence.' Unaware of his sinister connections, I met Hanson in London towards the end of 1974, and somehow, Healy found out about the encounter and made much of it in his party's press, hence the connection. Such slanders were standard practise in the WRP, and were in the same tradition as Stalin's tactic of branding all his critics as agents of Hitler, with whom he then signed a pact in August 1939. At the 1974 WRP conference, I for example was charged by Healy with being on the CIA payroll and conducting my campaign of subversion from an office in the US embassy.

Using their collaboration with me as the pretext, Thornett and his comrades from British Leyland were all drummed out of the WRP at the end of 1974, their real crime having been to doubt the infallibility of the party's General Secretary. Their place was taken by an influx from the other end of the social scale by well-intentioned but politically naïve recruits and fellow travellers from the acting and allied professions. Many of them were, and some still are, household names. In first place must surely be ranked Venessa Redgrave who, though she joined sometime later, I remember her supervising donkey rides at a Healyite fund raising event in the summer of 1971. Once enrolled by her brother Corrine, she vaulted into the party leadership, now playing the part of the authentic voice of the British, indeed world proletariat. In the second volume of his autobiography, *Inside Cowley*, Thornett describes her in full flight in this exciting and demanding new role at meeting of the WRP central committee shortly before he was expelled. Thornett had barely completed the critique of Healy's ultra-left polices that we had prepared some hours previously when, outraged by the Leyland truck driver's act of *les majesté*, 'Vanessa Redgrave leapt up screaming "bourgeois pig".' In the same interview with Callahan, Tim Wohlforth offers a plausible explanation for why she resorted to this kind of language: 'I think Vanessa just thought it was about being tough and being a Bolshevik. She was playing an acting role as a Party member.'

One of the first to sign up for Healy's world revolution was Corinne, to whom I was introduced in my Foreign Editor's office not long before I resigned from Healy's movement. Then followed, in no particular chronological order, and with varying degrees of commitment and levels of association, Judy Dench, Bill Oddie, Francis de la Tour, Georgia Brown, Stuart Hood, Kikka Markham, Judy Geeson, Jack Shephard, Ricky Tomlinson, James Bolam, Kenneth Trodd, Marty Feldman, Tom Kempinski, David Mercer, Tony Garnett, Margaretta D'Arcy, Ken Loach, John Arden, Roy Battersby, Suzy Kendall, Trevor Griffith, Tom Selby, Malcolm Tierney, Joe Melia, David Calder, Paul Jones, Slade, UB40, Adrian Mitchell, Christopher Logue, Annie Ross, Troy Kennedy Martin, Roger Smith. Frances Barber, Colin Welland, Neville Smith, Michael Parkinson, Eleanor Bron, Spike Milligan, Glenda Jackson, Dudley Moore, Helen Mirren, Larry Adler, Roy Kinnear and John McGrath. Little wonder that the WRP acquired the sobriquet West End Party. Neither was the appeal limited to stage and screen. When Healy wound up his *Workers Press* in 1976, and with a non- union print shop in Liverpool, the Gaddafi-funded Astmoor Litho, launched his more populist *Newsline,* the sports page featured regular columns by two football legends, comrades Jimmy Greaves and Malcolm Allison.

Needless to say, Healy was astute enough to ensure that the celebrities who adorned the public face of the WRP were hermitically sealed off from the sordid and often violent events that were increasingly becoming a back-stage routine. Those who took the final step of joining were consequently accolated to what was known as the 'Outer London branch', whose activities consisted almost exclusively of lectures and discussions on theoretical questions. Members of this branch were therefore never required to undertake the soulless, and what proved to be futile grind that was the lot of members organised in territorial branches. Placing Healy's sexual practices in a separate category, the harshest regime of all was reserved for male members of long standing or full time employees. I have already described the kind of treatment meted at the 1966 summer camp to myself, Bob Shaw and Jack Gale. Now let me relate two more incidents, which each demonstrate the mental state of the leader the movement had saddled itself with. The first has what proved to be a sexual dimension. Tim Cowan, the affable son of a wealthy farmer, was appointed by Healy in 1969 to manage the newly-acquired *Workers Press* premises. His wife, Claire, the daughter of a South African diamond magnate, was a school teacher, who in her holidays, did a variety of odd jobs at the same location. Claire was an attractive, intelligent young woman. She always wore a mini-skirt, like nearly all the younger female staff at party HQ, and this made it easier to admire her shapely legs when she brought me my morning and afternoon cup of tea in my office. Healy for sure must also have sized them up, as later developments proved because, quite quickly, Tim fell out favour. He could do nothing right. Things came to a head in the run up to the General Election of June 1970 when Tim was instructed by Healy to install a large notice board in one of the *Workers Press* offices. Unfortunately for Tim, he surrounded the board with blue gaffer tape. On seeing it, Healy rounded on

Tim, and accused him of being a Tory agent. Shortly afterwards, he was sacked, preparatory to Healy cuckholding him..

I have it on good authority that the final act of Tim's denouement came when, still a member, he was instructed by Healy to steal, or rather kidnap, a pig from his father's farm, which would then be used to provide greasy pig rides at an upcoming fund-raising event. And so, at dead of night, Tim drove to his father's farm in a van and parked it close by where the pigs were kept. His attempts to manoeuvre one of them into his van raised such a racket that it woke up his father, who proceeded to lay into what, in the dark he initially assumed was a professional pig rustler. I don't know what then ensued when Tim's dad recognised who the thief was, but it did lead, as Healy had warned, to his expulsion. With Tim out of the way, Healy (successfully, as was usually the way) made his move on Claire, an ordeal which, to give her full credit for her honesty and courage, she relates in all its sordid details in her memoire, *My Search for Revolution*.

The second affair also involves a kidnapping, only this time, a successful one. The kidnappee was another full-time party worker, the not very bright, but hard-working and mildly-mannered Larry Hands. He fell foul of Healy's wrath for dutifully obeying the Leader's instructions. It happened like this. The chain of events that to Larry's downfall began 200 miles away in Liverpool, where a League member, a young university graduate by the name of Rosemary Whip, quite possibly at the prompting of her party branch, had got herself a job in a factory. When just as I did at Johnson's in similar circumstances, she started to preach revolution, but unlike me, was sacked, a mass meeting was, called to decide whether to defend her. It voted not to do so because of her politics and student background. The incident briefly became national news, with headlines calling her 'Red Rosemary', and references to her membership of the SLL.

Back in London, anticipating a media onslaught on the

League's Clapham HQ, Healy declared a state of siege. No one was to enter or leave the premises. Larry was dispatched by Healy to the nearby Clapham Common tube station exit to turn back any members arriving there. This he dutifully did. A few hours later, in a small room next to my office, I heard a disturbance, and Healy bellowing at the top of his voice, punctuated by the sobs and whimpers of what turned out to be poor Larry. He was being 'worked over' because one of the league comrades he had turned back at the tube station was delivering to Healy a substantial sum of money Healy, judged by his reaction, urgently needed. Repeated protestations by Larry that he was obeying Healy's instructions simply made matters worse. The 'working over', and I mean physical, continued for an hour or more. The next day, the word was that Larry, to use the customary expression for a desertion from the class war, had 'taken off'. He had not turned up for work, and he had cleared all his belongings, such as they were, out of his flat across the road. But this story too has a sequel, though not a sexual one. The mystery of where Larry had got to was resolved some six week later, when a job centre in Canterbury requested that his previous employer, New Park Publications, Healy's publishing firm that legally employed all his full time staff, forward his P45. Acting on Healy's often-repeated maxim that 'we don't accept resignations', a van was duly dispatched to Canterbury, and a watch kept outside the job centre. Sure enough, a day or so later, Larry arrived to sign on. The waiting kidnap squad pounced on and bundled him into the van, which then headed back to Clapham, where a de-briefing awaited the runaway. But it was no good. Larry had had enough, and I never saw him again, neither was his name ever mentioned again. He, like so many others before and after him, had become an 'unperson'. I invite the reader to contrast the manner in which Tim and Larry, like so many others, loyal members both, were abused by Healy, with the kid glove approach he adopted towards the party's more exalted members. But I have to admit that even before the glitterati began to adorn

Healy's stage, he had already revealed and exploited an extraordinary facility for attracting into his movement both the sons and daughters of extremely wealthy capitalists, and highly talented people who, after they left the movement, pursued successful careers in areas far removed from revolutionary politics. Before working on Healy's journal, I was by week-day an academic, and for the rest of my waking hours, an activist, selling papers, conducting educational classes and attending long and in retrospect, utterly futile meetings. My branch was a typical cross-section of the London membership, overwhelmingly drawn, like other far left groups, from every social category except the industrial working class. Once liberated from the self-imposed shackles of Healyism and the requirement to do six impossible things before breakfast, many made their marks in a variety of fields. Just in my branch there was John Bird, who when I first knew him, was a typical street hustler, but who not so many years later, founded the *Big Issue*, and now gives after dinner speeches for a substantial fee in which he expounds the virtues of authoritarian conservatism, including the restoration of capital punishment.

Then there was Terry Monaghan. After attempting suicide after being cuckolded by Healy, I visited him in hospital without knowing why he had tried to take his life with an overdoes of sleeping tablets. He then drifted out of the movement, only to remerge many years later as the founder of the highly successful Jiving Lindy-Hoppers troupe and as one of the world's leading experts on Afro-American dance. Finally, and this was just in my branch, there was P.J. Arkell, heir to the West Country beer dynasty, and Dr Cyril Smith, a senior lecturer in mathematics at the London School of Economics, the very same who would later gleefully relate to my former flatmate how Healy had tried to ruin my academic career. Two young women from other branches in London whom I knew quite well were both heiresses to vast fortunes, one in bananas, the other in diamonds. But no 'workers'. And there was Ron Porta.

Being gay, Jewish and an extremely talented musician, finally escaping from a movement led by an anti-Semitic, homophobic philistine must have been a truly liberating experience.

And what of my flat mate, David, my first recruit to the SLL? After a couple of years as a full-timer, he fell out with Healy and took a job as London bus driver, obviously having more luck than I did with my failed attempt to become a Glasgow clippie. It must have been the Oxford degree and his military record that made the difference. That was the last I heard of him until, early in the 1980s, reading *History Today*, an academic monthly, I came across an article by David, now a lecturer in Russian history at Aberdeen University. It was the first in a series entitled *Makers of Modern Europe*. Not by chance, his chosen subject, or rather, target, was Lenin, and a fine demolition job it was, demonstrating, by reference to primary sources, that from its first days in power, Lenin's regime had usurped the expressed will of the Russian people. I thought it only right, in view of our past friendship and shared political conclusions, to pen a short letter applauding his article, adding another example of his subject's duplicity, namely Lenin's reneging on a pledge to introduce freedom of the press. This declaration of solidarity from one notorious renegade to another did not pass undetected. Shortly after my letter appeared in the next number of *History Today*, Healy's *Newsline* launched into yet another diatribe, only this time the object of its venom was a certain Blick-Longley.

When Mark and I launched our attack on Healy in 1974, we did so on the basis that his ludicrous claim that the leaders of Britain's trade unions were involved in the preparation of a military coup that would close down their own organisations constituted a radical departure from what was generally regarded as orthodox Trotskyism. And indeed, it was. But in doing so, it never entered our heads that we should become involved in an attempt to create a Trotskyist organisation to rival Healy's. And yet that is what did indeed happen. A fluent English-speaking delegate from our 'French connection', the OCI, visited Mark and myself in London to persuade us to join forces with a veteran of the Healy movement who had now turned against him. Her name, Betty Hamilton, was familiar to both of us. Around seventy, she was French-Swiss by birth, but had married a wealthy English businessman and was now naturalised British. Her maiden name was Dutois, being the aunt of the famous Swiss conductor Charles Dutois. When young, she had been a pupil of the ill-fated dancer and Bolshevik groupie Isadore Duncan, as chance would have it, played by Redgrave in the film *Isadore,* a role, so I was later told, that inspired her to emulate Duncan's example. Betty later became a dance teacher herself and, before the war, plying her trade at of all of schools, mine in Edmonton.

Betty had co-existed quite happily with Healy until the OCI, with whom she had many personal as well as political connections, broke with him in 1971. Mark and I first met up with Betty at her luxury apartment in Victoria. Unbeknown to us, waiting in another room were two other former members of the SLL, who comprised the rank and file of Betty's operation. After checking us both out, and deeming Mark and I kosher Trotskyists, without telling us their names, she informed us of her other two guests' presence, and brought them into the meeting. My heart sank. I knew them of old, Harry Vince and his side-kick and yes-man, Ken Stratford, a couple of chancers who, after dropping out of the SLL long before me, had worked their way through most of the outfits, factions and sub-factions that were multiplying like amoebae in the heady days of the late sixties Their promiscuous careers up to this point were best described. as political philately. And it soon became obvious that they had decided to throw in their modest lot with the wealthy and generous Betty for motives that were as much pecuniary as they were political. Not withstanding my reservations about Betty's acolytes, Mark and I agreed to combine our meagre forces. By this time, the spring of 1974, we had assembled a group of about ten or so ex-Healyites, while Hamilton's contribution amounted to no more than half a dozen at most. According to Wikipedia, 'by late 1974' there was 'a larger group around Blick and Jenkins' of 'perhaps 20', while the Hamilton group had 'perhaps 12'. The latter figure is too high, it was never more than half a dozen. The new formation took the name of the Bulletin Group, after the Bulletin we circulated to WRP members; and then, in 1979, three years after Mark and I had left, the Socialist Labour Group.

The OCI were very keen to adopt us as their 'British connection' as a rival to Healy's WRP. According to the Wikipedia account of this episode, the French organisation 'wanted Robin Blick to lead the Bulletin Group as open supporters of the OCI'. This had never been my intention. All Mark and I had wanted was to settle accounts with Healy. But it was certainly with the former intention in mind that Mark and I were invited to attend a number of conferences in Paris over the next two years. Despite our deep reservations about re-launching our revolutionary careers for a third time (we were also by now both approaching forty and the fathers of two young children), it did not take long for us to realise that in several ways, the OCI was a very different kind of movement to Healy's, not only in its policies, but in the manner it conducted its business. Instead of craven conformism and an all-pervading atmosphere of intimidation, debates were friendly, always accompanied by the consumption of wine and a French loaf.

In the course of my two-year's association with the OCI, I came to know most of its leading members quite well. I found them to be of a different calibre to the team of yes men and women Healy had assembled around himself. Just to take four that I knew personally, there was Pierre Lambert, a Jew who had been active in the resistance during the Second World War, with the ever-present threat of being betrayed to the Nazis by the Stalinists; Daniel Renard, who led a strike at Renault in 1947 that brought down the French government; Pierre Broué, an historian of international renown; and Stephane Juste, their most effective orator, who worked as an electrician on the Paris Metro. One I never met was Lionel Jospin, who was an OCI plant in the French Socialist Party, rising to become one of President Mitterrand's most trusted advisers. Jospin later ran, unsuccessfully, as the Socialist Party's candidate for the Presidency, though by this time, he had severed his connection with the OCI.

Mark and I also parted company with our 'French Connection', but in circumstances very different from those of Jospin. The break began when, after policy disagreements emerged in the Bulletin Group, the OCI backed Betty Hamilton's tiny minority. The main bone of contention was the division of Germany. I had written an internal policy document advocating the destruction of the Berlin Wall and supporting the unification of Germany *sans conditions,* as our French comrades would say. I had bluntly stated that the German people's right to a unified state was not negotiable, even if it resulted in their retention of the liberal democratic welfare capitalism of the nation's western sector. And, beginning on the night of November, 9, 1989 this is exactly what did happen. Ironically, the Wall was one of the issues that precipitated my break with the Stalinism of the British Communist Party.

The differences over German unification and more generally, the primacy of what were called 'democratic demands', combined with a series of intrigues by the Hamilton faction, led to what Wikipedia describes, quite accurately as 'the grouping around Robin Blick and Mark Jenkins holding secret caucus meetings within the Bulletin Group and moving away from support for the OCI'. It would not be long before Mark and I were moving away from Trotskyism altogether. Better causes and, more fruitful and enriching pursuits beckoned, as they did for many others who made the same break. As the same Wikipedia entry laconically observed, I was 'now a musician' and Mark, 'a playwright in Wales'.

After settling his several accounts with Healy, Mark did

indeed find fame if not much fortune as a highly-acclaimed playwright and film script writer for, amongst other productions, his BAFTA award-winning *Playing Burton,* which Maureen and I saw when it came to Swansea, *Rosebud, the Lives of Orson Wells*, and the film *The Scarlett Tunic,* premiered at the Cannes Film Festival and the Leicester Square Odeon. Across the pond there was another talented former Healyite, the already mentioned Tim Wohlforth, whom I first met on his visits to London to receive his instructions on how to organise a communist revolution in the USA. In later years, I got to know him really well when he revisited London, staying with me several times while he looked up old comrades from his political past. Tim had fallen foul of Healy when in 1974, at the exact same time as the eruption of the 'Blick-Jenkins conspiracy', his wife was accused of being a possible CIA agent. As Tim related it to Callahan, 'I felt very afraid when Healy moved in on me in his camp in Montreal and accused the woman I has associated with of being a CIA agent. The camp has all these guards and all I wanted to do was just get out of there. I was really worried about what might happen to me.'

Not surprisingly, Tim and his wife resigned. After a few more years of political activism with the anti-Healy Socialist Workers Party (not to be confused with the British party of the same name) Tim took to writing. First came his autobiographical *The Prophet's Children* (the prophet of course being Trotsky) and then *On the Edge*, a study of political cults. As was only to be expected, one of its chapters, appropriately entitled *Guru to a Star*, is devoted to Healy's.

His greatest literary success, however, came when he turned his hand to crime writing, which like Mark's dramas, has won him awards. I re-established contact with Tim when some years after I moved to Swansea, I caught up with the 21st century by acquiring a computer. I learned from Tim that although his main activity was novel-writing, he was also involved with a leftist grouping in the Democratic

Party, the Democratic Socialists of America. We both enthused over the victory of Obama in the 2008 Presidential Election, and even more so over his re-election four years later. And it seemed that on most issues, Tim and I were in broad agreement. This proved not to be the case, because when Putin invaded and then annexed a chunk of north Georgia in 2008, and then did the same to the Ukraine in 2014, and when later the same year Hamas launched its rocket attacks on Israel, Tim and found ourselves at odds, as I also did with Maureen's daughter. (But not, I hasten to add, with her mother, whose views about Israel and its many enemies, secular and religious, though arrived at independently of me, coincided exactly with mine.)

Matters came to a head when I sent Tim the first draft of my *Socialism of Fools*. He took me to task for failing to condemn what he called 'the crimes of Israel'. Since then, despite several attempts to re-engage with him, not a word, which is very sad, because I had always believed that our friendship, which went back the best part of half a century, would count for more than any differences we might have over politics. I have experienced a similarly sad parting of the ways with another friend, one whom I recruited into the SLL from the Communist Party early in 1963, and remained on the best of terms throughout our often-shared vicissitudes (it was to him that I confided my intention to seek out Maureen) until I emailed him the same draft of my *Socialism of Fools* that I had sent to Tim, with the same result. I later learned via Mark that my friend of more than half a century found my views on Islam proof that I had lost the plot. This, from a died in the wool atheist.

So far as my (and Maureen's) differences with Andrea were concerned, in time good sense prevailed when, after series of sometimes animated exchanges on the Hamas-Israel conflict of 2014, the First Amendment to the US constitution, the removal of Saddam Hussein, the Castro regime, the politics of Jeremy Corbyn, Islam, drug addiction, and whether the Holocaust was the greatest crime in history, Andrea and I agreed to confine our conversations to more humdrum matters. Perhaps my most fruitful as well amicable political (and philosophical) exchanges were with yet another ex-Healyite, Adam Westoby. In the Acknowledgments to Tim's autobiography, he makes reference to his 'close friends and intellectual companions in Great Britain who share with me some of the best and worst experiences chronicled in this book, Adam Westoby, Mark Jenkins and Robin Blick'. Mark, we already know. Adam, the unwitting intermediary in Healy's ruse to expose my connection with Thornett, joined the Socialist Labour League in the mid-1960s while an undergraduate at Oxford, so I only came to know him really well when he moved back to London shortly before I became Foreign Editor of the *Workers Press* in 1969. Amongst his many talents, Adam was fluent in both French and Italian, and when I was short of copy I was always glad to see him when he dropped into my office with a story culled from an Italian or French newspaper.

Adam was never a true believer like me, but he loved a political intrigue. So Adam needed little persuading when Healy asked him to undertake two under-cover operations. The first was to infiltrate a rival Trotskyist organisation, the 'Pabloite' International Marxist Group, then under the leadership of a fellow old Oxfordian, Tariq Ali, who would in later years follow the well-trodden path from 'street fighting man', the title of his autobiography, to pillar of the media establishment (More recently, doubtless impressed by the Labour Leader's fanatical anti-Zionism and Euro-scepticism, he became an enthusiastic Corbynista and campaigner for Brexit.) Adam's assignment involved feeding information back to Healy on the internal life of the group, while at the same time causing the maxim possible disruption by joining one of its feuding factions. Then it was my turn. A year or so after I had left the SLL, out of the blue, I had a phone call from Adam: 'Could we meet up for chat?' I was naturally a little suspicious, because I was ex-directory. How did he get my number? When I asked what he wanted to talk about, he was very evasive. I sensed something fishy, so I made some very nasty comments about Healy to test his reaction. When there was none, I just said goodbye and hung up.

Not long afterwards, Adam became involved in another intrigue, only this time against Healy, briefly joining the opposition led by Allan Thornett. So when he contacted me again in 1979, I assumed that this time, it was to resume our old friendship. To make sure, I put it to him bluntly: Was that call made on behalf of Healy? Rather shamefacedly, he admitted that it was. By this time, Adam had, like me, jettisoned most of his orthodox Trotskyists convictions, and was eager to explore the reasons as to why the entire leftist project had so clearly failed to deliver on its promises. Tim in the USA was also thinking along similar lines, so when he came to London to stay with me, the three of us sat down one day in my kitchen and tried, largely unsuccessfully, to reach some common understanding on where the left had gone wrong. But that did not matter. After spending a decade or more in a movement that imposed a mind-numbing conformity on its members, we were at last debating issues where there were no forbidden questions or answers. As Tim says in his autobiography:

'Robin and Adam were more than political collaborators. Together we had been possessed by the intoxicating dream of communism. We had given our lives totally to this movement and then each in our own way suffered from its degeneration. We found our ways of the movement individually yet came together through a common search to understand this experience. We did not come to the same conclusions in the end but were bonded to each other nevertheless.'

Tim describes how to give him a break from these intense exchanges, I took him to a social run by my local Labour Party branch.

'There was a raffle of course and the winning ticket was picked out of bowl by young man who proved to be Tony Benn's son [Hilary Benn]. Lo and behold, the fellow was calling out my number! I am not the kind of person who wins things. I went to the table to choose my prize. I could either have a complete set of the works of Kim Il Sung, North Korea's illustrious leader, or a set of beer glasses. I chose the beers glasses. Robin came over beaming. "Admit it, Tim, this is the first party that has ever given you something." He was right.'

Meanwhile, as Tim, Adam and I debated the future of socialism, the WRP seemed to be going from strength to strength, though this would prove to be an optical illusion. The cash flowed in from the Middle East, and the promotion from the West End. I have to confess that I played a modest part in the early stages of Healy's truly spectacular operation to enrol the elite of British drama into the ranks, and indeed with the two Redgraves, into the leadership of his movement. November 1967 was the 50th anniversary of the Bolshevik revolution, and as one of the few members of the SLL *au fait* with its history, I found myself saddled with the somewhat daunting responsibility of organising its commemoration in St Pancreas Town Hall on Euston Road. Naturally, the highlight and climax of the event would be a public meeting in the evening addressed by the British Lenin, Comrade Healy, while during the day, there would book stalls, refreshment's etc. To lend the proceedings an artistic dimension, I designed a mural portraying the history of radical movements from the French and Russian revolutions through to the Fourth International and concluding, rather fancifully, with the Socialist Labour League. Painted on to a continuous length of canvass by a team of talented artists, it was then suspended from the balcony surrounding the hall. This took care of the visual dimension.

As to the aural ambience, initially, my intention was to solicit the services of two playwrights who were close to the SLL, Roger Smith, who was writing and editing dramas for the BBC's Wednesday Play feature in the 1960s, and David Mercer, whose was already in the first rank as writer of scripts for stage, screen and TV. The idea I put to David when I met him at his St. John's Wood home was that he should produce a short sketch to be acted on the stage at the town hall. We talked through some possible plots, and finally came up with a short drama set in a Soviet prison cell, occupied by a Trotskyist and a Stalinist stool pigeon. He assured me that it would work, but the trouble was, he didn't deliver, leaving me with having to devise a substitute. Running out of time, in desperation, I turned to Trotsky for assistance, selecting dramatic passages from his superb *History of the Russian Revolution*, and with a team of actors, recorded them onto tape, later adding some mood music from Shostakovich's Tenth Symphony. As far as I know, this was the first occasion on which the SLL utilised the services of the acting profession.

My next encounter with the thespians reversed roles, with me doing the talking, and they as my audience. In the autumn of 1969, at the time of the launching of the Socialist Labour League's daily paper, the *Workers Press*, being regarded by Healy as something of an authority on the subject, I was enlisted to give a series of talks on the history of the Russian Revolution at film-producer Tony Garnet's spacious flat in Notting Hill. When I arrived, most of the students were already there. I vaguely recognised, without being able to put a name to most of them, faces I had seen on my TV screen. Also catching my attention and holding it considerably longer were a half a dozen or so attractive young ladies, who in their very short skirts, were displaying their wares on large cushions. Fruit bowls were distributed in strategic locations round the room. It could for all the world have been a scene from *I Claudius*, the only difference being that the talk was of the triumphs and tribulations of Trotsky, not Tiberius. Shortly after my arrival came the grand entry of Emperor Healy, accompanied as always on such occasions by the smartly dressed and immaculately groomed Aileen Jennings in her capacity as what today would be described as Healy's Personal Assistant. Aileen was by this time established both as Healy's favourite concubine and preferred chauffer, while officially remaining the wife of the cuckholded Paul

Jennings, the editor of *Workers Press*. She finally proved to be Healy's nemesis when sixteen years later, after being hospitalised by Healy when he assaulted her with a chair, she exposed him as a sexual predator.

My efforts at what I genuinely believed then was political enlightenment undoubtedly bore fruit, as the roll call of conversions to what became Healy's ever more exotic brand of Trotskyism testifies, though by this time, I had long left, and was engaged in putting an end what I had helped to start. What became of the WRP's Thespian battalions? It told much of their level of political sophistication, not to speak of their morality, that when the Healy sex scandal broke in 1985, most followed the example of the Redgraves, and Greater London Council supremo and later London Mayor Ken Livingstone by remaining loyal to their Lothario leader, while others far fewer in number, some of whom I later came to know, began a search for a different kind of politics altogether.

The Thornett affair must have hurt him badly, because in the years leading up to the implosion of the WRP in 1985, Healy kept returning to the so-called 'Blick-Jenkins conspiracy' of 1974, one that apart from the actor's union Equity, had effectively put an end to what little influence the WRP once had in the trade union movement, and had left him financially dependent on funding from anti-Semitic Arab dictators. As first renegade, then spy, provocateur and double agent, I had become Healy's public enemy number one. Even six years on, in a booklet melodramatically entitled *Thornett's Clique Unmasked*, Healy was still accusing myself and Mark, in this instance truthfully, of being 'the authors of the documents which Thornett presented inside the WRP as his own work', and of holding 'private talks' with Hansen, 'agent in chief [of both the CIA and KGB was meant here] of the Socialist Workers Party of the United States'.

The booklet claimed that having received its instructions from the CIA and the KGB via the double agent Hansen, the 'shadowy Blick-Jenkins group' then 'set up a secret clique in the party, organised disruptive and anti-party practices and then fed off the expulsions that resulted'. But a little further on we learn that I was not after all the author of the Thornett documents. Now it transpired that they had been 'written by Blick and Jenkins under the guiding hand of the agent [by which was implied of the CIA and KGB] Joseph Hansen'. But the plot thickens even further, because with or without the knowledge of Soviet and US intelligence, I was also involved in a 'cynical type of provocation worthy of Scotland Yard'. Then of course there was the 'French connection', the OCI, presumably acting as a front for the *Direction centrale des renseignements general.* So what had begun simply as the 'Blick-Jenkins' plot against the WRP had now blossomed into a vast transatlantic 'Blick-Jenkins-Hansen-OCI anti-party conspiracy.' To enable the general public to visually identify the main culprits in this nefarious enterprise, their photos were conveniently reproduced in the pamphlet, including one of the spymaster Joseph Hansen, one of myself taken at the 1963 conference of the WRP's predecessor, the SLL, and another of Mark selling the socialist (or rather 'corporatist') weekly, *Tribune*.

In answer to its own question, 'where are they now?' the booklet revealed that 'Robin Blick is "out of politics" and now plays with a large train set in his front room'. Again, more lies. I was not 'out of politics', only the kind that pursues the fantasy of a Lenin-style revolution in Britain. And for all his claims to political omniscience, Healy failed to predict that five years later, he would be out of his own party, expelled appropriately on my birthday, 19 October 1985, on charges of the sexual abuse of a score or more of younger female members. And to set the record straight, neither did I 'play' with what was condescendingly called a 'train set' in my front room'. I ran a vast layout in my loft, which after I moved in with Maureen in January 2000, I reassembled with her help in the loft at 169, Pentregethin Road, Swansea.

One of the many ironies of the Healy saga his was choice

of Mike Banda as his successor as General Secretary of the WRP, because it was none other than the tried and trusted Banda who led the revolt to expel Healy from his own party in 1985. However, in a letter to all branch secretaries, dated December 16, 1980, he was still strictly on message, recycling the same slanders that his predecessor had concocted against 'Blick-Jenkins'. Citing passages from my statement of November 6, 1980 detailing my dealings with Thornett, Banda arrived at the conclusion that 'the Blick group', 'a hostile clique of agent cultists' no less, had as its aim 'to act as a tool of a counter-revolutionary agency', namely, the FBI. However, I feel rather flattered by the letter's concluding instruction that that 'all comrades should read the Blick letters' and 'treat them as an indispensable part of the preparation for the Fifth [WRP] Congress.' (After his break with Healy, Banda at least had decency to apologise to me in the *News Line* for being complicit in the abuse I had suffered under the Healy regime.)

Some five years after Healy's death in 1989, the strange story of the Blick-Jenkins-KGB-CIA-FBI-Scotland Yard-OCI conspiracy surfaced yet again when there was published what to all intents and purposes was an official biography of Gerry Healy by two of his most dedicated acolytes, Paul Feldman and Corinna Lots, both of whom I had come to know personally in the course of my membership of Healy's organisation. The 370 hagiographic pages of their *Gerry Healy: A Revolutionary Life* were introduced in a Foreword by Ken Livingstone, which concluded with the assertion that 'it was a privilege to have worked with Gerry Healy. I know this book will give those who did not know him an opportunity to understand his contribution to the working class revolutionary movement.' If indeed Livingstone had read the book whose subject he was praising, he would have found on pages 262 to 264 an instructive example of how Healy and his disciples went about making one of many such contributions:

'Robin Blick and Mark Jenkins were disgruntled ex-members of the SLL who moved in Labour Party circles.

They were recruited as British agents of the OCI, who had set out to disrupt the work of the WRP. They circulated material alleging that Healy ran a regime of "terror and violence"[the very idea!] which the Tory press immediately picked up, embellished and published...Blick and Jenkins wrote documents for Thornett to present to the WRP central committee. Aiding this conspiratorial group was none other than Hansen, the leader of the American Socialist Workers Party, who would be exposed [that is, by Healy, with no more proof than was forthcoming at Stalin's infamous purge trials of the 1930s] as a double agent of Soviet and American intelligence.'

Did Livingstone really believe that Hansen, Mark and I were agents of the KGB and the CIA? Quite possibly, because he too liked to see conspiracies where none existed. The downfall and disgrace of Healy in 1985 apparently was not caused by the long-overdue exposure of the scale and manner in which he indulged his Gargantuan sexual appetites. According to Livingstone, 'the split in the WRP during 1985 was the work of MI5 agents'.

But that spectacular *denouement* lay in the future. After the successful accomplishment of our assignment on behalf of British, US and Soviet intelligence, Mark and I decided to undertake a freelance operation that did not sit too well with one of our previous employers. Throughout the 1970s, leading up to the emergence of the Polish free trade union *Solidarnosc* in the summer of 1980, the Soviet regime had adopted a new tactic to supress the mounting internal resistance to its totalitarian rule. Abandoning rigged public trials of so-called 'dissidents', which attracted some, but far from enough criticism in the West, opponents of the system would be diagnosed as suffering from one or more of a number of mental disorders and then detained in KGB 'hospitals' until they proved their return to sanity by renouncing their political convictions. Now, with our far leftist politics well behind us, Mark and I helped to initiate and co-ordinate a series of campaigns on behalf of the victims of Soviet persecution.

There was the case of Victor Fainberg, arrested in Red Square in August 1968 for protesting against the Soviet invasion of Czechoslovakia, and confined to a KGB psychiatric prison. The same treatment was meted out to the organisers of SMOT, the illegal Soviet trade union, advocates of independence for the USSR's national minorities, writers and artists opposed to censorship, Christian denominations such as the Pentecostals and the Reformed Baptists, which unlike the age-old pillar of the Russian State, the Russian Orthodox Church, had not been legalised by the Soviet authorities, and Jews demanding the right to emigrate from a country that with more than a little encouragement down the ages from its rulers, had lamentably failed to cure itself of the disease of anti-Semitism. Remarkably, given the odds, persistent lobbying, letter writing, demonstrating and holding public meetings did secure the release of some, but far from all of these beneficiaries of Kremlin justice. One who made it to the West was Victor, whom Mark and I came to know very well after his arrival in London. I remember introducing him to the delights of Indian cuisine in a restaurant in Southall, just down the road from where I then lived in Ealing. In the middle of the meal, he produced a pocket chess set and insisted on challenging me to a game, though the result now escapes me.

One of the most satisfying and also moving experiences of this time occurred when I was invited, in the spring of 1976, to appear on the platform at a meeting convened at the Paris *Mutualitie*, the traditional venue for radical political gatherings, to protest at the continued persecution of dissidents in the Soviet Union and Eastern Europe. The event had been organised by our 'French connection', the OCI and it was indeed impressive. The vast hall, with a capacity of around 2,000, was packed to overflowing. The main speakers included the biologist Vladimir Bukovsky and the Ukrainian Leonid Plyushch, cofounders of the Soviet Union's first human rights group, both being two former Soviet political prisoners who had recently been freed from the clutches of KGB psychiatric prisons as a result of aggressive and persistent campaigning in the west by Amnesty International and a tiny group of human rights activists, among who I am proud to number the KGB agents Blick-Jenkins.

After the meeting, the platform entourage was treated to a sumptuous meal at Maxims, Paris's most famous restaurant, which had been privately booked for the occasion. I had been seated between two Czech exiles from the crushed Prague Spring of 1968, State TV Director Jiri Pelikan and student leader Jan Kavan, the plan behind this arrangement being that I was to persuade them of the necessity of adopting a Trotskyist perspective in the fight for political freedom in the Soviet bloc. They listened politely, and then tucked into their meals. I looked around the tables. We were just a handful, and the Kremlin's hold on its empire, despite the occasional disturbance here and there, still seemed unshakable.

Then in the summer of 1980, everything changed. The isolated and largely unheeded protests of a handful of dissidents against the might of the Soviet state were now joined, first on the Baltic coast in the port and shipyards of Gdansk, and then across the whole of Poland, by a mighty mass rebellion for workers' rights. In a matter of weeks, a new trade union, *Solidarnosc* had enrolled almost the entire industrial work force of the country, while in the countryside, farmers poured into its rural counterpart. Mark had by this time moved to Cardiff with his second wife and two girls to take up a lecturing post at the University of Wales, leaving myself and my wife, now joined by Adam Westoby, by this time a leading academic at the Open University and author of several studies of communism, to organise a meeting in London in support of *Solidarnosc*.

At that meeting, chaired by myself, came the launching of the Polish Solidarity Campaign. Subsequently, I was elected its secretary, and set about drumming up support for *Solidarnosc* among its trade union counterparts in Britain, as well as from prominent members of the Labour Party. I reasoned that the more such support was forthcoming from the British left, the harder it would be it for the Polish authorities to depict the new movement as an anti-socialist conspiracy. In this I was only moderately successful. The most prominent Labour MPs publicly associating themselves with our campaign were the future Labour Leader Neil Kinnock, Robin Cook, later to serve as Tony Blair's first Foreign Secretary and Peter Shaw and Eric Heffer, former government ministers under Harold Wilson, together with a small sprinkling of back benchers. The response was no less patchy when I approached trade union leaders who, in theory at least, one would have supposed would been only too willing to extend the hand of solidarity to their embattled Polish brothers and sisters. The National Union of Mineworkers thought otherwise, with Arthur Scargill preferring instead to lend his public support to the military regime whose security forces, after the declaration of Martial Law in December 1981, shot dead seven coal miners at the Wujek collier and four years later, as if to rub salt into an open wound, exported coal to Britain to help Margaret Thatcher's government break the miners' strike.

Meanwhile, Scargill's Polish comrades in the UK were also busy, making several attempt to subvert our campaign, with intelligence agents merging with our demonstrations to incite acts of violence, and attending our public meetings. This however was small beer compared what in the lingo of the trade, goes by the name of 'special operations'. Let me quote from the official history of the PSC, *For Our Freedom And Yours*: 'The most worry case was that of Lujan Latala, a Pole stranded in Britain due to Martial Law, who was highly active with SWS. [this was a break-away group from the PSC] In September 1982 he was found dead in a park, hanging by his neck from a tree, with his hands tied behind his back.' Just as was the case with the death of God's Banker, Roberto Calvi, who three months earlier, had been found hanging from Blackfriars Bridge, also with his hands tied behind his back, the verdict was one of suicide. In the light of what ensued, I have good reason to suspect that as it did with with the Vatican, preserving normal diplomatic relations with Poland played a part in arriving at this ruling. Shortly after it was announced, SWS held its monthly demonstration outside the Polish embassy in Great Portland Street. I was one of the speakers, and so witnessed the following incident. There was an unusually heavy police presence at the meeting, and it soon became evident why. The first speaker was Tardek Jarksi, founder of SWS. Early on in his speech, he described the circumstances of Latala's death, and had just begun to pour scorn on the verdict of suicide when the police pounced, dragging him off the improvised speakers' podium, the pedestal of a statue, and bundling him into a nearby police van. I never got to speak, because the police closed the meeting. So much for free speech in the UK.

Given my high-profile role in the campaign, it was inevitable that Healy should make it his business to slander me yet again, an undertaking that naturally needed to take precedence over giving support to the Polish workers. Already it was going the rounds on the far left that I was, as recounted in *For Your Freedom and Ours*, the official history of the Polish Solidarity Campaign, 'CIA funded and to the right of Genghis Khan'. I also learned that a namesake (but not relation) of mine, the NALGO committee member Mike Blick, had to reassure his more leftist trade union colleagues that he did not share my genes. Then on 4 February 1981, Healy's Gaddafi-funded daily paper, now changed from its title of *Workers Press* to *News Line*, carried an editorial entitled, *Beware, Fake Solidarity*.

In the best Healy tradition, it did not mince its slanderous words. 'Trade unionists and Labour Party members must be warned against an outfit calling itself the Polish Solidarity Campaign', the reason being that 'the self-styled secretary [I *was* the secretary] of this pill-boxed sized organisation is Mr Robin Blick, the infamous anti-communist. He was a principle figure in the political conspiracy against the Workers Revolutionary Party in 1974. He and Mark Jenkins [why no Mr?] worked in secret to set up a party within a party in order to try smash the WRP...Since those heady days Blick has been careering even further to the right. His main fascination, apart from toy trains [wrong again, model railways], is whipping up anti-Soviet causes.' The article did however correctly quote me as saying 'the reason the TUC had not recognised the new Solidarity union in Poland was because they had been corrupted by trips to the Soviet Union. They would "hate to have their noses torn out of the nose bag", he said.' Dead right.

One might have thought this was enough. But not for Healy, for whom my part in the 'Thornett conspiracy' evidently still rankled badly. On 16 February, he resumed his slanders against me, this time with a feature on page 11 of the same paper, together with a large photo of myself taken by a WRP photographer (the heir to Arkell's beers no less) at a recent PSC press conference in the House of Commons. Healy was clearly furious that the Sunday *Observer* had 'published a letter to the editor which perpetrates a political hoax on the workers' movement'. The target of Healy's ire was not so much the twelve signatories, who included four Labour MPs and a number of trade union officials, but that the letter carried a certain address. 'This is the home address of one [sic] Robin Blick,' the same Blick 'who worked from the sidelines to create a party within the WRP with the declared purpose of smashing the WRP and destroying its leadership by a mixture of lies and slanders. Now Blick is up to his old (and filthy) tricks, using the names of MPs in a letter to the *Observer*, but remaining well in the background himself.' So much in the background, that not only my address, but my name, appeared at the head of all PSC correspondence. For how else would *News Line* would have known that this was my address, since I no longer lived at the Acton flat with the Thornett fire escape exit?

The PSC's 'fake solidarity' consisted not only of holding public meetings and demonstrations in support of democracy and trade union rights in Poland, and soliciting public declarations of support for Solidarity from British trade union leaders, but buying and shipping to Poland a Roneo Duplicator for their maligned, besieged, and resource-strapped brothers and sisters. This desperate predicament meant nothing to a WRP whose only concern was to undermine the solidarity actions of those who, despite their meagre resources, were doing what they could to help them overcome it.

Having lost its only foothold in the labour movement, the WRP was by this time serving chiefly as a propaganda and publicity agency for its Arab paymasters. Tim Wohlforth describes in his autobiography how Vanessa Redgrave fronted Healy's fund-raising campaign: 'With Healy in tow, Vanessa toured the Middle East capitals soliciting funds from the Iraqis, various sheikhdoms, including the royal family of Kuwait [whose kingdom was invaded by Iraq in 1990], Libya and Iran [also invaded by Iraq in 1980]. Everywhere Vanessa went, large sums were raised.'

Gaddafi took a special interest the WRP, referring to it as 'my party'. This in a sense was true, since he was far and away its main financier, a status reflected in the extensive covering devoted to his deeds and speeches in the WRP's press and from its launching in 1981, by the weekly *Labour Herald*, printed on Healy's Gaddafi-funded printing press Astmoor Litho, and under the joint editorship of the already mentioned long-standing Healyite and former Lambeth council leader Ted Knight, GCL leader Ken Livingstone (suspended in 2016 from the Labour Party on charges of anti-Semitism) and his deputy John McDonnell, Corbyn's shadow chancellor and declared opponent of the existence of the state of Israel. Asked why the *Herald* was being printed by the same company as the WRP's *News Line* and the Libyan embassy's *Green March*, Knight disingenuously said he first learned of Astmoor Litho through reading *News Line*. 'They are very capable printers. That's why we chose them'. A likely tale. Knight was a Healyite entryist in the Labour Party back in the 1950's. I was present with him and Healy at top-level SLL meetings held at the League's headquarters in the 1960s. The lie that Knight had told the *Sunday Telegraph* reporter was what Healy used to call 'a class truth'.

Unlike those of the *Labour Herald,* Healy's Libyan connections were never a secret. His official biography relates how he 'met Colonel Gaddafi on a number of occasions, even flying back to Heathrow in the Libyan leader's jet'. But for all its bluster, bravado, and A list celebrities, the clock was ticking for Healy's movement. Despite, and indeed because of the lavish funding from Muslim dictators, it was failing to balance its books. Even without the sex scandal that brought Healy down, his party was heading for bankruptcy, political as well as financial. So much so in fact, that secret plans were afoot to remove him for any positions of influence in the party.

In his book on political cults, Tim described in some detail the regime that Healy imposed on his movement in his last years in power, one which crumbled overnight when the same leading members who had hounded the Thornett opposition eleven years previously finally summoned sufficient courage to rebel against him. And it did need courage, as both Mark and myself can testify. After Healy's ousting, a party member related how for questioning one of his rulings, after being punched by him 'several times', he was 'given a good kicking by about six comrades [sic)]' while two party leaders 'urged them on, shouting, "Break his legs" several times'. Was it perhaps incidents such as this that that Ken Livingstone had in mind when he wrote so approvingly of Healy's 'massive impact on the working class socialist movement'?

When the story broke on October 23, 1985, with the *News Line* headline, 'G. Healy Expelled', there were no specific reasons given for his expulsion, other than that he had 'abused his power for personal satisfaction.' When over the following week, details began to emerge of his sexual relations with female party members, derived mainly from Aileen Jennings' letter to the WRP central committee, the tabloids knew they were in for a field day, with a potent mix of sex, celebrities and far left politics. For the first time in the history of British Trotskyism, thanks to Healy's genitals, it was front page news. The *Daily Mirror* of October 31 set the pace and the tone, with its headlines 'Red In The Bed' and 'Sex scandal of sacked Trot chief and 26 women', complete with a mug shot of Healy. (The *Star* trumped this with 'Reds in the Beds') This was followed by the *Mirror's* Sunday stablemate on November 3, which carried the front-page headline, 'Secrets of Randy Comrade Casanova'. One of Healy's concubines had revealed to the paper that Healy had 'lured women members back to his flat by offering to give them "special training"', and 'pretended to each of them [all 26 presumably] that they were the only love of his life.' Is this what Ken Livingstone had in mind when in his introduction to Healy's official biography, he praised the priapic septuagenarian's 'freshness of approach'?

The *Daily Mail* went for the celebrity angle, with its headline plus photos of November 1, 'Exit Left the Two Redgraves', and the story, culled from the *News Line*, that Healy had gone into hiding. (His official biographer, Karina Lotz, relates how he spent 'three months underground' at a series of 'safe houses'.) On the same day, the down-market *Star* plumbed for straight sex, 'Girls Lured To Red Gerry's Casting Couch', while the *Daily* Telegraph went for sexpol, with an editorial headed 'Revolutionary Sex'.

In its coverage of a press conference held by the two Redgraves (never was a surname more appropriate, given the circumstances) on November 4, *The Times* quoted Venessa as saying, 'the allegations are all lies and the women who are supposed [sic] to have made them are [sic] all liars. I don't care whether it's 26, 36 or 236. They are all liars.' Echoing Redgrave, Livingstone, as we have already noted, attributed 'the split in the WRP' to 'the work of MI5 agents', a view shared by Healy's biographers, who added an extra ingredient of *cherchez la femme*: 'A key figures in Healy' political[sic] life, Jennings was an obvious target for destabilisation. Someone had "turned" her and created conditions for her disappearance.' The list of Healy's 26 sexual conquests was dismissed as 'poisonous allegations'. However, for cartoonists, they were gift of a lifetime, with one cartoon featuring a naked Healy pursuing a nubile nude woman past two policemen. One says to the other, 'Don't worry - it's probably a recruiting drive by the Workers Revolutionary Party'. Another had a queue of decrepit-looking old men outside the premises of the WRP. Two ladies are standing at the entrance, and one says to the other, 'Isn't it wonderful the way recruitment's gone up, Vanessa?'

I can't remember exactly how it came about, but through a contact with an ex-WRP journalist friend, both Mark and myself were approached by the press for inside stories about life in Healy's party. Of course, we were only too happy to oblige. Interviewed by the *News of the World*, Mark understandably focused on the disgraced leader's penchant for cuckholdery and wife-snatching. In a double-page feature entitled 'Randy Red Supremo Grabbed My Wife; Sexy weekends in flats says husband', complete with a photo of Mark's 'ex', Mark told 'how a lecherous "Red in the bed" had a sneaky affair with his wife and wrecked their marriage.' It was a tale of a holiday romance with an unusual twist, philosophical, but hardly Platonic. Healy had 'invited himself along on our holiday. He insisted on driving away with my wife for afternoon discussions on philosophy. The pair of them knew as much about philosophy as Bugs Bunny. It was obvious they were having an affair.' Mark's marriage to Dany, a full-time, in fact, like most of Healy's female staff, an over-time worker at the party's headquarters, was over. 'I packed my bags and then left Dany and Healy in the caravan and joined the human race.' What was already, by conventional standards, a bizarre episode, was rendered doubly so by the fact that accompanying the threesome on their holiday were Aileen and her husband Paul. Did Aileen fear that she was about to be displaced as the Leader's most favoured concubine?

Both Mark and myself related to the same reporter how we had been physically assaulted by Healy. As Mark put it, 'if you disagreed, you got thumped. It was simple as that'. Mark's story had a sequel, which he told to me many years later. A few days after returning home early from his holiday, a big car pulled outside his flat. It was Healy and Mark's wife. Dany had come to collect her personal effects. She was moved into one of a block of flats rented by the SLL across the road from the League's office just off Clapham Common, joining the other female staff who had been installed there to cater for the Leader's seemingly insatiable sexual appetite. All Gerry had to do when he felt the urge was to nip over the road for a quick one. I am not joking. I have been told by an unimpeachable source that this was an established routine. Healy called it 'cadre training'.

The *Star,* in a report entitled, 'Red Boss Stole my Wife', told how Paul Jennings, the husband of Healy's longest serving concubine, Aileen, had related a similar but in his case, tragic story to a WRP conference convened to discuss the Healy affair. He revealed that his wife had been 'in hiding for four months for fear of Healy.' After being beaten by Healy, 'she needed hospital treatment and has been receiving physiotherapy ever since.' Even so, Livingstone for all his profile as an advocate of women's rights (but, like Corbyn, so long as they are not those of Muslims) was able to conclude his Foreword by saying that 'it was a privilege to have worked with Gerry Healy' Maybe so. But not for the scores who like Aileen had experienced at first hand his brutality and sexual exploitation.

Like so many others in his situation, Paul admitted 'I suspected nothing until she suddenly told me all one night'. The next morning, 'she left our home and I haven't seen her since'. I have been told by a mutual friend of the couple that Paul soon afterwards emigrated to Australia to start a new life, while Aileen returned to her native Nottingham, where she married again. Through a mutual friend, she sent her best wishes to me, and I if I could, I would return them, as I would send them to Paul, because, unlike many others whom I had dealings with in my ten years as a member of

Healy's movement, even when I was out of favour, they always behaved decently towards me.

Apart from herself, Aileen quite rightly did not name any of the 26 women who had had sexual relations with Healy. I do know who some of them were, but like Aileen I will not betray a confidence. Some on the list, those that I worked with for two years at the party's headquarters, were, to put it crudely, but for all that, accurately, office tarts on the make (I have two especially in mind who fit that description exactly), but others obliged Healy out of a misplaced sense of duty. I know this for a fact, because when I attended a meeting at the Conway Hall in London to mark the tenth anniversary of Healy's expulsion from the WRP, Dot Gibson, already a full-time party worker at the time I joined the SLL in 1961, and married to Pete, a London bus driver, explained how it all began. She did not put a date on it, but some time back in the middle 1960s, she and Aileen Jennings had decided that as Healy's leadership was indispensable to the success of the fast-approaching British and world revolutions, all his needs, not least those of sexual nature, had to be catered for. Whether this imperative was conveyed to others in Healy's female retinue she did not say, but I know for certain that even at this early date, Dot and Aileen were not the first to service Healy in the manner indicated.

An intriguing episode occurred in the course of my dealings with the press in the wake of the Healy expulsion. A top *Daily Mirror* journalist came to see me at my home to discuss an editorial he was preparing on the Healy affair. I suggested to him that rather than yet another salacious story of sex and the Redgraves, he should focus instead on a subject no-one had yet touched upon…Healy's dependence on funding from Arab dictators. The next day, November 4, page 2 of the *Mirror* carried two Healy items, both by the reporter who came to see me, David Thompson. One was entitled 'Our Sex Nightmares, By Red Gerry Girls', which in addition to reporting claims by WRP female members that they had been sexually assaulted by

Healy, carried a comment by 'former central committee member Robin Blick' that Healy's party was 'a little Cambodia' where 'people were beaten up almost every day'. The other item was the 'Mirror Comment' which said exactly what we had agreed and drafted on the previous day. Entitled 'Readies in the bed', it ran as follows:

'Although it is the antics of what the Reds did in the bed that have hit the headlines [including his story on the same page], the current rift in the Vanessa Redgrave-Gerry Healy Workers Revolutionary Party raises a far more important question about its finances. The WRP is awash with ready money. It has funds well in excess of £1 million. That is FIVE TIMES more than the general fund of the Labour Party. Where does the WRP's money come from? Where does it get its cash for its printing plant and presses, its offices and considerable property? It is well-known that some has come from Colonel Gaddafi's Libya through perfectly legal, if abnormal printing contracts. But how much? How is it paid? And from what other sources, if any, does it come? These are important questions. The Workers Revolutionary Party - and other far left groups – have a disruptive significance way beyond the size of their membership or popular appeal.

If funds are coming into this country from a foreign government that harbours terrorists and which was responsible for killing a policewoman on the streets of London, the people of this country have a right to know. And to know what is being done about it. The Special Branch must have been investigating the funding of the WRP. If the Government doesn't know the results of those investigations, it should find out. And tell Parliament and the nation. The sexual excesses of the WRP's founder, Gerry Healy, hold no threat to this country. But if Gaddafi money is being used to try to subvert Britain, that is quite different and must be exposed.'

David Thompson rang me up the day his editorial appeared

to tell me that the editor of the *Mirror* wanted a follow-up piece on Healy's funding. Could he come over to discuss it? Of course, I said yes. Then, a short while later, he rang me again. He was angry. His editor had cancelled the story, hinting that he had been advised to leave the subject alone. Evidently someone in the security services had read the editorial and decided that investigating Healy's terrorist connections was a matter best left to themselves.

Certainly, there was much that needed investigating, and well before the Healy affair, the quality press had been busy doing it. The *Sunday Telegraph* of September 13, 1981 reported that 'prominent Libyan exiles abroad and expert political observers maintain that he [Gaddafi] has contributed considerable sums to the Workers Revolutionary Party and its publication *News Line*.' A clue as to the source of the funding was provided by the list of the publications printed by Astmoor Litho, the WRP's printing company. In addition to the *News Line*, they were Editor Ken Livingstone's *Labour Herald* and *The Green March*, an English language Libyan government publication. In addition to carrying regular features and reports promoting the Gaddafi regime, *News Line* 'has also carried advertisements from the Libyan government', one can safely assume not free of charge. As further proof of the party's close links with Libya, the report cited the WRP delegation, headed by Vanessa Redgrave, that had just participated in the celebration of the twelfth anniversary of Gaddafi's military coup in September 1969.

Definitive proof of just how dependent the WRP had become on Arab funding finally came to light on February 7, 1988, in a document passed to the *Sunday Times* by a former party member detailing the sums involved, their sources and the services the WRP agreed to provide in return. Between 1977 and 1983, the party received a little over £1million, with Libya, at £542000 being the main provider. Arafat's PLO and Saddam's Iraq each stumped up £20,000. In what the report described as a 'secret pact', 'signed in Libya between a Tripoli government representative and Corinne Redgrave', the WRP undertook to provide information, and here it quotes from the document, on 'the activities, names and positions held in finance, politics, business, the communications media and elsewhere of Zionists', that is to say, *Jews*.

Six years previously, in reply to a letter in *Tribune*, the left wing weekly, that had accused both the *News Line* and the *Labour Herald* of being dependent on support from the Gaddafi regime, the editors of both publications hotly denied this charge in the issue of October 22, 1982. Both letters attributed the accusation to the machinations of the 'Zionists', in other words, a classic *Jewish* conspiracy. My old colleague on the *Workers Press*, Alex Mitchell, now editor of the *News Line*, acting in accordance with his party's agreement with its Libyan paymasters, was quite explicit. As it had been down the ages, it was once more simply a matter of *cherchez le Juif*: '...it does not come as surprise that *Tribune* should publish a letter signed by Anthony Julius. He presents himself as a dispassionate observer, but he is a member of the editorial committee of *Vanguard*, the magazine of the Poale Zion British Labour Zionist Movement...The Zionists [i.e., *Jews*] work on the "big lie" theory that if you tell the "Libyan gold" story often enough, then some people are bound to start believing it.'

The BBC Money Programme obviously thought there was more to the story than either Mitchell or Livingstone claimed. Its investigation, broadcast in March 1983, revealed that the London-based Libyan Jamahiriya News Agency received an annual subsidy of £1.5 million from the Libyan government, and that nearly all the journals published by the Agency were printed by Astmoor Litho. A printer at the Colchester printers QB was quoted as saying that *Labour Herald* could not possibly cover even its printing costs at a cover price of 20p, let alone distribution and staff salaries. The same considerations obviously also applied *a fortiori* to the WRP's daily paper *News Line*, selling at 5p less and with a much larger full-time staff. As the *Sunday Times* revelations were to prove, it was Mitchell and Livingstone who were telling the big lie, or, in Healyease double-speak, a 'class truth'.

In retrospect, the anti-Semitic undertones of the relationship between the WRP and the Gaddafi regime were a portent of things to come, with the surge of Jew-baiting in the Labour Party that followed the election of Livingstone's old comrade and fellow anti-Zionist, Jeremy Corbyn, as its Leader in 2015. That is why it is a serious mistake to dismiss the events I have been chronicling as storms in a tiny Trotskyist tea cup. What was once seen as the politics of the lunatic leftist fringe, with its obsession with Zionist conspiracies and dealings with Arab terrorists, with the election of veteran anti-Zionist campaigner Jeremy Corbyn as Leader of the Labour Party in September 2015, they now moved centre stage.

While it remained under Healy's leadership, the WRP never missed an opportunity to demonstrate to its Libyan paymasters that it was fulfilling its undertaking to sniff out the hidden influence of the 'Zionists' on British politics. The *News Line* of December 6, 1980, carried an editorial entitled 'Wither the Anti-Nazi League'. The League's secretary, Paul Holborow, was taken to task for saying 'the main fight is now against anti-Semitism'. This 'sudden switch to anti-Semitic issues reveals the deep [sic] Zionist [i.e., *Jewish*] influence in ANL'. Who then was pulling the strings of the ANL? 'This change in policy has been done to facilitate the participation of another pro-Zionist, Mr Anthony Wedgewood Benn'. Trust the Jews to hide behind a *goy*.

But the *News Line* had not done with the 'Zionists' of the ANL. As a further objection to the League's campaign against anti-Semitism, the editorial offered its own version of Holocaust revisionism, one that would some twenty or so years later become the norm on the Corbynista left, with the claim that the 'gas chambers of the Third Reich did not discriminate. They were used to exterminate Jews, Christians, gypsies, Russian, Poles, Czechs, socialists and communists'. This was a lie. The gas chambers *did* discriminate, on purely racial grounds. Only Jews and gypsies were targeted for extermination. There was no equivalent Nazi 'final solution' of a Christian, Czech, Polish, socialist or communist 'question'. In a leaflet distributed at an anti-BNP demonstration in Derby in 2008, the far left-dominated 'Unite Against Fascism', one of its Honorary Presidents being Ken Livingstone and another Corbynista zealot Dianne Abbott, went one better, omitting any reference to the Jews from its list of victims of the Holocaust.

What on that occasion was explained by those responsible for the omission as being an oversight (some oversight!) has now become standard procedure, and not only on the far left. Given his long-standing and well-advertised collaboration with Islamic Jihadis who seek the destruction of Israel and the murder of its Jews, it should have been no surprise when in his 2018 Holocaust Remembrance Day message, Labour Leader Jeremy Corbyn made no mention of either the Jews or anti-Semitism, any more than should have been his declining invitations to attend the celebration of the 100th anniversary of the Balfour Declaration of November 1917 promising a homeland for the Jews and to visit the Holocaust Museum in Jerusalem, and his rejection of a proposal by party colleagues that he should visit the most notorious of all the Nazi death camps, Auschwitz in Poland. But then in their Holocaust Remembrance Day messages Tory Prime Minister Theresa May and Liberal Democratic Party Leader Liam Fox (and US President Donald Trump the previous year) also chose not to mention either the Jews or anti-Semitism…Hamlet without the Prince.

Corbyn's omission surely could not have been an oversight and, in the light of his track record on matters Jewish, predictably caused outrage amongst Britain's 370,000 Jews. But given its attitude towards Israel, his omissions would I suspect have elicited a less censorious response from the UK's tenfold larger and overwhelmingly Labour-voting Muslim 'community'. As for all three party leaders omitting any reference to the Jews, could this huge disproportion in the Jewish and Muslim electorates have played any part in what is otherwise an inexplicable coincidence? According to one analysis of the Muslim vote, it can decide the outcome in 28 parliamentary contests, which given their zero-sum nature in most seats, could amount to a gain or loss of up to 56 seats for the two main parties. As for the Jewish vote, analysis has shown that it decides little or nothing, and is therefore hardly worth pandering to at the risk of alienating one ten times larger. Finally, we have a survey conducted in 2015 which suggested that around 40% of the UK's (not just Muslim) population harboured anti-Semitic prejudices. I leave it to the reader to draw their own conclusions.

As for Healy, he would have struck his deal with Gaddafi and other anti-Semitic Arab leaders irrespective of whether or not he was himself an anti-Semite. But it so happens that he was. On two occasions, I witnessed his giving vent to his feelings about the Jews, humiliating an older party member who still lived with his mother by calling him a 'Jewish mummy's boy', and advising me 'never to trust pale-faced Jews with glasses.' I can't say whether he would qualify as pale-faced, but Trotsky certainly was a Jew who wore glasses.

The WRP was not the sole beneficiary of the Colonel's largess. He not only contributed to the slush funds of two corrupt right wing politicians, French President Jaques Chirac and Italian Prime Minister Silvio Berlusconi, but funded and hosted far right, anti-Semitic organisations in Europe and north America. Neither was the WRP the only movement to promote Gaddafi's *Green Book*, which it praised in the Party's 1981 Manifesto: 'The WRP salutes the courageous struggle of Colonel Gaddafi, whose Green Book has guided the struggle to introduce workers' control of factories, government offices and the diplomatic service, and in opposing the reactionary manoeuvres of [Egyptian President] Sadat, [Israeli Prime Minister] Begin and Washington'. Who needs Trotsky, Lenin or Marx when we have the profundities of Colonel Gaddafi?

Gaddafi's guide to struggle also found equal favour on the far right in the Neo-Nazi National Front's *NF News*, which carried an advertisement which implied the Front had a contract with the WRP's Libyan comrades to be the book's sole outlet in the UK: 'This vital book cannot be obtained from any other book suppliers in Britain. Read the ideas which the Zionists [i.e., *Jews*]and Capitalists want to supress. Only £3.000 incl. p&p.' The NF's claimed monopoly on sales was no obstacle to the WRPs access to the book, since it had a generous contract with Libyan regime to print 250,000 copies of the English langue edition on its own printing presses. What the WRP printed at inflated cost, the NF sold on the cheap. If the National Front was not selling the Healy edition, where did their supply come from? Was it case of the joining of hands across the extremes of left and right, which in the Corbyn era, became almost routine? Such a convergence most certainly did occur when when *The Palestinian*, a 66-minute WRP film starring Vanessa Redgrave, was hired for a screening by Australian Neo-Nazis. Connections of this kind were understandably a matter the WRP wanted kept well under wraps, because when my friend Adam Westoby, in an article in the 'Pabloite' weekly, *Socialist Challenge of January 22, 1981,* drew attention to a speech by Gaddafi in which he made some sympathetic comments about Hitler (this was nothing out of the ordinary for an Arab leader or Muslim cleric), instead of dealing with the matter in hand, the *Newsline* created a diversion from it by fabricating a new version of the Thornett affair. Now, it was not Blick-Jenkins, but Blick-Westoby who were the villains of the piece. In a page spread entitled '"Hitler" slur is repeated against Gaddafi', accompanied by photos of Adam and myself, Adam was accused of having 'linked up with the notorious anti-communist Robin Blick in a conspiracy to try to smash the Workers Revolutionary Party in 1974'. This was pure fiction. As I have already related, my only contact with Adam between my leaving the WRP in 1971 and meeting up with him again in 1979 was a phone call he made to me on behalf of Healy. As to Gaddafi's speech, it would have surprised no-one conversant with the recent history of Arab and Islamic politics. For reasons that should not need elaborating, Hitler was their hero. (My *The Socialism Of Fools* examines this subject in detail.) As a last salvo at a Healy who, after the sex scandals, was effectively finished as serious figure on the far left, I penned a feature for the *New Statesman* entitled *The Life and Times of Comrade H* that compared the WRP to religious cults, in particular the Flagellants of the 13th century. The parallels were uncanny There were of course the always fast-approaching day of judgement and the privileges accorded the cult leader, including the sexual services of his female devotees. But it did not stop there: 'In medieval Flagellant sessions, the master of the cult would add his own blows to the self- inflicted of his disciples, a practice which for many WRP members, will recall the spectacle of the organisation's leader berating members in sessions of self-criticism. As one member told me: "Self-criticism was Healy cricising you and you criticising yourself."'. From examples such as this, I argued that the WRP 'shouldn't be treated as a purely secular political movement but as one in the tradition of the millennial movements of the middle and early modern ages, along with religious cults like the Moonies and the "People's Temple" of Jim Jones.' My American friend Tim Wolfforth agreed. In his *On the Edge*, he generously conceded that 'Robin Blick, Mark Jenkins and the late Adam Westoby were among the first to point out the cultic nature of the Healy group and to encourage a look at the political cult phenomenon as a whole'.

His expulsion, public disgrace and ridicule were pretty much my swan song so far as the vendetta was concerned though in 1988 I did undertake an abortive attempt to attend a Healy function with my wife and my son Andrew, who by now, nearly 15 years of age, was eager to see the so-often talked about semi-legendary figure in the flesh so to speak. The meeting, held at Kensington Town Hall, was in support of the PLO. Up on the platform I immediately spotted Healy and next to him, Vanessa Redgrave. Healy must have spotted me just as quickly, because seconds later, we were approached by a bulky steward, who politely but firmly asked us to leave. I ingenuously replied that Healy did not have a monopoly on support for the PLO. At this, the steward became more insistent, so, not wishing to create a scene that could easily result in not just myself, but all three of us getting a taste of Healyite thuggery, we left.

My final, and even briefer encounter with Healy was a posthumous one, his funeral at Mortlake cemetery in December 1989.This time I did not even get in. I was excluded by guards who had been posted at the door of the crematorium to ensure that only those of the approved political persuasion and loyalties would be allowed to witness the proceedings. It must have been on this basis that among of those made welcome were Ken Livingstone and one the chief mourners, Vanessa Redgrave, and a delegation, judging by their and their car's appearance, an impressive vehicle with darkened windows, of Middle Eastern provenance. My wife and Andrew meantime had slipped in undetected, and witnessed the whole performance, much to the chagrin of mourners who recognised my wife, but too late to stage a repeat of the Kensington eviction. Amongst the mourners were a number of women 'of a certain age', all dressed in black, and deeply distressed to the point of tears.

Healy's unique status on the far left was reflected in the number and length of the obituaries he received in the quality press. Three were by past and present members of Healy's movement, one being an irreverent memoire, replete with sexual *double entrendres*, by Brian Behan, brother of the playwright and one-time industrial organiser of the SLL, and another, devotional, by Vanessa Redgrave: 'I owe to him my subsequent development as a political woman and artist.' But perhaps the greatest tribute of all also came from the Thespian Tendency in the person of Sir Lawrence Olivier, who took the part of what was so obviously Healy in *The Party*, the play by the leftist dramatist Trevor Griffiths, first at the National Theatre in 1974, and then, in his last stage appearance, at the same theatre in 1985.

Despite the continued adulation that he received from Ken Livingstone and the West End faction, headed by the doting Vanessa Redgrave, after the 1985 debacle and the public ridicule that followed, Healy's cult had shrunk to coterie of devotees so tiny that it was simply not worth bothering about. And when the Berlin Wall came tumbling down four years later, neither was the crumbling empire founded by his two mentors, Lenin and Trotsky, together with its labour camps, KGB hospitals and hounding of dissenters. Mark, Adam and I were out of a job.

Adam, with Mark my closest friend and political collaborator, was truly remarkable in so many ways, not least for his indomitable spirit. Afflicted since birth with a spinal deformity inherited from his father that progressively inhibited his mobility until in his last few years, he was confined to an electrically-powered wheel chair. Born, like Maureen's daughter and the day of Healy's expulsion, on my birthday, 19 October, though eight years after me, in 1944, he died of Leukaemia on 27 November 1994, but lived long enough to bear witness to the collapse of a system he had devoted so much of his mental powers to understanding and energy to combatting. His contribution to the cause of Polish freedom did not go unacknowledged. Some twenty years on, in recognition of our services on behalf of *Solidarnosc*, Adam, posthumously, and I were awarded medals by the trade union in a ceremony conducted at the Polish Embassy in Portland Place.

It was a strange experience to be a guest of honour in the very same building that I had previously only seen from the outside as a hostile speaker and demonstrator. I did, however, on one memorable occasion get as far as the front door, when with Shirley Williams I handed in a denunciation I had drafted of the suppression of *Solidarnosc* by martial law on 13 December 1981. I was much gratified to see that one of the signatories on my certificate was the first Chairman of *Solidarnosc* and later President of Poland, Lech Walesa. When I got back to Swansea and showed it to Maureen, she was truly proud and, by way of an exception, actually said so.

But what had followed the award ceremony left a nasty taste in my mouth and, I hope, not mine alone. Two members of the audience had requested permission to speak. Playing to his largely Catholic audience, the first enthused about the newly-elected Pope, Francis II, but then added, perhaps being not as well informed as he should have been about the track record of some of them, 'but of course, I admire all the Popes'. Familiar as I am with the shenanigans and debauchery some of them got up to (far more so I suspect than the mainly pious audience) I found this comment more amusing than anything else. But the second speaker pandered to a prejudice that is more prevalent in Poland than any other European nation bar Russia. After accusing the Israeli government of collaborating with the USA in the 'rendition' of Islamic terrorists, he launched himself into attack on 'Zionists' of such a ferocity that it left me in no doubt as to who his target really was. I found it hard to resist the urge to walk out of the hall in protest.

VIII

By the time of my early retirement from lecturing in 1997 at the age of sixty, I had written two more books: the two volume *Fascism in Germany* (again, the title is self-explanatory), and *The Seeds* of *Evil*, a critique of Lenin's political philosophy and tactics that demonstrated, with citations from their writings, that they had little if anything in common with those advocated by the founders of modern communism, Marx and Engels. The reaction of the leftist press to the latter work was predictably of the kind the Roman Catholic Inquisition reserved only for heretics. Typical was one review by a not so ex-Healyite which, without refuting any of the instances I cited of Lenin's ruthlessness, airily dismissed them with the comment 'Blick's allegations are worthless'. To a disciple of Lenin, maybe. But they were true nevertheless. Indeed, as I pointed out to him, some of these 'allegations' (against Lenin, and there was the problem), far from being 'worthless', I had validated by citations from a book he himself had helped to edit, namely, the WRP's English translation of the verbatim record of the proceedings of the 1903 Second Congress of the Russian Social Democratic Labour Party at which the Bolshevik and Menshevik factions first emerged,

Now a man of leisure, I was becoming quite busy musically with session work, recording and gigging with a number of bands. It had always saddened me that Maureen had only heard me play in her front room, and not with a band in a live gig. Incurable romantic that I am, once I took up playing again, I used to have this fantasy that one day, I would see in her in the audience where I was playing. How could I have possibly guessed that this fantasy would soon become a reality?

My musical comeback began quite by accident. My son Andrew, a more than handy trumpeter, could not make a gig with Tortus, the band he was currently playing with, so he asked me to replace him. There was no time to rehearse, so

I had to go in the deep end and play by ear. Luckily, the numbers were not too complicated and I was able to avoid making a fool of myself. Modesty does not prevent me from citing the *Melody Maker* review as proof. 'Blowing guests breeze in and out from gig to gig, but tonight the valves belong to Robin Blick's E-flat baroque trumpet. He gives this tiny instrument an enormous voice which may be muted, but it won't be gagged. It prowls around Lucy's vocals and weaves in and out of her flute like a snake through grass.' A few weeks later, the band asked me to add some trumpet parts to a single they had recently recorded. Again, the results were reviewed by the now sadly long-defunct *Melody Maker*. 'Tortus' seamlessly integrated brass section means they make avowedly experimental music without sounding inaccessible.' The 'brass section' was me multi-tracking.

Around this time, early 1996, the band's programmer created his own project, first called Pipe and then a little later, Blowpipe, which Andrew and I were invited to join. A well-known radio DJ, John Kennedy, became interested, and financed the recording, production and distribution of the album *First Circle*. Considering the music was purely instrumental and well to the left of the usual pop fare, its reception by the critics was surprisingly positive. *DJ* magazine gave it nine out of ten. 'What a treat to have a grown -up album in my possession. And when I say grown up I mean sophisticated, thought-out and brilliantly executed new music that has genuinely exited me.' Other reviewers also caught on to what Blowpipe was up to. It was 'blowing genres out of the water', '21st century chamber music', 'music that takes from any source', 'uncategorizable', 'adventurous to say the least, quite magical'. Another album, *Pendulum*, now minus the Tortus programmer, followed in 1998, with again the same press response.

Our radical profile even secured us two headline gigs at Ronnie Scott's, the ultimate accolade. Then later the same year, Andrew and I were approached by Roundabout, a new

German label based in London, who wanted to add us to their roster of acts. We signed a three-album contract, and within a matter of months, we had recorded the first, *Epilogue* with its release coming only a matter of weeks after I had moved in with Maureen. Again, the critical response was almost entirely positive, 'a mesmerising swirl of musical vibrancy' capturing the feel of our best effort so far. Even so, one review in *Making Music*, the trade monthly, was I think a little over the top. 'This is the type of groove explosion that every "jazz-funk and acid jazz creation" tried desperately to induce in the early 1990s. Few came this close to the holy grail of groove, the mystical vision of brooding jazz extrovert funk and every type of percussion from tablas to decks co-existing in spine chilling harmony. Miles [Davis] himself would've had to concede this is just breath-taking.'

Family connections, this time Katharine's, secured me some session recording with Octopus, a Brit-pop band. Her then current boy-friend, Dave Francolini, was producing the band's debut album, *From A to B*, for Food, the EMI label. He required two trumpeters for a couple of demo tracks that he needed to clinch the deal, and Katharine suggested that Andrew and I would fill the bill. The tracks in question must have been up to scratch, because unusually, they ended up on the album. Andrew then became a full-time member of the band, touring as far afield as Japan.

The oddest gig I ever did occurred about this time when I was approached by BBC Radio Four to appear on a programme devoted to of all things, vacuum cleaners. Somehow or other, the producer of the programme had learned that I had played industrial tubing on one of our Blowpipe albums and wanted me do something similar on his programme, only using a vacuum cleaner. Andrew generated a short track which combined the sound of a switched-on vacuum cleaner with me blowing down its hose with the aid of a French horn mouthpiece inserted at one end. We called the track FBI, as in Edgar J. Hoover. (We were hardly breaking new musical ground. Back in 1956, in a music festival promoted by the prankster Gerard Hoffnung, one of the works performed, to a capacity audience of 3,000 at the Royal Festival Hall, was Malcom Arnold's Grand Festival Overture for orchestra, three vacuum cleaners, a floor polisher and four rifles.) We turned up at the BBC in Great Portland Street with three vacuum cleaners and a hose, complete with mouthpiece. After a short interview in which I made the case for the vacuum cleaner as a legitimate musical instrument, and demonstrated the kind of sounds that can generated by blowing down a vacuum cleaner hosepipe, the presenter played a short excerpt from FBI. The programme, which had been recorded, went out a few days later. My younger brother Gerald happened to be listening to Radio Four that same evening, and rang me up afterwards, much amused.

Another band I played with was Horsepower. Again, Andrew provided the introduction. Horsepower were a spin-off from Rosa Mota, who had been quite a hit on the Mute label. Andrew was due to guest for the band at a big gig at the Borderline venue in Charing Cross Road, and asked if I could play along with him. It went well enough for the two of us to be asked to record a trumpet duet for the same band on an album they were recording at the Abbey Road, in the very same studio that had been inaugurated in 1931 by Elgar conducting his First Pomp and Circumstance, and where the Beatles recorded their epoch-making Sergeant Pepper album. Shortly after that, I became a regular member of Horsepower, playing French horn, piccolo trumpet and soprano sax. We recorded three albums, two just before I found Maureen, and the other shortly after we began living together. Maureen rather liked Horsepower, and a review of the first album, *Fayetteville*, helps to explain why.

'Horsepower now sound like a band you need to get to know. They've made a very restrained, very adventurous, very quiet, very reflective rather beautiful album. You can see still see the scares – it's a melancholic album a peaceful album, a beautiful shimmering album. *Death of a Man* is probably one of the most simple, beautiful reflective pieces of music you'll ever hear.'

Journalistic hyperbole to be sure. But the album's description fits in several respects Maureen's temperament, as did Sibelius for the same reasons, above all melancholy and reflective, and in nearly all situations except the most intimate, when she could be adventurous in the extreme, restrained. The second album, *Fairy Tales*, was cast in the same introspective, dark mood, with what one reviewer in the NME described as its 'mournful trumpet and willowy vocal'. The second track, Summer Song, on which I play French Horn (just two repeated notes), is truly beautiful, with words and melody by Ian Bishop that still move me to tears at the lines, 'One day I'm going to take you my arms and keep the world at bay'…because I did. About a year after I moved to Swansea, Maureen saw the band play live at the 12 bar Club in Denmark Street.

So much for my life up to the time I began my search for Maureen. As for my two children, after attending the Purcell Music School, my daughter Katharine, who was born in 1970, made her mark in the music world, first as the founder of Miranda Sex Garden, and then, famously as the founder and musical director of the three times classical chart-topping all-female Medieval Baebes.

Miranda Sex Garden, with its three ex-Purcell School vocalists, began life as a straight *a capella* madrigal trio, releasing their first album, *Madra*, on the Mute label in 1991. Largely at Katharine's instigation, with the addition of percussion, keyboards, violin and electric guitars, MSG evolved into a gothic and industrial band, generating a sound 'full of colour and chaos' to quote my daughter. In all, they released six albums, one of which I recorded on.

Katherine launched the Baebes in 1996, halfway through the life of MSG. The ensemble has recorded songs, all arranged or composed by Katharine, in a vast range of languages ancient and modern, including Latin, Middle English, French, Italian, Russian, Swedish, Gaelic, Manx, Spanish, Welsh, Provencal, Irish and Cornish. In addition to their dozen or so albums, the Baebes have provided music for the title music and soundtrack of the BBC production *Virgin Queen* and the theme song for the ITV production *Victoria* and twice sung in the New Year at the televised Edinburgh festivities. In 1999, the Baebes went on the road with the Jools Holland Rhythm and Blues Orchestra, followed up by a two-night gig at the Albert Hall. Her most recent release is a left field, rather dark nursery rhyme double CD album, *A Pocketful of Posies*, in which I am featured playing a variety of instruments: bass clarinet, flugal horn, trumpet and piccolo trumpet, French horn and euphonium as well as plastic watering cans and cardboard tubes.

Perhaps wisely, in view of my notoriety in certain circles, Katharine chose Blake as her professional name, after her favourite poet. She kept things in the family, however, when she very kindly invited both Andrew and myself to record as guest artists for both groups. Katharine is a shrewd operator in the music world, and she hired very effective PR teams to promote both her ventures, with features, photos and interviews appearing in the tabloids, celebrity magazines and even the spread sheets.

It always amused me how when giving details of her family background, my political CV used to vary somewhat. In her wilder Miranda days, she had me down as a 'jazz trumpeter and anarchist'. Where she got that from I will never know. Anarchism has always intrigued me, as it has much to tell us about the dangers of centralised power, and I have written on several occasions for an anarchist journal. But I find their vision of a stateless society hopelessly impractical. Katharine, whose grasp of the nuances of left-wing doctrines she would admit was hazy at best, knew none of this. I think the idea was to make her background sound as underground as her music. With the Baebes, whose target audience was the thoroughly middle-of-the-road, middle-aged, middle-brow and rather twi middle class, Katharine adjusted my political profile accordingly. I now became 'a political writer, jazz trumpeter and lecturer', while another feature simply said I was 'politically active'. My mask of respectability was, however, allowed to slip a little in the *Sunday Express*, where I featured as an 'ex-writer for the Workers Revolutionary Party paper and Jazz trumpeter'. A small detail...I was never a member of the WRP. I had left its more modestly titled predecessor, the Socialist Labour League, more than two years before its foundation.

One of my daughter's self-promoting stunts was to display her well-proportioned body at every possible opportunity, both in photo shoots for magazines and *in situ* at 'happenings', in the latter case, never failing to ensure that the press was tipped off well in advance as to when and where it would be on view. Her intentions in this respect were signalled in a feature on the MSG in the *Independent,* when Katharine, much to my double shame as a father and as an anti-fascist, was described as appearing in a German Cabaret Night sporting an 'outfit' that 'included an SS cap and bare breasts'. Early in the life of the Baebes, Katharine rang to alert me to the imminent appearance of an item in what was new territory for her, *The Tines Diary*. Having advised me as to its subject matter, she added, as if to prepare me for the worst, 'forewarned is forearmed'. Headed *Bare Baebe*, the story ran thus:

'A Mediaeval Baebe has taken her madrigal [wrong...madrigals are post-mediaeval] group's idea of a fun a little far. The twelve girls were celebrating one of their number's birthday in an Islington pub when a man inquired if they wished to join him for a drink at his stag party upstairs. Joining the throng, Katharine Blake [not, thank goodness, Blick] found that a stripper had not been booked. So she offered to fill in for forty pounds. Blake then proceeded to strip down to her stockings. "The party was dying until we arrived" she tells me. "I am not inhibited. Being a stripper paid for me to start as a musician."'

This last was a bare-breasted lie, at least as far as I am aware. Katharine's was not the only appearance of a member of the Blick family in the *Dairy*. A far more elevated tone had been struck some years previously, when it carried two items concerning a controversy that has been provoked by the publication of my book, *The Seeds of Evil*.

If he will forgive the cliché, my son Andrew, born in 1973, followed more in my footsteps than his less academically-inclined sister. He shared her musical gifts, playing trumpet in a number of bands, including two in which I partnered him on a variety of wind instruments, first Blowpipe, and then its successor, Gyratory System. But his greatest achievement has been to have become one of the leading authorities on British constitutional history, having to date written eight books on this and related subjects. A Reader in Politics and Contemporary History at Kings College London, visiting professor at the Washington and Lee University of Virginia, consultant for the Constitutional Society and advisor to democratic reform movements in Pakistan, Tunisia, Turkey, Iran, Morocco and Ukraine, he also regularly features as a TV and radio pundit on constitutional issues. Yet another of his many duties is as expert adviser to a Parliamentary panel on devolution and the future of the UK constitution, and Research Fellow to the first-ever House of Commons inquiry into the possibility of introducing a written constitution into the UK. So, I am naturally immensely proud of what they have both achieved in their chosen fields. I was a poor, sometimes faithless husband. But I think I did better as a father.

And what of Maureen during the time we were apart? She had of course married Terrence Stewart (he of the Duke Ellington concert), whom like me, she met at Lentheric, in 1967. When Maureen broke the news of their engagement to her mother, all Alice said, as I later learned, was, 'pity about Robin'. Indeed, it was, and not just for Maureen and myself, who by this time should have been married and possibly beginning a family. It was no less so for my wife, who after more than thirty years of marriage and a number of infidelities on my part, I deserted to be with Maureen, both the worst and the best deed that I have ever committed.

Until four years later, when their only child, Andrea was

born. Maureen continued to work at Lentheric as a highly successful cosmetic chemist. In 1973, her husband began an affair with a barmaid he met while on holiday, followed by their divorce. Maureen firmly believed that the main reason for Terry's infidelity was his inability to face up to his responsibilities as a father adding, on one occasion, 'how wrong can you be about somebody.' Whatever the causes after six years of marriage, Maureen was single again, leaving her, with the support of her mother, to raise Andrea on her own. To be closer to home, Maureen never returned to her career in the cosmetic industry, and took up a less demanding, but also less well-paid job in off-license closer to where she lived in Enfield. And so the patterns our widely contrasting two lives were set, seemingly never to merge again. But neither of us forgot.

IX

When I found Maureen again, she told me that my reappearance in her life had been no great surprise. She used to predict to those that knew of me that one day, quite how she never said, I would find her, provided that my politicking did not have fatal consequences. 'He won't make it to thirty,' she used to say to her daughter, even though by this time, I had left that age some way behind me. As she grew up, Andrea learned more about the man Maureen called 'my friend Robin', that I was very left wing and something of an academic, and also, that we had been lovers. When we were together again, Maureen told me that in the years after she broke up with Terry, from time to time she used to entertain the idea of contacting me by sending a message in the personal adds section of a newspaper. Not that I think she would have done it, or that if she had, it would have reached me. But it proved that she still not only cared for me, but missed me, though probably not as much as I missed her.

If proof were needed that she had never forgotten me, I found it when not long after we began to live together, rummaging one day through her desk, I came across a plastic wallet containing every single one of the many poems I wrote for her nearly forty years before. And there was the painting I gave her as a Christmas present at about the same time. She made a point of telling me that until its backing board cracked, she kept on her wall what was a reproduction of a red-dressed flamenco dancer, one which I had I chosen because with her Iberian-hued skin and jet-black hair, Maureen looked every inch a Spanish beauty.

Maureen's conviction that one day I would be ringing on her doorbell yet again, though she put it down to pure instinct, must surely have at bottom been due to a certainty that my profound love for her would not fade, and would one day compel me to seek her out. For what other motive than love could I possibly have? And indeed, that is exactly what did happen. My longing and determination to meet Maureen, even if it was only once, before one of us died, became an irresistible obsession with me partly as the result of an entirely unrelated chain of events. But even before that, in all the years we had been apart since our brief but passionate encounter in the winter months of 1965–66, she had never left my thoughts, and it was this state of mind that I described in my first letter to Maureen after I succeeded in locating her address in Swansea:

'16-8-99

Dear Maureen,

I am Robin. Please, if my sending you this letter shocks, disturbs or offends you in any way, forgive me if you can. But, even if you cannot, please read what I have to say. When we parted all those years ago (I can tell you when…February 1965) we both understood, without saying so, that it was for ever. Do you remember the last words I spoke to you? They were to ask you never to forget me. And you replied, and these must have been your last words to me, 'never never never'. This is what I must, I have to tell you. Not a day in my life since our parting have you escaped from my memories and my thoughts. Not a day…and especially not at night. I have one dream that recurs more than any other. I am searching for you, sometimes in places I recognise (your old home street, your old work place), others, where I am a stranger and no one knows you. But always the end is the same…I never find you. As I said, this is the dream I had the most often. But in the last year or so, it comes nearly every night and is ever more real. So real, that it crowds into my waking life, until sometimes I can think of little else.

Quite aside from my dreams, any number of events or things would trigger my most cherished memories of you…particularly music, which we both loved and shared.

As the years passed, I tried to imagine your life as it

might have unfolded. First, you would marry, I assumed (perhaps wrongly) that you married the man who took you to a Duke Ellington concert just before we parted. Next would come a family, and then? And as it went on...imagining, guessing and hoping. Yes, hoping that you had fulfilment of kind, a purpose for living.

What else? Let me tell you. From when I first knew you, you were and have remained the love and the light of my life. Yes, like you, I married and, for better or worse, wisely or otherwise, helped to perpetuate our often-benighted species. But through it all you have never faded...more than that...the memory of you envelops me more and more. This last year – I don't understand quite why – the pain and the joy of those memories compelled me to act. Contrary to all my past assumptions, and perhaps to good sense (I will let you be the judge of this), I found myself devising (hypothetically at least) ways in which I could perhaps do what I am doing now. Maybe it was thoughts of my (and your) mortality. I am as atheistic as ever, and if I was ever to find you, it would have to be in this life. Anyway (as you used to say) the cumulative effect led me a couple months ago to see if I could find you. Let me make it clear. I have no wish or intention to interfere in your life. You do not have to reply to this letter, and if you do not, there is an end to it, and I will, however sadly, accept that is what you wish. You are the last person in the world I would want to inflict any gratuitous distress upon. I am hoping that, at least, you might reply to this letter, to tell me about your life, the good and the bad. And, at the most, that I might hear your voice and even see you, after all these years. The decision is entirely yours.'

My letter then concluded

'I would dearly love to hear from you. But whether I do or not, I want you to know and never forget this. I will go on cherishing your memory and loving you with all my being, to the day I die. I want to thank you for all the joy

you gave me, the light and warmth that you let into my life, for being willing to share with me a precious part of yours. If you can, then please reply.'

I did not go into details in this letter as to the precise circumstances that led to me take the actions that I did. Music, more specifically, the recording of it, conspired to force my hand and led me to try to find Maureen before it was too late. What happened was this. The previous year, 1998, my son and I had recorded a second album, Pendulum, with our band, Blowpipe. We financed the pressing ourselves, and after collecting the finished CDs from the factory in Wembley where they had been manufactured, I drove with my son to the warehouse of Shellshock, the company that was to handle their distribution to the record shops. It was located at the end of a cul de sac in South Tottenham. Pulling up outside the entrance, I suddenly became aware that I was in familiar territory. A few yards away to the right, on the other side of a wall, stood the Lentheric building where I first saw Maureen forty years before. It was then, as all my memories of that glorious, magical moment flooded through my brain, that I resolved that whatever the consequences, I would seek Maureen out.

And yet, for the best part of year, I took no active steps to do so. I sensed, in fact I should have known, because looking back now it was so obvious, that if I ever did find Maureen, and if she were to respond in some positive way to my approach, it could not but have consequences, not only for my inner emotional life, but my marriage. My children by this time had long gone, but my wife, who knew nothing of Maureen, would become the entirely innocent victim of what had become by now my obsessional pursuit of my first and greatest love. Knowing this stayed my hand for a whole year until, in July 1999, I began the search that would lead me once again to Maureen's front door, but this time, at last, to a shared life that brought us both our greatest joy and fulfilment.

I know to the day the experience that pushed me over the threshold and compelled me to take the first steps to this final decision. It was 12 March 1999. On that day, or rather evening, I was due to record on some tracks for Horsepower's first album, *Fayetteville*. The recording was to be done at the home of a band member in Stoke Newington. *En route*, I had to drive along Marylebone High Street, by the entrance to the same Great Portland Street underground station where I met Maureen thirty-eight years before, the time when she came to visit me at my West End flat. The memories of that evening came flooding back, of how on my bed we embraced and kissed as we had never done before. A few minutes later with my head still full of the most vivid memories of Maureen, I was brought back to earth by an announcement on my car radio that Yehudi Menuhin had just died in Berlin at the age of eighty. The date was 12 March 1999. That was the day I finally decided that the waiting was over. I would find Maureen. Would it have happened otherwise? How can one tell? I think it would have done, somehow, sooner or later, so much was it becoming an obsession with me.

But how? Where to look? The first step was surely to trace her movements after we last parted. At the time, I remembered her telling me that the terraced houses in her street were due to be demolished to make way for a number of high rise flats, and that their current occupants would be given first option on the new accommodation. I made an appointment with the Enfield Historical Society to consult their archives, which held copies of the Electoral Register as far back as the period in question. Feverishly, I went through the names of occupants of each tower until I found a Maureen, with the surname of Stewart, together with her husband Terry on the 14th floor of Sark House. I had no way of proving it was my Maureen. Her name was then common enough to give grounds for doubt. Even so, because I desperately wanted it to be her, I easily convinced myself that it was. I then consulted a later register for the mid-1970s and found that the Stewarts had moved. Where had Maureen gone? How could I pick up the lost trail? After asking a close friend to conduct what proved be a fruitless search on the internet, I hit on the obvious solution – a private detective.

In order to go ahead with the search, all the firm required was a copy of Maureen's birth certificate, which I duly acquired after a visit to the Public Records Office near the Angel tube station. Whilst there, I also located the details of Maureen's marriage in 1967 to Terry Stewart, and of their daughter Andrea's birth on 19 October 1971, also my own birthday. After I had handed over Maureen's birth certificate and paid the £150.00 fee to the detective agency, I pondered my next move. What I had in mind at that stage was at best, assuming she still lived in London, a meeting at some convenient location, perhaps a café. But there was a serious problem confronting me, to which I could see no easy solution. Given that Maureen was still married, which at that stage I had no reason to doubt, then how could I contact her without risking some mishap? Even if I obtained her phone number, there was the very real possibility that her husband would answer my call. Or if I wrote to her, supposing her husband opened my letter by mistake? Or what was more likely, her husband was to ask her whom it was from when she opened it?

Such concerns evaporated when, a few days later, I received a telephone call from the detective agency, fortunately, when my wife was out. Not only had they found where she was living, they were also able to tell me that she was no longer married, since there was no Terence Stewart living with her at her address. That information simplified matters more than somewhat. In a state of mounting excitement and anticipation, I wrote it down as it was dictated to me: 169, Pentregethin Road, Swansea SA5 8AY. How could I have known that five months on, that this would also be my address the address where I am typing these lines now? My next step was now obvious. Without considering for one moment what the consequences might be for my marriage, I instantly realised that I could now write to Maureen without fear of causing any damage to hers. The result was the letter which I have partly reproduced above.

It was enclosed in a package of items which helped to fill in at least some of the details of my life since we last parted in February 1966...a copy of my latest book, some press reviews and CDs of my music making and such like. I wanted her to know that I had not entirely wasted the talents she believed I possessed. I included in the letter an address she could use if she was to reply, this being of the record company I was under contract to at the time. Days went by, then a week...but no reply. To have come this far, and fail, was more than I could bear...or allow. Fortunately for me, my wife had arranged to visit her parents in Cardiff, leaving me on my own for three days. I booked a cheap day return at Paddington (I still have the ticket) on 21 August, and two days later, boarded the first train to Swansea. Though I did not know it, though on reflection, perhaps I should have done, the die was cast.

My arrival in Swansea some four hours later was less than auspicious. I was wearing a pair of quite smart black shoes, a gift from my father-in-law, who in his retirement, believed he had developed an eye for a good bargain in second hand shops. One such was the pair of shoes I was wearing. (Another was no less ill-fated, a bike that buckled under me on the first day I used it.) On the way down, the shoes had started to pinch me, and by the time I reached Swansea, they were unwearable, such was the pain. I hobbled down the High Street, and found a shop which sold cheap footwear. I bought a pair of trainers for around six pounds and dumped the shoes in a bin. I walked back to the station, and hired a mini-cab to take me to 169, Pentregethin Road. Already on the train, all manner of questions had been crowding my brain. Would she be in? On the two previous occasions, I had rung on her door bell, she had been. Would my luck hold for a third time? She could easily be at work. In which case, having come all this way, I would stage a vigil outside her house until she returned home. But then, even if she was in, how would Maureen react when she opened the door? Perhaps she had company...Surely, knowing I had travelled nearly two hundred miles to see her, she wouldn't send me way. But then again, why hadn't she replied to my letter? And now that she was sixty, what would she look like? All these thoughts churned around as the taxi made its way out of the city centre towards my destination. When we reached the bottom end of Pentregethin Road, I told the driver I would walk the rest of the way to 169, which as it turned out, was some distance up a steep hill. I gave him a ten-pound note and told him he could keep the change. As I made my way up the hill, all my doubts and fears vanished. I was now once again in a trance-like state as memories flooded back of my walk down Eastfield Road to ring on Maureen's door for the first time forty-two years before. As I counted off the house numbers, I somehow became ever surer that at last, I was going to see Maureen again, and that as she had done before, she would welcome me in. I reached number 169.

Like most of the other houses in the road, there was no front garden, just a couple of steps up to a gate on the right, and a path that ran along the front of the house to the front door on the left. I was now quite calm. Unlike on previous similar occasions, without any hesitation, but with a pounding heart, I rang the doorbell. Seconds later, through the door's frosted glass, I saw a figure clad in white. The door opened. At the sight of Maureen standing there in her dressing gown, not it seemed the least surprised to see me, I burst into tears, and putting my arms around her and holding her tight, sobbed as I had never done before, and have only done since at her death bed. As I still held her, I heard her voice for the first time in thirty-three years, when she promised never to forget me, asking softly, 'What's the matter?' As if she didn't know.

When I had regained a little of my previous rather fragile composure, Maureen ushered me into her large double living room. Such was my emotional state, now one of elation, that I cannot remember all the details of that day. I do, however, recall very clearly her telling me, and this was early on in the proceedings, that she had indeed never forgotten me. I also learned, around forty years after the event so to speak, how much she had admired me as 'this brilliant genius who excelled in so many fields', and that my poems had reminded her of Robert Browning. Perhaps, to put it mildly, the over the top nature of these compliments was compensation for there being among the very few she had made in entire the five and a half years of our friendship. True to form, they were among the last, with Maureen often preferring instead to ironically describe and address me as 'the Great Blick' when I believed I had done something worthy of note.

Inevitably, seeing that we had been once been lovers, there were moments of more than a hint of *je ne sais quoi*. In the course of our reminiscences, Maureen insisted that had we married, 'we wouldn't be together today', a strange remark, because even though we had become lovers, no such possibility had ever arisen or been alluded to in the more than five years of our friendship. Was this a guilty conscience speaking? And I can still see her now, standing with her back to the walled-up fire place, assuring me that she had no interest in sex, and that she should have been a nun. Before the year was up, Maureen would be laying naked on her bed, asking me to stroke her still firm breasts, 'especially around the nipples'. After waiting for thirty-four years, how could I not oblige?

Unlike on the three previous occasions when I had called on her, this time my arrival had been anticipated. There was after all, my letter. That perhaps partly explains why, despite our shared excitement at meeting again, the atmosphere was so relaxed, even convivial, more like old friends meeting (which of course we were) than former lovers, though she knew from my letter that my passion for her was undiminished. However, she did rather pointedly ask me, since my first letter had finally told her the truth about my marital status, 'Where does your wife think you are?' to which I replied, more than a little caught off guard by her bluntness, but nevertheless truthfully, 'At home, because she is visiting her parents in Cardiff.' We talked of many things, of the past, naturally, but without recriminations or regrets, and of course of my now long dissipated revolutionary zeal: 'How could you think there was going to be a revolution in this country when everything was getting better?' to which I had no answer. Her dad had been right.

En passant, I learned a little of her life since we last parted, in particular of her failed marriage. Without bitterness or rancour, she described Terrence as a 'silly man', which amongst things, he indeed was to have deserted such a beautiful and intelligent woman for a bimbo of a barmaid. She told me of her daughter, who had recently begun a degree course at the Open University, proudly showing me the high marks which she had been awarded for some recent essays. But there was the also the immensely sad story of her mother's last years. When Maureen's daughter left home, Alice, long since widowed, joined Maureen in the move to Swansea, which was of course her hometown. Then she contracted Alzheimer's, and Maureen had to give up her job as a saleswoman in a department store to become a full-time carer on a pittance of around fifty pounds per week. The little that she told me about the trauma of coping with her mother's ever worsening condition, which compelled Maureen to become virtually housebound, revealed a side to her that I had naturally not encountered in previous times; her resilience in adversity, her compassion, and her almost stoical readiness to forego the normal pleasures of life for the sake of those dear to her. I could not but help contrast the sacrifices Maureen had made in her life for the good of both her daughter and mother to my own political commitments, which however genuine and often time-consuming, never remotely involved the same degree of self-denial. But for all that, Maureen did not remotely look her sixty years When she said that 'I still feel like I'm thirty five and 'I've worn quite well', biased though I was, I could in all honesty not disagree. Some of the photos of her at the end of this book are the proof. As if we were making up for our thirty and more lost years, the minutes and then the hours flew by while we talked of our cabbages and kings. Only once was I caught off balance. I can see her now, still in her dressing gown, standing with her back against the kitchen door that led to the garden. Entirely out of the blue, she said in a very matter of fact way, 'I don't want to die'. Stumped for a response, because the idea of Maureen dying, or death in general, were the last subjects I wanted to talk about, I shrugged it off with rather lame quip 'you'd better take it up with your MP'. She smiled, and that was that. Aside from her dismissal on one occasion of the prospect of eternal life as both absurd and horrific, only once did death, mine as well as hers, arise, and at that, by implication. As I have already related, Maureen's was open house for stray cats, and all the time we were together there were always at least two, and sometimes three or four in residence. Two of them had litters, which ended up in a local cattery. Not long before she died…it must have been a year or so…she said to me, in a way that left no doubt as to what she was getting at, 'we mustn't take in any more cats'. Since then, none has arrived. And of the two that we had, one died, and the other, after Maureen died, deserted me. So now I am catless for the time in half a century, just when I have needed feline company more than ever before. But every evening, I put out a bowl of cat food in the garden for a fox that first arrived a couple of years before Maureen died, and that she used to feed. But I run ahead, so back to our reunion of August 23, 1999.

Since she pressed me on the subject, much of our talk was about what I had doing in the many years since we had last met, in the course of which she said something that filled me with sadness. 'As for me, I've done absolutely nothing.' Yet she had done so much. Without the advantages of full-time tuition, she had achieved the highest qualifications in her profession. Virtually on her own, she had brought up her daughter, and as best she could, prepared her for adult life. And once again, in the last seven years of her mother's life, again putting aside her own needs, she chose to become her full-time carer. And what she had given me was beyond measure. Was all this *nothing*?

Finally, after a lull in our animated exchanges, Maureen looked at her watch. 'That's the first silence in four hours.' It was time to eat, because I had to catch the last train from Swansea to London at 8.30pm. Maureen cooked a meal, and we toasted each other with red wine. As the time approached for me to get a cab back to the station, I asked Maureen if she would like to stay in touch, possibly even to meet up again. Without hesitation, she said yes. 'I've been getting a bit rusty', meaning I think that she enjoyed our verbal jousting. She gave me her phone number. The doorbell rang. It was my cab. As we stood at the open door to say goodbye, I pulled it to, saying, 'We don't want anyone to see us, do we?' She smiled invitingly, and I held her and gave her the gentlest of kisses. She watched as my cab hurried off to the station. I did not know it then, but my second wooing of Maureen was about to begin. And unlike the first, it would succeed.

What I most clearly remember of my state of mind on my journey back to London was a feeling of euphoria, even of elation. And with good cause, for had I not succeed in my quest against all the odds? And it was obvious to me that Maureen was no less overjoyed than myself to meet again after so many years apart. As for her pointed query about my wife, even if it was not intended as such, it accorded with my impression that what had taken place was not the overture to a new affair, which even if had been in the offing, had never been my intention anyway, but the renewal of an old friendship. And yet...

My wife returned home from Cardiff a day or so later and our lives resumed their humdrum routine. Naturally, I never told her about my encounter, and I saw no reason why I should. At least this time, I was able to convince myself, I had not been unfaithful, only dishonest...as if one could not lead to the other, with of all women, Maureen. Sure enough, within a few days, the urge to contact her became too strong to resist. I phoned her from a phone box. Either then, or during another call, I asked if I could come to Swansea again. She said yes. But hadn't we been in this very same situation twice before, when after believing we had parted for ever, I had visited her and then made love? Only on those two occasions, Maureen had known nothing of my marriage. Now she did, and yet fully aware that I still loved her passionately, she said yes. Given all that had gone before, from that moment on, neither of us could claim innocence of what was to follow.

With my wife back at home, this time, I would have to devise a pretext for being away all day. I told her quite plausibly that I had been offered some session work conveniently situated at a studio in Neath, a few miles away from Swansea, and that I would need the car to get there. So as to extend my time with Maureen, I arranged to stop over at my wife's parent's home in Cardiff overnight, and complete my journey back to London the next day. And so one bright sunny morning in early September, while my wife still slept, I loaded a couple of instruments into the car and headed off down the M4,

From the moment I arrived, I sensed, and I am sure Maureen did too, that this visit would not be like the first. The passage of but a few days had already done its work. Yes, there was, at least initially, the same banter that predominated at our first encounter. Implying that my dress sense hadn't improved since my student days, she said, 'You're still a tramp,' I subsequently replied to this accusation by enclosing in a letter I sent her on my return to London a cutting from what I described quite truthfully as 'the prestigious international style magazine *Dazed and Confused*' (circulation a million plus). There I can be seen in all my sartorial glory, complete with a much-prized fashion accessory; to wit, one piccolo trumpet.

The first part of the day was totally relaxed. After calling in at her doctor to pick up a prescription, we headed for central Swansea so she could show off to me a little of her adopted home town.. It was a warm September day, so we had coffee outside a smart café. Then we went shopping in the covered market, where Maureen bought some items for the evening meal. Everything felt so natural, so normal so relaxed, for all the world just another couple chatting about this and that as they did their weekly round. But then not long after our return to Maureen's home, our exchanges took on an altogether different, more intense timbre. Quite how or even exactly why the change occurred, I cannot now recall, but sometime into the evening, I confessed, with some anguish, that I was torn between loyalty to my wife and my love for Maureen, and it was all too obvious, without my having to say so, which was the stronger. She too was wrestling with a similar dilemma. This time my rival for Maureen's affections was Les, a postman, with whom she had become friendly while still living in London. There was, said Maureen, a little hesitantly, as if fearing she might upset me, 'an understanding' that sometime in the future, Les would get a transfer to Swansea. The rest was kindly left unsaid. I remember resolving to myself that this time, I would fight back. I would try to win Maureen, come what may. Some weeks later, I recalled in three letters to Maureen what had been, unlike the first, an emotion laden, even traumatic visit, and one that looking back now, I can see far more clearly than at the time, foreshadowed the consummation of a love affair that would endure for seventeen wonderful years.

'This will be a strange letter. I miss you so much, I have to write to you every day. Firstly, if I make so bold, this sex business. I was not I, but your good self, who from the beginning of our renewed whatever who has inserted it (if I may give scope for your penchant for double entendre) this topic into our conversation. At our first encounter, apropos nothing in particular, I was regaled more than once as I recall, with strictures on the banalities of sex (to which I did not respond) and the attractiveness of a career as a nun. But, then, on my second visit, when strange things began to happen, a notably different spin was put on the same theme, when you said, in making love, "Why hold back?" Why indeed. When we first met again, or rather the second time

I came, I was in some distress, as you will recall, about my divided loyalties. I told you I did not love my wife as I love you, but wished her no harm. I could tell that your feelings for me were stronger than mere affection. But you explained that you too had ties. Yet, knowing this, we continued. I thought it better to stay away for a time, and perhaps you agreed, so I wrote and we talked instead. And despite our ties, we both came to realise that our old love, for me the only true love of my life, had survived and was, in me at least, stronger than ever. What has happened, begun by me it is true, has been willed by us both. That responsibility we must both share.

As you said the other day (on the phone), the second time I saw you (or maybe between the first and the second) things began to happen which neither of us had intended. I told you afterwards, during that angst-ridden talk we had on the phone when I was supposed to come and see you (you see, even that far in, I was trying, hopelessly ineffectively as it turned out, to resist the irresistible) that the second time I came, I asked you take your glasses off (yes, your glasses). To see you without them brought back such memories as I cannot find words to evoke them that would do them any justice. You looked back at me with a look that I felt was not so far from what I was feeling. For me, everything changed at that moment, or perhaps what had already begun had become self-evident. I think you knew then not just what I felt; after all, I had written to you at some length about that, and madly maybe (but I do not think so), about what I wanted. I remember, when I was about to leave, I had given you such a gentle kiss, just like I did the first time, and was about to go when you hugged the breath out of me in a way you never did all these years ago. Then, a few days later, much distraught over the phone I fumblingly inquired, for the first time, as to what, in your opinion, was going on between us. Up to that point, our numerous and often long phone chats had been about what I was up to musically (it was the time when Blowpipe's single was coming out), the weather in London and Swansea, and general chit chat and banter. Very light stuff you might say, and nothing wrong in that. But I had to tell you, however awkwardly, that as I remember putting it, I could not countenance the thought of not knowing you again. I asked you, "What is going on?" In your customary forthright manner, you replied, "You mean where is all this leading?" to which I replied in turn, "Yes." Then you said, "I don't know."'

When I returned home the next morning after my second visit to Maureen, I was beset by feelings of acute guilt and decided that I owed it to my wife to give her at least a partially truthful account of what I had really been up to the previous day. Without telling her about my first visit, or going into details about the second, I explained how I had taken it into my head to look up an old friend from a time before I had met my wife (which was true after a fashion), and that on a sudden impulse, I decided to see how she was getting on. Entirely justifiably, Karen was not at all pleased. 'I don't like it,' she said with some vehemence. There we let the matter rest, with me giving the impression as best I could that my trip to Swansea had been a one-off. (When I told Maureen at my next visit that I had confessed some, if not all, to my wife, she was a little cross with me. Did she fear that telling my wife meant that I would no longer be able to see her? Could she already have been considering perhaps that an affair was in the offing? In either case, what about Neil mark two, Les?)

Given our somewhat unconventional past, I found it hard to resist the temptation to wheedle out of Maureen an explanation for her behaviour towards me in those distant times. In particular, I wanted to know why, after five years of friendship, the first two of which had been effectively platonic, she agreed to make love with me. So, in one phone conversation I asked her straight out. Unfazed, she replied: 'Because I owed it to you.' Owed it to me? For what? And whatever it was, why this particular form of payment? I think rather than settling a debt, it was Maureen's way of saying, too late in the day, that she loved me.

X

It was around this time, in mid-October, that I decided to tell my two children what was going on, and where it might, or rather, where I wanted it to lead. I arranged to meet Katharine at an entrance to Leicester Square tube station, and we went for a coffee. Even though I didn't tell her why I needed to speak to her so urgently, when we met, and I told her why, she replied she had immediately guessed what our meeting would be about, even though she knew nothing of the lady in question. I began by saying, like one does with a child at bedtime, 'Let me tell you a story.' And indeed, she listened as if spellbound to my extraordinary tale of a love that had endured in me, and I believe in Maureen too, for forty years. When I reached the point where I found Maureen again and visited her Swansea, Katharine, who had been listening with mounting excitement, could contain herself no longer: 'What...you've *found* her again?' and then, approvingly, 'Dad, you're so romantic.' By this time, I was near to tears, and between sobs, told Katharine that if she would have me, I would spend the rest of my days with Maureen. As we parted, I asked her to tell her brother Andrew what I had told her, and she did.

I had two other similar encounters at this time. One with was Ian Bishop, a close friend of those times and lead singer in Horsepower, a band I played in that was under contract with Mute Records. He too quickly guessed why I needed to see him, and I related the same story as I had told to Katharine. Quite apart from needing to talk about my predicament to people whom I knew I could trust and whose friendship I valued, I particularly wanted Ian to understand my situation because Maureen had already expressed concern that my moving to Swansea could create difficulties for my musical career. I asked Ian to speak to Maureen on the phone and persuade that certainly in the case of Horsepower, who only did a gig about once a month, this would not be the case. This he kindly did.

Afterwards, I wrote to Maureen, partly because I was curious about a remark she had made to Ian during their conversation.

'Something I still (obtuse though I may be) do not understand, despite discussing it with you more than once, Ian told me that you said you were not surprised when I found you. Did he mean, turn up on your doorstep (this, I appreciate would not have so unexpected, given that I had already written to you and my impulsive nature) or does this refer to me finding you in the first instance? If so, I am still at a loss as to how you did not find this something totally out of the blue or should it be red? That's one. The other is a mystery of a totally different order. I keep going back to this in my thoughts, and I have written about this, as you know, and when I told our story to Katharine and Ian (who know each other by the way, and in some ways, resemble each other) I began with that day forty-two years ago (Christ, that long!) when I first saw you, and you changed my life. How did I know, because I did and I was right (for once) that you would be, exactly as makes no difference, like you proved to be? My life would I am sure have turned out not only very different, but probably much less, what shall we say, complicated, if I had been wrong.'

In another letter, I related to Maureen the effect on me of recalling seeing her for the first time after we last parted.

'Why is it that the two times I have told this story to Katharine and now Ian, I break down exactly the same point, when I describe how, on my first visit, I see your outline through you frosted glass front door? I suppose it is that moment when, after so many years of remembering you as you were, and then picturing you as you might have become, I was about to see the real you. It was the most overpowering moment of my life when you opened the door and I saw you as you are now. You see that face every day in a mirror (I presume not to know your cosmetic routine,

but surely this is a reasonable assumption) but I had not seen it for thirty-three years, and yet pictured it over and over again in my dreams and awake, every one of those years, the face that I first saw on those stairs so long ago and whose memory will never leave me. When I described that moment to Ian, as I did to Katharine, I could not help myself dissolving into tears. I am not ashamed or embarrassed by this you understand. I am just mystified how these feelings which I cannot put words to (but music could convey) have taken hold of me with such force. I do not behave like this normally you know. I have very strong feeling about many things, often misguidedly so perhaps, but they do not do that to me. I watched you doing your ironing the other day, and it nearly happened then. Bent to you task, you did not notice that tears were running down my cheeks from thoughts that, at the moment, I cannot really speak to you about.'

They were of course, thoughts of living with Maureen as man and wife. Having told my tale to Katharine and Ian, that left Maureen's daughter Andrea. In addition to being regularly appraised as to most of the details concerning my reappearance in the life of her mother, she had from quite an early age been told about the man Maureen used to call 'my friend Robin' and of whom she said, as she had to myself, Ian and others that knew of me, that I would one day sometime, somehow, find her. Andrea had already met me, briefly, when a few weeks previously she came with her partner Jess to a Horsepower gig near Kings cross. Just before I was due to go on stage, she came in, recognised me...how I am not sure...came over, put her arms around me and gave a frankly passionate kiss. At last, she had met the almost legendary 'Mum's friend Robin'. Soon after this first encounter, we met up, again at Leicester Square, where over a meal, I poured out my heart to her about my love for her mother. Again, I was reduced to tears as I told her of my constantly recurring dream about fruitlessly searching for Maureen, and of my yearning to at last be with her.

Although my hopes and fears concerning Maureen naturally dominated my thoughts, music, and to a lesser extent politics, still played a large part in my life, and from time to time featured in my letters to her. And there was also philosophy and theology, both being subjects Maureen and I shared an interest in, albeit at times from different perspectives. During the five years I first knew Maureen, religion rarely featured as a subject for discussion. She knew I was an atheist, while I could never quite work out what she did or did not believe in, though she did have a number of friends who unlike herself, were regular church goers. When me met up again, matters had changed somewhat. On my very first visit, I learned, much to my surprise, that Maureen regularly attended services at the local Jehovah's Witness Bethel, not as a member, thankfully, but as a guest. As she explained it to me, she respected the Jehovahs because they knew their Bible, and tried to live by it. Another reason for Maureen's involvement was, I believe, that living on her own, she welcomed the company of people she found to be friendly and decent.

A few weeks after I had moved in with Maureen, two of her best friends from the Jehovahs dropped by for a chat. Without any embarrassment, and in the very matter of fact way so typical of her, in introducing me, Maureen explained who I was, my status so to speak, and that I was an atheist. 'You know we can't approve of that,' one of her friends replied, meaning I think not my atheism, but the fact that Maureen and I were living in sin, which debarred her in future from attending Jehovah services even as a guest.

Unlike my first years with Maureen, on my visits to Swansea, religion, and its philosophical implications were from the beginning a subject of animated debate. Perhaps Maureen was playing devil's, or rather God's advocate to my atheism, because she advanced an explanation for the origin of the universe that was essentially the same as the deists of the late 18th century, who argued that having created the universe and the laws that govern its behaviour,

God lets events take their natural course. After spending many hours debating this hypothesis, pedant that I am, I felt it was time I summarised her argument in a letter.

'Going back to what we talked about last time I saw you, you offered a non-orthodox explanation for a supposedly divine act of creation, namely that of vast cosmic experiment, with God as the scientist, the universe as his laboratory, and us human beings endowed with free will, as the guinea pigs. Defined thus, the outcome of the experiment cannot be predicted even by God (why else the experiment, if the result is known in advance?). This hypothesis, while suggesting a solution to one problem (namely, the purpose of God's initial act of creation) creates others not answered only by just mainstream or traditional theology, but by all schools that I am aware of. For example, God is invariably ascribed, amongst his other qualities, that of omniscience. Knowing all surely means knowledge not only of the past and the present but also of the future. Your hypothesis, let us call it the Griggs Thesis, implies that this ability to know the future is jettisoned. God's knowledge is thus reduced to human levels, it becomes finite and, as such, he becomes fallible. Now, if this deduction is integral to the Griggs Thesis, then a problem arises. Assuming firstly that the past is known to God, and also the present at the moment of the creation of our species, the subject of the experiment, and secondly, that the future is contained in, will be generated by all the elements, factors, forces, properties etc. that constitute this present, and thirdly, that the laws of causation apply without exception and in the same regular manner, then it follows that the future, in its entirety, can be deduced not by revelation, but by extrapolation from an entire knowledge of the present. Unlike God, we humans cannot do this because our knowledge of the present is incomplete, likewise our knowledge of the laws that govern it.

All this follows, unless we put into the cosmic equation one random factor...human free will, whose consequences are the subject of the Griggs Experiment. Disputes as to whether such a thing as free will exists predate by centuries modern science, where opinion is no less also divided on the subject. While Roman Catholic theology insists that God endows us with free will so that we have the ability to choose between good and evil, Calvinism subscribes to the doctrine that even before we are born, God has predestined our souls either to go to heaven or hell, irrespective of how behave on this earth. Because it is so old and enduring, this dispute must tell us something about what we are, about our human condition. We surely on the one hand like to think of ourselves in one sense at least as being free, in the sense of making choices that are real and not illusory. On the other hand, our minds seek order, regularity, meaning, purpose, causation in the processes of the natural world, in the sweep of history, and in our everyday routine existence. When we turn on a light switch, we expect the light to go on. Yet the world cannot, at the same time, be subject to the whims of our free wills, which will not obviously not always concur, and will often seek opposed outcomes, as in a sporting contest, and at the same time, be governed by laws whose outcomes, if only all the constituent factors were known, are totally predictable. I confess that I cannot prove the existence of free will, however limited. It seems to me, by the way the issue defines itself, it is unprovable, and that belief in it derives from some (who knows, possibly wholly conditioned) psychological need that our choices matter, and that we are not acting out, word perfect, a part already written.'

In this letter, I refer to Calvin's doctrine of predestination, one to which Islam bears a close resemblance, where it is called in Arabic, *Qadar*. Like the God of the Bible, Allah knows and determines the future, being both omniscient as well as all-powerful: 'No calamity befalls on earth or in yourselves but is inscribed in the Book of Decrees, before we bring it into existence. Verily, that is easy for Allah.' (*Koran*, Chapter 57, Verse 22) So the story goes, the Decree in question was written on a tablet by Allah before he created the universe, and is unchangeable. The doctrine was invoked by the Saudi monarchy when on two occasions, stampedes by pilgrims visiting Mecca that led to more than two thousands deaths were decreed to be the will of Allah.

This age-old conundrum, fate, or determinism, versus free will, continued to exercise our minds once Maureen and I were together, not least because it goes to the heart of what the more philosophical among us call the human condition. Are we puppets on strings pulled by what we, mistakenly, call sheer chance? Just think for a moment of the links in the chain that brought Maureen and I together. Remove or change just one, and I would not be writing these lines. For example, if I had bought myself a mute for my trumpet practice, I would not have been evicted from my digs in Brimsdown. Or if Maureen had taken the first job she was offered after leaving school, and not the second. Yet strictly speaking, these were not chance events. What we call chance or an accident is, viewed from a broader perspective, simply an event that was not intended or expected to happen. A car crash is called an accident, but the police nevertheless look for its causes, which in their turn, could lead to the prosecution of the driver... over the limit, on drugs, speeding etc. Each event has its causes, and in its turn, itself becomes a cause of what follows. In that sense, there is no chance or accident.

There is no way to scientifically either prove or disprove that our lives, and our deaths, are mapped out for us before we are even born. We cannot, beginning from the same starting point, re-run our lives to see if they vary, as one can with an experiment in a laboratory. So was Maureen my destiny, as I said in my poem about our first meeting? That indeed is the mystery that lies at the very heart of the human condition, because to questions such as this, there is no provable answer. Not long before Maureen died, sitting side by side in our armchairs one evening, I asked her, 'Just supposing the Big Bang that created the universe was to exactly repeat itself, would we be sitting here in this same living room, 7.8 billion years later, asking that very same question?' A strict determinist would probably give an answer that goes something like this:

'Given that at any moment in time, what is at that moment the present has been determined by what has gone before, it must surely follow that though we cannot accurately predict the future, because there are too many unknowns, nonetheless, that future has already been determined by what has preceded it. The objection that chance must play a part in all natural processes, the so-called butterfly wing effect, rests on the illusion that what we call chance happenings are not subject to the same physical laws that produce events that we able to predict and explain. A game of chance played with dice is in fact nothing of the sort. Its outcome, though it cannot be predicted, is governed by the same laws of motion that were first described by Isaac Newton. By this reasoning, and I have yet to encounter a totally convincing refutation, free will and chance are illusions.'

It will be objected that quantum mechanics has established that the behaviour of sub-atomic particles, the very 'stuff' of all matter, cannot be predicted, thereby rendering causality itself a cosmic lottery. In which case, no matter how times we re-run the history of the universe from the big bang, the result will always be different. But is this true? Granted that sub-atomic particles behave in what we call a random manner, but, with each step upwards in scale, through atoms, then molecules and to the matter they form, this ceases to be the case. Once all the variables are known, as Newton established with his three laws of motion, the movement of solid bodies can be predicted with total accuracy. 'Chance', at this level, is removed from the equation. If this is the case, where does it leave 'free will', since the brain, from which the 'will' emanates, being composed of organic matter, is subject to the same laws that govern inanimate matter. The frequently invoked counter argument is that while physical processes are indeed undeniably subject to the inexorable laws of cause and effect, the human will, being thought, electrical charges, is, admittedly in a limited way, autonomous, so that we can and do make choices that are real, and it is this ability to make choices that leaves open the possibility of an infinite range of future outcomes, hence not condemning us to a future that cannot be changed. But here too the same objection applies. Electricity, however generated and whatever its source and function, like matter, always obeys the same laws. So we arrive back at square one.

Many are the philosophers who have insisted that we do indeed possess the capacity and indeed have the obligation to make moral choices, whether it is the 'Either Or' of Soren Kierkegaard, the categorical imperative of Emmanuel Kant, or the Existentialist *engagement* of Jean-Paul Sartre. Irrespective of the truth or otherwise of these assumptions, all legal systems and notions of justice have as their bedrock the principle that adult individuals of sound mind are responsible and therefore accountable to society for their actions, and without this principle's enforcement, civilisation would in an instant descent into barbarism. Even so, determinists, among them leading neurologists, continue to object that there is no evidence to suggest that the workings of the human brain should be exempted from the laws of causality. What we call our will, our seeming ability to make choices is no less determined by what has gone before than any other law-governed process, including the thought that we have free will. The brain receives information from one or more sense organs, and makes what it calls a decision on the basis of its past experiences, stored as memory.

And so it goes, to and fro. Perhaps this counterposing of free will and determinism is a false dichotomy. So I am tempted to accede to the intermediate position perhaps best conveyed by Karl Marx, even though he was speaking of man in the collective: 'Men make their own history, but not in circumstances of their own choosing'.

These questions fascinate me, though I freely admit that

even if answers were forthcoming, they would more than likely have no practical value. The human brain would go on working just the same. Being the down to earth person, she was, Maureen used to say that such speculation was so much hot air, and that all that was required to sort out the big issues was the application of common sense. I could never accept this. I argued that philosophy, like science, from whose findings much of it is derived, is uncommon sense. For thousands of years, common sense said that the sun went around the earth, that life could be generated spontaneously without reproduction, like maggots from rotting flesh, that labour pains, disease and natural disasters were divine punishments for sin. And incredibly, even today, there are people who still believe this. It required not the common sense of the untutored multitude, but the science of seismology, the genius of a Galileo and a Pasteur to prove otherwise, and of an Aristotle to systematise the rules of logical thinking. And though we had both read Stephen Hawking's book on the subject, we did not agree about the nature of time either. While Maureen believed that time must have existed before the big bang, that time is in some way an objectively existing 'thing', I tended towards the view that time has no meaning independent of the sequence of events that it measures. *Ergo*, no universe, no time.

Rather than sweet nothings, such was often our pillow talk before making love. As we once jousted thus into the early hours, a *risqué* thought occurred to me, I asked Maureen, 'Which do you prefer, my penetrating remarks, or my remarkable penetrations?' She really liked that one. However, her more usual reaction to my attempts at word play and puns (as distinct from foreplay) was to dismiss them as worthy at best of a fourth-year schoolboy. Maureen could also 'talk dirty' when the mood took her. On our first visit to Florence, we were resting on our hotel bed after a hard day's sightseeing, and she said, in a very matter-of-fact way, 'Blicky' (that was one of her pet names for me) 'I fancy you.' Somewhat taken aback by the directness of her approach, I asked her, 'What do fancy, exactly?' 'You inside me,' she replied.

Another mutual interest was of course music, including mine. Maureen was a devotee of left field, and especially electronic genres, and so immediately took to *Epilogue*, the third Blowpipe album that I had recently recorded with my son Andrew. The single from *Epilogue*, with my daughter singing the vocals, had just been released when I first visited Maureen. (Blowpipe featured two musicians with a somewhat dark pedigree. Our harmonica player was Nick Reynolds, the son of the brains behind the Great Train Robbery, while Patrick Mosely was the son of Max of Formula One, and grandson of Sir Oswald, the pre-war *Fuehrer* of British fascism.) When I told Maureen, our single had been reviewed in a music journal, she headed into town to buy a copy.

Maureen had no time for Mozart operas. She sat through the Marriage of Figaro and was, she told me afterwards, bored stiff. Though she did not say so, I think it was because like most Mozart operas, and indeed much else of his music, Figaro lacked the brooding inwardness, depth, darkness and yes, even pessimism that is the distinguishing characteristic of her favourite composer, Sibelius. And what Maureen valued in music, she also was herself. It was what drew me to her from the very beginning, and held me in thrall to her to the very end.

XI

As for politics, by the time I found Maureen, my active career was long over, except for a vendetta against comrade Healy's legacy. He had been dead for some ten years, but Ken Livingstone, one of his most prominent admirers, and in the political orientation of his weekly *Labour Herald*, which was identical to that of the WRP, one of his closest collaborators, was still very much in business. It was Livingstone more than anyone else who was to provide the link between the Zionist baiting of the Healy movement and its return, no longer on the leftist fringe, but as far more toxic strain at the summits and in the heart of the Labour Party under the leadership of Jeremy Corbyn.

Active in local government politics from the early 1970s in Lambeth with the veteran Healyite Ted Knight, and then Hampstead, his association with Healy began no later than May 1981, when he was the subject of an in-depth interview in *News Line* by Paul Feldman, the co-author of the official Healy biography published in 1994. Then in September of the same year came the launching of *Labour Herald*, printed by the WRP's Gaddafi-subsidised Astmoor Litho. More interviews followed, together with regular appearances, prominently promoted and pictured in *News Line*, on the speakers' platform at WRP rallies alongside Ted Knight, Healy, Venessa Redgrave and other party stalwarts.

In his new high-profile role as GLC Leader, Livingstone had been the subject of criticism for what some regarded with good reason as anti-Semitic comments about the Jews, for example, that British Jews had 'suddenly become reactionary, turned right, nearly to fascism', and 'extremist Jews' were organising 'paramilitary groups', presumably, given their fascistic tendencies, akin to Hitler's anti-Semitic Brown-Shirted stormtroopers. While some Jews were allegedly turning fascist, others were exerting an undue influence on the left. It seems that whatever the Jews do, they just can't get it right: 'There is a distortion [sic!] running right the way through British politics...a majority of Jews in this country supported the Labour party and elected a number of MPs.' Another case of *cherchez le Juif.*

Even back then, Livingstone had already acquired a penchant for the kind of Holocaust revisionism that is now common coin amongst much of the far left, and which bore an uncanny resemblance to the version that we have seen expounded by his comrades in *News Line*. According to Livingstone, speaking on Irish radio, 'what Britain has done for [sic] the Irish nation, although spread over 800 years is worse than what Hitler did to the Jews'. Hitler was also compared favourably with 'international finance', which 'every year [sic] kills more people than World War Two'. And by way of mitigation, Livingstone added, 'but at least Hitler was mad'. Here we have two falsehoods. All experts on the subject concur that Hitler was not mad, and of the 72 million deaths in the Second World War, 80% were caused by the Nazis and their allies.

Press headlines of the time highlight illustrate just how fixated Livingstone was even then on the 'Jewish question': 'Livingstone is lashed over "anti-semitism"'; 'Jewish fury at GLC Leader'; 'Ken caned for "racist" cartoon'. This concerned a cartoon in Livingstone's *Labour Herald*, which portrayed Israeli Prime Minister Menachem Begin with a huge nose, wearing a Nazi uniform, giving a Nazi salute and standing on a heap of human bones from which streams of blood were flowing, and with the caption, in Gothic lettering, 'The Final Solution.' On September 24, 1982, the *Jewish Chronicle* carried a story headed 'Jews ejected from pro-PLO rally'. 'Supporters of Israel' had been 'ejected from a stormy pro-PLO meeting addressed by Livingstone. A 'small number' of Jews had been 'punched as they were bundled out the hall by stewards'. They chanted *'Am Yisrael chai'* – 'May the people of Israel live'. The official policy of the PLO at that time was for the destruction of the state of Israel. What was to happen to its Jews was anybody's guess. (Those Corbyn was to call his 'friends', Hamas and Hezbollah, came up with the answer.

They were to be exterminated.) In addition to his support for the PLO, the meeting had a strategic significance so far as Livingstone's future political career was concerned. It had been organised by Brent East Labour Party, where a faction of anti-Zionists was campaigning for Livingstone to replace the Jewish Reginald Freeson as its MP.

Another controversy involving Livingstone and the Jews erupted after *Labour Herald* published a review of book which claimed the Zionist movement collaborated with the Nazis in the Holocaust in order to win sympathy for a Jewish state in Palestine. According to the reviewer, 'Israel is a state built on the blood of Europe's Jews, whom the Zionists deserted in their hour of greatest need'. Shortly after writing this review Harry Mullin joined the neo-Nazi British National Party. (Livingstone has his own spin on this lie. He was suspended from the Labour Party in 2016 not only for saying that 'Hitler supported Zionism', but his no less mendacious and preposterous claim that the SS 'setup training camps so that German Jews that were going to go [to Palestine] could be trained to cope with a very different country when they got there'. How considerate. The only SS camps German Jews saw the inside of were those where they met their deaths with millions of other Jews.)

Given their shared and well-advertised visceral hatred of all things Zionist, it was inevitable that sooner rather than later, Livingstone and Corbyn, who in the 1983 general election, had made his debut as Labour's MP for Islington North, would recognise each other as kindred spirits. Their first 'joint enterprise' was the founding of the Labour Movement Campaign for Palestine, which eventually morphed into today's anti-Semite-infested Palestine Solidarity Campaign, one of whose Patrons is Corbyn. It would have been more honest if its two founders had described it as what it was, a campaign to eradicate the official recognition of any Jewish presence in the British and international labour movement. Its two stated aims were the recognition by the Labour Party of the terrorist PLO as the legitimate representative of the Palestinian people and, as complimentary to that objective, the elimination of 'manifestations of Zionism' in the Labour Party. Pursuant to the second objective, at a meeting on May 19, 1984, the campaign approved a resolution calling for the expulsion from the Labour Party of Poale Zion (now the Jewish Labour Movement), an affiliate of the party since 1920. A second resolution demanded that the 'Trade Union Congress and its affiliate trade unions' sever 'all links' with their Israeli counterpart, Histadrut, a *bona fide* trade union affiliated, like the TUC, to the World Trade Union Federation and which, contrary to lies about an Israeli apartheid, organised and represented both Arab and Jewish workers. But so far as Livingstone and Corbyn were concerned, none of these indisputable facts counted for anything. It was simply a matter of Jewish socialists and workers out, lavishly-funded PLO Jew-killers in. But it was not only Poale Zion and Histadrut, the only free trade union in the Middle East, that were to be flushed down the anti-Zionist memory hole. Israel, likewise the only democracy in the same region, was itself to be swallowed up and devoured by the creation of a so-called 'bi-national Palestinian state', in which, given the demographic balance of the time, its Jews would find themselves heavily outnumbered by its projected Palestinian majority and, as an inevitable consequence of that preponderance, ruled by the PLO. Given the virulent anti-Semitism of their new masters (in 1972, the PLO's ruling Fatah wing was responsible for the 'Black September' terrorist operation at the 1972 Munich Olympics operation that culminated in the massacre of eleven members of the Israeli team), it requires little if any imagination to envisage what their fate might be. under such a regime. Suffice it to say it would be less respectful of their rights than the equality accorded Israel's Palestinian minority since the establishment of the Jewish state in 1948. Such was final solution to the Zionist question being advocated by the Corbyn-Livingstone axis. And as they must surely have known, it could only have been achieved, as it had been attempted, and defeated, on three previous occasions in 194t8, 1967 and 1973 by Israel's Arab neighbours, by force of arms. The demise in 1991 of the PLO's Soviet sponsors and military quartermasters left Arafat with only one option…a US-brokered agreement with Israel to work towards what became known as a 'two-state solution' of the Palestine-Israel conflict, enshrined in the Oslo Accords of 1993. There then followed the establishment of the Palestinian Authority, which assumed all civilian responsibilities and functions in the West Bank and the Gaza Strip. In the wake of these agreements, there arose to prominence two movements in the Middle East that regarded the PLO's recognition of the state of Israel as a heinous betrayal of both the Palestinians and of Allah. The despised Jews - the Koran calls them offspring of 'apes and swine' – had stolen land that been gifted to the Arabs by Allah. The two movements in question were Hamas, an Arabic acronym for 'Islamic Resistance Movement', sponsored by the theocratic Egyptian Muslim Brotherhood, and based in the Gaza Strip, and Hezbollah, the 'Party of Allah', based in Lebanon, and sponsored by Syria and the Iranian theocracy. It was these to these two terrorist, theocratic movements, both dedicated to the total destruction of the 'Zionist Entity', that Livingstone and Corbyn, together with those on the far left associated with their many and various front organisations, would in due course turn, now that the PLO, at least on paper, had made its peace with Israel.

Three decades on, and now enjoying the patronage and protection of his old comrade-in-arms as Labour Leader, Livingstone was still tirelessly waging his far from one-person war on Zionism. In the midst of the furore over the abject refusal of the Labour Party to expel him for his comments associating Hitler with Zionism, he claimed that in his 47 years' membership of the Labour Party, he had 'never heard anyone say anything anti-Semitic.' Either Livingstone has his own, highly idiosyncratic definition of anti-Semitism (and he has indeed said that hating the Jews of Israel does not qualify as such), or he needs to see a doctor about his hearing and an optician about his eyesight. To cite but two of several cases of blatant anti-Semitism that either passed him by, or did not merit this description, we have the on-line postings of the Labour Councillor for the High Town Ward of Luton, Aysegal Gurbuz, one which because of its topicality and extreme nature, attracted media attention, though it seems not Livingstone's: 'If it wasn't for my man Hitler [sic], these Jews would have wiped Palestine years ago.' Then we have Naseen Khan, prospective Labour candidate for the Little Horton Ward of Bradford. She complained that schools were 'brainwashing' pupils into 'thinking the bad guy was Hitler.' 'What good have the Jews done in the world?', she asked rhetorically, perhaps unaware that Jews, despite the ravages of the Holocaust, and who today comprise less than 0.2% of the world's population, have won 25% of all Nobel Prizes; 35 for chemistry, 54 for physics, literature 15, peace, 9, economics, 29, and the one she, together with the rest of the world's Muslims, must surely have benefited from the most, 54 for medicine, making a grand total of 196. Muslims, who are 24% of the world's population, have won 12, a little over 1%; of the total; 7 for peace, including Yasser Arafat (who says Scandinavians don't have sense of humour), one for physics, 2 each for literature and chemistry, and none for medicine. Accused of anti-Semitism (obviously not by Livingstone) Khan replied, 'I am an ordinary [sic] Muslim that has an opinion and put it across. We have worse people in the world now than Hitler. Stop beating a dead horse. The Jews have reaped the reward of playing victim.' I cite scores of similar cases, many quite openly anti-Semitic and some, even enthusiastically genocidal in their intent, in my *Socialism of Fools*. Here I provide just a small sample of such postings by Labour Party members that one would have expected, before the advent of Corbyn, only to see on a Neo-Nazi or Jihadi website. They were published by the *Sunday Times* on December 8, 2019:

'You have to think with a scientific method...with clarity of thought. No emotion. We need to eliminate this infection. We kill viruses every day.'

'The Jew is worse than the Black Death [which, like Covid19, they were accused of causing and spreading], worse than Ebola virus. The Jew represents pure evil.'

'Can we hope for the complete extinction of all Jews by 2017?'

'I call for the complete annihilation and [sic!] extermination of every Jew on the planet.'

Despite the mountain of evidence to the contrary, like other prominent Corbynistas (Dianne Abbott being one of the most vocal), Livingstone insisted accusations of Labour Party anti-Semitism were an invention of Corbyn's enemies, the result, he claimed, of a 'well-orchestrated campaign by the Israel lobby to smear anyone who criticises Israel as anti-Semitic.' Another conspiracy.

It is easy to see why numerous commentators over the years, not all of them Jews by a long way, have suspected that Livingstone may have an issue with anyone who defends the right of Israel to exist. As we have seen, well before the Tory government wound up the GLC in 1986, Livingstone had staked out a safe Labour seat, Brent East in north west London. Was it just by chance that this seat was currently occupied by a Jew and Zionist, Reginald Freeson, and that he was also Chairman of Poale Zion, the Jewish organization that together with Corbyn, Livingstone had been campaigning to have expelled from the Labour Party? Only Livingstone can answer that question.

It so happened that with the help of the *Jewish Chronicle*, I had been collecting over the years a dossier on Livingstone's many hostile comments on Israel and Zionism, some of which shaded over into what many, including myself, regarded as anti-Semitism. As far back as

1985, when he was still closely associated with Healy's party, Livingstone's attitude towards the Jews had elicited a protest from Poale Zion. Reginald Freeson, whom after a dirty campaign, Livingstone had ousted to become the constituency's new Labour candidate and then MP at the 1987 general election, expressed the group's concerns in a letter to the Labour Party's National Executive Committee:

'This letter is by way of a friendly warning about a situation that I fear could deteriorate soon if the Party does not unequivocally dissociate itself from the crude populism which Mr Livingstone's anti-zionism and anti-Jewish remarks represent. It could permanently alienate the Jewish community collectively and many Jews individually from the very Party to which so many members of our community have looked for support and their own political involvement.'

In 1999, with the election pending in May 2000 to the newly created mayoralty of London, and with Livingstone, even though running as an independent candidate, a possible, even the likely future Mayor of the city which is home to most of Britain's Jews, I thought his views on this subject were deserving of more scrutiny than they had received up to that point, 'Red Ken' then being the darling of the popular press.

With this in mind, I wrote to the official Labour mayoral candidate, Frank Dobson, a letter dated 27 October 1999, which he neither acknowledged the receipt of nor replied to.

'I am writing to you in confidence as a Labour Party member of some twenty-five years standing who views with horror the prospect of Ken Livingstone securing nomination as the official Labour candidate for the Mayor of London. I therefore hope that it might be of interest to you that over the last twenty years or so, I have closely followed the political career of Mr Livingstone, in the process collecting a mass of well-documented information which, if placed

before the Labour Party and voting public of London, would place his candidature in the light that it deserves. I might also add that the nature of this material would have led to the publication of a book on the subject by Harper-Collins but for two considerations, one being that at the time the proposal was made, Livingstone was regarded as a passé politician, and, secondly, for fear of litigation on the part of Livingstone himself. Time is short. If you or any of your campaign colleagues are in any way interested in what is being offered, please do not hesitate to reply. I can, of course, furnish evidence and testimonies as to my bona fides.'

Having drawn a blank with Dobson, I approached the Jewish journalist and political broadcaster Peter Kellner, who had made his views known about Livingstone's attitude towards the Jews. He requested that I send him my dossier, which I promptly did. And then again...nothing. As I had found so often in the past, nobody seemed prepared to take Livingstone on in the manner he deserved. Seven years later, in March 2006, my attempts to nail Livingstone were vindicated when the Adjudication Panel for England suspended him from office for four weeks after he had insulted a Jewish journalist by likening him to a Nazi concentration camp guard.

Just before my move to Swansea, in December 1999, politics and music merged in a novel manner when my son Andrew, who had been working as an intern at Number 10 Downing Street for Fiona Millar, adviser to Cherie Blair and the partner of Press Officer Alastair Campbell, received the following letter, dated 2 December 1999, from the Political Office.

'*Dear Andrew*

Hi, how are you? Sorry to bother you but we are trying to organise some entertainment at the opening of the Christmas party this year and both Fiona and Laura strongly recommended you and your band. I hope it is not too cheeky to ask if you could come along and do a spot for myself and the other organisers of this event so that we can have some idea of what you do. Or if you have such a thing as tape could you send it in. Also, can you offer any Christmas theme type materials, even carols?'

How did they know Blowpipe would fit the bill? Earlier that year, in September, Andrew, my wife and I had been guests at an afternoon tea party at Chequers for the families of interns, hosted by the Blairs. Not one to miss a trick when it came to promoting our music, Andrew suggested to Mrs Blair that she use our latest album as background music for the event. Hence the invitation. When we arrived by car for the gig, at the gates at the end of Downing Street there was a noisy demonstration underway, comprised of Serbian émigré nationalists and Trotskyists. They were protesting against the Blair government's military action in defence of the Muslims of Kosovo, who were being ethnically cleansed by the Serbian President and later indicted War Criminal Slobodan Milosevic. (Acting on the principle that the enemy of my enemy is my friend, two years later, after 9/11, the Trots switched partners, dumping the Serbs and backing Islamic jihadis in their war of terror against the West.)

Some kind of operation must have been immanent, because when we arrived at Number 10, the hallway was filled with military brass in full regalia, presumably on their way to a council of war with the Prime Minister. Upstairs, the mood was festive, and the food and drink, as one would expect, first class. Halfway through our usual jazzy repertoire, the Blairs made a carefully staged low key entry. When we had completed our programme, it was Cherie's turn to be in the spotlight, and I found myself accompanying her on my euphonium, along with my daughter, in a fair rendition of *Silent Night*. Dancing had been scheduled for later on in the evening in an area adjoining the main room where the party was being held, but with drinking and networking in full flow, nobody seemed interested in taking to the floor. Seeing that I was driving, and had no one to network with, I suggested to Katharine that we kick start the dancing. Andrew, who was networking with the best of them, became very embarrassed at the sight of his dad galumphing to the strains of someone called Fat Boy Slim, but in no time at all the floor was heaving. Later, Andrew apologised to me for being so shirty, and passed on Fiona Millar's thanks for keeping the party going. Though like me no fan of Mrs Blair's, when I gave Maureen an account of the proceedings, she was rather impressed, particularly with my dancing which, to put it mildly, has never been one of my strongest suites.

But so far as I was concerned, a gig and dancing at Number 10 were mere sideshows compared to my future with Maureen. By this time, we both understood that a decision had to be made, and soon, not least because of the effect it could have on the lives of those closest to us. The stress of the situation was getting to both of us. Our phone conversations, though they continued to touch on other subjects of mutual interest, were consequently about little else. My letters became more desperate. I implored Maureen to make a decision, one way or the other.

'I am more hopelessly in love with you than ever...partly I think because there is more to love, or perhaps I see even more now than I did I did all those years ago. I have to tell you this, not to indulge my own feelings, but because you should and need to know. The last thing I want is for me to be a nuisance or embarrassment to you. I tried, without much success, to talk about this with you last week. You said, prompting my semi-articulate mumblings, "where is all this going?" I know, and I have told you, where I would wish it to go. I want to be with you. I know that quite apart from whether you would find this a desirable state of affairs in other circumstances, this raises all sorts of problems for you if not for me. So I ask for your help, even if, or especially, this means being what I might find cruel so as to be kind.'

No wonder Maureen felt, as she put it, 'hit by a hurricane.' After one torrid evening, when Maureen said things, perhaps unintentionally, that made me despair of every being with her, I wrote of the pangs of 'grief and utter desolation' that 'from, the very first day I saw you until now have swept over me and through me, and never left me'. But I went on, as if to mitigate any feeling of guilt Maureen may had for causing such pain, that

'to me it seems a self- defeating and futile exercise to spend one's whole existence avoiding pain. At the risk of sounding patronising, I should remind Maureen the scientist that pain performs vital functions in the human organism. We humans are built to feel grief, to cause it, deliberately or otherwise, and through our unique faculties, transform it creatively into the most sublime works of art. Isn't that the true purpose of tragedy, viewed philosophically? It comprises the core of 'la condition humaine' from which we can never in reality escape...our mortality, or ultimate futility and in a sense puniness, but which are our spirit refuses to accept and even in its doomed struggle against it, transcends and illuminates the narrowness and confinements of our everyday routine-clogged lives. Did I seek pain when I fell in love with you? Of course not. But through a terrible inner conflict, I learned to accept it. I cannot say it was my choice, because I found and still find you totally irresistible. I will also say this, because for honesty's sake, I have to tell you, however absurd it might seem to you, that I would do anything I held to be on balance morally acceptable to be able to live out the rest of my life with you. The pain in me comes from knowing that the realty is very different.'

In the same vein, yet another letter assured her that whatever the outcome, 'seeing you again, despite the emotional stress that it has visited upon me has in the midst of all that given me moments of wonderful happiness'. Maureen was not toying with my feelings. Even in small matters, she had always found it hard to make up her mind.

Here she faced a decision which would not only bring dramatic changes to her life, but also no less so to those of others. True to her cautious nature, and entirely contrary to mine, Maureen refused to be rushed. And not only was there the traumatic legacy of her failed marriage to consider. Maureen was a both very honest and moral person, and she was all too aware that by agreeing to live with me, she would be taking upon herself some, if not equally, the responsibility of ending my marriage to Karen, in effect, doing to my wife what Terry's barmaid had done to her. However, there was an important difference between the two situations, that whereas Maureen had been left with a small child to bring up on her own, my two were long gone. Had this perhaps played a part in Maureen's final decision? I do not know, because I never asked her then or later. It is not the kind of question one asks, given the circumstances. What I do know is that in the end, her love for me overrode such considerations, just as mine did for her much more easily when it came to the fate of Les.

From what I have been able to glean about Les, partly from Maureen, but mainly from her daughter, he was a decent enough chap, but passionless and rather boring. What also proved in the end a minus was that despite living with his mum and having a well-paid job with the post office, he always seemed to be on the brink of insolvency, the consequence of all-too-frequent visits to the betting shop. The simple fact is that Les was a gambling addict, and like most of his kind, a loser, something that worked to my advantage. While I was wooing Maureen, Les visited her in Swansea, as he did from time to time when he could afford the petrol. The plan was that they would spend a few days motoring around Wales. As my luck would have it, Les ran out of cash, leaving Maureen, whose sole income was her state retirement pension, to pick up the bills. That was *finis* for Les. Once back home in Enfield, he rang Maureen to apologise, and Maureen, very unusually for her, told him to 'sod off' and put the phone down. A few days later, she phoned Les to tell him she was 'making a clean break'. All

Les could say was, 'I've blown it.' Indeed, he had. As Maureen told me a little later, 'Once you arrived on the scene, he didn't stand a chance.' With Les out of the way, the situation had become somewhat less complicated and stressful for both of us. Even so, I knew I could not convince Maureen to accept me just by bombarding her with love letters and angst-ridden phone calls. I had to plead my case face to face, and to spend such time with her as might help to persuade her that we could live together as lovers, as I put in one such impassioned letter, 'until one of us dies'.

So much for my rival. What of my domestic situation? Even before I had visited Maureen the first time, my wife had sensed that my thoughts, and possibly a lot else besides, were somewhere else. One day she confronted me, demanding to know what, if anything, was going on. Truthfully, at least as far as I knew and indeed intended at that point, I assured her she had nothing to worry about. Even if Maureen did reply to the letter I had sent her, or, and this was wildest extent of my hopes, even agreed to allow me to visit her, I could not envisage anything happening that would give grounds for her concerns. It is so obvious to me now that I was deceiving myself, and in so doing, also deceiving my wife. When I told her about my second visit, which as far as she knew, had been my first, she said, almost triumphantly, 'I knew it.' What she had known, precisely, she never said, but she knew 'something' was going on and she had been proved right. And now that 'something' was on the brink of becoming an affair with a woman I had loved for more than forty years, a liaison that I hoped would lead to us sharing what remained of our lives. If only I could find a way to see her again just a few more times, perhaps I could convince her.

Without being aware of it, Ian of Horsepower became my pretext for coming home in the early hours of the morning. I told my wife that Ian and I were working on some new songs for the band (this was in fact true), and I needed the car to get back late at night from Ian's place in Tottenham. My wife, who is six years younger than me, was still employed as nursery teacher, so once she had left for work, I would head off to Swansea, getting to Maureen's at around 11.00am. After about twelve hours with Maureen, I would then head back to London, arriving home at about two o'clock in the morning.

Maureen not only knew these visits were secret (how they have been anything else?) but, also from my letters, why I was making them. We established a routine of a sort. Weather permitting, we would go out in the afternoon, either into town, or to admire the splendours of the Gower Peninsula. On one such excursion, as we stood admiring the view, she suddenly clasped her arms around me, and held me tight. On another, while we walking side by side close to the sea, she gently rubbed her right breast against my left arm. In true Maureen fashion, she might say one thing, but her body was saying something else. Back at Maureen's we have would a meal and talk, for a while maybe about matters of mutual interest, but more often, and at greater length, about our possible future together. It was during one such torrid exchange in which she, as was her way, had raised all manner of doubts as to what I was proposing, that she blurted out as if to mitigate them, 'I do you love.' Stunned, for this was first time I had ever heard say those magical words, I asked her to repeat them. This time she simply said, 'I love you.' I took this unprecedented affirmation of her love for me as a sign that the barriers that she had been raising were beginning to tumble. It must have been on my next visit that I felt bold enough to take matters a step further, to a place where we had been so long ago.

Early in the evening, I asked her, in a very matter-of-fact way, making it as easy as possible for her to say her favourite word, if she would go to bed with me. Without any hesitation, she said yes, knowing full well what it would lead to. Not wanting to put her under any pressure to do something she might later regret, I said nothing more about it, leaving the moment to her. A while later she invited me up to her bedroom. We lay down side by side on her bed, initially fully dressed. We kissed, and I began to caress her.

Now aroused, she said to me, as if I could have forgotten, 'I love having my breasts stroked, especially around the nipples.' Soon she was lying on the bed, naked, with me gazing at her still beautiful body. I said to her, not to flatter, but because it was true, 'You have the figure of a woman half your age.' I so madly wanted to possess it. And she wanted me to no less. Like our very first attempt at love making all those years ago – thirty-six to be precise – not all went according to plan. It was all still very novel. But given time, I knew it could and hoped it would, once we were together. Having crossed one Rubicon, I wrote to her some days later, reminding of how far we had come since my first visit, and pressed as never before to come to a decision, so that we might cross a second.

'You can manage to say, without being prompted, that you love me. You also say in the latest lingo that you 'cannot get your head round' the idea of what living an everyday life with me would be like. Perhaps not. Nor can I with you. If I could picture it all before, where would be the joy, the magic and the surprise (and shocks) of the adventure, for such it would and should be. But Maureen, some things, quite important ones you might agree, we do know already. Aside from that we have always shared, and which is as rich and exiting as ever (more so now because you no longer defer to me), we have shared, in the times I have visited you (six now) many quite ordinary hours doing ordinary things together without, I trust, serious mishap. We also, I seem to recall, shared your bed. Did any of these things prompt you to think we were not suited to live together not just now and again, but every day until one of us dies? Each time we meet, or talk it seems to me (correct me if I am wrong) we draw closer together. I cannot believe you continue to indulge me because you are little bored and need amusement. I implored you, sometime ago now, in a letter, that if this was to lead nowhere, then you must be cruel to be kind.'

XII

As can so often happen, what, as I have already said, we call chance events finally forced Maureen's hand. The approach to her street was via a dual carriage way that led off the M4. Failing to notice that the speed limit was only forty miles an hour, on one of my visits, and this would have been early in December, I was caught by a police camera without my being aware of it. A few days later, there arrived in the post a police notice addressed to my wife, since the car was in her name. When she opened it, but before she had a chance to read it properly, I told her it must be me, and where I was when it happened. Naturally, and justifiably she was furious. Even though I had not confessed to all my other visits, she understood that what she had sensed and feared at the very beginning was now a reality. It was time for me to tell all, or at least as nearly all that made no difference. This I owed to my wife, who unlike me had been so loyal over all the years of our marriage.

I had to tell her what Maureen meant to me, that she had been my first love, and that I had never forgotten her. When she demanded to know who exactly Maureen was – including of course her name – I said nothing about Maureen and I becoming lovers all those years ago, only that we had been very close friends for a number of years, and that by the time I had met my wife, Maureen and I had parted. Even without knowing the truth, she sensed at once what had really happened, that she had been a replacement for Maureen. 'It was too soon…you should never had married me,' she sobbed. And she was right. What I did all those years ago had come back to haunt us both, and was now destroying her marriage. And I alone must take full responsibility for that. I did not have to marry Karen. Neither did I have to seek out Maureen. I had used and abused Karen's love for me as a means to heal my own self-inflicted emotional wounds, and now, thirty-six years later, she, not me, was paying the price of my deceit.

Due to another chance happening, the crises in the lives of all those involved – myself, my wife and Maureen – escalated rapidly. Since my retirement from full-time lecturing, I had taken up private tutoring, and after this confrontation, just before I went out to tutor a student, I phoned Maureen firstly to tell her what had happened, and secondly, to ask her if I could come to see her that very same night. Although her daughter was staying with her at the time, she said yes. Then, without telling my wife where I was going, I took the car and left to visit my student. A little more than an hour later, I was on the M4 to Swansea. Needing to fill up with petrol for the trip, I stopped at the Reading service station, and while there, phoned my wife to tell her where I was going. As far as I was concerned, I had burned my bridges, and I was about to throw myself on Maureen's mercy and, I hoped, her love. But I quickly discovered that my wife had no intention of letting me go quietly. After I left, she had retrieved Maureen's number by dialling 1471, and then rang her up to find out what was really going on and, whatever it was, to try put a stop to it.

What little she told me about that exchange very strongly suggested that my wife had succeeded. Not knowing all the details of what had passed between my wife and Maureen, and therefore whether to continue to Swansea or turn back, I opted for the latter. I asked my wife, 'Shall I come home?' She said yes. That same evening, I was given the full story. This time I was left with no doubt that Maureen had been effectively warned off. My wife began by telling me that Maureen had assured her she was 'not a marriage wrecker', to which my wife replied that even if we did get together, it would not last five minutes. My strange ways would make me impossible to live with. 'You mean his obsessions,' Maureen is supposed to have replied. And more in the same vein. 'Have you been to bed with Robin?' my wife asked. 'No' Maureen lied. I once had an affair with a student, my wife lied back. Maureen later told me, when I truthfully denied it, that she didn't care if I had. I don't blame my wife one little bit for behaving as she did. She was fighting to salvage a marriage that, with all its ups and downs, had lasted thirty- six years, and a few lies or half-truths here or there were as nothing compared to the catalogue of my deceptions and infidelities.

Over the next few days, life at home returned to a semblance of normality. My wife truly believed – and so did I to be frank – that it was over. But even so, the pull of Maureen was too strong to resist. What must she be thinking of me know? Had she believed everything my wife had said about me? Early the next week, I think it was a Tuesday, my band Blowpipe was playing a gig in Camden. After the sound check, I found a phone box close by, and in state of great trepidation, l called Maureen. 'I wondered when you were going to call,' she said almost triumphantly. Overjoyed, I asked, are we still friends? Can I see you again? Each time, the answer was yes. Assuming that the threat to our marriage had been quashed, and I said or did nothing to disabuse her of that illusion, my wife's vigilance slackened sufficiently to enable me to engineer one last visit to Maureen before the final denouement that took place, some might say symbolically, on the first day of the new Millennium. And again, it was quite by chance.

As she regularly did, Maureen came to London that Christmas to stay with her daughter and her partner in Enfield. My wife was visiting her sister's family in the West Country, so I arranged to meet Maureen off the train at Paddington, and help with her luggage. It felt so strange to see and be with her in London again after so long, travelling together on the tube and then the bus, the last time being back in September 1960 on our West Side Story date. I stayed for a while at Andrea's and then made my way back home. A desultory Christmas came and went. Then just after midnight on New Year's Day, I rang Maureen at her daughter's home on our upstairs extension to give her my new Millennium greetings. Downstairs, my wife had picked up the other phone and was listening in. Whether she had intended to make a similar call, or had suspected what I might be up to, I do not know. It made no difference anyway. Once I had finished my call to Maureen, she confronted me, and said I had to go. 'You're a philanderer,' which given the circumstances, was fair comment. She was not sharing me with another woman. A few days later, I went to see Maureen to tell her what had happened, wondering how she would react now that I had received my marching orders. A few weeks previously, she had she had made the rather unrealistic, from my point of view, suggestion that I could come and stay with her for a few days to see how we got on. And now, partly because of her, I was effectively homeless. But it was not so much that which pushed Maureen over the brink, but the sudden death of a very good friend. Why wait any longer? *Cape diem.* She said we should go back to Swansea together.

When I told my wife what I intended to do, there were no scenes, no histrionics. She simply said I had gone mad, which in a way was true, and that she wished I was dead, which was also understandable, because I had treated her abominably. She calmly told me she wanted me out of the house by no later than 16 January, and that she would be seeking a legal separation, which I said I would not contest. As the totally innocent party, I said she would have the car, the house, and all its contents except for my books, my personal effects, my musical instruments and the rolling stock and locomotives of my model railway. We split our joint bank account down the middle, and that was that. On the day before my departure was due I hired a van, loaded up some, but far from all of the items I would be taking to Swansea, and drove over to Enfield to collect Maureen. A few hours later, we were on the M4, heading for a life together that should have begun so many years before. We had a lot of catching up to do.

Our journey back to Swansea was none too auspicious. The fuel indicator in the van I hired had stuck, and we ran out of diesel in of all places on the middle of the Severn Bridge. With the assistance of the AA, we got moving again, and arrived at 169 Pentregethin Road late that evening, leaving the unloading of the van to the morning, after which I intended to head back to London to collect the remainder of my books. But even in those first few hours with Maureen, it became evident that she would initially find it much harder to adjust to the reality of living with me than I with her. True, I had chosen not only to leave my home and my wife, but also to put two hundred miles between myself and my two children, my friends, and my musical life, and because of that choice, had found myself in a strange city where I knew no one except Maureen. On the other hand, Maureen had given up nothing except her independence. And therein lay the problem.

Maureen had not shared her life and her home with a man since the break up her marriage twenty-seven years previously. In between myself and Terry, there had only been the decent but dull and predictable Les, he with his mum in Enfield and Maureen for most of that time in Swansea. It was only five months since I had burst in on her life as she once put it 'like a whirlwind', and now here she was giving me a key to her front door! And then there were my books. Maureen had always liked order in her life, with everything in its right place, and now, stacked up on her living room floor were umpteen piles of books, several feet high. And when I told her there were at least as many still to come, she, uncharacteristically, panicked. All her bookcases and shelves were full to bursting, so where would they go? Matters were not helped when a day or so later, in the middle of the night, all the stacks toppled over and woke her up. Relations between us did not improve when, the next day, I returned with another van load of books, which just like the first, toppled over in the middle of the night, with the same result. (Today, after a steady flow of additions to our collections over the next seventeen years, our combined total of volumes is in the region of three thousand.)

The main problem, however, was not my books, but me. Having lived as a single woman for twenty-seven years, it had only now dawned on Maureen that her life was about to change radically, in ways both practical and emotional, that she had probably not previously considered. When I went into her bedroom on the first morning to see if she was awake, she gave me an almost terrified look, as if I were a total stranger. And in a way, I was, because I was no longer an occasional visitor, but living with her. Simply my presence threatened to and in fact unavoidably did disrupt the routine and rhythm that had been her life since she moved to Swansea more than a decade previously. Because, unlike me, Maureen was very much a creature of habit, a trait accentuated by the fact that for much of her adult life, she had lived on her own. Not having to share her home with anyone else, it had been easy enough for Maureen to keep her home just the way she liked it. As I quickly discovered after I moved in, everything in every room had to be kept in or returned exactly to its place. Cushions had to be plumped up, curtains had to be drawn so far, but no further, and with no folds, sheets tucked just so. Conforming to these exacting requirements posed no technical problems that with a little effort, I could not overcome. But the same was not true of my eating habits, or more precisely my seemingly congenital propensity to spray crumbs in all directions but the plate when I consumed biscuits, cakes or sandwiches. Even holding the plate directly under my mouth failed to prevent the accumulation of detritus under my chair.

For the first few days, the emotional stress was such that it told on Maureen's appetite. For the next week or so, she had to virtually force feed herself, a reoccurrence of an eating disorder, which though I did not know it at the time, she had experienced when Terry walked out on her in 1973. However, in at least one important matter, we had already reached an understanding. Maureen had become so used to sleeping on her own that she felt unable to accommodate my wishes in that respect. This did not inhibit our love making, because when the need, or rather the urge arose, we would visit each other's bedrooms, an arrangement that undeniably added a certain *frisson* to the proceedings.

With all my belongings in Swansea, I now had to drive back to London yet again to return the van to the hire company, and buy myself a car. Both tasks accomplished, I rang Maureen on my recently acquired mobile phone and told her I would be coming back that same evening. I could tell by the tone of her voice that something had changed. In the middle of our conversation, she suddenly said, almost desperately, as if she feared I would not be coming back, 'I love you.' A matter of a few hours later, I was given all the proof I needed. We made love for the first time. The next day, I was back on the road again, this time for a gig in London with Horsepower. Ian had agreed to put me up for the night before and after the gig. Ian, as I have said, lived in Tottenham. What I didn't say was that his house was but a stone's throw from Lentheric. That first evening, I crossed over the road from Ian's house in Mount Pleasant Road and walked the few yards down Lawrence Road to the Lentheric building on the left. There was my yard, deserted. So was the building. It was undergoing renovation. The side door leading from the yard into what had once been Lentheric was open. I climbed the stairs to the first floor. Could this be real? Could I be standing at the very spot where, forty-three years before, I first glimpsed the glorious beauty of the woman who was now my lover? I rang Maureen on my mobile phone, and my voice breaking with emotion, described where I was. She too was greatly moved. We had both come full circle.

Soon our lives settled into a routine, for the most part like any other retired couple's, the only difference being, and it was big one, was that we were not approaching the end of our lives together, but just beginning. There was the weekly visit to Tesco's, followed by a snack at our favourite café. Every other weekend I would drive back to London for my round of tutoring, sometimes staying overnight with Maureen's daughter. One bright February day, we made our first excursion out of Swansea via the Brecon Beacons to Hay-on-Wye, home of the famous book fair, where we had our first meal out, the first of many, in a pub. All very ordinary, but for me, sheer joy. On the way back, she asked me, out of the blue, although it must have been playing on her mind since the day I had moved in, 'Do you miss your wife?' I replied, 'Yes of course I do.' But I could not leave it at that. So I added, 'I have chosen to live with you because after all our years apart, I want to give you what remains of my life.' We left it at that, though the subject did come once more some days later, when we were in bed together. Obviously, still unsure about my commitment to her, Maureen said to me, 'Absence makes the heart grow fonder,' and asked if I had any regrets. I replied, quite truthfully, 'None whatsoever.' That subject was never raised again.

As I had hoped, in many respects, the move to Swansea had little or no impact on my previous activities and commitments. Now that I had my own car, a Ford Escort, I was able to make the round trip to London every other weekend to continue with my private tutoring, which brought in an extra five hundred pounds or so per month. And of course, there was the music, both with Horsepower, and my own band Blowpipe, whose album, *Epilogue* had just come out on the Roundabout label. Only a couple of weeks after I moved in with Maureen, I had to go to London for a meeting with the company that was promoting the album. I met Andrew outside their office, and the first words he said to me were, 'You've done the right thing.' What he said did not rid me of my feelings of guilt but I was glad that he bore me no malice for the distress I had inflicted on his mother.

Because of our very different marital histories, my relationship with Maureen's daughter was inevitably different from hers with my two children. I had arrived back in Maureen's life long after her separation from Terry, whereas Maureen, as she would later acknowledge, still felt guilty for her part in the ending of my marriage to Karen. As she once explained to me, for this reason she felt unable to have any dealings with Andrew, because she assumed that given the special relationship that she believed existed between mothers and sons, he would always harbour resentful feelings towards her for being instrumental in breaking up his mother's marriage. I told her many times this was not so, but it made no difference. The only contact between Maureen and Andrew, apart from a very brief encounter in London when we sat in the car while I waited for Andrew to come home, was on the odd occasion when she took phone calls to me from him.

With Katharine, though for similar reasons, it was totally different. Maybe because of Maureen's special love for her Freddy, she rightly assumed that Katharine was closer to me than she was to her mother. Maureen first met Katharine at a Baebes gig in Carmarthen, one that echoed the provenance of the music with vintage medieval food and beverages. Katharine had arranged that Maureen and I were given the best seats in the marquee, and just before we took our places, I persuaded a rather hesitant Maureen to say hello. And Katharine had news for me. I was going to be a grandfather. The ice broken, Maureen never had any problems on the later occasions she met up with Katherine at Baebes gigs. At one, she even took on the role of baby minder. We had been invited to a New Age extravaganza on Bodmin Moor, and while she was on stage, Katharine asked Maureen to look after her recently born daughter, Ava. We then spent the night at the nearby home of one of the Baebe's singers, Emily Ovenden, whose highly eccentric artist father Graham was engaged in building single-handed in his sprawling twenty-two-acre estate a replica Gothic castle, 'Barley Splatt', which remained uncompleted until it was sold in 2008 and converted into a B&B hotel.

The next morning, Katharine took the Baebes on a country hike, while Maureen again looked after Ava. Katharine had been most insistent that Graham and I should meet, fulfilling a long-harboured wish that what she described as 'two mad geniuses' could indulge their various mutual obsessions. In that respect at least, she was right.

Graham was undoubtedly a man of many talents. Before taking up painting and writing books on art, Graham had trained as a musician, graduating at the Royal College of Music. He then switched careers, and graduated at the Royal

College of Art in 1968. In 1975, he founded the Brotherhood of Ruralists, and over the next thirty years, in addition to his painting and photography and authoring a large number of books on art, his work has been the subject of television programmes and films.

However, it was our mutual musical interests which occupied us that morning. He revealed to me his vast collection of first edition records going back as far as the end of the 19th century. It was a collectors Aladdin's cave, worth millions. I selected for playing one that especially caught my eye, a violin solo by Josef Joachim, whom Brahms chose as the soloist for the first performance of his violin concerto back in 1879, one of Maureen's favourite compositions as well as mine. And now I could hear him, more than century after he made this record, clear as a bell, perfect intonation, such a pure, sweet sound. It moved me to tears. I was listening to a friend of Brahms. Graham's musical knowledge was as vast as his record collection. Discussing our likes and dislikes, he made clear to me his dislike of Mahler, and attributed what he regarded as his excessive play-time on Radio Three to a Jewish plot at the BBC. At this, my ears pricked up. A little probing revealed that he was a devout Christian. 'How can you believe all that nonsense?' I asked him. 'I'm too old to give it up,' he replied, more than a little embarrassed. And then he made a cryptic remark whose significance I only later came to appreciate. 'Besides, the local vicar has been a great help to me.' Over what was no business of mine, so there the matter ended, and we resumed our conversation about music until the Baebes returned from their hike, and it was time to head back to Swansea. I was so happy that Maureen and my daughter had really hit it off.

It was only after our overnight stay with the Ovendens that I learned from Katharine that in addition to his other personal quirks, Graham had something of a track record as a suspected paedophile. Many of his art works had children as their subjects, and childhood as their theme, but this in and of itself is no proof of paedophilia. After numerous brushes with the law and customs officials, none of which led to criminal charges being brought, in 2013, a couple years after our visit, Graham was found guilty at Truro County Court on six charges of indecency with a child and one of indecent assault on a child, and was given a twelve-month prison sentence, suspended for two years, which on appeal, was converted into an immediate prison term of twenty-seven months. His wife, who was also an artist, left him, while his daughter, Emily of the Baebes, coped as best she could, and continued with her musical career. The sequel does little credit to the integrity of our artistic institutions. Following his conviction, works by Graham Ovenden that had been on display for years at the Victoria and Albert Museum and the Tate Gallery were removed from public view.

XIII

When I moved in with Maureen, I quickly discovered that aside from the Jehovah Witnesses, Maureen had no real friends in Swansea. There were of course relatives from her mother's side of her family, but all her long-standing friends had been left behind in London when she made the move to Wales. Not that it troubled her greatly because both by temperament and of necessity, she was self-sufficient to a degree. I too had left both friends and family in London. But nevertheless, after I moved in, we always had company, indeed, a substitute family. On my arrival, there were two cats in residence, Mitch and Richard, like all their predecessors and successors, both strays. They were then soon joined by Pippin, ginger like Richard. Mitch then died, to be replaced the burly Eric, my favourite, yet another ginger tom. Two female strays then deposited their litters in our living, room, which together with their mothers, we were able to offload onto a cattery. Then yet another ginger tom arrived, Tristan, making four in all. It was one too many for Eric, who gave Tristan rather a bad time. Tristan soon took the hint, heading for cat flaps and feeding bowls anew, and who knows, an Isolde. The last two to arrive were the all-black Sophie, being female, the only one to take a fancy to me rather than Maureen, and the all-white Frankie. One by one, the ginger toms died, followed by Sophie. Then, shortly after Maureen died, Frankie left me, though a cocky little black tom we called the intruder carried on popping in for while when the fancy took him, striding up and down on the kitchen work top until he was fed.

Some years ago, our garden became a home for a family of hedgehogs, who in season came up in the night to the kitchen doorstep for their feed from a cat bowl, and also for foxes, who were fed from a larger bowl up the garden path. Sadly, the hedgehogs have gone, but I have inherited from Maureen the obligation to ensure that the fox or foxes are properly nourished.

Among our shared joys was in the spring to drive along the coastal road to the Mumbles, on the way viewing the masses of daffodils then bursting into bloom, to a café at the road's end, where on a clear day there is a glorious panoramic view across the Bristol Channel of Devon and the Quantocks Hills. Coming and going, at Maureen's instigation, we would make-believe that at certain location along the way, where the road passes through a cutting between high rocks on either side, there dwelt the spirits of our departed cats and her beloved Freddy. We would say a cheery hello on the way out, and on the way back, a fond goodbye. The last time was a sunny day in September 2016, four months before I bid Maureen farewell at the nearby Singleton Hospital. It was only when, a year later, my daughter and her two children came to stay with me that I was able to summon the courage to return to this sacred place, where my Maureen used to reveal the child-like nature that I so adored.

And then there was our love making, the initial frequency of which prompted Maureen to comment after the first few weeks of our living together that we were 'going at it like teenagers'. True, but we had a lot of catching up to do. And whatever happened to Maureen the would-be nun? Her explanation, one that I found very flattering, was that it was not sex as such, but me, that turned her on. 'You only have to touch me and my knees start to wobble.' I was even more flattered with her compliment that I was 'a very unselfish lover', a mode of approach to the task in hand that she contrasted favourably with what she called 'wham bam thank you ma'am'.

When two people decide to live together, from the outset, all manner of personality quirks that previously were not so obvious quickly reveal themselves. Maureen's were of a pattern; essentially concerned with a profound need for order and routine in her life and home, and related to that, stubbornness, to the nth degree. Once Maureen got an idea or an opinion into her head, it was a truly herculean task to dislodge it, no matter what evidence might say to its contrary. I had forewarning of this trait when I discovered after I found her again that she was a great admirer of Catherine de Medici, the wife of Henry II of France, and the mother of three useless brats who all became French Kings, Francis II, Charles IX and Henry III. Maureen simply would not have it that Catherine was in any way complicit in the massacre of the protestant Huguenots unleashed by Charles IX on St Bartholomew's Day, 24 August 1572. Even when I sent her a photocopied excerpt from a biography of Catherine that contained irrefutable evidence to the contrary, Maureen would not have it. As if by way of either refutation or mitigation, I was regaled with the *non-sequitur* of a fourteen-year-old Catherine being raped on her wedding night by Henry II, and of her husband's subsequent carryings-on with his official mistress, Diane de Poitiers. When she saw her coat of arms prominently displayed at the Chateau de Chenonceaux in the Loire Valley near Amboise, she came as near to I have seen to exploding, because it was then that she realised that the chateau was a gift from Henry to Diane.

Let me relate another instance of Maureen's stubbornness. On my very first visit to Maureen we talked about many things, including her involvement with the Jehovah Witnesses. We were sitting in the kitchen at the time, having a cup of tea, and I happened to make the remark that the authors of the Bible were scientifically illiterate, offering as proof what I understood to be their belief that the earth was flat. Maureen insisted I was mistaken. In the Bible, (she did not say precisely where) the earth is described as a 'globe'. There we let the matter rest, since I assumed that the source of this claim could well have been her Jehovah friends, who certainly knew their Bible, and had as I later discovered, supplied Maureen with reading material that included articles upholding its scientific validity. Then some years later, I found a website on the internet that cited numerous passages from the Bible which, it claimed, in some cases tenuously, proved that whoever wrote them believed the earth to be flat. So, I asked Maureen, where exactly is this reference to a 'globe'? I never found out, because it isn't there. But Maureen went on believing, or at least claiming, it was.

Another friendly bone of contention was Maureen's monarchism, or from her point of view, my republicanism. From time to time during our seventeen years together, I had what I believed to be legitimate cause to criticise the intrusion of Prince Charles into the process of parliamentary legalisation, demanding, and being given the opportunity to scrutinise bills before they became law, and even securing changes in their wording to accommodate his own idiosyncratic preferences. While not defending this particular abuse of royal influence, Maureen's argument in favour of monarchy was that it acted as a check on the otherwise excessive powers of the Prime Minister. I have lost count of the times I tried to explain to her that the theoretical powers of the monarchy, namely, the royal prerogatives, are in practise exercised by the Prime Minister, thereby not acting as check on the office, but the reverse. It made no difference. Unlike many of mine, Maureen's views on such matters were set in concrete and nothing, least of all fact and rational argument, was going to dislodge them. I think it was more matter of honour and pride than any deeply rooted political philosophy that was the cause of this inflexible attitude. I say this, because it even extended to music.

Though Maureen's favourite composer was Sibelius, she had a great liking for Bach, or rather I should say some of it. While hooked on his Preludes and Fugues and Brandenburg Concertos, she had somehow got it into her head that she couldn't stand Bach's church cantatas. When I tried to explain to her that Bach's B Minor Mass, which she once famously described as 'glorious', was assembled largely from segments borrowed from his cantatas, it made no difference. B Minor mass good, cantatas bad. It left me wondering where and when had she heard any of Bach's cantatas? There were none in her record collection, while when I arrived back on the scene, her main radio listening was The Wave, a local Swansea news and pop music station.

It was in arguments such as this that Maureen, with perhaps more than a little justice, used to accuse me of treating her like one of my students. So in the matter of the monarchy, I appealed to a far higher authority than mine, and one that as a lover of the classics, she greatly respected, namely Edward de Veer, the 14th Earl of Oxford, whom Maureen and I agreed wrote the plays attributed to the illiterate imposter of Stratford. (He, the supposed author of Hamlet and a score or more similar masterpieces, on the five attempts he made to spell his name on a legal document, did so on each occasion differently and with a barely legible scrawl, and in his will, left not a single book to his next of kin, including his two daughters, who were also both illiterate.) I persuaded her to read a speech by Richard II in the tragedy of that name, worth of the quoting because it encompasses all who, however briefly, have wielded the sword of state:

'For God's sake, let us sit upon the ground
And tell sad stories of the death of kings;
How some have been deposed, some slain in war,
Some haunted by the ghosts they have deposed,
Some poison'd by their wives, some sleeping killed;
All murder'd; for within the hollow crown
That rounds the mortal temples of a king
Keeps Death his court, and there the antick sits,
Scoffing his state and grinning at his pomp;
Allowing him a breath, a little scene,
To monarchise, be fear'd and kill with looks,
Infusing him with self and vain conceit,
As if this flesh which walks about our life
Were brass impregnable; and humour'd thus
Comes at the last, and with a little pin
Bores through his castle wall, and farewell king.'

For someone who academically had excelled in subjects that place a premium on evidence and proofs, Maureen found it very hard, and in some respects, impossible, to admit she had got something wrong. This was not the Maureen that I first knew all years ago, who if anything was a little deferential to what she assumed was my superior knowledge in matters of mutual interest. Her mental toughness could sometimes become a rigidity that inhibited her from embracing new ideas and doing new things. I believe this stubbornness was a trait acquired out of necessity in her later years of stress and sacrifice. However, when the boot on the other foot, my political past was fair game for not only criticism, but ridicule, a conclusion I had as a matter of fact come to some good few years before we met again. I was a sitting and deserving target for Maureen's derision, with my delusion, one with no more foundation in reality than the myths of the Bible, that Britain was ripe for a re-enactment of the Bolshevik Revolution of 1917, compared with which her admission that she voted Tory in 1979 was a minor *faux pas*.

Disputes over the Bible aside, while neither of us believed in the hereafter, with the exception of our shared loathing for the Catholic Church, we never quite saw eye to eye over religion, chiefly I think because when it came down to it, Maureen was non-religious whereas I am unashamedly anti-religious, not in the sense that I want it banned, since I believe that freedom of expression is everyone's right, no matter what their opinions, but because, as in ages past, religion is responsible for most of the misery, mayhem and murder being visited on our planet today.

Maureen was half-Welsh by birth, but wholly so in her appreciation and advocacy of the culture and natural beauty of her chosen homeland. Though not a Welsh speaker, she could get her tongue around the place names with some facility. Again, on my very first visit, I was submitted to an impassioned harangue about the attempt by the English to eradicate the Welsh language, including the beating of school children who slipped back into their mother tongue. She was also far more knowledgeable than me about Welsh history, what little I did know only having to do with its trade union and political movements of recent times. And of course, there was rugby.

Swansea, as I quickly came to learn, is in many ways two cities. One, as depicted in the film *Twin Town*, of junkies, drug dealers, joy riders, tattooed and grossly obese men and woman and Saturday night punch-ups, and another of high culture, with its proliferation of male voice choirs (also, to be fair, featured in the film, at its end), brass bands, jazz and classical music festivals, live drama, art exhibitions and legacy of renowned musicians, artists and writers. To give but one example. We were in town on the day the box office opened for the performance of Bach's B Minor Mass by the Leipzig Sankte Thomas Kirke boys choir and orchestra at the Brangwyn Hall, so just to make sure we had seats near the front, we called in at the Grand Theatre to make our booking. When I looked at the plan of the seating, I was stunned to see that at least half of its 1070 seats had already been sold. And it was the same with Handel's Messiah. Twin city indeed.

Until my arrival in Swansea, without ever having watched a top-level match, I had always dismissed rugby, with its randomly bouncing ball, as a game of chance and brute force, not and skill and. brains. This proved to be a typical footballer's prejudice. Even though to this day I still do not understand all the rules, it did not take me long to realise how wrong I had been. Watching the Six Nations with Maureen, it became obvious to me that the muscle power on display was being deployed with as high level of tactical sophistication as could be seen on any Premiership football pitch. And not only that, I had become accustomed to watching prima donna multi-millionaires who, after the slightest body contact (and even none at all) theatrically topple over and writhe on the pitch in simulated agony, and in flagrant violation of the rules, surround the referee in invariably futile attempts to secure the reversal of his decision. Now I was watching real men who played not for the money but the pride, and with passion, relentlessly pounding the daylights out of each other without wincing, and accepting the rulings of officials without whinging. The difference was well captured by a Welsh commentator of a particularly bruising Six Nations encounter between Wales and Ireland. Wales, hanging on to the slenderest of leads, for the last ten minutes of the game, had withstood a relentless Irish siege feet from the line. He said it was 'all about brotherhood'. How non-PC can you get?

Compatibility does not imply or require similarity. It was a matter of frequent comment, mainly by Maureen be it said, that our personalities and temperaments could hardly be more different. And though as I came to know her again, it became obvious that as before, we had many interests in common, the same was not necessarily so with regard to our opinions, tastes and beliefs. And that was all to the good, for otherwise, what would we have had to argue about? It was what I call creative friction. The breadth of Maureen's interests are partly reflected in some of the titles which fill her shelves to bursting: Novels by Dickens, Trollope, Cordell, Buchan, Delderfield, Orwell, Tolkien, Hardy, the Brontes, Elliot and Austin, poetry anthologies and the poems of Dylan Thomas, John Betjeman, Byron, *The Mabinogion*, Homer's *Iliad* and Virgil's *Aeneid*, the Oresteian trilogy of Aeschylus, Aristotle's *Ethics*, *Birds of Europe*, *The Observer's Book of Wild Flowers* and *A Brief History* of *Time* by Stephen Hawking.

Differences there were in plenty, but nothing that harmed our love for each other. On the contrary, they added spice to it. And there were more important matters on which Maureen and I were in total agreement, more often than not of a moral nature. Top of the list was anti-Semitism and the increasingly fashionable hostility on the left towards Israel, which in addition to mine, led to several altercations with her daughter, whose views on the subject may well have contributed to her enthusiasm for Corbyn following his election as Labour Leader in September 2015. Maureen could not to bear to watch TV programmes that depicted the Holocaust, whether they were documentaries or films such as *Schindler's List*. She once said to me, with much feeling, 'We should be down on our knees before the Jews,' and she meant not only for what has been done to them, but for what they have done for others. And yet the classic anti-Semitic stereotype, one that gained a foothold in the Corbynite Labour Party, is of Jews constantly scheming to their own advantage. Strange, because as I have already pointed out, Jews, who comprise less than 0.2% of the world's current population, have been awarded 26% of all Nobel Prizes for medicine, which have been calculated to have contributed to the saving of 2.8 billion lives, including, we can be sure, of those who not only loath them but want them dead.

The first years of her childhood that she spent in the countryside implanted in Maureen a profound respect for and love of nature in all its variety, one that remained with her for the rest of her life. She totally rejected the arrogant assumption, originating in religion, and until recently subscribed to by many naturalists, that that we humans are uniquely endowed with the capacity for love, compassion, reasoning and grief. The more we observe and learn about animal behaviour, and discover about the mechanisms and workings of heredity, the more obvious it becomes that the human species has inherited not just some but all of its faculties from its evolutionary predecessors. Otherwise, where did they come from? *Ex nihilo*? A miracle? Or maybe another of Archbishop Cary's 'mysteries'. But evolutionary science has proved that we are merely the most recent link in an unbroken chain that reaches back four billion years. It is a sobering thought that we share 99% of our genes with chimpanzees. Along the way, long before our arrival on the scene, species evolved the capacities that the naïve believe are special only to us. Maureen was fascinated no less than myself by TV programmes that showed how elephants grieve, primates make as well as use tools, paddle makeshift boats, how insects devise, debate and decide on strategies for survival, swans and penguins fall in love, dolphins rescue drowning humans and whales compose songs which others learn. Often with the current state of the world obviously in mind, Maureen would turn to me and say triumphantly, 'And what do we humans do?' as if there was only one possible answer. And, no longer the naïve optimist I once was, I must concede she had a point.

Still waters ran deep in Maureen. Reserved and with her feelings only rarely not on the tightest of leashes, she revealed her other self in her musical preferences, which were anything but restrained. It was the human quality of the violin, with its lyricism, pathos and above all passion that for Maureen ranked the concertos of Brahms, Mendelssohn, Tchaikovsky and Sibelius among the compositions she loved the most. For similar reasons, Maureen preferred the intimacy and subtlety of the Modern Jazz Quartet to the brashness of the big bands. Modern pop music she abhorred, her tastes having being shaped in an era long past.

Our mutual interests were many, and no less our differences, both in opinions and what might be called lifestyles, so much so that to casual observer we might have seemed completely incompatible. Maureen, as I have said, was in all things inflexible to a degree, seemingly resistant to change on principle, whereas in many respects I am the diametric opposite, impetuous. This divergence of temperament led to many clashes, some of them in their own way retrospectively quite amusing, at least to me. I will give one example illustrative of many. I shall call it the battle of the pond. When Maureen bought her home in Swansea, she inherited a small pond in the garden. By the time I arrived at 169, its moulded metal lining had partially caved in. I must have lost count of the number times I suggested to Maureen that she let me get it back in proper working order, but each time I was fobbed off with one pretext or another. Several years went by until finally I took the law into my own hands. Early one sunny morning, long before Maureen was due to rise, I removed the old lining, enlarged and deepened the pond, and cemented in a lining of bricks around its walls. All it now needed was a new lining of waterproof sheeting. In a matter of hours, my act of insubordination was detected. Nothing was said, but it didn't have to be. For several days, relations were distinctly frosty. But within a week, Maureen was happily transforming the pond into the centre piece of her garden, as if that is what she had wanted all along. In fact, it was, but she just couldn't say it. How she came to say yes to me, when she couldn't say yes to a pond is beyond my comprehension.

Give our many divergences, it was just as well we could and did agree on issues that really mattered. One such was assisted suicide. Neither of us could see any valid objection to someone who is proven by those qualified to do so to be *compos mentis* seeking help in the ending of their lives, if that is their clearly expressed wish. Since suicide ceased to be a crime in 1961, the law has in effect recognised that our lives are our own. Despite this view being shared by a sizable majority of the British population, out of deference to unelected clerics, not one political party has had the courage or common decency even to raise the issue as a subject worthy of public debate, let alone argue that assisted suicide should be made legal, as it has been in a growing number of countries more civilised than my own.

Maureen being by habit a late riser, what her daughter called our joustings, were usually reserved for the evenings or in bed. A typical Griggs day would begin more mundanely around 1.00 pm with Maureen confronting me with a verbal list of misdemeanours that I had committed, knowingly or otherwise, over the previous twenty-four hours, usually prefaced with 'Oh, and by the way' or, less often, 'I'm sorry to be such a nag, but…' In fact, she wasn't sorry at all. It was her way of letting me know who was boss. My one and only complaint about Maureen, and in my estimation if not hers, it outweighed all Maureen's about me put together, was her smoking, because it tore us apart long before her time.

XIV

Although I still had musical commitments in London with Blowpipe and Horsepower, not long afrer I moved to Swansea, I discovered there was quite a scene just five minutes' drive away. The city's pubs specialised in open mike nights, when half a dozen or so acts would turn up and take turns to play a few numbers. However, my debut in Swansea came when I sat in on my cornet with a New Orleans band at the same venue. It was the first time Maureen had heard me play in public. She must have been impressed, because afterwards, as we walked to the car, she called me her hero. (The other occasion was after I released a beaver from a lakeside trap at a hotel where we were staying at in France. Not by accident, they both involved Maureen's two greatest loves...music and animals.) My next gig came when after answering an ad in the local paper for a saxophonist, I found myself playing at a lavish wedding party in the Mumbles. The star of the band was the lead singer, who did indeed have good voice, though the songs he sang were all cover versions of pop songs...not my thing at all. In the course of the evening, it became evident that he resented sharing the limelight with me, and said as much to the other members of the band, so I was not surprised when I was not asked to play with them again. However, the drummer, whose band it was, felt a little guilty, and by way of restitution, introduced me to Super Czar, a band he occasionally played the drums for in open mike nights at a pub called the Celtic Pride. The number I sat in on immediately hit a steady bluesy groove, and this time, on my muted trumpet, I felt entirely at home. At the end, the audience went wild, and I was signed up on the spot.

Over the next couple of years, the open mike nights became a regular evening out for Maureen and myself. Some of the acts were first class, and it was a real blow to the Swansea music scene when they came to an end after the pub changed hands. However, there were the monthly

Jazz open mike jazz sessions at the St James Social Club, where one could play a couple of numbers backed up by a top-class resident rhythm section. Super Czar carried on gigging around town for a while, recorded a couple of rather good albums, and then folded. I guested for a couple of other local bands, but nothing regular. Meanwhile, back in London, it was the same story. After also recording two well-received albums, Horsepower broke up when its lead guitarist emigrated to the USA after marrying an American lady, and its American bass player moved to Glasgow to pursue his legal career. Many years later, I discovered that my old friend and confessor Ian was in New York, still making good music. That left just Blowpipe.

When Andrew and I signed up with Roundabout, it did not take long for us to discover that not all was we had been led to believe. Bank-rolled by a multi-millionaire former school friend of one of its two producers, its real purpose, at least in the opinion of the other producer, the over-indulged scion of a wealthy Bavarian land-owning family, was to serve as the vehicle for his own inflated musical ambitions. The role allotted to Blowpipe in this scheme of things was to serve as visiting card and piggy back to his vanity project, Bridge and Tunnel. The critical success of our Epilogue album ideally suited his purpose. The trouble was, promoters did not want Bridge and Tunnel, only Blowpipe, despite a high-powered publicity campaign by the label that dwarfed the label's token efforts on our behalf. Andrew and I had no problem with Revolution, the company engaged to secure press reviews and radio play for our album. Their angle was to present Blowpipe as a family affair. 'Sultry jazz from the Blick family: legendry session brass and reeds player Robin Blick, his son Andrew, trumpet, and daughter Katharine, usually known as Katharine Blake, Mediaeval Baebes and Miranda Sex garden.' Given the opportunity, Andrew quite enjoyed exploiting the father-son dimension. In one interview entitled *Dad Rocks*, he was asked if it was 'weird' playing with his father. 'I try not to think about it,' replied Andrew. 'But when we play I forget he is my dad. It's a shame he's not here so you could ask him too.' When asked where I was, Andrew replied, 'He's out siring more children to join the band at a later date.'

After a gig at Le Batofar, a night club on a large boat moored on the Seine in Paris, followed by two more in the same city at the prestigious *La Scene* venue, we were, offered a UK tour by a leading promoter, but without Bridge and Tunnel. That was not the plan, so we found ourselves being cold-shouldered. No attempt was made to promote our album, despite offers of sales deals around the world. The result was boxes of unsold CDs ending up on the label's office floor. Once Andrew and I rumbled what was going on, we exercised our legal right to withdraw from our contract with the label. However, *Epilogue* proved a hit with two BBC radio shows that every week-day for about a year used tracks from the album as their theme music, resulting in a royalty pay out of around four thousand pounds, which Andrew and I split evenly between us. We recorded another album, *Sphere*, our fourth, under our own steam, and then called it a day. For some time to come, my musical life in London would consist only of the occasional recording session for my daughter's various projects. And with the demise of Super Czar and the open mike nights at the Celtic Pride, apart from the monthly sessions at the jazz club nothing much was happening for me in Swansea either. But I kept practising, just in case something turned up. And it did…Gyratory System.

Named after the enormous roundabout at the Hanger Lane, North Ealing, intersection of the A40 and the A406 North Circular Road, Gyratory System, like its predecessor Blowpipe, won acclaim for its innovatory vision. I thought of the name, but it was Andrew who conceived of the format, and was responsible for all the technical production. A little tongue in cheek, Andrew was quoted in one review of the band's first album, *The Soundboard Breathes* (a quote from Milton) as to how the music was assembled. 'Gyratory System is the malevolent, quivering creation of Dr Andrew Bick, by day a House of Commons employee, by night a musical scientist creating a surreal kraut-dance for true outsiders. His concept album The *Soundboard Breathes* was formed around a principle he calls "The process". In his own words, "We devise a formula to produce a backing track, then layer random performances on top of that, then re-arrange them using the original formula." In layman's terms, an accomplished trumpet player jams the hell out of series of mechanical one-man bands, then shuts himself in a laboratory to hone the results with his panpipe playing dad.'

In reality, it didn't quite work like that. Andrew in London would create or sample a backing track and email it to me in Swansea. I would then either improvise or work out parts to play on top of his track on a variety of instruments, and send the result back to Andrew in London. He would then select the parts he liked best, and produce a final track. The critics loved the final result, even if they didn't quite understand 'the process' that generated it. 'Liquid ecstasy', 'modern music for the dance scene in the *Wicker Man*', 'the light weary remnant of an alien marching band', 'processed through a myriad of deluded wobbly synthesisers and spat in your grimacing face', 'slightly maddening and totally compelling', 'this lovely, lurching thing', 'giddy shonky, maddening bleeps and shuffles, more demonic than harmonic, and all the better for it', 'the UK's oddest but most satisfying dance group', 'an utterly individual sound that makes you feel like you're going slightly unhinged', were just some of the attempts to capture the essence of the Gyratory sound.

We did a UK tour and recorded three albums on the left field Angular label before Andrew's academic duties and family obligations (he now has two boys) compelled him to retire, I hope only temporarily, from the music scene. I think Andrew would agree that Gyratory's greatest accolades were the invitation we received from the mega duo Soul Wax (in their other persona, Too Many DJs) to share the bill with them for two nights at the Brixton Academy after they had heard our first single, and to perform at an international electronic music festival in Neuchatel, Switzerland, in 2012. Several high-profile DJs took to the Gyratory sound, resulting in frequents plays on the BBC's Six Music, where we did a live studio session, and on Radio One and Radio Two.

Shortly after Maureen died, on February 2, 2017, I stayed for few days with Andrew's family in Acton, West London. While there, I met with up with James, the bass and keyboard player in Gyratory System, at a pub in Holborn. Seeing I was at very low ebb, he suggested we form a new group with a friend of his, another Andrew, a very competent drummer. Warming to the idea, I suggested that it should not be a mark two Gyratory System, but one that while also using a backing track, should allow space for me to improvise. (The parts to Gyratory System never varied by so much as single note, being played as if read from a musical score.) So was born the Blick Trio. (James proposed the name). Until the advent of Covid19, we gigged around London and recorded six tracks, one of which, *Ascension*, which I wrote in memory of Maureen, had radio play. Also since Maureen's death, I have recorded on several of my daughter's commercial projects, playing a wide variety of brass and reed instruments. But nothing in Swansea. For reasons that I should not have to explain, that era is over.

After I moved to Swansea, in 2000, I retained my interest in British and world affairs, but my two ruling involvements or rather passions, were now Maureen and music. Nevertheless, I transferred my Labour Party membership from Ealing to my local branch Swansea, but apart from some social events that Maureen came to, the only meetings I attended were two that selected the Swansea East parliamentary candidate, both of which, in view of the genes of all eight of those short-listed, looked to me suspiciously like female-only stitch-ups.

As for writing, I thought I had said all I wanted to say about the twin curses of the modern age; totalitarianism of the left and right. Now both were fading memories, never to return. Or so I thought. The UK far left seemed to be going the same way. Outside the Labour Party, the Healyites had split into half a dozen warring fragments, each barely visible even under a microscope. The Socialist Workers Party (the 'state capitalists'), once the largest group on the far left, were rocked by their own sex scandal, with multiple accusations of rape against some of its leaders, followed by mass resignations after a cover-up. The 'deep entryists' of the Militant Tendency also split after the fiasco of its attempt to Bolshevise Liverpool. The Communist Party that I was once a member of and then expelled from for factionalism had also split, into Stalinist pro-Moscow and democratic factions. The former were known as the 'Tankies' because of their enthusiastic support for Red Army invasions and occupations of Hungary, Czechoslovakia and Afghanistan, (Israeli occupation, bad, Soviet occupations, good). The Tankies retained the party name, its Muscovite loyalties even after the fall of communism and its daily paper, the *Morning Star* (previously the *Daily Worker*) in which appeared, from time to time, articles, chiefly on foreign policy, by a then obscure Labour MP, a certain Comrade Corbyn. The other fragment, composed largely of disillusioned ex-Stalinists, called itself the Democratic Left. The membership of the two combined could not have been more than a few hundred. All in all, the far left seemed to be following the Soviet bloc into terminal decline, while under Tony Blair's leadership, the Labour Party seemed to have finally laid the ghost of its own kamikaze leftism with its largest-ever general election victory in 1997, followed by two more in 2001 and 2005.

As for religion, everywhere in the western world, disbelief was on the rise, even, apart from the White House, in the USA. Christians had stopped killing each other in Northern Ireland and the Balkans. True, Islam had brought scenes redolent of the Third Reich to Britain's streets following Ayatollah Khomeini's death sentence *Fatwah* on Salman Rushdie, with Nazi-style burnings of his *The Satanic Verses* in Bolton and Bradford. But nobody was hurt, let alone killed. Then came 9/11, 7/7, al-Qaeda, Bin Laden, the Taliban, Hamas, the Islamic State, followed, like 9/11, seemingly out of nowhere, by another suicide operation, this one mounted by Comrade Corbyn and aimed at the Labour Party. A comprehensive account of its antecedents and consequences can be found in my *Socialism* of *Fools*, so I will only sketch their outline here.

The US response to the suicide attacks on September 11, 2001, was to invade Afghanistan to remove from power the Taliban regime that was harbouring the instigator of the operation, Osama Bin Laden. In its turn, the far left, with the Socialist Workers Party being the prime mover, launched the Stop the War Coalition with the aim of staging demonstrations to oppose the US military intervention. Amongst its founding members were Jeremy Corbyn, Labour MP for Islington North since 1983, the Labour veteran leftist Tony Benn, Tariq Ali, student protestor of the 1960s turned media mogul, the Saddamista former Labour and then Respect MP George Galloway, Kamil Majid of the British Stalin Society (!) and Andrew Murray, veteran of the Stalinist wing of the Communist Party, who served as the Coalition's first chairperson until replaced by Corbyn in 2011. (Murray later served as one of Corbyn's key advisers) This was far from being Corbyn's only involvement with what might be termed an Islamic cause. As we have seen, in 1982, he co-founded with Ken Livingstone what later became the Palestine Solidarity Campaign, and had been active in support of Unite Against Fascism, an organisation that has been criticised by human rights campaigner Peter Tatchell for being 'silent about Islamist fascists who promote anti- Semitism, homophobia, sexism and sectarian attacks on non-extremist Muslims'.

In the case of the Palestinian Solidarity Campaign, it is not a matter of silence about anti-Semitism that prevails, but its quite blatant and unashamed promotion. This scandal has been the subject of three surveys of the PSC's on-line postings, a selection of which I reproduce in *The Socialism of Fools*. Here I will only cite one that reflects directly on the integrity of one of its Patrons, Jeremy Corbyn. (Another was until 2018 the former Liberal Democratic Party Peer, Baroness Tonge, sacked from her party's front bench after accusing Israeli relief workers of harvesting the body organs of victims of the 2010 Haiti earthquake, and who in 2016, after being suspended, resigned from the party following another anti-Semitic outrage. After yet one more anti-Semitic scandal, (she insinuated that the murder of eleven Jews at a Pittsburgh synagogue by a far-rightist gunman was in some way provoked by Israel's treatment of the Palestinians) she was obliged to resign as a Patron of the PSC. Amidst all the PSC postings about Jews harvesting the body organs of children, Holocaust denials, a Holocaust approval, world Jewish conspiracies - 9/11 (of course), the Islamic State and the Paris massacres - we read the following, a posting by Tony Gratrex of Reading PSC:

'A century of deceit. Iraq, the World Wars, Holocaust, Zionist imperialism…In an effort to white-wash their own egregious war crimes, the Allies went along with the Zionists' premediated fictitious account of six million dead Jews. At the post-war Nuremberg trials, an Allied kangaroo court staffed to the brim with Zionist Jews and their Allied lackeys, the truth was buried under a tidal wave of falsehoods. The Zionist motives for the war were purposefully obscured and a cartoonish narrative of "Nazi evil" was foisted on the world. to advance the victors' post war aims for Europe and accelerate the Zionists' ambitions for Jewish ethno-state in Palestine.'

Here we see the totally uninhibited on-line ravings of a Neo- Nazi…and also of a member of the Reading branch of the Palestine Solidarity Campaign. But we see more than this. On the same website, we also see Jeremy Corbyn with his right arm around the Neo-Nazis' shoulders, smiling as they pose for a photo. Gratrex is clearly no stranger to Corbyn, nor, it is reasonable to assume are his views, which are there for all to see on the Reading PSC website. But most damning of all for Corbyn is another photo, taken at the 2016 Labour Party conference, where once again, he can be seen, again smiling, with the same right arm round the Neo-Nazi's shoulder. And I do mean the Labour Party conference, and not that of the British National Party

I have already related how Healy's WRP, as a direct consequence of its financial dependence on the Gaddafi regime, became entangled with anti-Semitic movements of the extreme right in their shared opposition to Israel. In the case of Corbyn and the neo-Nazi Gratrex, we see a similar alignment, with the crucial difference that it is acknowdged and based upon a shared membership of two organisations; the Palestine Solidarity Campaign and the Corbynised Labour Party. But Corbyn has also received unsolicited endorsement from a no less unsavoury source, namely David Duke, former Ku Klux Klan Grand Wizard and founder of the white supremacist National Association for the Advancement of White People. In a radio interview conducted by Duke just after the election of Corbyn as Labour Party Leader in September 2015, the Jewish conspiracy theorist James Thring, who had been a speaker the previous year at a Westminster meeting hosted by Corbyn, introduced himself as a 'long-standing friend of Jeremy', and then described how 'people like me and Jeremy are coming together over the Zionist and Jewish power....He doesn't mention Jewish power actually [correct , always "Zionist"], but you know, it's obviously behind his mind...I think it's quite clear from people like Jeremy and some of the people he's chosen for his [shadow] cabinet, like John McDonnell [on record as opposed to the existence of the state of Israel]...that they do know who is really running the country and they are itching both for an opportunity to make it known to the public and to do something about it.'

Revealingly, this comes from someone who regards himself as a 'long-standing friend' of Corbyn. And while Duke and Corbyn had never met (though they had both appeared on Iran's Press TV channel and been guests of war criminal President Assad of Syria, along with BNP Fuehrer Nick Griffin - three times no less - and three delegations of

European Neo-Nazi movements,) Duke's reply illustrates how, as was the case with the endorsement of Gaddafi's *Green Book* by Healy and the National Front, the far left and the far right can converge in a common cause: 'We must keep looking for sunshine and I do believe we are going to find sunshine in this world. Things are opening up.... I know you are a friend of Mr Corbyn and I know that you respect his position on the Middle East. It's a really good kind of evolutionary thing isn't it when people are beginning to recognise Zionist power and ultimately the Jewish power in Britain and the Western world?'

In addition to his involvement with Middle Eastern Jihadis and their equally anti-Semitic British apologists, Corbyn has yet another Islamic connection, being closely associated with the Shi'a theocracy in Iran to the extent of taking up paid employment as a host presenter on Iran's Press TV channel, together with an exotic galaxy of Zionist haters and baiters, including, Livingstone, George Galloway, a Tory MP, a Maoist, a Holocaust denier, a Jewish conspiracy theorist, Cherie Blair's half-sister and Islamic convert Lauren Booth, and a German neo-Nazi. In this capacity, as the House of Commons register of shows, Corbyn was paid £20,000 for four four-hour appearances, which calculates at £1,250 per hour. Nice work if you can get it. Corbyn made his last appearance in August 2012, eight months after Ofcom had fined Press TV £100,000 and banned it from broadcasting in the UK after it screened a Iranian political prisoner, who had obviously been tortured, making a forced confession. How did that Corbyn mantra go? Wasn't it 'A Kinder Politics'?

Corbyn and Livingstone, who both say they are opposed to capital punishment, were working for a regime that has the highest execution rate per capita per in the world, accounting for more than half of all global executions, and under which death is the punishment for 133 offences. each being dictated by the laws of the Religion of Peace. In the first six months of 2015, the year Corbyn was first elected Leader of the Labour Party, his former employers carried out 694 executions. Numbered amongst the tens of thousands who have been executed in Iran since the clerical fascist 'Islamic Revolution' of 1979 are leftists, trade unionists, poets, children, Kurds, feminists, secularists and homosexuals, who unlike the rest are sometimes not publicly hanged, but hurled from cliff tops, as required by Sharia Law. Adulterers, usually women, are stoned to death, again as per Sharia Law, while virgins sentenced to death are raped by guards the night before their hanging, because Iranian law states that virgins cannot be executed.

Even though Corbyn was reportedly too busy to visit the Holocaust Museum in Jerusalem, and declined a suggestion by his colleagues that he should visit Auschwitz, he has had no such difficulty in finding the time to do his bit for the Ayatollahs who want to wipe Israel off the map. Corbyn has been a speaker at the annual anti-Israel 'Quds Day' rally in London. (Quds is the Arabic for Jerusalem, the Israeli capital which Muslims, even though they have Mecca, claim exclusively for their religion.) It is convened at Ramadan by the Iran-sponsored terrorist movement Hezbollah, whose founding charter, like that of Hamas, calls for destruction of Israel, and whose leader, Sheikh Hassan Nasrallah, has called for the extermination of not only all the Jews of Israel, but of the entire world. Quds Day rallies held by Corbyn's former paymasters in Iran are always accompanied by chants of 'death to Israel', while Iran's Supreme Leader Ayatollah Khamenei has on several occasions declared his intention to 'wipe Israel off the map'. In 2009, Corbyn invited to a meeting he had convened at Westminster representatives of two movements that share Khamenei's goal. Announcing the event, this is what he said:

'It will be my pleasure and my honour to host an event in Parliament where our friends from Hezbollah will be speaking. I have also invited friends from Hamas to come and speak as well, so we can promote that peace, that understanding and that dialogue. The idea that an organisation that is dedicated towards the good of the

Palestinian people and bringing back long-term peace and social justice and political justice in the whole region should be labelled as a terrorist organisation by the British government is really a big, big historical mistake.'

Let us see who is making a big mistake. The Hamas Charter in operation at that time, dating from 1988, said nothing about either peace, understanding or dialogue with Israel. This is what it did say: Article 8: 'The Prophet of Allah says: "The last hour will not come until the Muslims fight against the Jews and the Muslims would kill them, and until the Jews hide behind a stone or a tree and a stone or tree would say: Muslim or Servant of Allah there is a Jew behind me; come and kill him, but the tree of Gharqad would not say it, because it as a tree of the Jews."'. Article 13: 'Peace initiatives, the so-called peaceful solution and the international conferences to resolve the Palestinian problem are all contrary to the beliefs of the Islamic Resistance Movement...There is no solution to the Palestinian Problem except by Jihad. The initiatives, options and international conferences are a waste of time and an exercise in futility.'

So much for Corbyn's 'peace' 'dialogue' and 'understanding'. Section three of the New Hezbollah Manifesto of 2009 says exactly the same: 'Our stance...is a total refusal to any kind of compromise with the Zionist entity [sic]'.

According to Wikipedia, between 1993, the year of the Oslo Accords between the Israeli government and the PLO in which both parties agreed on a 'two-state solution' to the Palestinian question, and 2005, Hamas was responsible (in most cases claimed responsibility) for 87 of the 171 suicide attacks against Israeli Jews, nearly all of whom were civilians. Just in the period between 2000 and 2005, of the 805 Israeli Jews killed, 503 were victims of Hamas, for example, the 21 killed at the Tel Aviv Dolphinarium and, the Haifa bus and Mazta Restaurant bombings, both with 15 victims. And Corbyn says it is it is a 'big, big mistake' to accuse Hamas of terrorism? One has to conclude either that Corbyn had not bothered to avail himself of these facts or read the Hamas Charter, and was therefore unwittingly acting as a Hamas 'useful idiot', to quote an apt phrase of Lenin's, or that he had, and therefore was lying. Or perhaps he does not regard these atrocities as 'terrorism' but necessary and therefore justified measures against the 'Zionist entity'.

If indeed Corbyn had done what any half-competent politician would have done as matter of routine, that is, check out the profile of an organisation before lavishing such unqualified praise upon it, he would have discovered, no doubt to his bemusement and horror, that he was included on the list of Zionist accomplices against which Hamas was fighting. Article 22 of the 1988 Hamas Charter identified movements and historical events which it claimed have served exclusively 'Zionist interests', among them 'the French and Communist revolutions' and 'most of the revolutions we hear about here and there'. So, the left is just one more manifestation and proof of the existence of that ubiquitous but always elusive world Zionist, or rather Jewish conspiracy. Hardly a novel idea, since it fills up page after page of Hitler's *Mein Kampf*, (in Arabic, *Li Jihad*) which in turn was but an elaboration of that notorious anti-Semitic concoction by Russian Orthodox clerics in the late 19th century, *The Protocols of the Learned Elders of Zion*. And sure enough, in Article 32 of the 1988 Hamas Charter we read the following:

'Zionist scheming has no end, and after Palestine they will covert expansion from the Nile to the Euphrates. Only when they have completed their digesting the area on which they will have laid their hand, they will look forwards to more expansion, etc. Their scheme has been laid out in the Protocols of the Elders of Zion, and their present conduct is the best proof of what said there.'

Such are Corbyn's 'friends'. So enamoured are they with Islam, the religion, not of peace but, if one actually reads the *Koran* rather than genuflect before it, of *Jihad*, both

Corbyn and his comrade- in-arms in the anti-Zionist struggle, Livingstone, have each nominated their favourite Muslim preacher. Livingstone's is Yusef al Qaradawi, whom in 2004 he hosted as his 'honoured guest' when Mayor of London. On January 9, 2009, in a sermon on Al-Jazeera TV, his honoured guest said the following:

'Oh Allah, take the treacherous Jews. Oh Allah, take this profligate, cunning band of people. Oh Allah, they have spread much corruption and tyranny in the land. Pour your wrath upon them Oh our God. Oh Allah, take this oppressive Jewish, Zionist band of people. Oh Allah, do not spare a single one of them. Oh Allah, count their numbers and kill them, down to the very last one.'

Here he is preaching again on the 28th of the same month:

'Throughout history, Allah has imposed upon the Jews people who would punish them for their corruption...The last punishment was carried out by Hitler...He put them in their place [sic]. This was divine punishment for them.
Allah willing, the next time[sic] will be at the hands of the believers.'

This was not only a prediction. Livingstone's esteemed but aging Muslim cleric still wanted a piece of the action: '...the only thing I hope for is that as my life approaches its end, Allah will give me an opportunity to go to the land of Jihad and resistance [sic], even if in a wheelchair. I will shoot Allah's enemy, the Jews, and they will throw a bomb at me, and thus, I will seal my life with martyrdom'.
Writing in the *Muslim News* of September 2010, that is, more than a year *after* these two broadcasts, Livingstone, a Vice-President, would you believe, of Unite Against Fascism, lauded this Islamo-Nazi preacher as 'one of the leading progressive voices in the Arab world'. But then Livingstone does not believe that anti-Semitism is 'the same

thing as racism'. Just to complete the picture, Qaradawi is the author of *Our War Against the Jews in the Name of Islam,* and is on record as approving the death penalty for leaving Islam, female genital mutilation and wife-beating, all on the grounds that they are rulings of the prophet, and the suicide bombing of Israeli civilians.

Such are the stated convictions of the preacher Livingstone has described as an 'absolutely sane Islamist' and praised as 'the strongest force for the modernisation of Islam', and who unashamedly announces to the world that he eagerly looks forward to the day when Islam will complete the genocide of the Jews that was begun by Hitler, 'down to the last one'. In the light of his more than thirty years of controversy in matters Jewish, a question surely needs to put to Livingstone: How can he reconcile his refusal to share a platform with the Neo-Nazi British National Party in a BCC radio husting for the 2012 London mayoral elections, and his Vice Presidency of Unite Against fascism, with his hosting and unqualified praise of a theocratic Nazi?

Now for Corbyn's number one preacher, Hamas's Sheikh Raed Salah, on 9/11:

'A suitable way was found to warn the 4,000 [sic] Jews who work every day in the Twin Towers to absent themselves from their work on September 11, 2001...Were 4,000 Jewish clerks absent by chance, or was there another reason? At the same time, no such warning reached the 2,000 [sic] Muslims who worked every day in the Twin Towers, and therefore there were hundreds of Muslim victims.'

And here he is, resurrecting the vile medieval Christian 'Jewish blood libel': 'We are not the ones who allowed ourselves to eat a meal based on bread and cheese and soaked in Christian blood.'

Again, as was the case with Livingstone, long after these two anti-Semitic slanders entered the public arena, Corbyn praised their author on Al-Jazeera TV in 2012: 'I look forward to giving you tea on the [House of Commons] terrace because you deserve it'. Salah was an 'honoured citizen' with 'a voice that deserves to heard'. It is a pertinent judgement on Corbyn's and Livingstone's choices of Muslim preachers that their anti-Semitism has led to their both being banned from entering the UK.

It also a fitting comment, although one of an entirely nature, on the ethics of those whom Hamas and Qaradawi wish to exterminate that shortly before the kidnap and murder of the three Jewish teenage boys that triggered the Gaza war, Jewish doctors at a Jerusalem hospital treated the mother-in-law of the Hamas leader Ismail Haniyeh, just as they performed an emergency operation on Amina Abbas, wife of Palestinian Authority President Mahmood Abbas at the Assuto Medical Centre near Tel-Aviv one day after the murders. They also treated his brother-in-law at the same facility in the Autumn of 2015 while, urged on by Abbas, Muslim fanatics were carrying out a series of stabbing attacks in Jerusalem on Jewish civilians; and finally, his youngest brother for cancer in April 2016. How strange then that leaders of Hamas and Fatah, movements that routinely accuse the Jews of Israel of carrying out a genocide of the Palestinians, entrust to them the care of their nearest and dearest rather than to any of their own medical staff.

When Corbyn has been accused of at the very least, acquiescing in prejudices against the Jews, his allies have claimed that this is a case of guilt by association. Diane Abbott adopted this line of defence when she said 'Jeremy has done thousands [sic...as a now notorious TV interview demonstrated, maths is not her strongest suite] of meetings, rallies and memorial events. Now if over those thirty years he has been on a platform with someone who is clear is now [sic] an anti-Semite, given the chaotic [sic?] nature of the liberation [i.e., anti-Zionist] movement, that will happen. That doesn't make Jeremy an anti-Semite.'

This is a puerile excuse, as if Corbyn by accident, just once or maybe twice, over a period of 'thirty years', in 'thousands' of events on behalf of the anti-Zionist cause, found himself, by sheer chance and not choice, sharing a platform with someone who only afterwards, proved to be an anti-Semite. If by chance, Corbyn were to find himself sitting on a bus next to a total stranger who is also, though he does not advertise the fact, an inveterate anti-Semite (surveys of the incidence of anti-Semitism in the UK have suggested this is a far from improbable scenario) and during the journey, they exchanged a few pleasantries about the weather and such like, it would of course be absurd to accuse Corbyn of sharing the anti-Semitic views of his fellow passenger on the basis of this fleeting and unsolicited encounter.

But, if as been the case with Corbyn and Livingstone, over a period of 'thirty years', someone praises, seeks out precisely because of their hostility to Zionism, and associates and collaborates politically with individuals and organisations that make no secret not only of their desire to destroy the state of Israel, but have approved and could have assisted in the preparation of terrorist operations that deliberately killed Israeli Jewish civilians, as in the case of Hamas and the PLO; those whose TV channels feature children's programmes where girls swaddled from head to foot and as young as four years recite the Jew-hatred that has ensured that for as long as it endures, there can be no peace between Israel and the Palestinians; who treat as good coin the lies of the *Protocols of Zion*; if someone, as Corbyn most certainly has, shares platforms not once but repeatedly, for 'thirty years', with speakers who subscribe to Jewish conspiracy theories; if someone takes paid employment, as both Corbyn and Livingstone indubitably have, with a regime that hosted a conference dedicated to proving the Holocaust never happened, and has declared its intention to 'wipe Israel from the map'...all this is indeed guilt by deliberate, repeated and calculated association, and would be proved as such if tested in a court of law.

Whatever the creationists may claim to the contrary, the Bible has nothing to tell us of any worth about the origins and nature of the universe. But it does contain much wisdom about the human condition, especially in the Old Testament. For those who truly believe, as Corbyn's apologists evidently do, that one can spend decades of one's life pursing a common cause in regular association with anti-Semites, and remain uncontaminated by their vile and murderous prejudice, I recommend Ecclesiasticus, Chapter 13, Verse 1: 'He that toucheth pitch shall be defiled therewith.' Corbyn did not so much touch pitch as wade in it up to his neck.

So much for the Allah connection. But there is also a Kremlin one. In the year Corbyn became an MP at the 1983 general election he also began to write the occasional article for the pro-Moscow *Morning Star*, which became the daily paper of the re-launched British Communist Party after its split with the Democratic Left in 1988. The origins of this split go back to 1968, when an ultra-Stalinist minority went against party policy by supporting the Soviet-led Warsaw Pact invasion of Czechoslovakia to crush its 'Prague Spring' of democratic reforms, thereby earning the title of 'tankies'.

One can legitimately ask, why did Corbyn, who from his membership of CND in 1966, has always presented himself as a peace-campaigner, chose to associate himself with a Stalinist faction with a reputation and policy of supporting the use of Soviet military might to crush movements for democracy? Even after the collapse of the USSR in 1991, Corbyn continued to devise excuses for Moscow's expansionist strategy in the *Morning Star*, blaming NATO for Putin's incursions into the Ukraine, and denouncing the European Union as a 'tool of US foreign policy'. Together with Livingstone, Corbyn is a prominent member of the Cuba Solidarity Campaign, whose two main functions, apart from junkets in Havana and at the Cuban embassy in London, seem to be acting as a propaganda agency for the country's one-party communist regime and lauding the achievements its late dictator, Fidel Castro, one of which was to order three days of official mourning on the death in

1975 of his fascist counterpart, General Franco, and another, to appoint Ramon Mercader, the assassin of Leon Trotsky, as Inspector General of his regime's full to bursting prisons.

Domestically, Corbyn's appointments after becoming Labour Party Leader revealed a tendency to favour those with marked Stalinist leanings. As his advisor for strategy in the general election of 2017, Corbyn hired Andrew Murray, his replacement in 2015 as chairperson of the Stop the War Coalition and a forty-year veteran 'tankie' of the British Communist Party, who defiantly proclaimed on one occasion, 'we are all Stalinists' and on another, his support of North Korea. Of all people, why hire him?

In the 2016 London Waterloo Theatre's satirical production *Jeremy Corbyn the Musical*: *The Motor Bike Rides,* the story line revolves around a tour of East Germany (the ludicrously mis-named 'German Democratic Republic) the then current Labour leader undertook in the 1970s, with his shadow Home Secretary and most devoted apologist Dianne Abbott riding pillion. The 1970s takes us back to the time of the Berlin Wall, erected in August 1961 to ensure that all those on the wrong side could no longer escape, as they had been doing in their tens of thousands, from Walter Ulbricht's proletarian paradise to the capitalist slavery of the West. Corbyn evidently did not share the qualms that when it was erected in 1961 led to me to question the pro-Soviet polices of the British Communist Party. After all, he was going in as a tourist, not risking his life trying to get out. And a risk it certainly was. In the period between the Wall's erecting in 1961 and 1970, East German border police killed 89 would be-escapees. Did Corbyn know this? It he did not, why not? And if he did, then what was a member, and, from 1974, a councillor of a Labour Party that has always stood for democratic socialism, doing taking a holiday under a regime that imprisons its subjects behind a wall and murders those who simply want to live somewhere else? Did he know, did he care, that in June 1953, the workers of East Germany rose in a revolt against their Stalinist oppressors that could only be put down, as in

Hungary in 1956, by the intervention of the Red Army and hundreds of summary exactions? Why not be like Che Guevara and take a holiday in Franco Spain as well, which treated its workers just the same?

As a footnote to Corbyn's Soviet bloc sympathies, I reproduce excepts of a story that appeared in *The Sun* on February 15, 2018 Headed, 'Corbyn and the Commie Spy: Jeremy Corbyn met a Communist spy during the Cold War and "briefed" evil regime of clampdown by British intelligence.', it continues: 'New-found comrade, who was given the code name COB, even warned the Soviet-backed spies of a clamp down by British intelligence. Jeremy Corbyn met a communist spy at the height of the cold war and warned him of a clamp down by British intelligence, according to secret files obtained by *The Sun*. Mr Corbyn [a Labour MP since 1983] was vetted by Czech agents in 1986 and met one at least three times – twice, it was claimed, in the House of Commons.'

The Sun then reproduced documents it claims substantiate this allegation. The first, partly printed in Czech, has Corbyn's name written in ink at the top, then his correct birthday and nationality, and under that, 'L P, House of Commons'. *The Sun* also reproduced another text, first in Czech, then translated into English: 'RS "COB". On 24.10.1987 at the time from 4.00 to 5.30 PM I carried out a meeting with COB at the House of Commons with the objectivate strengthen mutual recognition and the deepening of trust. The topic of discussion was the national liberation movement, the position of Britain and the USA concerning the situation in BSV or Persian Gulf. Knowledge could not be used for purpose of information as they were limited to a general nature.'

Professor Anthony Glees of the Oxford Intelligence Group said: 'These files show that Jeremy Corbyn has been targeted by Czech intelligence services…At the time dissidents were under attack and being imprisoned in Czechoslovakia. In the struggle between the dissidents who were trying to overthrow the communist government and the Czech government, Corbyn is working on the side of the Czech government.'

'Working' implies complicity. Irrespective of what were his undoubted sympathies with the Soviet bloc, and *prima facie* evidence of a number of conversations with a Czech intelligence operative, I am sure as one can be that Corbyn was not spying, an undertaking which demands possessing confidential information of value, a high level of intelligence and extreme discretion. Corban lacked each of these desiderata. As his record of association with dictatorships and Irish and Islamic terrorists has demonstrated, he belongs that that category of dupes that Lenin once described as 'useful idiots', a naive fellow traveller. Why else his occasional article in the tankie *Morning Star*, and his motorbike tour of the Kremlin's east German bailiwick?

Corbyn is far from being the only British leftist to have been identified as a target or collaborator with Soviet-bloc intelligence. Others so named have included the trade union leaders Jack Jones, Hugh Scanlon, Ted Hill and Richard Briginshaw, Labour MPs Tom Driberg and Ian Mikado, and Dick Clements, editor of the left wing weekly, *Tribune*. Irrespective of the truth or otherwise of any of these accusations, I can personally vouch for the fact that neither Corbyn nor any of those in his current inner circle responded to the repeated appeals made by the Polish Solidarity Campaign to support publicly the ten-year struggle of *Solidarnosc* for workers' rights and democracy in Poland. And it is surely also reasonable to ask, is it by sheer chance that in this same inner circle, there are those who share their leader's soft spot for Lenin and his heirs?

Writing in the Communist Party's *Morning Star* of September 25, 1991 Livingstone made the extraordinary claim, no more rooted in reality than those of his about Hitler and Zionism, that the reforms of the Attlee government elected in 1945 were due 'largely [sic] to the presence of post-war developments in Eastern Europe'. What Livingstone coyly calls 'these developments' could not have had any bearing whatsoever on Labour's creation of the Natoinal Health Service and massive expansion of the public sector of the economy, since they occurred after and not before the adoption and much of the implementation of Labour's 1945 election manifesto, *Let us face the future*, which was itself largely derived from the Beveridge Report of 1942, at a time when the whole of Eastern Europe was under Nazi rule. As to Stalin's and his successors' 'developments', they involved the enslavement, purging and economic exploitation of Eastern Europe on such a scale and level of intensity that they provoked a series of rebellions against Soviet rule and workers' uprisings in Yugoslavia in 1948, East Germany in 1953, Hungary in 1956 and Poland in 1956, 1970, 1976 and 1980, Czechoslovakia in 1968 and the entire Soviet bloc in 1989.

Seamus Milne, recruited from the *Guardian* as Corbyn's first Director of Communications, who in his Oxford student days sported a Mao uninform and moved resolutions against Israel, shares Livingstone's rose-tinted view of Stalin, claiming, that 'for all its brutalities' (at least 20 million killed by famine, terror and slavery) his regime had been motivated by 'genuine idealism [sic!!!]', and had 'delivered rapid industrialisation, mass education and job stability'. One thing Stalin's vast army of industrial slaves could be sure of was indeed 'job stability.' And did not Nazis apologists once say of Hitler that he built the Autobahn, restored Germany's pride and got the unemployed back to work?

Corbyn's Shadow Home Secretary Diane Abbott struck a similar balance sheet for Mao, only with three times as many victims. On a TV programme hosted by ex-Tory MP Michael Portillo, when asked what could possibly justify the deaths of 60 million people, she did not contest this number, but replied, 'he [Mao] led his [sic] country from feudalism, he helped to defeat the Japanese, and he left his [sic] country on the verge of the great economic success they are having now'. She failed however to explain why this necessitated killing 60 million of 'his' people. Portillo could have pointed out that the 'great economic success' was largely being enjoyed by a new class of immensely wealthy capitalists, and were due to the ditching of Mao's ruinous polices after his death in 1976, and the adoption of those of Portillo's former party leader, Margaret Thatcher.

One-time deputy to GLC leader Livingstone and with Livingstone and Knight, co-editor of the Healyite *Labour Herald*, shadow chancellor John McDonnell advertised his Maoist leanings when in the debate on his opposite number's Autumn Statement, he quoted from the mass murderer's *Little Red Book*, perhaps as a portent of things to come. If so, it would have been time to buy a large extra freezer, and lay in stocks for the famine.

I only came about most of above information concerning Corbyn's Jihadi and Stalinist associations as result of two related events: the Hamas-Israel conflict in the Summer of 2014, and Corbyn's election as Leader of the Labour Party the next year. Not long after I moved to Swansea, I had resumed my friendship with Mark of Blick-Jenkins infamy, who since the early 1980s, had been living just a short drive down the M4 in Cardiff. The Gaza war started on June 12, 2014, with Hamas kidnapping and murdering three Jewish teenagers. Since 2006, when Israel withdrew from the Gaza strip, leaving it to be governed by its Palestinian inhabitants, Hamas has been using child labour to tunnel into Israeli territory to carry out such operations, and since 2007, firing thousands of rockets at Jewish civilian targets. Yet the world's media overwhelmingly took the side of Hamas when Israel acted, fully in accordance with international law, to protect its own territory and people from these attacks. It was this that led Mark and I to jointly write an article in support of Israel, and about the unholy alliance of anti-Zionist leftists and anti-Semitic Muslims and neo-Nazis that had taken to the streets of the west in T-shirts that proclaimed 'We are all Hamas' and in at least one instance, had chanted 'Hamas, Hamas, Jews to the gas.' In scenes redolent of the Middle Ages, Tsarist Russia and the Third Reich, Jews were assaulted on the street, Jewish shops ransacked, Jewish-owned department stores and supermarkets picketed, and synagogues attacked. In France, despite the unprecedented mobilisation of the army to protect Jewish citizens and buildings, including schools, from attack, the level of intimidation was such that in its wake, 40,000 Jews decided to emigrate.

Mark assigned the first draft to me. Once I had started, the article developed directions and a momentum of its own as I delved more deeply into the dark sides of the far left's obsession with Israel, which dated back to the Healy's connections with Arab dictators and the terrorist PLO that began back in the late 1970s. Then came the Corbyn campaign for the Labour leadership and following his election, reports of a sudden surge of anti-Semitism in the Labour Party (dismissed by Corbynistas as a Zionist plot) of which the suspensions of Livingstone for claiming Hitler was a supporter of Zionism, and the Muslim MP for Bradford West, Naz Shah, for proposing the deportation of the entire Jewish population of Israel to the USA, were but two of its many manifestations.

Then came the sinister Corbyn cult, a phenomenon that in British (but not continental) politics had, until its emergence in the Labour Party, been confined to the fascist fringe, with the black-shirted adulation of the tin-pot Fuehrer Sir Oswald Mosely. Now it had moved centre stage, literally, with red-shirted Momentumistas rhythmically chanting, Nuremberg-style, their leader's name at rallies and pop concerts, singing a Jeremy song and sporting T-shirts vilifying the only Labour Leader to have won three successive general elections. The cult has even generated a booming Corbyn memorabilia industry. These are just some of the items that can bought on line: children's colouring-in books, miniaturised and life-size cardboard cut-outs of the Dear Leader, Corbyn garden gnomes and playing cards, broaches, knit-wear, under-pants, fake tattoos (though two women have had real ones done), shopping bags, pillow cases, mugs (sic), Corbyn's Lenin-style cloth cap and Lego figurines. All this, and much more as the Corbyn story unfolded, swelled what had been intended as an article of at the most 2,000 words to a book of over half a million.

It was 9/11 that for me announced the arrival of Islamic terrorism in the west, after being confined largely to the Middle East, where its target had been almost exclusively the Jews of Israel. Aside from its impact on the Left, I was both fascinated and disgusted by the cowardly and dishonest attempt of politicians generally to define Islam in ways that separated the religion entirely from the terrorist actions carried out by its followers and in its name. In my quest for the real Islam, and not the fictitious varieties concocted by the likes of Blair, Cameron, Merkel, Obama, the Pope, Corbyn *et al*, I was fortunate in having at my disposal no less than three English language editions of the *Koran*, all gifts from Muslim students concerned for the welfare of my heathen soul. There I found an Islam totally at odds with what I had been assured by our political and clerical establishments was a (or the) 'religion of peace'. To refute this lie, in one of its appendices, my *Socialism of Fools* cites 61 verses of the *Koran* which unambiguously command the faithful to wage war against the enemies of Allah. To set the scene for what follows, the work begins with a series of contrasting statements about the nature of Islam, a small sample of which I reproduce here:

UK Prime Minister Tony Blair on 9/11: 'Islam is a peaceful and tolerant religion, and the acts of these people are contrary to the teachings of the *Koran.*'

Koran, Chapter 8, Verse 12: 'I will cast terror into the hearts of those who disbelieve. Smite them above the neck and cut off their finger tips'

German Chancellor Angela Merkel: 'Islam is not the source of terrorism.'

Koran, Chapter 4, Verse 56: 'Those that deny Our revelations, we will burn in fire.'

US President Barack Obama: 'Islam has a proud tradition of tolerance.'

Koran: Chapter 5, Verse 33 'Those that make war on God

and his apostle and spread disorder shall be put to death or [sic] shall be crucified and have their hands and feet cut off on opposite sides.'

(One of my three *Korans* provides an anatomical footnote to the second citation that could be taken as guidance for prospective executioners: 'The upper part of the neck which is just below the head and is considered to be the most vulnerable for dealing an effective blow with the sword.')

It is not only at the summits of society that truths about Islam cannot be spoken. I have been an occasional contributor to the letters page of my local daily paper, the *Swansea Evening Post,* and since my arrival in the city I must have submitted at least a dozen letters on a variety of topics, some of them highly controversial. All but one had been published, while another was edited. In the latter case, the letter concerned the imminent deportation back to Nigeria of a gay man who had been denied political asylum in the UK. The edited sentence, as I wrote it, ran thus: 'After reading you story in Tuesday's *Post*, I was outraged and ashamed that this country is deporting a Nigerian man to face the near certainty of either rotting in a Christian jail or being stoned to death by Muslims simply because he is gay.' After the *Post*'s censors had done their work, the words 'Christian' and 'by Muslims' had being deleted without any ellipsis, therefore fraudulently presenting the letter as the one I had actually written.

It is sometimes the practice to carry on a correspondence page a statement to the effect that the editor reserves the right to edit readers' letters. But since the *Post* does not do so, my letter should either have been published exactly as I had written it, or not published at all. Equally to the point, my reference to stonings by Muslims was factually correct. Indeed, the article in the *Post* to which I was responding had itself said the punishment for homosexuality in Nigeria was either 20 years imprisonment or death by stoning. All I had done was to allude to the reason for the difference. Nigeria is a Federation, and its northern states, being Islamic, have adopted Sharia Law, under which the punishment for homosexual acts is death. In the states of Gombe, Jigawa, Zamfara, Kano, Bauchi, Kaduna, Katsina, Kebbi and Yobe, the execution of those convicted of homosexual acts is carried out by stoning. As Obama says, 'Islam has a proud tradition of tolerance'. The letter that was not published ran as follows:

'I read with interest the item "dispel myths" (|*Post*, February 12) concerning the 'Discover Islam' week in Cardiff being hosted by the Ahmadadiyya Muslim Youth Association. The report quotes Dr Nassir Domun as saying that "Islam means peace". I have checked a number of Islamic websites, and they all disagree with Dr Domun. This is what one of them, Islamic Learning Materials, says: "Islam does not mean peace...The word 'Islam' means submission, to give up and cease resistance against a stronger power." It is of course possible to argue that submission can lead to peace, but that does not alter the fact that strictly speaking, the words peace and submission have different meanings.'

Despite this letter's making no critical comments about either Islam or Muslims, and citing only Islamic sources, the editor of the *Post* had felt it was not fit for publication. That is the level of submission we have been reduced to.

On university campuses, intellectual life is increasingly regulated by an Orwellian thought police, with its 'trigger warnings' alerting students to topics and even words that might cause them distress, 'safe [from disturbing controversy] spaces', and 'no platforms' for outside speakers deemed politically incorrect. While no such restrictions apply to Muslim students and speakers, Jews are anything but safe. They are the target for a hostility that can and has turned violent. My son was witness to one such incident.

In January 2016, sitting in his office at Kings College, London, where he is a Reader in British Constitutional History, just down the corridor outside the next room, he heard the chant of 'Two, four, six, eight, Israel is a fascist state', followed by the sounds of a commotion and uproar that was in fact an assault by a mob of pro-Palestinian students from the nearby School of African and Oriental Studies on a meeting called by the college's Israel Society. In the ensuing *melee,* witnessed without protest or intervention by the college's 'Safe (sic) Officer', chairs were broken, windows smashed and fire alarms set off. The meeting was abandoned, which was the purpose. of the attack. More than twenty police arrived on the scene, but made no arrests.

Two years later, a similar scenario was played out, again at Kings, when anti-Zionists attempted to shout down former Israeli Deputy Prime Minister Dan Meridor with constant chants throughout his speech of 'terrorist' (sic) and 'criminal'. Jewish students leaving the meeting had fingers poked in their faces. Such scenes were a commonplace in the universities of the late Weimar Republic. Now they are being re-enacted at universities, not only in London, but across the UK and even in the USA, the land of the First Amendment. (Evidence of this concerted assault on campus free speech can be found in my *Socialism of Fools*).

Maybe in relating the details of my renewed crusade (no apologies for the word by the way) against the recrudescence of the left's unholy alliance with Arab and Islamic anti-Semitism, I have created the impression that my last years with Maureen were largely spent in pursuing, to the exclusion of nearly all else, yet another of my all-consuming passions. True, Maureen often used to come into the back bedroom where my computer is situated, and exclaim, in mock surprise, 'You're not still at it are you? I thought you said you'd finished it'. Indeed, I had, not once, but at least a dozen times. But the events and the facts kept coming until, as I have already said, what began as an article of 2,000 words mushroomed to a treatise the size of three normal books. Luckily, in view of the time and energy I devoted to the subject, Islam in general, and naturally enough, in particular, its oppression of women, was one of the few topics Maureen and I never had cause to argue about.

Though modern in her outlook in many matters, she was very much of her generation when it came to feminism. Though she would never apply the term to herself, partly because of its recent excesses, hers was of the now unfashionable kind that recognised the unnegotiable right of all women to equality with men, irrespective of culture, race or religion. This put her at odds with current 'third wave' feminism, which in fact is not feminism at all, but a white, western upper middle-class narcissistic and racist movement concerned exclusively with what it calls the struggle against the 'white patriarchy' and the 'glass ceiling' (most being already well above it), and which denounces any criticism of the misogyny of Muslim men as Islamophobic, racist and culturally imperialist.

One such *faux* feminist, writing in the *Guardian* (despite the glass ceiling) dismissed all reports from the Islamic world of the abuse of Muslim women as mere 'horror stories'. Yet on YouTube, if one has the stomach for it, one can see videos of women, surrounded by a mob of men, being stoned to death for alleged offences under Sharia Law that in any civilised country would, if they in fact did commit them, be perfectly legal. Is it any surprise then that there was little or no feminist outcry when, as a result of a series of trials, beginning in Rotherham, it was revealed that over a period of in some cases more than thirty years, in something like thirty towns and cities across the UK, various public agencies...the police, social services, councils and the like...had been concealing and in some instances actually conniving at the pimping, trafficking, grooming and gang rape, with but few exceptions by Muslim men, of tens of thousands of under-age, white, vulnerable mainly working class girls. I am convinced that had the reverse been the case, and white men had been pimping and gang raping under-age Muslim girls, it would not have taken thirty years to bring the culprits to justice.

Corbyn's response to these appalling crimes was as predictable as it was incoherent: 'The problem is that crime is committed against women in any community. Much crime is committed by white people. Crime is committed by people in other communities as well.' Corbyn evades the central issue in two ways; by referring only to crimes in general, and not those that gave rise to his comment, which were of a very specific sexual nature, namely the industrial-scale grooming, trafficking, pimping and gang rape of under-age girls; and secondly, by categorizing the perpetuators of crime according to race and not religion, which is also what the far right does. Yes, 'much crime' is indeed committed by 'white people'. But this is hardly surprising, since they make up around 90% of the UK's population. But what is cause for comment, and some would also say concern and not denial, is that men from the Muslim 'community', which constitutes less than 5% of the UK population, made up approximately 90% of those convicted of the crimes in question and are, according one study of the subject, 180 times more likely to commit them than non-Muslims.

Perhaps because they cannot envisage a time or situation when they will, like their Muslim sisters, become subject to Sharia Law, third wave feminists also have their blind spots when it is matter of how Islam sees and treats Muslim women. Judging by their silence on such matters, many seem untroubled by the *Koran's* sanctioning of wife beating (Chapter 4, Verse 34) and rape within marriage (Chapter 2, Verse 223), the marriage of little girls to men who can be five and more times their age (following here as in other sexual matters the example of the Prophet, who married his final wife, Aisha, at the age of six, when he was nearly nine times her age); the requirement of four adult male witnesses to prove a charge of rape, and female genital mutilation, for which there has only a single conviction in the UK since it was made a crime in 1985, even though the number of cases is believed to be in the region of 20,000 per year. When it comes to choosing between the right of a Muslim woman not to beaten and raped, to decide for herself whom she marries and at what age, and to control what she does with her own body, and the demands of 'cultural sensitivity', as far as third wave feminists are concerned, (and not they alone) political correctness wins every time.

I know exactly what Maureen would have said about the nauseously patronising charade of 'World Hijab Day' of February 15, 2018, when prominent western women including, predictably, leading politicians, all of whom can chose what they want and do not want to wear, paraded in front of cameras sporting what is for millions of their Muslim sisters the symbol of their humiliation and subjection by men, while in Iran, brave young women were being arrested and jailed, in one case for more than fifty years, for removing the hated object in public. Try criticising in the wrong company this cynical, Sharia-appeasing, Muslim vote-grabbing stunt and the odds are you will be called either an Islamophobe, a racist, a cultural imperialist, a Nazi, a Zionist, or any combination from all five. You will in all probability also be given a lecture on the need to respect equally all cultures (except, it goes without saying, one's own) because all cultures (again with the same exception) are equal, with one, the Islamic, being more equal than the rest. The best reply to this nonsense is to suggest, especially if they are either gay or female, that they exchange the inferior culture of 21st century Britain for the superior culture of Iran, Yemen, Somalia, Saudi Arabia or the outbacks of Pakistan and Afghanistan.

While engrossed in my researches into the origins and ramifications of the Corbyn phenomenon, I was struck by a blast from the past. My good friend Mark rang to tell me that he had been contacted by Healy's daughter, Mary, who wanted to interview me about my dealings with her father. Of course, I said yes. Mary was a total stranger to me, having never met her, though I did know his son Allen quite well. He was a gifted flautist, and when I was Foreign Editor for the *Workers Press* he used to wander into my office playing his flute for a chat about music, both jazz and classical. But never about politics. He was obviously a disturbed boy…hardly surprising, given his dad's lifestyle.

Shortly after his father's death, I learned he had died of an overdose.

I met Mary in the café of a hotel opposite Swansea's railway terminus. Dispensing with formalities, over coffees, she asked me a series of prepared questions about my experiences with her father, mostly to do with his darker sides. She explained why. After decades of semi-denial, only now was she able to confront the monster she now accepted he was. A monster of a father to be sure....but for me, it wasn't as simple as that, and I told her so. It was in a way similar to the Wagner case. Yes, Healy was a lousy father and husband, a bully, a thug even, and a sexual predator. But none of that invalidated the truth and continued relevance of what he taught me; that, to quote Trotsky, 'Stalinism is the syphilis of the workers' movement'. Because of Healy, I, and many like me, were cured of the infection of Stalinism, and for that, I told Mary as we parted, I am still grateful.

XV

When I moved in with Maureen, she had a pretty good idea of what she was taking on, even though at the beginning it could be heavy going at times for both of us. But what really changed things was our first trip abroad, to Paris in June 2000. In the six months before that, we had settled into rather humdrum routine more befitting a couple who had been married for thirty years...shopping in town on a Friday, the occasional trip to the coast, the Gower or inland to the Brecons. Evenings, it was a meal and TV or a video and, as often as not, a bed-time quiz or debate, and love-making, the highlights of an otherwise usually routine day. Every other week-end, I would be in London tutoring, and less frequently, gigging with Horsepower. One evening out of the blue, in her usual matter of fact way, Maureen said to me, 'it isn't going anywhere'. She didn't elaborate, and I didn't ask her too, because I knew she meant. This was supposed to be, and in fact it, was the consummation of an extraordinary love affair... and yet we hadn't even had a honeymoon. Where better to go than Paris?

When I suggested this to her, she was thrilled - a rare condition for one normally so *sangfroid*. We travelled by Eurostar, and stayed at a modest but tidy hotel on the south side, not far from the Pantheon. With only two full days to see the sights, we did the usual tourist trek...the Latin Quarter, Montmartre, the walk up the Champs Elysee from the Place de la Concorde to the Arc de Triomphe, the Pantheon (Voltaire, libertarian and father of the French Enlightenment, and his antagonist Rousseau, Robespierre's exemplar and father of the terror) and les Invalides (the tomb of Napoleon, the maker of modern Europe). On the Champs de Mars, I took a photo of photo of Maureen. Framed by the Eiffel Tower she has the exited smile of a school girl. And deep down, as one of the fascinations of her complex nature, so she still was.

By sheer coincidence, Blowpipe had been engaged to

play a gig in Paris a couple of days after we were due back in Swansea. (I stayed in London, then went back to Paris to do the gig, while she went straight home to Swansea on her own.) It was on a boat, the *Batofar*, by another co-incidence moored on the Seine only a short walk from our hotel. Not being one to pass up such an opportunity to impress, at least where Maureen was concerned, as we strolled along the river bank, I suggested we check out the venue. And there it was on the bill-board…Blowpipe.

A few days after I got back to Swansea, a letter addressed to me arrived in the post. It was from Maureen.

'My Dearest Robin,

You will probably think I am very strange, demented even, but I have something important to say to you and decided that I would prefer to write it down. Too often when I tell you how I feel or try to pay you a compliment you appear not to take me seriously or interrupt me with some trite remark. This guarantees me a captive audience and hopefully proof of my sincerity. I want to tell you that I had the most amazing time in Paris. I loved every minute I was there and cannot imagine being in Paris with anyone but you. Thank you so much for taking me and sharing the experience with me.

I also have to tell you and you must believe me, that I have been very happy the past six months despite the little twinges of guilt that beset me. I really do like living with you and even though I enjoy the odd days that we're apart, I always look forward to you coming home. I enjoy your company, your music and most of all just being with you and I hope that you'll stay with me always. You often say that we're not suited and I'm never sure if you mean it or you're just joking. Consequently, even though I believe you when you say you love me, I still get this feeling that you may get bored and decide to go. I hope not, because I've realised (a little late I know) that you are the love of my life and I can't imagine my life now without you. I think that we are very well suited and dissimilar enough to make it interesting. So Blicky, it's down now in blue and white and finally you have your letter.

All my love, Maureen.'

In the darkest moments of my despair after Maureen's death, it was reading this letter over and over again that sustained me, affirming as it does that she returned my love for her in full measure. It was only out embarrassment that sometimes times I responded, as she says as I did, to her protestations of love for me. There was also a degree of incredulity…they had been a long time coming. As for her 'twinges of guilt', although I can understand why she felt them, they were as I saw it largely groundless. It was after all my decision to search for Maureen that led to the chain of events that brought us together.

Twenty years on from that first trip to Paris, our fridge is still covered with magnets, some 120 in all, that we collected in our odyssey around Europe. I recently calculated that of our seventeen years together, just over one of them was spent abroad. For me, and I believe for Maureen too, exploring Europe as we did, wherever possible by car, was to travel through all four dimensions; not only down by the coasts, the rivers and the lakes, up amongst the peaks of the Alps and the Pyrenees, from Italy and Spain in the south to Sweden and Iceland in north, and from Ireland the west to Poland and Estonia in the East., but also back in time, from the collapse of a Soviet empire that gave the world nothing, through the Enlightenment, Renascence, and Reformation to classical Greece and Rome that between them gave us nearly everything. The ravages of time and two world wars have grievously damaged much of the architecture of this priceless heritage, but thankfully not obliterated it. In some cases, buildings have been lovingly restored to their former glories, as we discovered when we visited that baroque gem on the Elbe, Dresden, and the medieval old town in Tallin.

Although never by inclination or background a big city girl...why else her move to Swansea...Maureen relished her stays in some of the jewels in Europe's urban crowns, above all in Florence, which contains, so I am told, 40% of the world's art treasures. Surely the most glorious of them is Michangelo's David, the symbol of Florentine liberty and independence, still facing south, as his creator intended, to defiantly confront the despised Goliath in the Vatican. Unlike Florence, where one meanders, strolls, snacks and gazes in awe and wonder, Rome is, as Maureen used to say after trudging up and down the seven hills from one semi-ruin to another, 'a city you do.' As we were waiting in the queue for St Peters, I looked up that towering monument to clerical hubris and said to Maureen, 'Is this what Jesus had in mind?'

According to the Greeks, hubris is followed by nemesis, or as we say, pride come before a fall. And sure enough, it was the Vatican swindle of making the poor and the gullible foot the bill for St Peters by the sale of indulgences, promising a fast track to paradise, that sparked Luther's rebellion against Rome and the Protestant Reformation. I can easily imagine Leo X, as one would expect of a Pope from the banking house of Medici, rubbing his hands and saying, 'Blessed are the poor. So let us make them even more blessed by making them even poorer.' As a direct consequence of his pride and avarice, two of the seven deadly sins, today's Vatican City, although it is still fleecing the poor and the gullible, is all that remains of a once-mighty empire, the 'Holy Roman', the first Reich to Hitler's Third, one that once embraced all of Central Europe. What goes around comes around.

Of all the other cities we visited...among them Copenhagen, Malmo, Lyons, Tours, Bruges, Antwerp, Amsterdam, Utrecht, Marseilles, Avignon, Aix en Provence, Luzern, Locarno, Metz, Dijon, Sienna (glorious), Prague, Strasbourg, Colmar, Troyes, Konstanz, Regensburg, Reykjavik, Venice, Lucca, Verona, Lille, Barcelona and Cork, only two proved to be a real let- down...Dublin and Bordeaux

Both lacked what Maureen would call 'a scene', and both had failed to exploit their rivers for social life and cuisine.

It was as result of our stay in Colmar, a beautifully preserved old town in Alsace near the German border, that our exploration of Europe took on another dimension and brought us our greatest happiness together. Maureen had told me many times, with more than hint of nostalgia, of her Easter holiday school trip to the Swiss Alps, where the party stayed at a hotel, the Beau Site, in the ski resort village of Adelboden. Down below in the valley was Lake Thun, and at its western end, the town of Thun, which straddled the River Aar as it made its way out of the lake and then north to join the Rhine. Colmar lies west of the Rhine, about forty miles north of the Swiss border at Basel. Thun is another eighty or so miles further south again.

Having explored Colmar, and for the first time crossed into Germany for a drive through the Black Forest, and now pondering what to do on our last day, I looked at the road map, and saw that Thun was a mere two hours' drive away. Thun for me was the town where towards the end of his life and having as he believed retired from composing, Brahms stayed with a friend for two summer holidays, and inspired by the Alpine setting, created some of his most lyrical works. But I also knew what Thun meant for Maureen, so early the next morning, we were heading south on what I expected to be just another pleasant day excursion. Maureen knew differently.

After a short stay in Thun, where we had coffee in a square overlooked by the distinctive red roofs of the *Schloss*, without saying why, Maureen suggested we drive on to Interlaken, at the other end of Lake Thun. Once out of Thun, the road ran along the north side of the lake. On the other side there reared up from almost the lake's edge the full, overpowering majesty of the Alps. I was so overcome with awe I had to stop the car at the first layby and just gaze in wonder. True to form, Maureen effected a typical *blasé* air, as if to say, I've seen it all before, which of course she had…fifty years ago. But I could see that she was as moved as myself, and perhaps more so, since it must have evoked in her fond memories of the school excursion she had related to me so often and with such enthusiasm. The very touristy Interlaken would have proved something of anti-climax but for its view of the Jungfrau, with the snow-capped peak glistening in the sun. A year later, we were back by Lake Thun, but this time as guests at its famous Hotel Hirschen at Gunten. Our love affair with the Swiss Alps had begun.

Over the next dozen years, we must have stayed by Lake Thun at least eight times, always visiting Thun and driving up to Adelboden to have a coffee at Maureen's school trip hotel. There were also spectacular Alpine rail excursions, including one to almost the very top of the Jungfrau, the train on the way climbing up a tunnel inside the mountain featured in the Clint Eastwood film, *The Eiger Sanction,* in which, incredibly, if you have seen them, he did all his own stunts. And for once, the cliché was true. The views from the top, where we could see for a hundred miles and more in any direction, were beyond description.

Maureen like myself was a pantheist at heart. We both found our greatest joy and peace of mind when worshiping at the shrines of mighty rivers like the Rhine, Elbe, Seine, Danube, Rhone, Moselle and Loire, serene or bustling lakes like Thun, Como, Maggiore, Luzern and Garda, and the soaring peaks of the Alps, Dolomites and Pyrenees. In the midst of these glories of nature, Maureen was I believe happier and more fulfilled than at any other time in her life since her schooldays. And when we were not savouring nature in the raw, we were sampling the oldest, most historic and finest urban centres of Western Europe.

For logistic reasons, as much as any others, the country we saw most of was France. In addition to our four stays in Paris, there was Reims, with its magnificent restored cathedral (but after four years of bombardment by the Kaiser, little else); Rouen, scene of the trial and burning of Joan of Arc in 1431 by the same Church that nearly five centuries later, somewhat belatedly discovered that all along, she had not been a heretic but a saint; Cabourg, close to the Sword Beach in the Normandy landing of June 1944, and where there are still Nazi fortifications to be seen along the coast; Lyons, where the mighty Rhone and Saone rivers converge; Chamonix, at the foot of Mont Blanc, and where Byron and Shelly once stayed during their exiles from England; Besancon, situated in the coils of the Doubs River and birth place of Victor Hugo; Briancon, at 1,326 metres, the highest altitude city in France; Avignon, with its imposing Papal Palace and where Maureen danced on its bridge; Marseille, heaving, buzzing, and a little dangerous (Gene Hackman would vouch for that); Lille, with its wonderful free entry zoo and Flanders-style central square; Blois, dominated by its massive chateau, where Maureen and I stood in the very room where in 1588, Henry III murdered his fanatically Catholic Guise namesake; Strasbourg, home of the EU parliament and another glorious cathedral; Colmar, where from the hotel room window facing the station, Maureen train spotted far into the night, marvelling at the speed and number of freight trains that roared by.

Alsace has always had a special interest for me as an historian because it still contains within itself, as the inheritance of the limits and rupture of the Roman empire, the division of Europe between the Germanic peoples in the centre and north and the Latinate peoples to the west and south, one which bequeathed to the continent so many of its wars and religious conflicts. In Alsace, though French is the only official language, as it is everywhere else in polyglot France, Alsatian, a German dialect, is still spoken by around 40% of its population. Why so? The answer lies in the Treaty of Verdun of 843, which shared out Charlemagne's Holy Roman Empire of the German Nation, to give it its full title, between his three grandson, dividing it into three vertical slices. The western slice became what is now modern France, the eastern, modern Germany. The central one, running from what is now Holland in the north through eastern France (Burgundy, Alsace, Lorraine) and Switzerland to north Italy in the south was divided linguistically and, lacking the internal cohesion of its two neighbours, became a bone of contention between east and west that was only resolved at the end of the Second World War. Just as one example; in the space of only 74 years, Alsace (and to its north also eastern Lorraine) as a result of three wars, had oscillated from France to Germany in 1871, back to France in 1918, then to Germany against in 1940, and back to France in 1945.

The 'middle kingdom' of Charlemagne's grandson Lothair (from which Lorraine), is long gone, but most of its components, after many vicissitudes, are with us as independent states: Holland, Belgium, Luxemburg, Switzerland and Italy, just as its linguistic divisions endure, from Dunkirk on the English Channel, where Flemish still survives, east through Belgium, with its Flemish, French and German; then down through Luxemburg, where French, German and Luxembourgish are spoken; Alsace with its German and French; Switzerland, with four; German, French, Italian and Romansch; and so to the Mediterranean and north Italy; French, German and Italian. We speak our history. Though we may not know it, we owe our mother tongues and our passports to events that in some cases occurred some two thousand and more years ago.

Neither can one escape history if one travels around the western coast of France. We stayed at Dieppe, where we were both moved by the number of beautifully-kept graves of the Canadian serviceman, who in 1942, died in the near-suicidal rehearsal for the Normandy landings, and at Quineville, just a short drive from where the US Marines (or, if you are of a Corbynista disposition, Yankee imperialists) were slaughtered in their thousands on Omaha beach, depicted so graphically in *Saving Private Ryan.* How different from the relaxed sun-drenched south of Aix en Province, with its street after street of tempting Provencal cuisine restaurants, and the little gem of Amboise, where on one of our many stays, Maureen gazed across the broad but languid Loire and cried out, again most uncharacteristically, 'I could live here.'

Knowing Maureen and her love of mountains and the sea, I very much doubt if she could have. But I think she meant it at the time. Our two stays in the Pyrenees, on the Atlantic side in the Basque country a little way inland from Saint Jean de Luz, and on the Mediterranean, also close to the Spanish border at Le Boulou, allowed her to enjoy both. Being so near to Spain also enabled us to visit San Sebastian and Pamplona on the west side, and spend a day in Barcelona in the east.

One of our visits to France took us down, via a short stay at Amboise, to Perigueux. From there, I planned to pay a visit to an old-school friend, Don Harrison, who had settled with his second wife near a tiny village a little way north of the central Pyrenees. Don was a really interesting character. He had been a brilliant footballer, and was one of the stars in a very successful team we both played for after we left school. (Undefeated league champions three seasons in a row…and I still have my medals.) Around the same time, he bought himself a trumpet, on which I used to give him lessons at his home in Enfield. Then, when he began his National Service, I lost touch with him. I found him again some ten years after I moved to Swansea, via the Edmonton County Old Scholars website. Don, as I learned from a mutual friend (the very same who sold me the clarinet that I bought for Maureen), had become a very successful artist, and on the proceeds, had moved to a luxurious home in the south of France. 'Would he mind if I looked him up?' I asked. Not at all. My friend gave me his email address, and a few days later, we were swapping stories about our lives in the intervening half century.

Don told me his life had hit the skids for about five years after being divorced by his Indian wife, who had retained custody of their two children. 'An alcohol-fuelled sex binge' is how he described it to me. Then Don, who to this point had earned his living as a commercial artist, decided that he should put his exceptional gifts as an artist to better and, as it turned out, more profitable use. Under the brand name 'Watching the Paint Dry', he produced a series of videos and books designed to instruct amateur artists in the techniques of easel painting. The venture proved so successful that he was able to make the move to his purpose-built spacious bungalow, together with a full-size outdoor swimming pool complete with sliding roof. It was there that Maureen and I drove to from Perigueux, a journey of around two hours, to socialise, catch up on life, talk about old times, have a meal at a nearby restaurant, and admire Don's paintings.

As Don and I spent a good deal of time reminiscing, Maureen paired up with Don's partner. Having no wish to be the cause of any unwarranted friction during our short visit, as we chatted, I steered clear of any subjects over which we might disagree, especially politics, since Don had already made it pretty clear in one of his communications that in recent years he had moved from the left to the right. I naturally assumed that Maureen, normally an exemplar of decorum in such situations, would do the same. So I could scarcely believe my ears when, in a reversal of roles, I overheard Maureen launch into a diatribe against creationism. I did my best to switch off, fearing an awkward moment. As far as I could tell, there was none. But it set me thinking, imagine if that had been me, and I had put had put my foot in it.

When visiting Belgium, we always preferred picturesque Flanders to industrial Wallonia, with its spectacular gothic central city squares and lovingly preserved medieval architecture. With Bruges, the jewel in the crown, as our base, we visited Antwerp, Ypres and Ghent. Maureen had a strong aversion to most modern art, and so our visit to it to Antwerp's contemporary art museum was not exactly a success. One exhibit, a heap of orange balls, really set her going. Maureen nearly staged a walkout in protest. In the land of Rembrandt and Vermeer, we stayed three times in Amsterdam, one of Maureen's favourite cities. She loved the rattle and clank of the trams and the buzz and bustle of the Leidseplein. Utrecht, where we stayed once, is in many ways a smaller version of

Amsterdam, and also, because of its central location, ideally placed to take a train to anywhere else in Holland. From there, we went to Leiden and Amsterdam, where we visited the newly refurbished Rijks Museum, with its incomparable collection of old Dutch masters. On the way back to the station, Maureen of course insisted we had our customary coffee and session of tram spotting at the Leidseplein.

In Italy, Maureen's favourite country after Switzerland, we stayed at Bellagio on the ravishingly beautiful Lake Como, with its Alpine backdrop and non-stop to-and-froing of ferries; Riva on Lake Garda; a rather run-down San Remo on the Med; sublime Florence, awash with art treasures like no other place on earth; car-less Venice, where in the Piazza San Marco, Maureen was nearly enveloped by pigeons after offering them a bag-full of peanuts; Sienna, with its breathtakingly gigantic and magnificent Piazza del Campo; Verona of Roman theatre fame, and Lucca, with its scores of hand-made shoe shops, and statues of Rossini, a native of Lucca, and Garibaldi, whose army of Red Shirts helped liberate Italy from the Bourbons, the Austrians and the Pope. Milan, we both found a real let-down. Banks and shops, but little else.

On one of our grand tours, driving down from Innsbruck to Lake Garda, we took a detour off the Brenner Pass *Autostrada* to climb up to the snowline of the Italian Tyrol and then down to Merano, a small town on the River Adige, for a snack before completing our journey. Here indeed there was history, much of it that the Catholic Church would have prefer, like so much of its past, to remain a closed book. Until the end of the First World War, Merano was part of Austria, and even today, half of its population of about 40,000 still speak German as their first language. Together with being off the beaten track, perhaps that is why it was chosen by the Vatican as a staging post after the Second World War for wanted Nazis on the run to Catholic South America and the Islamic Middle East...the so-called 'Rat Line'.

The operation was run by Bishop Alois Hudal, who

supplied the Nazis entrusted to his care, many of them guilty of involvement in the Holocaust, with new identities, false passports and booked passages to their final destinations. Among those he saved from the hangman's noose at Nuremberg were Franz Stangl, Commandant of Treblinka, where nearly one million Jews were gassed, Gustav Wagner, Commandant of Sobibor, responsible for its gassing of 200,000 Jews, and Adolf Eichmann, Heinrich Himmler's chief executant of a Holocaust that claimed six million Jewish lives. Stangl, after a stay of three years in Syria, and Wagner, known by his victims as 'the beast', both began new lives in Brazil, courtesy of the Teutonica de Santa Maria Dell Anima in Rome. When Wagner's whereabouts were discovered after being identified by one of the 300 escapees from Sobibor, the Brazilian government refused all requests for his extradition. Interviewed by the BBC in 1979, Wagner showed no remorse. 'It became just another job. In the evening we never discussed our work but just drank and played cards. 'Yes, one needs to unwind after another busy day at the gas chamber.

A year later, Wagner was found dead in Sao Paulo with a knife in his chest…surely another case of revenge tasting best when served cold. Retribution of a kind also caught up with Stangl, who was extradited by West Germany to stand trial for the murder of 9000,000 Jews. Like Wagner and those Roman Catholic clergy who facilitated his escape, he also felt no guilt. Interviewed in prison after being sentenced for life, he told the author Gitta Sereny 'my conscience is clear about what I did.'. Eichmann's end was by far the most fitting. Tracked down by Israeli intelligence to Buenos Aires, he was kidnaped to stand trial in Jerusalem for his leading role in the Holocaust, and hanged there on June 1, 1962. In its seventy-year history, this was Israel's only use of the death penalty, which is reserved exclusively for convicted Nazi war criminals. Having done little or nothing to bring Eichmann and fellow mass murderers to justice, despite Churchill's pledge to 'pursue them to the uttermost ends of the earth', the ten members of the UN

Security Council voted by eight votes to nil, with two abstentions, the USSR and Poland, to condemn the Israeli operation as a violation of Argentinean sovereignty.

Any Roman Catholics reading this sordid story should ask themselves why the Vatican, which throughout the entire war never uttered a single word to condemn, let alone lifted a single finger, to prevent the hounding and extermination of the Jews, was only too eager to deploy its manifold resources to spirit away their murderers. Yet all that was required was the reading out to congregations a pastoral letter from Pius XII forbidding Roman Catholics, on pain of ex-communication, to take part in any way in the persecution and murder of Jews. On Easter Sunday of 1937, a pastoral letter from the previous Pope, Pius XI, entitled 'With Burning Concern', was read out from every pulpit in Germany, protesting against violations by the Nazis of the Concordat agreed between the Third Reich and the Vatican in July 1933. So why no similar protest on behalf of the Jews? As for excommunication, the only one of a number of Nazi leaders of the Roman faith (including Hitler) not to die in good standing with their Church was Goebbels, denied the sacraments, not for his complicity in the greatest crime in human history, but for marrying a Protestant.

In his memoires, Bishop Hudal explained why his and his fellow clergy's sympathies lay with the Nazis and not their victims. In their war against the Third Reich, the Allies had 'used catchwords like democracy, race [?], religious liberty and Christianity as a bait for the masses. All these experiences were the reason why I felt duty bound after 1945 to devote all my charitable [sic!] work mainly to former [sic] National Socialists and fascists, especially [!!!] to so-called [!!!] "war criminals".' As with the Inquisition, we still await the Vatican's *mea culpa*. But going on past form, I have good cause to suspect it will be a long wait, perhaps forever, because, as the catechism says, the church 'cannot err', even when it once insisted, *contra* Galileo, that the sun revolved around the earth. What better reason can there be than the Vatican Rat Line to endorse Voltaire's war cry in his life-long battle against the obscurantism and persecutions of the Roman Catholic church: '*Écraser l'infame!*'.

Rarely did our itinerary miss a stay in Switzerland, our greatest love. In addition to Gunten on the magically serene Lake Thun, framed by the peaks of the Bernese Oberland, we dallied by lakes at Luzern, Locarno and Neuchâtel, and in the Alps at Crans Montana, which overlooks the Rhone Valley and where from our hotel we had a clear view of the Matterhorn. Our stay at the hotel was enlivened by an entertaining display of one-upmanship at our evening meal. At the table, next to ours there sat a married couple and two other diners, both male. The elevated social tone was announced from the outset by their selection of venison from the hunting menu. In the course of their rather noisy exchanges, I learned that the husband had set next to Bill Gates in a recent jet trip, and that he and his wife had once played a round of golf with Seve Ballesteros. Their son, Gideon, was 'doing very well in California', as was his mother's company, which manufactured aeroplane wings. Gideon's father then reminisced about his time studying for a Master's degree at University College London. This called for a response from their dining companions.

One of the pair, a scientist of some sort, related how he had flown into Hong Kong from an island in the South Pacific, and even though he was a member, had been barred from staying at the Jockey Club because he was wearing jeans. Then came the punch line. He checked into the Five Star Hilton instead. Now it was the turn of the fourth diner. Adopting the tone of an aristocrat, he dismissed the wines on the menu as 'bourgeois'. And so it went on through the meal. I said quietly to Maureen, 'I could play this game as well. I have accompanied the Prime Minister's wife on the euphonium at Tony Blair's Christmas party. And that's just for starters.'

In Germany, we stayed three times at Trier on the Mosel, the western capital of the Roman Empire and the birthplace of Karl Marx, where I bought the bust which now sits on our mantelpiece alongside a statuette of another famous Jewish revolutionary, Michelangelo's David. Trier is saturated with history, not all of it pleasant or enlightening. In addition to its Roman and revolutionary heritage, Trier was witness in the 16th century to a ferocious outbreak of witch-burning, instigated, naturally, by the city's Roman Catholic Archbishop, Johann von Schônenburg. Between 1587 and 1593, 368 women were burned at the stake as witches. Two local villages were left with only a single living woman. A scholar who protested against the massacre was himself arrested, and forced to recant after being threatened with the same fate. And quite right too. Does not the Bible, in Exodus 22:18, say, 'Thou shalt not suffer a witch to live'? I also have on a bookshelf the current edition of the Roman Catholic Catechism, which assures me that the church not only does not, but *cannot* err. So let there be no doubt: the Archbishop acted correctly.

We also stopped off three times at Lahnstein, near Coblenz, where the Rhine meets the Mosel, *en route* towards Switzerland. Always on our way up the Rhine we stopped at the place called the Lorelei, whereas legend has it, a jilted Lore Lay took her revenge on men by luring sailors to their deaths on the rocks below. Nearby there is a monument to the most famous German poet of them all, Heinrich Heine, who immortalised this story with his poem of the same name. Hounded from his homeland by those who deemed his political convictions too dangerous for the times, in Paris Heine found friendship and comradeship of a sort with another radical Jew on the run from his native Germany, Karl Marx.

Cologne, like Reims a casualty of war, presented a similarly sad sight. Flattened by 'Bomber' Harris's thousand bomber raid, also like Reims, its sole remaining glory is the soaring twin-towered cathedral. From there, we took a boat trip on the Rhine to Bonn, the birthplace of Beethoven. Further south, we explored the Black Forest and the ancient city of Freiburg, and further south again, stayed twice at Constance by the Boden See, where the already mighty Rhine turns west before finally swinging north along the German-French border. Constance is also where in 1415, the Bohemian religious reformer Jan Hus, after being given safe conduct to attend a Church Council, was burned alive for daring to criticise the corruption, worldly ways and false teachings of the Roman Catholic Church, and where today, one can visit, as we did, the museum devoted to his memory, in the house where he spent his last days of freedom. How I loath the Catholic church...but no more than Maureen did. Briefly married to it, she witnessed it from the inside...not a pretty sight at the best of times.

My special interest in the outer reaches of the old Soviet Empire took us to Dresden, now again resplendent in its former Baroque glory after incineration by allied bombing in the Second World War. But first I had to break our journey across Germany to visit the small town of Eisenach, the birthplace of Johann Sebastian Bach, where Maureen insisted on taking a photograph of me in front of a statue of my greatest hero. I took another of one of only slightly lesser rank, Martin Luther who, inspired by the teachings of the martyred Jan Hus, struck his historic blow against the Pope in this very same town, where he translated the Bible into German. For what was a small town (population even today only around 40,000) Eisenach has witnessed several other momentous milestones in German history. It was here in 1817 that a gathering of students launched the movement that would in 1871 culminate in the unification of Germany, and in 1869, another, of socialists, many of them comrades of Karl Marx, who founded the party that today, still dominates the German left, the German Social Democratic Party.

Dresden had for me a special significance quite aside from its restored beauty. I first visited Dresden with my wife and Andrew shortly after the Berlin Wall came down. Forty-five years after its destruction, its once glorious Elbe façade was still a just a heap of shattered masonry, as if its communist rulers had intended to preserve its ruins as a testimony to the evil ways of the west. Ironically, the raid had been carried out as gesture of solidarity to Stalin whose troops were approaching the city from the east. The war was nearly over, and the city had no war industries worth bombing, yet the raid was one the biggest mounted by the Allies in the entire conflict. The plan was to disrupt Dresden's rail connections, but in the event, the central train station escaped virtually unscathed. Instead, the bulk of the bombs, including the incendiaries, were concentrated on residential areas and the historic buildings of the river front, resulting in an estimated 25,000 deaths, among whom were a large number of refugees fleeing from the advancing Red Army. I came to know the full story of the Dresden raid when I first knew Maureen, and its tragedy, and the guilt of those responsible, moved me to include this couplet in one of the poems I wrote for her:

Young man over Dresden you are a maggot
The apples gone but still you bite.

Standing outside a tourist shop, Maureen caught sight of a display of post cards with photographs contrasting graphic views of Dresden before and after the raid. We had discussed the rights and wrong of the Dresden raid in the past, and unlike myself, she had never been able to make up her mind as to whether it had it had been justified. Maureen was no more a pacifist than I am, and had no doubt that the Allied cause was a totally just one. But the stark horror of what she saw, an entire city gutted, and the knowledge that thousands of its civilians had been burned or boiled alive for no good military reason finally convinced her. For Maureen, that was quite an achievement.

Leaving Dresden, we then embarked on what was our most ambitious and, as Maureen's chauffeur (she liked to call me Parker), easily my most demanding itinerary. Staying within the confines of the old Soviet Empire, our next destination was Prague, due south along the Elbe. However, I was set on paying homage to the land of *Solidarnosc*, so we headed even further east, and stopped off for a snack at Jelenia Gora, a small Polish town near the

German border. Here too there was a testament, even if in this case of a not too distant past. Until the end of the Second World War its name was Hirschberg, and its German inhabitants German Lutherans. Today, they are Polish Roman Catholics, thanks to an agreement between the 'Big Three', the USSR, Britain and the USA, at Potsdam in the summer of 1945, that vast tracts of German territory should be transferred to the Soviet Union on the Baltic, what had been East Prussia, and further west and south, to Poland.

Although estimates vary, it is safe to say that at least six million German civilians, mainly women and the young and the old, were either driven to the west, deported to the Soviet Union for slave labour or killed to make way for the new Polish and Russian settlers, resulting in the largest 'ethnic cleansing' in modern history. In what had previously been German Silesia, industrious Protestants had been replaced by largely rural, less-well educated Catholics, and the result around and in Jelenia Gora was an area that had a neglected, run-down look about it, while the only visible signs of economic activity in the town itself were a car park, a prostitute sitting on a door step with her legs apart, a café and a mobile stall selling memorabilia.

From Jelenia Gora we then doubled back to the Czech Republic and made for Prague, as we did so passing through another territory that had witnessed a post-war 'cleansing' of Germans, those of the Sudentland of infamous memory, handed over to Hitler in exchange for what Chamberlain promised would be 'peace for our time'. Here there was not so much neglect as abandonment. It seemed as if the descendants of the Czechs who moved in after the war had largely gone. Factories, obviously of pre-war vintage, stood empty, as did boarded up shops and homes. The streets were silent. As we neared Prague we saw evidence of a revitalised Czech economy, even if it was mainly Japanese high-tech factories. On the approach to the city centre along the right bank of the River Vltava, a tributary of the Elbe, we passed the spot where Reinhard Heydrich, the Nazi overlord of the 'Protectorate of Bohemia and Moravia' and together with Himmler and Eichmann, one of the chief architects of the Holocaust, was assassinated on May 27, 1942, by two members of the Czech resistance, Josef Gabnik and Jan Kubis. Betrayed by a fellow Czech, Gabnik committed suicide rather than be captured, while Kubis was killed in a shoot-out.

The centre of Prague is as beautiful as it is historic, with the main attractions being for us its heaving with tourists King Charles Bridge and massive monument of Jan Hus in the city's Old Town central square. I had visited Prague just after the so-called Velvet Revolution of November 1989, when most of the traffic was trams running on scenically bumpy rails, and the only decent restaurant in town was situated in the North Vietnamese Cultural Centre, and a meal for three cost less than a pound. Now we were spoilt for choice, but the prices had escalated somewhat, while the traffic was so dense it took us nearly an hour to battle our way from the river to our hotel.

For our next stop, we headed west over the German border into Bavaria for Regensburg, once the capital of the Holy Roman Empire, and the home after the Second World War of Schindler of the list. Situated on the three arms of the Danube, its main attractions were yet another magnificent cathedral and a well-preserved old town.

Still we were not done. Our *Alma Mater* on Lake Thun beckoned, a drive of about 570 kilometres. After being trapped in a traffic jam that began near Munich and continued off and on for the best part of the day, and then, having finally escaped it, driven over a tortuously winding Alpine pass in near darkness, by the time we reached our hotel in Gunten, we had been on the road for at least twelve hours. Forgoing my usual cup of coffee, I took a shower and went straight to bed.

The lure of the East also took us to a fourth former Soviet colony, Estonia, this time by plane, where we stayed in its immaculately restored medieval capital of Tallin. I was intrigued by the way that with the Soviets gone, the native population had assumed the dominant status once enjoyed by their Russian masters. All the shops and cafes inside the Old Town wall, judging by their names, were owned by Estonians, while outside the wall, Russians plied a miserable trade. Up on a hill overlooking the city towered the three-domed legacy of Estonia's departed overlords, the Russian Orthodox Cathedral named after folk hero Alexandra Nevsky, the prince who defeated the Teutonic Knights at the battle of Lake Peipus in 1242. Restored by the Estonians after decades of neglect by the Soviets, its interior, aglow with gold and icons, is a wonder to behold.

Of all our excursions abroad, the one that for Maureen proved to be the most spectacular and memorable was to Iceland. The terrain, composed almost entirely of volcanic lava, more resembled the surface of Mars than planet Earth. Geysers gushed up everywhere, and hardly a blade of grass or any other vegetation could be seen outside the capital city of Reykjavik. Just as unreal was the sun still shining at midnight, since we were there on the longest day. And to cap it all, running north to south down the island was the ever-widening gap caused by the gradual separation of the tectonic plates supporting Europe to the east and North America to the west. It was at the very place where this rift is most clearly visible that the Vikings chose to convene the world's first parliament, the *Thingvellir*, in AD 930, predating that of England, supposedly the mother of all Parliaments, by more than three centuries. The unique starkness of the topography, and its geological and historical import, moved us both deeply. It was the one experience that more than any other Maureen returned to when recounting to others our adventures abroad.

Finally, from the majestic and momentous to the minuscule, there was Lichtenstein. *En route* on a car trip from north Italy to south Germany, Maureen insisted we made a slight detour to stop briefly in the Principality (blink and you will drive straight through it) even if only to buy a fridge magnet to prove we had been there.

It would not be an exaggeration to say that the time we

spent abroad, and where we spent it, not only transformed Maureen's life, enabling her to see things, as she once told her daughter, 'that I could not possibly have imagined', but, as travel always should, also broadened her mind no less than mine. On my first visit to Maureen in Swansea, when we inevitably got around to talking about politics (I clearly remember it was in her kitchen over a cup of tea) I quickly discovered that she was what today would be described as a Eurosceptic, and had a referendum been held then, in 1999, on Britain's membership of the European Union, I have sneaking suspicion she would have voted to leave. But in June 2016, she voted to remain, and what is more, with some conviction.

What had changed her mind were not my occasional onslaughts on the Eurosceptic lies, half-truths and sheer xenophobia peddled by her *Daily Mail,* but encountering and experiencing and in time savouring and acknowledging the fact that Europeans had more to teach us about civilised living than we them. No marauding gangs of drunken young men up for a fight, and shoals of screaming young and not so young woman, already out of it on a couple of pints, ruining a pleasant evening for anyone with a few grey hairs. Little or no litter (partly due to a dearth of junk food outlets), and public transport not only superior but ludicrously cheaper than back at home, where it is the costliest in all of Europe. In the town centres, a coffee and wine culture prevail, with couples and their children out for a relaxed Saturday evening meal. No intimidation, no gangs, no boorishness. Everywhere we went, we met with not just politeness but a genuine friendliness we hardly deserved, seeing that on the continent, Brexit Brits have acquired a largely merited reputation for looking down on its inhabitants as a collection of semi-barbarians who haven't learned to speak English proper.

Not that Maureen's conversion to a Europhile was instant. On one of our early trips abroad, when were in Dieppe, we met up with what proved to be a loquacious British truck driver, who tagged along with us as we strolled through a quayside market. In no time at all, our truck driving acquaintance had become *persona non-grata* with Maureen when, comparing his own country to the European states he was constantly visiting, with unconcealed scorn he described Britain as an 'insignificant little offshore island'. When we ran into him again a little later, Maureen said to me, 'I want to keep well away from him.'

Ten or so years on, we were in Cremona, the birth place of the father of opera, Claudio Monteverdi, and of the Stradivarius violin, of whose maker there is a statue in the lovely city's main square. On the first evening, just before were due to go out for a meal, we could hear through our open hotel window clattering, banging and scraping sounds. We looked down, and saw hundreds of chairs and small tables being neatly assembled in the square below. Later that same evening, after our meal, we were back in our room when another sound began to rise up from below, this time a low buzzing. Again, we looked out. Now all the tables, and there were literally hundreds, were occupied by mainly young men and women, sipping their coffees and chatting, the combined effect of which had produced the buzzing we heard from our widow. Maureen and I did not have to say what we were both thinking, even though we did. It just so happened to be a Saturday, and in our minds, we contrasted the civilised and convivial scene below with the mayhem and even murder and rape that a few hundred miles away to the north-west, were being unleashed by rampaging drug and alcohol fuelled barbarians on the city centres of our proud offshore island.

It was in the same city that we witnessed what I afterwards referred as the Cremona effect. It is a well-known and long-established fact that woman have always been and still are now more likely to be religious than men, and when they are, to be more devout. On Sunday, on our way back from a walk by the Po, Italy's longest river, we passed by a church, where in the car park were half a dozen or so cars, each with a man setting at the wheel. Inside, mass was underway for what can only have been their wives, rather like the scene from the film *Manon des Source*, except that the men are all in the bar. The sight recalled for me how Darwin, and Verdi similarly used to accompany their wives to church, wait outside, and then take then home.

It has always puzzled me how a religion that denies women the right to conduct its services is still able without much difficulty to sustain their belief in its teachings. How many Roman Catholic women are aware that the partition in the confession box was introduced to protect women from being raped by their confessors?

It was such cultural variables that added an extra dimension of interest and edification to our travels aboard. For example, when we were Ireland, after three nights in cosmopolitan Dublin, which proved something of a disappointment, we headed down to Cork, a traditional centre of militant Irish republicanism. I noticed in a café that unlike everywhere else we had been in the EU, all the European Union flags were on display except one, ours. Old memories die hard, especially in Cork, where there stands a massive monument, erected in 1906, to the memory of the risings against English rule of 1798, 1803, 1848 and 1867.

On four occasions, we were joined on our foreign ventures by Maureen's daughter and her partner Jess. The first was to the Basque region of the western Pyrenees, where we self-catered for a week, while the next three, ranging from the Rhineland to Switzerland, Provence and Tuscany, were officially conducted under the auspices of Blick Tours. One of the features of the package was a pre-recorded in-car commentary that provided detailed historical, political and cultural information on the locations passed through and visited. I am not joking.

Maureen's profound attachment to Wales ensured that not all our excursions were to Europe. We spent four nights at a hotel in the heart of Snowdonia, from where we circumnavigated the Island of Anglesey and visited the location for the cult TV series *The Prisoner* at Portmierion, and via the Beacons made frequent day trips to Brecon, where visits to a labyrinthine second-hand book shop necessitated the installation of yet more shelves in the loft. Nearer to home, a 30-minute drive would take us to the Gower, with a half a dozen bays and beaches on the south side, and utter tranquillity, and the glorious vista of the Loughor Estuary on the north. And always a pub for a coffee or a snack.

It might seem from this account that ours was always a life of leisure. Not quite. On my arrival at 169, it was obvious to us both that was serious renovation work to be done on Maureen's property. An old building, typical of most of Swansea's housing stock, it had fallen into serious disrepair due to Maureen's lack of means do much about it. For years, Maureen told me, Les had talked about undertaking some serious DIY, but predictably, with the betting shop commanding first claim on his spare cash, it was just that, talk. Ridding the structure of damp was the first priority, followed by a new back door to replace one that Swansea's all too frequent relentless rainfall had rotted away. In an act of defiance against the Swansea gloom, we had the outer walls painted a bright yellow, which when caught by the odd moments of sunshine, positively glowed. Another priority for Maureen was creating a space to store my books by covering the floor of her spacious loft. Later it would also serve as a perfect location to reassemble my model railway.

With the house now secure against the worst the elements could hurl at us, we could set about gradually upgrading the interior. Even some of the basics were lacking, again for the same reason. We bought a washing machine to replace the one that long ago had given up the ghost, and a micro-wave oven. Strictly according to designs and colour schemes devised by Maureen (I was merely the labourer), all walls were repainted. In the living room and the hall, old carpets were removed and replaced by wooden flooring, new carpets laid on the stairs and the landing, chairs and sofas re-upholstered, the bathroom re-floored, banisters replaced, books shelves inserted into living room alcoves, and new pictures hung on walls. Finally, the *piece de la resistance*, came the installation of an entirely new kitchen, courtesy of a cut-price offer from B&Q. What newly married couples normally do in their twenties or thirties, we were doing in our sixties!

The garden was likewise in need of serious attention, again, not because of any neglect on Maureen's part – she was at her happiest when potting her plants or manicuring the lawn – but simply through lack of funds. The wooden shed had rotted away, while the wooden fencing running along the access lanes at the end and down one side of the garden was on its last legs. The extra I was earning from tutoring was more than enough to cover the cost of putting matters right. The same local handyman who did our inside work erected breezeblock walls to replace the fencing, and I somehow managed to assemble a flat pack green plastic shed. A visit to the local garden centre for a boot-full of potted plants and Maureen was in business.

That just left Maureen's clarinet. It must have been getting on for fifty years old by the time I had moved to Swansea, but even so, like its owner, its body was in pretty fair shape, likewise the keys. Only the pads needed servicing, and once they had been fixed, the instrument was as good as new. With two hours practice most days, it wasn't long before Maureen was sight reading the slow movements from Mozart's clarinet concerto and quintet, and the Swan from Saint Saens' *Carnival of the Animals,* and with a lovely rounded tone. She was a natural. Maureen was quite hot on her scales too, partly because sometimes when we were in bed, I used to test her by calling out some of the trickier ones, and she had to recite the notes in the correct ascending order. It was so sad that she had to give up playing when her breathing became more difficult.

XVI

My daughter Katharine's romantic involvements were invariably with fellow musicians. After numerous such liaisons, usually with drummers, the dodgiest of the lot, in 2006, she finally settled down and made a home with Nick Marsh, a highly talented and successful vocalist and guitarist who was currently a member of the Urban Voodoo Machine, an uncategorizable but highly entertaining and successful ensemble led by a thoroughly Anglicised Norwegian, Paul Ronney Angel. I had known Nick from my Horsepower days, when he appeared on the same bill as a solo act, and from the time a little later, after I had moved to Swansea, when I recorded on some of the tracks of albums he produced with Katharine. Only a few years on, with the birth of first Ava and then Rosa, he had become the father to two of my four grandchildren.

Naturally concerned that living in Swansea could lead to my becoming estranged from my children's offspring, in my stays in London, I split my time between staying with Andrew in the west, in Acton, and in the east with Katharine in Walthamstow. In Acton, where Andrew's wife Nicola reigned supreme, everything went by the numbers. In Walthamstow, benign chaos ruled. Then in 2014, Nick contracted throat cancer, possibly, though I do not know all the details, as a result of smoking. Katharine never allowed smoking in her home by anyone, but I believe Nick indulged his habit elsewhere nevertheless. And he was a terrible boozer. Despite several treatments and operations, his condition deteriorated, and after being transferred to a hospice, died in June 2015. I came to London to see Nick and say goodbye shortly before he died, but he was unconscious, because at Katharine's insistence, he had already been sedated. Katharine was wonderfully resilient throughout this terrible time, and with the unflagging support of my wife, ensured her two children survived the ordeal as best as could be hoped.

Katharine being Katharine, she intended that Nick's open-air humanist funeral should be conducted on the grandest of scales. After refreshments and listening to a programme of music, several hundred mourners would make their way to Nick's open grave in the nearby woods, led by the Urban Voodoo Machine's New Orleans-style marching band, an *ad hoc* spin off from the original act. As Nick's father-in-law, Katharine very much wanted me to play on my piccolo trumpet in the band, and Paul Ronney, who was a close friend of Nick's, agreed. It so happened that the Voodoo Machine were playing a gig in Swansea a week before the funeral, which gave me the opportunity to turn up early at the venue and run through the four tunes they intended to play, two slowly, to the burial, and then two up-beat on the way back, as was the tradition in New Orleans funerals. The ceremony at Nick's grave was superbly conducted by a lady in Nick's band. She moved me, and not only me, to tears. She spoke not of God and an afterlife, but of the return of the elements that composed Nick's body to the star dust from which it came, to create new life in what is the grand cycle of nature. Five years after Nick's death, Katharine became engaged to yet another musician, a really decent and very intelligent bloke called Michael, who made bagpipes (yes, bagpipes) for a living. Trust Katharine!

A while after the funeral, Katharine rang to tell me that Paul Ronney intended to keep the marching band going, and would like me to join it. With nothing happening for me in Swansea apart from a monthly open mike night at the jazz club, and with Gyratory System on its last legs, I naturally said yes. Paul Ronney called a few days later, and gave me the dates of two upcoming engagements for the new band. Was I hearing right? The first was at the Camden Roundhouse, providing the musical entertainment for the annual *Classic Rock Magazine's* Roll of Honour Dinner and Awards. The second was at the 02 Millennium Dome, as a support act for an American band. Apart from Ronnie Scotts and the gig at the Brixton Academy, this for me was a different league entirely. Even though the world of rock music is an entirely alien one for me – after all, it helped to kill off jazz – I still recognised some of the names of those being presented with awards for this, that or the other. Living Legend, Re-issue of the Year, Film of the year, Band of the year, Comeback of the Year, Classic Album of the Year, Album of the Year, Maestro of the Year, Showman of the Year…it was as if the number of awards had been calibrated to ensure that just like a children's birthday party, nobody went home empty handed. The Marching Band made its entry into the main arena just before the dinner was due to begin, to the cheers and applause of an audience of mainly aging rockers accompanied by ladies who looked half their age or less.

After we had done our stint, I picked up a free copy of the event's sponsor, the magazine *Classic Rock*. I did not read it until I arrived back in Swansea. Leafing through, there on its centre spread, was a feature entitled *Magic and Loss*, with a full-page colour picture of Katharine and Nick. Katharine, like her father would do two years on, had felt compelled to express and preserve in print her grief at the loss of her lover. Much of the talk in the first part of the interview was of the music she had made with Nick over the previous decade, and of their last collaboration, *From the Deep*. Then came Nick's death and his funeral.

'I was still numb and in denial at the time, so it put me in my comfort zone because I'm used to organising events. It gave me something to focus on. Paul Ronny came over every night for about three weeks, we'd get drunk, commiserate and obsessively organise it all. It turned out to be a really epic, rock'n'roll funeral in Epping Forrest. We got all our musicians to play, people made amazing speeches and there was lots of dancing. Paul Ronny led all the horn players and drummers through the forest in a New Orleans style band to Nick's grave.'

Katharine is more resilient, much more, than me. Perhaps it is also a matter of sheer necessity, since unlike myself, others depended on her to keep going, not only her two young girls, but those with whom she makes her musical career. 'You can't just fall apart. If my kids need to keep going to the same school, I need to keep doing the things that I was before. There's been so much change lately and music is a lifeline. The Medieval Baebes is a walk in the park compared to the rest of my life. I'm a survivor, you know.' More than that, my Katharine. You are a winner. Since Maureen's death, I too have continued to make music, which I am sure is what Maureen would have wanted me to do. As I have said, I have formed a new trio with James, the bass player from Gyratory System, and a top-class drummer friend of his, which James insisted on naming, over my objections, The Blick Trio, and I now play occasionally with the Urban Voodoo Machine as well as the marching band when the gigs are in London or not too far from Swansea. Without music, and my memories of Maureen, my life would have very little purpose and meaning.

So much for music. What of politics? Back in London, I had for some years been an almost totally inactive member of the Labour Party, and this continued after the move to Swansea. I did, however, attend two meetings for the selection of the Labour Party's parliamentary candidate and took note of the fact that on both occasions, all four of the prospective candidates were women, and that at the second meeting, the candidate selected worked in the office of the retiring MP selected at the first. Both Maureen and I suspected that perhaps there had not been a very level, gender-free playing field. I should point out that when I first knew her, Maureen had been all for women's equality, but in recent years, had become increasingly critical of what today passes for feminism, with its demanding special treatment, obsession about a largely imaginary glass ceiling while ignoring and even justifying the appalling treatment of their sisters in the Islamic world. Apart from the two selection meetings, the only other Labour Party events I attended were socials, where I was joined by Maureen. At one, there was a team quiz on the First World War. As it was one of my specialities, I suggested to my team that if they wanted to win, they leave the answering to me. The prize, a bottle of whiskey, I handed over to Maureen. I am strictly a wine and occasional port man, whereas Maureen was also partial to stronger brews.

When I arrived in Swansea, I would say that in some respects, mainly in matters of economic policy, I was to the left of Maureen, though in elections, we both always voted Labour. After the election in 2008 of Cameron, Maureen edged ever so slightly to the left, while I moved in the opposite direction, resulting in our sharing pretty much common ground on most issues in the last few years; that is, for a mixed economy, with the railways and the utilities back under public ownership and no privatisation of the NHS. We both were dismayed by the capture of the Labour Party by the Corbynistas, with their pandering to the primitive prejudices of Islam, and Corbyn's associations with Muslim terrorists. These were issues that we learned were best avoided with her daughter.

As I have already related in another context, when Israel replied to the Hamas terrorist tunnelling and rocket attacks in the summer of 2014, the anti-Zionist response of much of the left, and in fact beyond it, compelled me, with the encouragement of my friend Mark, to write what finally resulted in the book initially entitled *Allah's Useful Idiots, or, The Socialism of Fools*: *Islam, the Jews and the Sharia Left*. Despite the warning of 9/11, I did not anticipate when I began it that the next years would witness an escalating series of terrorist attacks on civilians throughout the West, and that the Labour Party would be subverted by those who sympathised with their perpetrators. I completed the substance of the book only a matter of weeks before Maureen's death, and as I knew from her many often-acerbic comments that her views on its subject largely coincided with mine, I dedicated the work to her shortly after she died.

When the far-leftist takeover of the Labour Party brought with it an upsurge of hatred against Israel and, in some case, against the Jews, after Corbyn was re-elected as

Leader of the Labour Party in September 2016, I resigned my forty-two years of membership, explaining my motives for doing so.

'*24 September 2016*

The purpose of this communication is to formally inform you of my resignation from the Labour Party, effective as from the date of this email. I owe it both to you and myself to provide the reasons for this decision, which I can assure you I have not taken lightly. I joined the Labour Party forty-two years ago, believing that it was the only political organisation that could represent and advance the interests of working people. The re-election of Jeremy Corbyn as party leader has convinced me, and I have good reasons to believe many others, that this is no longer the case. The party has allowed itself to be hi-jacked by infiltrators, many of whom have been proved to have either belonged to or voted for parties other than Labour, or to organisations whose ethos and methods are totally opposed to those of the Labour Party, and are incompatible with its rules of membership.

Since the election of Corbyn and the emergence of Momentum as the dominant force in the party, electoral support has been in catastrophic decline in those very areas of the country that are its traditional strongholds, not least because the party has become the vehicle for the ambitions of self-indulgent political playboys who care nothing for those the party was founded to represent. However, important though they are, these are not my main reasons for leaving the Labour Party.

As a life-long opponent of anti-Semitism, I cannot remain in a party led by someone who throughout his career as an MP has collaborated with individuals and movements who make no secret of their enmity towards the Jews, and in the cases of his 'friends' Hamas and Hezbollah, have as their avowed goal not only the destruction of Israel but the murder of its entire Jewish population. Corbyn has also taken paid employment with the state-run Iranian Press TV channel, that is, with a regime whose Supreme leader proclaims that it is his aim to 'wipe Israel off the map' and which amongst its many victims that include poets, secularists and Kurds, publicly hangs homosexuals from cranes.

I do not believe that it was by co-incidence that Corbyn's election as leader was accompanied by an upsurge of quite open hostility towards the Jews, to such a degree that he was with some reluctance compelled to commission what predictably proved to be toothless inquiry into Labour Party anti-Semitism. What sort of party has Labour become that a Jewish MP critical of Corbyn's leadership, after receiving 25,000 abusive messages, some of them death threats and many of them anti-Semitic, has found it necessary to attend the party conference accompanied by a bodyguard?

Robin Blick, Swansea CLP.'

Maureen understood why I had left the Labour Party, that it was part of my general disenchantment with the modern left, which with the Corbyn take-over of Labour, I shared with thousands of other veteran members who made the same decision. Ironically, the election of Corbyn as Labour Leader in September 2015 had exactly the opposite effect on Maureen's daughter. It did not greatly surprise me. The previous year, we had fallen out over Israel's response to the kidnapping and murder by Hamas of three young Israeli men, and the terror group's tunnelling and firing rockets into Israeli territory. In one of a series of emailed exchanges that passed between us, she argued that my support for Israel's military reaction to these attacks lacked 'nuance', which was indeed true, the reason being that as I say in my *Socialism of Fools*, Israel was reacting in the same way as would any other country if its citizens were murdered, and its territory attacked and invaded by terrorists. Israel's response to these violations of its sovereignty was entirely in accordance with resolutions on the subject approved by the United Nations in 1974. After an on-line debate that failed to narrow the wide gulf that separated our respective positions, we agreed to call it a day.

Now fast forward a year, to September 2015. Meantime, Andrea and her partner Jess had moved to Swansea. As we did every Friday, Maureen and I were doing our big weekly shop in town, stopping off as usual for a coffee and a snack at Gershwin's, our favourite café As Andrea worked a four day week, with Friday off, we had arranged to meet up at Gershwin's. Only a few days previously, Corbyn had emerged as the winner of Labour's leadership contest. Fully appraised as to his political agenda which, as a fanatical anti-Zionist, naturally included his support of his 'friends' Hamas and Hezbollah, and of his Stalinist pedigree and record of associations with anti-Semites, I said to Maureen as we approached Gershwin's, 'I'm dreading this…I know Andrea's going to be overboard for Corbyn.' And so she was. Expecting me to respond in kind, and quite taken aback when I did not, she asked me, 'Is he too left wing?' 'No' I replied. 'It's the company he keeps.' It was evident from her reaction that this was an aspect of Labour's newly-anointed Messiah that she knew nothing about, even though it had been the subject of comment in the media. When my attempt to remedy this oversight met with a marked degree of scepticism, I said I would email to her the sources of my information, which a day so later, I did.

A few days later again, back came her reply. Being, like her mum, both highly intelligent and of a liberal (with a small l) disposition, I had reason not just to hope but expect that it would say something like 'That's awful – thanks for telling me' or 'That's disgusting'. The reply she did send proved something of a disappointment. It consisted of just one word: 'Interesting'. Not wanting a re-run of our rather testy spat over the Israel-Hamas conflict, I let it rest there After all, Andrea was far from being alone in her enthusiasm for a politician who, throughout his long career, had consistently associated himself with individuals, movements and even regimes whose ideologies and objectives were in almost every respect diametrically opposed to hers. For example, Andrea has described herself to me a feminist. But Corbyn, as she must have been well aware, sang the praises of a religion that relegates its female adherents to the status of second class citizens, with its holy book sanctioning wife-beating (80% of Pakistani husbands beat their wives), marital rape and the sexual enslavement of captive infidel women and, following the example of the religion's founder, child marriage and the practice known as 'thighing', a form of masturbation which involves inserting and rubbing the penis between a child's or even a baby's legs. Then of course there is female genital mutilation, sanctioned by the prophet in a so-called *hadith*, an allegedly recorded saying of Mohammed. Anyone in the UK found guilty of committing any of these offences would be due for a long prison sentence and, for most of them, have their names entered on the sexual offences register for the rest of their lives. Yet in Corbyn's book (and not only his by a long way) anyone criticising the religion that sanctions these crimes would be accused either of racism (absurd, because Islam is not a race) or Islamophobia, a word invented back in the 1970's by Iranian clerics for the specific purpose of criminalising criticism of Islam, one which subsequently was adopted by western legal systems with same end in view, now defined as 'hate crime'.

Then there is racism. Andrea is no less an anti-racist than she is a feminist. But Islam is racist, specifically, anti-Semitic, as have been scores of Corbyn's closest political collaborators, infidel and Muslim alike, in the anti-Zionist movements that he either sponsors. or promotes in various ways. And Islam sanctions slavery, and to this day, its Arab followers still practice it in the slave auctions and markets of Libya and Yemen. Andrea once told me she considered slavery a greater crime than the Nazi extermination of the Jews. Some Muslims practice the first, while others either deny or applaud the second. But none of these abominations has elicited any condemnation from Corbyn. His eyes and meagre intellectual powers are trained on only one enemy...Israel and the 'imperialist west'. Here too, in the normal run of things, Andrea would have found herself totally at odds with Corbyn's global allegiances. She believes in democracy and human rights. Yet all the regimes Corbyn has directly associated himself with, publicly defended and, in one instance, actually worked for, rule over peoples whose human rights are either distinctly in short supply, or non-existent: Cuba, Venezuela, Nicaragua, Iran, China, Russia, Syria, Gaza.

Finally there was Europe. While Andrea was no less a Europhile than her mother or myself, Corbyn, like his Stalinists associates, and for the same anti-Western reasons, was a dyed in the wool Europhobe, in the year before his election as Labour Leader denouncing the EU in the Communist Party's *Morning Star* as a 'tool of US foreign policy'. (According to another article by Corbyn in the same journal the USA in its turn was in the grip of what he called the 'Zionist lobby'.) Previously, in a speech in 2009, he had described the EU as a 'Frankenstein' and called for a referendum on the UK's membership. In 2016, he got the referendum and the result that he wanted, the very next day being the first party leader to demand the activation of Article 50, which set in motion the process of the UK's withdrawal from the EU. His Johnsonian determination to 'get Brexit done' should have come as no surprise to anyone acquainted with Corbyn's voting record in the House of Commons. Defying the Labour whip, he had from the beginning of his parliamentary career invariably voted with Tory Eurosceptics against every bill emanating from Brussels. As was the case with thousands of converts to the Corbyn cult, so far as I was able to ascertain, none of this seemed to register in the same way for Andrea as it did for me. The result was that as I and those of a like mind exited through the party's revolving door, Andrea joined the flood of those who, like her, many for the best of motives, poured in.

What Andrea thinks of the so- called 'Project' now, after

it has ended, as I predicted it would, in the proverbial tears, I have never asked and have no intention of doing so in the future. And anyway, who am I to crow over one *faux pas* when I committed more than my fair share in a political odyssey that began with Stalinism and then, via various schools of Bolshevism, has ended with my subscribing to a mildly leftist First Amendment libertarianism and, after Keir Starmer's election, returning to the Labour Party at the age of 83. To repeat Hegel, 'The owl of Minerva flies only at dusk.' Neither have I sought her opinion about what is in some respects, the successor to the failed Corbyn 'Project', Black Lives Matter, though I have emailed her reports of some its activities and policy statements, both of which have revealed the movement as intrinsically and even at times explicitly racist and anti-Semitic. What I do find extraordinary even in these woke times is how a movement which has much to say about the enslavement of black Africans in centuries past, but nothing about their enslavement today or the scourge of London's 'black on black' knife attacks and murders, a movement which calls for the abolition of the police and the nuclear family, and which claims that the UK is a racist country, and yet despite its blatant double standards, racism and lies, has been able effectively to hi-jack some of the UK's, and in some cases, the world's most hallowed institutions. For example, in the wake of the British Library Chief Librarian, Liz Jolly's, claim that racism 'is the creation of white people'(where? when? which 'white people'...all of them? How? In a laboratory perhaps?) came the announcement that pursuant to the de-whitening and de-colonising of the library, it would be considering the removal of its statues of Beethoven and Mendelssohn, as they were symbols of the alleged supremacy of white western civilisation. Had these ignoramuses but know it, the cultural fascists responsible this truly Talibanesque proposal were emulating the two most repressive regimes in human history. In 1936, the Nazis pulled down statues of the Jewish Mendelssohn in Leipzig and Dusseldorf, while a dozen or so years later, his portrait was removed from display at the Moscow Conservatoire as part of Stalin's murderous campaign against so called 'cosmopolitans without kith or kin'…code for the Jews. As for Beethoven, far from being a symbol of white supremacy, it was at his insistence that George Bridgetower, a black musician, played the violin part, Beethoven accompanying him on the piano, in the first performance of his so-called Kreutzer sonata, opus 47. And Beethoven it was who chose Schiller's *Ode to Joy* (originally to Freedom) as the text for his ninth symphony, the choral, with its humanist message, now, sad to say, no longer in season, that when joy 're-unites all that custom has divided, all men become brothers'. Surely, the Chief Librarian of the world's best-stocked library would be better placed than anyone else to avail themselves of these facts before making such an inanely ill-informed proposal.

To leave no one in any doubt as to the sincerity and import of the library's Damascus moment, and the new tasks it imposed on its employees, the library's Chief Executive Roly [sic] Keating told a staff meeting that 'the killing of George Floyd and the Black Lives Matter movement are the biggest challenge to the complacency of organisations, institutions and ways of doing things that we are likely to see in our lifetimes'. Let us test the validity of Keating's extraordinary but, so it would seem, uncontested assertion.

Rather than seeking to impugn his powers as a prophet, let us see how he makes out as an historian. Along with several other million current inhabitants of the UK, my 'lifetime' had already begun before September 3, 1939, the day Britain and France declared war on Nazi Germany. I would submit that the Second World which ensued, ending six years later, with the unconditional surrender of Japan on August 14, 1945, subjected Britain's 'organisations, institutions and ways of doing things' to an immeasurably greater challenge than the killing of George Floyd and the emergence of Black Lives Matter. And if Mr Keating made the time to do so instead of delivering ill-informed agitational speeches to his staff about the epoch-shaping significance of Black Lives Matter, he will find ample proof to support my claim in either the military or the British history sections of his library. There he will learn that the UK's casualties as a result of enemy action in that war were 383,000 military deaths, and 376,000 military wounded, and civilian deaths, 67,000. In London alone, deaths through bombing were 30,000, with 50,000 wounded. Again, just in London, 70,000 dwellings were destroyed, and 1.7 million damaged.

The library's lead was rapidly followed by the British Museum, which announced that on the grounds of a fictitious complicity with British colonialism, the hitherto exalted status of Charles Darwin, an outspoken opponent of slavery, would be under review.

Meanwhile, the BBC provoked a furious backlash against its announced intention to the stage the last night of its severely Covid19-truncated and audienceless Proms season with no-vocal renditions of the traditional Land of Hope and Glory and Rule Britannia. The BBC let it be known that it no longer approved of the lyrics of the second song, since they could be interpreted as a justification of British colonialism and slavery. One has to assume, given the objections to the song's alleged message, that these are offending lines:

> The nations not so blest as thee
> Must, in their turn, to tyrants fall
> While thy shall flourish great and free
> The dread and envy of them all…
> Rule Britannia, Britannia rules the waves,
> Britons never never never shall be slaves.

The first five lines are simply statements of indisputable historical fact. From the Spain of the Inquisition in the West to the Russia of the Tsars in the East, continental Europe, with the exceptions of the Netherlands and Switzerland, was ruled by tyrannies, while England, thanks to Oliver

Cromwell, whose statue, along with Churchill's, was on the BLM hit list, had a century previously already taken the first steps towards the Parliamentary democracy that it is today. Precisely because England had, as early as the Magna Carta of 1225, (hence the line, 'this was the Charter, the Charter of the land') established the principle that all, including the monarch, were subject to the same laws and, with the Glorious Revolution of 1688, in its *Bill of Rights*, that of the supremacy of Parliament, it had indeed earned the envy of those in Europe who were denied but desired these freedoms and institutions, among them being the anglophiles Beethoven, Mendelssohn and Voltaire, the father of the French Enlightenment. And it just so happened that during his exile in England, Voltaire shared membership of the radical Beefsteak Club with the author of the lyrics of *Rule Britannia*, the poet James Thomson. The whiggish Thomson was famed in his day for his epic poem entitled, not 'In Defence of Slavery' but simply 'Liberty', which celebrated and charted the rise of freedom from its origins in ancient Greece through Magna Carta to its triumph in the Glorious Revolution, an event which did indeed, whatever the BLMistas at the BBC might say, make England one of the freest, if not the freest of nations on our planet.

Voltaire was far from being the only freedom-seeking exile to land on Britannia's shores. From as early as the 16th century, with the arrival of the Huguenots, through the revolutionary exiles of the mid to late 19th, Karl Marx being the most famous (or notorious) and Jews fleeing Tsarist pogroms, to refugees from Nazi and Stalinist tyranny in the 2Oth century and the horrors of the Religion of Peace's fratricidal holy wars in the 21st, Britannia has been a beacon of freedom and haven for the persecuted like no other country in Europe, or the world for that matter, save for the no less institutionally racist USA. History records no comparable movement in the opposite direction.

As for the fifth line, when this song was composed in 1740, Britannia did indeed 'rule the waves', having over the previous half century established a world-wide naval supremacy that it retained until the Second World War. This too is simply an assertion of an incontestable fact. Now we come to the sixth line which, by the same alchemy of 1984 Newspeak, in which war became peace, and freedom slavery, has likewise had its meaning transformed into its opposite, being construed as justifying slavery. And here we have a case of truly nauseating hypocrisy. Those who hunt down and seek to erase all traces of crimes the West has committed in what is now a distant past, as they fondly believed was about to be achieved with the banning of Rule Britannia, are silent about the very worst of crimes being committed, not centuries go by Beethoven, Darwin and Mendelssohn, but today, by Arab slave traders. These black lives do not matter, any more than do those of the young black men being gunned down every day on the streets of Chicago, and knifed on the streets of London. And it is for the same reason, because their killers and attackers are not white. Dare to say 'all black lives matter', and you will be called a racist, as happened to me on of all places, a Jewish website.

When it became the turn of the Proms to be decolonised, on this occasion, after a public outcry, the denizens of BLM met with a rebuff. But elsewhere, the bandwagon, or rather juggernaut, rolled on, with knee-taking and BLM shirt logos at football games, and a Bristol medical school announcing that it would be de-colonising its teaching syllabus. On Radio 3, I heard a prominent figure in the musical establishment explaining how 'the murder of George Floyd [sic…this was said before the trials of the accused had even begun] and Black Lives Matter' should 'affect how we think about classical music.' Just how was left unsaid. The UK was going woke-crazy, and any public figure who dared say so ran the very real risk of being accused of any number of unforgiveable sins, the worst being racism.

The self-appointed judge and jury in such cases will either be Black Lives Matter or, as is more likely for tactical reasons, those who, irrespective of their private thoughts on the subject, have deemed it expedient to dance to its socially divisive, racial supremacist tune. As an example of the emergent BLM groupthink, we can do no better than two on-line postings by Yusra Khogali, the Religion of Peace co-founder of Toronto Black Lives Matter, that she made in the summer of 2020.

'Melanin enables black skin to capture light and hold it in its memory mode, which proves that blackness converts light into knowledge. Melanin communicates directly with cosmic energy. This is why the indegeniety [sic] of all humxnity [sic] comes from blackness. We are the first and strongest of all humxns. Menaline [sic] is essential for the efficient performance of all the body [sic] natural functions. Therefore white ppp [sic] are recessive genetic defects. [sic] This is factual. White ppp need white supremacy as a mechanism to protect their survival as a people because all they can do is produce themselves. Black ppl through their superior genes can literally wipe out the white race if we had the power to do so.'

What was that about whites creating racism? Another posting, much briefer, and directed heavenwards, read:

'Plz Allah give me the strength not to cuss/kill these men and [?] white folks out here today. Plz plz plz.'

Ironically, many of those who criticise BLM from the right have defined it in the same way as its founders, as a Marxist movement Yet what we have depicted and advocated here, as in many of BLM's other pronouncements, bears not the remotest resemblance to Marx's struggle of classes. However, what it not only resembles, but replicates almost exactly is the Nazi struggle of *races*. The only difference, and it is a minor one, is that whereas with Nazis, 'Aryan' or 'Nordic' thinking was done with the blood, according to Ms Khogali, blacks do it with their skin. We can be reasonably sure that the *Fuehrer* of

BLM Toronto did not invent this racist nonsense herself. It is more than likely, given the current predominance of wokeness and 'critical race theory' in academe, that it first saw the light of day on a university campus. How did we come to find ourselves in a situation where not only politicians but the heads of our cultural, informational, sporting and educational institutions feel obliged to genuflect before a movement that embraces and promotes such rancid racism?

The rise of Black Lives Matter (ironically, for all its alleged 'Marxism' largely dependent for its funding on a $100 million grant from the Ford Foundation, itself now dependent on donations from Wall Street) is part of a more general decay of the global Left, whose detachment from its traditional roots in what is now a shrinking industrial working class has in the UK led its more radical elements to explore and exploit pastures new far removed from the Labour Party's origins in the British trade movement... Islam, black supremacism, the younger of the well-heeled metropolitan middle class, students, sexual, gender and ethnic minority activists, professional victims...the list is ever-expanding, and the trend reflected in the changing demographic of the Labour vote at the 2019 general election, which dramatically increased among higher income groups, and fell by even more in the lowest.

If we exclude for a moment the Islamic and Stalinist influences helping to drive the Corbyn 'Project', which are without precedent in the entire history of the Labour Party, the Corbynite lurch to the far-left that energised Andrea and tens of thousands like her was just the most recent, albeit most extreme, spectacular and self-destructive example, of a long-established pattern. From its very beginnings, the Labour Party has been characterised by series of oscillations between left to right. If we just go back to 1945, Attlee won a huge majority on a leftish programme which created our welfare state and, until the arrival of Margaret Thatcher, a Keynesian mixed economy. After two election defeats Attlee was replaced in 1955 by Hugh Gaitskell who, following a massive defeat in 1959, moved rapidly towards the centre. With his death in 1963, his successor, Harold Wilson, edged back to the left. Succeeding Wilson in 1976, Jim Callaghan drifted to the right, and after losing the 1979 general election, made way for the far-left Michael Foot. Slaughtered in 1983, Foot was replaced by the more moderately leftist Neil Kinnock, who after another hiding in 1987, began to ease the party back towards the centre left, where he lost more narrowly in 1992 to John Major. The re-alignment was completed under the leadership of the now-despised Tony Blair, who not only secured Labour's largest ever majority in 1997, but went on to win two more successive general elections, the only Labour leader ever to do so. He achieved this by re-positioning the Labour Party just to the left of centre, thereby pushing the Tories further to the right.

In earlier times, this would have opened up a space on the far left for the likes of Tony Benn and the Trots, but with both largely spent forces, and Labour and trade union activists desperate for a Labour victory at any price after eighteen years of Tory rule, the territory remained largely unoccupied. Then, after the resignation of Blair in 2008, the reverse drift began again. First under Gordon Brown, then Ed Miliband and finally Jeremy Corbyn, there was an accelerating shift back to the left, leaving the centre to be occupied first by the Liberal Democrats and David Cameron, successfully, and then by his successor Teresa May, disastrously. Following the rout of Corbynised Labour in the general election of December 2019, the party's worst defeat since 1935, came yet another swing back to the centre with the election of Keith Starmer as party leader. As for the Right, under the pro-EU Cameron, UKIP temporarily occupied the space that opened up on the far right, but with the Brexit victory, the party lost its relevance, and its vote was hoovered up by the Eurosceptic populism of Boris Johnson.

Long before me, Maureen instinctively understood that elections are in most cases won in the battle for the centre ground, either by the Tories, slightly to the right, or by Labour, a similar distance to the left. This is what the despised Blair understood, and his leftist election-losing critics scorned as a sell-out. The centre-left is where Maureen, like her dad, had always been, ever since I first knew her, whereas it took me the best part of half a century to get there, ironically, just at the time when the Labour Party decided to head off in the opposite direction.

There is no compelling reason why children should inherit the politics of their parents any more than their views about religion. If fact, if they always did, nothing would ever change. So it was with Maureen and her daughter. No matter how many times it was explained to her, Andrea could never understand why her mother, given her mildly left leanings, took the Tory *Daily Mail*. To me, the answer was obvious. Maureen was perfectly capable of distinguishing between an informed and well-written feature, of which the *Mail,* when compared to other tabloids, has more than its fair share, and political spin. The impact of the paper on Maureen's political judgement was best measured on polling days, when mother and daughter voted for the same party. For all her moderation, Maureen had strong convictions on political and on social issues. She was a staunch advocate of free speech, and despised racism and homophobia. Neither did she follow the current fashion on the left of either ignoring, denying or even justifying the oppression of Muslim women. By her nature, she was above all a compassionate, noble-spirited and intensely serious person, and was valued as such by all who knew her. But there was another side to her that few if any knew as well as I did.

From when I first knew her, she rarely smiled or laughed, and her beautiful eyes at times conveyed a deep inner sadness. Yet Maureen grew to maturity in the 1960s, a time of optimism and for many, liberation from the prejudices of older generations. Capital punishment was abolished, and abortion and homosexuality legalised. Materially too, things were on the up. Livings standards were rising. Everybody who wanted to work could find a job. People were becoming healthier and living longer. All this seemed to pass Maureen by. Hers was not a life spent in pursuit of happiness, let alone fun. There was a darkness in her soul, one that she found reflected in the music of Sibelius and the poetry of Dylan Thomas, and which I found irresistibly alluring...and challenging.

Maureen's last years by contrast with the sixties were spent in a world beset by economic crisis, intolerance, political confusion, religious fanaticism, and the ever-present threat of terrorism, each of which served to confirm her long-held and deep-seated conviction that unlike all other species, the human race was morally so flawed that it was doomed to self-destruction. Fortunately for both of us, her innate pessimism did not impinge unduly on our personal lives together, though it was often a matter for lively debate. I retained a residual optimism that perhaps, but only perhaps, by a process of natural selection, good ideas will win out over bad ones, though the evidence for such an assumption becomes ever harder to find. This subject pre-occupied us more than any other, and our exchanges could at times become somewhat heated. At such moments, Maureen was want to say, 'You are talking out of your anus.' Looking back, she often had a point.

Philosophical matters apart, after the first few weeks of mutual adjustment, the practical domestic routine was very much like most couples of our vintage. There was, however, one problem which, except when we were on holiday, we never managed to overcome. Our body clocks were grossly out of sync. I am and always have been an early riser, whereas Maureen, after her retirement from work, had lapsed into the sleeping pattern of a night owl, staying up to around three in the morning and sometimes not getting up till as late as one in the afternoon. Though I would have preferred more of her company, at least I could use the 'free' time to do some practising, and after I acquired a computer some ten years ago, check out the latest news and, more recently, work on my book.

Depending on the weather and the time of the year, ignoring her protests, I would get her out of bed to drive the few miles out to one of the Gower Peninsula's many beauty spots, sometimes having a pub meal. Friday was always the big shop day in town, invariably accompanied by a snack at our favourite café. Most evenings, we would watch TV together or, if it was all rubbish, which it frequently was, a film DVD from our large collection. Such, with very little variation, was our domestic life for nigh on seventeen years. And I would not have changed it by one iota. This was my fantasy of all those years ago come true…a life together as lovers, and as if we were man and wife.

XVII

For all the many and radical changes, we had wrought to the building and the garden of Maureen's, home, it is still for me the same place that I first entered when I rang on her doorbell on 23 August 1999. Everywhere I look, I see and hear and even sometimes feel my beloved Maureen. She still lives for me in her books; her tiny china figurines and ornaments; her miniature hedgehogs and cats; the solar lights around the pond; the trinkets on her book case and the mantelpiece; her stuffed animals that like a child, she still took to bed; in her perfumes and creams in the bathroom; her coats on the pegs in the hall, with beneath them on a small chair her woolly winter hats and brightly coloured scarf, and on the floor under the chair, her tiny pointed shoes; in the kitchen her slippers and garden shoes; on the microwave, her little blue bag in which she kept her Nivea cream; in the cupboard, the tins of food she bought for meals which she never lived to cook, and which I cannot bear even now to open; in her underclothes and dressing gown in the airing cupboard, her folding kitchen chair; her gardening tools by the back door, in the garden where she spent so many hours tending her beloved potted plants, and the now empty armchair next to mine in the living room, where most evenings we would sit together to watch television. This home is her secular shrine, where on its wall hang pictures of her life story, images which I with no shame worship in her memory. Each day, I see these holy relics and weep.

It is now approaching four years since her death, yet still I am still seized and overwhelmed by a grief so profound that I cry out Maureen's name over and over again, not caring where I am or who hears me, as if to deny or defy the death that has stolen her from me. For no apparent reason, several times a day my body begins to convulse and my breath quickens. I have not yet been able to go into town to our old haunts, where for seventeen years, every Friday, Maureen and I would do our weekly shopping round and take a snack at our favourite café. I push my trolley down the aisles at our local Lidl, where we used to shop every other Monday, sometimes with tears streaming down my cheeks, sobbing Maureen's name and thinking, *is this my lot until I too die?* Is it just me, or are others in my situation just better at hiding it? Perhaps the hardest to bear of all is coming home and opening the front door to a house I know will be empty, and going to sleep in a bed that I know I will never share again.

Those few who know me well would I think agree that I value reason above all other human faculties. Indeed, not so long-ago Maureen's daughter said she found me 'too cerebral'. She now knows differently. What her mother once described as my 'obsessions', be they music, politics, philosophy, theology, model railways or history, are as nothing compared to mine for Maureen herself, and that is why her death has left in me a void so vast that that nothing can fill it. I am not by nature a masochist. Neither am I a hedonist. I am above all a seeker of knowledge, about the world without, and of ourselves within. As Spinoza, the 17th century Jewish pantheist once said, 'neither weep, hate nor laugh, but understand'. But still we weep.

Nothing else in my life has had so profound effect upon me as my love for Maureen and now of her death, and it is the attempt to understand why this is so that continues to preoccupy my thoughts. Like I am sure many others in my situation, I have pondered long and hard about the nature of grief. Unlike love, it is at bottom a selfish emotion, caused by what at times is unbearable loss. True, it can give rise to actions which are not intrinsically selfish, for example, works of art. But even these serve a cathartic purpose, as I am well aware. Evolution tells us that love by its very nature serves a creative purpose of a very different kind…the perpetuation of our species. But about the function of grief, Darwin has nothing to say, because it has none. For a possible answer we could do worse than turn from biology to physics. Grief is to love in a manner akin to Newton's third law of motion, in which for every action there is an opposite and, mark this well, equal reaction. The greater the love, so the greater the grief.

I have no plans to 'move on'. Nor could I, even if I wanted to, which I do not. Move on to what? To a life that requires that I bury a past that brought me such joy simply because it has brought in its train grief in equal measure? Unavoidably, love is a sword with two edges, and they cut with equal depth into the soul. Even so I will neither remove nor hide anything in our home or garden which even catching the merest glimpse of can inflict so much pain. To do so would be for me, an atheist, an act of sacrilege. He who loves as I did Maureen must be prepared when the time comes to pay love's price.

My grief is compounded by the knowledge that had what we call chance, or if you will, fate, decreed otherwise, Maureen would still be with me today. I said Maureen was a creature of habit. One of those habits killed her. It was smoking. When I first knew her, Maureen was not a smoker. In fact, in all respects, she had what today would be called a healthy lifestyle. She was an outdoor girl who enjoyed long walks in the countryside. She had played for her school at netball and hockey, and still swam in the sea on her summer breaks in Swansea. Then about a year or so after I began my visits, it began. Looking back now, I cannot recall thinking at the time that there was anything amiss when in the course of an evening, she would smoke a couple of cigarettes. I did not smoke because I had suffered from acute asthma as a child, and still experienced the odd spasm, so simple common sense suggested that pumping smoke into my lungs, at a cost I could not anyway afford, was not a good idea. However, like nearly everyone else outside the tobacco industry, I did not know then that smoking could kill.

In those distant days, when tobacco companies had yet to be exposed as the mass murderers they knew they were and still are, smoking did not carry the opprobrium that it does today for most intelligent people. Indeed, for women of Maureen's generation, it could be seen as being rather cool and even seductive, something which before it was curtailed and then banned, cigarette advertising of the time exploited to the full. But as Maureen told me many years later when I asked her how she had started, her smoking did not begin at a party, but at work. Stocktaking is a wearying and boring business at the best of times, and though Maureen did not give me the details, I believe it is safe to assume that to relieve the tedium, her supervisor offered Maureen a cigarette, which she foolishly accepted. While on her modest income, she could not afford to become a chain smoker, by the time we parted for what we then believed was for the last time in 1966, she was well on the way to becoming an addict. The next two men in her life, Terry and Les, were hardly like to challenge her addiction, because they too were smokers, and heavy ones at that. Maureen even smoked throughout her pregnancy and beyond…proof positive of how firmly her addiction had taken hold. Yet in all other respects, Maureen was a devoted and responsible mother, even resisting to the bitter end her daughter's insistence she should have her ears pierced.

By the time I first visited Maureen in Swansea, she had been smoking for about forty years, as I quickly discovered, though not so much to my surprise as disappointment. On my first visit, and sitting in her kitchen a short while after my arrival, in a momentary lull in our conversation, she produced a cigarette, and was about to light it when instinctively, as if it had been my daughter (who as far as I know, only smoked pot), I made to take it out of her hand. Her equally instinctive reaction, which was to almost desperately cling on to her cigarette, told me that this was the classic behaviour of an addict, and the realisation greatly saddened me. Not a word was spoken by either of us in the awkward moments that followed, and I knew better than to attempt anything similar again, because for as long as I was only visiting Maureen, there was simply no sense in pursuing the matter further. She knew how I felt about smoking, and since I was not living with her, it was none of my business what she did in her own home. Once I had moved in with

Maureen, however, it was different story, although one with a tragic ending.

I made it clear almost from day one that I did not approve of her habit, and that I would try my best to persuade her to give it up. I also quite early on insisted, since it was now as much my home, though obviously not my house, as hers, that to prevent passive smoking on my part she should not engage in her active version in the living room, where I spent a good part of my time. She readily agreed to this, since it placed no limit on how much she could smoke, only where. Until sometime later, when I objected again, but this time for reasons of food hygiene, she smoked mainly in of all places, the kitchen. It was obvious to me that it could quite easily poison our relationship just effectively as she was poisoning her lungs if I constantly nagged her about her habit. And in fairness, she did ask me to not to give up on her. So from time to time, I tried pressing her on the subject. She would readily concede that smoking was 'stupid', but then carry on just the same. Taking her at her word, when I found her smoking outside the back door, I would lock it for a few seconds, and then as I let her back in, call her a cretin. But she carried on just the same.

To lighten things up a little, (no pun intended) I even tried a little *risqu*é humour, threatening her with sexual blackmail. When we were in bed together, whether before or after I cannot now remember, I said to her, mock seriously, that since she had now become addicted to my body as well, she had to choose. 'It's either nicotine or nickers off, fag or shag, smoke or poke.' She was much amused, but she carried on smoking. If ever there was an empty threat, this was it, because I was as addicted to Maureen's body no less than she was to nicotine. And unlike Maureen's, for my addiction, there was no cure.

It now occurs to me that I could have attempted another approach. Maureen, as I discovered in one of our many lively political exchanges, was a monarchist. So perhaps she could have taken heed of the advice of James I, whose views on the effects of smoking were vindicated nearly four centuries later by medical science. He described it as a 'custom loathsome to the eye, hateful to the nose, harmful to the brain, dangerous to the lungs and in the black stinking fume thereof, nearest resembling the horrible Stygian smoke of the pit that is bottomless'.

One of Maureen's strong points was her stubbornness, a characteristic that had served her so well in times past. But now it was doing her no favours. All my attempts to persuade her to at least investigate the many aids now available for kicking the habit met with the same response, 'You don't know what it's like.' That was of course quite true, but also irrelevant. How was it then that millions of other smokers had managed to kick the habit? No answer. Yet she must have known that sometime in the future, her addiction would pay her out, as indeed it did. True, when I first met Maureen again, her general heath was quite good. And as she said, she had worn well. But when some three years later, she contracted polymyalgia, an acute form of rheumatism caused by sticky blood, a very gradual but steady decline in her mobility set in, one that made it more imperative than ever to quit her addiction. And around the same time her vision had become so restricted that she had to undergo the removal of cataracts from both eyes. Some four years before she died came another blow to Maureen's already fragile heath. She was diagnosed with breast cancer, resulting in the removal of her right breast. Once again Maureen's stoicism proved an asset, helping her to a full recovery. But she carried on smoking.

Only in the last month of her life could Maureen be described as an invalid, unable even to walk as far as the front gate, wheezing, coughing and struggling for breath, and suffering from muscle pains so severe that at times she could only climb up the stairs on her hands and knees. But even a good many year previously, when we were abroad, she had begun to find it hard to walk up steep inclines. Then there was her cough, which was becoming steadily more persistent. Maureen put it down to what she called a 'tickle' in the back of her throat. Afraid that she might have throat cancer, I pressed her to do something about it. 'But what's causing the tickle. Shouldn't you see your doctor?' But she never did. I said to her on more than one occasion, because it was true, 'I know why you won't see your doctor. It's because you know the first thing he'll ask you is, do you smoke.' Again, there was no reply. Her stubbornness had now become her worst enemy, and there was nothing I could do about it. I had tried pleading, begging her to stop for my sake if not hers, but to no avail. Only one occasion did I allow my frustrations turn into anger. I had been brooding all morning over Maureen's blunt refusal to even discuss her addiction, and the effect it was having on me. When later that day we were out shopping, not caring overmuch about who might hear me, I let fly, using language that normally I would never have used in Maureen's presence. 'Can't you see what your smoking is doing to me? I don't want you die before you have to, but you don't seem to give a fuck how I feel.' Again, no reply. I was nearly in tears. It was as if she neither cared about her own life nor my love nor need for her.

But I knew that wasn't true. Maureen did not have a death wish. She savoured and enthused over what her life with me now had to offer, and I know she loved me. Those who specialise in such things will attribute such seemingly fatalistic behaviour to her being in denial about her addiction, while being dependent on it. For want of any more other plausible explanation, I will settle for that. And yet despite her declining heath, and the occasional friction caused by her inability to conquer her addiction, and my refusal to become reconciled to it, our lives remained as rich and fulfilling as they ever been, in fact more so, as with time, we grew closer together and in so many ways became as one. Yes, our love making was less frequent, but it was also more lingering, more tender. And in the year before Maureen died, even though her problems with breathing and mobility were now clearly becoming more serious, we once again made our annual pilgrimages to Lake Thun and Amboise on the Loire.

XVIII

Fearing, though I never said so, that this could perhaps be Maureen's last opportunity to re-live the memories of her childhood, in 2016 I booked our stay at Lake Thun for the end of April, to coincide with the time of her school excursion, when the snows had still to melt, reaching down from the peaks almost to the lake's edge. Everywhere one looked, the views were spectacular, the snow glinting in the strong sunlight that blessed nearly all our stay. Once again, we drove up the valley to Adelboden, to the hotel where she stayed with her school party more than sixty years before. (I am sobbing as I type this) Unlike on all our previous visits, which had been in September, it was closed. The skiing season was over and the summer one was still far off. So we found a café down in the main part of the village, which was almost totally deserted, and then headed back to our hotel and an evening meal. As I feared, that would be the last time Maureen saw Adelboden. And so it was with Amboise. Again, the weather was sublime. Every day, blue skies and dawn till dusk sunshine. After our buffet breakfast, we spent the rest of the morning in the spacious grounds of our usual hotel, situated five minutes' drive out of town and close by the Loire. Early in the afternoon we would meander by car around the Loire and its tributaries, stopping when the mood took us at a village café for coffee, and then off again, we cared not where. Maureen was as relaxed and happy as she had ever been, amidst nature and the serenity of the valley's great rivers. Back at the hotel, we would change before going into town for a meal at our favourite restaurant, next to the Chateau. Before heading back to the hotel, we would stroll, hand in hand like young lovers, by the bank of the Loire just as the light was fading and the air cooling. These were beautiful moments, and I will always cherish their memory. Because five months later, in the early hours of 2 February 2017, my Maureen, the light and love of my life, would be dead, and I would be grieving. And it is about love, death and grief that I now need to speak.

Not all love ends in grief. Maureen's did not. But all grief is born of a lost love, as mine was and is. Just as no two human beings are the same, so neither are two loves. Like a snow flake or a crystal, or any other of nature's creations, each of us is unique, and those who we love are likewise unique. It follows that the grief suffered by the loss of those we love is in each and every case also unique, special to the loved one we have lost, triggered time and again by the memories that we alone carry with us to our deaths.

We now know enough about the functions and workings of the gene to understand that that there are different kinds of grief, just as there are different kinds of love. There is the love of a child for its parents. But since it is in the natural order of things that a child outlives its parents, the death of a parent who has lived out his or her normal lifespan, and has therefore become biologically redundant, does not precipitate the same kind or magnitude of grief experienced by a parent's children, who are more likely than not to be already raising their own children; as does the reverse, of a parent losing its child, a loss that violates the purpose of our genetic programming, which is for parents to nurture and raise their offspring so that they in turn can perpetuate the species. Unlike two adults who have chosen to spend the rest of their lives together and over time, become ever closer, as did Maureen and I, parents and children will in due course separate, the offspring in their turn to reproduce, and their parents to grown old and die. Evolution has seen to it that all life, including our own, is admirably equipped to perpetuate itself, and by a means that we are programmed to pursue obsessively and enjoy more than other human endeavour. But evolution has done nothing to shield us from the grief caused by life's loss. And why should it, for the selfish gene's work is done with the procreating and nurturing our offspring.

Having known the love of and for a parent, a child and a

sibling, I have come to the conclusion that the most profound love of all is that of two lovers, with me, the shared love of a man and a woman. When a man and a woman make love as Maureen and I did, that is, make love, not 'have sex', two, however fleetingly, become one, not only emotionally, but literally, as by the sex act, their bodies are joined in a unique ecstasy of passion. Unless we allow for incest, there is no remotely comparable degree of intensity and intimacy in the relationship between siblings, or between parent and child. This is because in loving and making love, we are responding to the prime directive of our genes, which is to perpetuate themselves through the act of sexual reproduction.

But love is a great deal more than just making love and reproducing. We go on loving, and making love, long after our reproductive task is done. Love also and indeed primarily defines itself by its capacity to enrich, to sublimate, to transcend the simple sex act, and even sometimes to be able to dispense with it altogether. I loved Maureen for five years before I made love to her, and afterwards carried on loving her for more than thirty years without even seeing her once. Over the last hundred years, twice husbands and wives have continued to love each other when separated for years by war. We need to ask ourselves, why is it that of all loves humankind can experience, it is the love of lovers that down the ages and in all cultures, has inspired so many of our most sublime and enduring works of art, literature and music, not that of the love between parents and their offspring? What poetry would remain if we took away all the verses devoted to a man's love for a woman?

If it is true, as I contend, that the love of lovers is not only quintessentially different from all others, but also richer, and greater, much greater in its degree of intensity, then it helps us to explain the utter desolation, the loneliness, the despair visited on the one who survives the death of their lover. Love comes at a price. The longer we have loved and the more intense the love, the more we invest in it, the longer and more intense the grief that we experience when the one whom we love it is torn from us by death. This can only be because love reaches to, and comes from the core of our being. It answers to no superior force. Its creative and yes, its destructive powers are beyond measure.

From the very dawn of civilisation, and though we lack the same tangible proofs, we can safely assume long before it, mankind has been aware of the dichotomy between reason and emotion, and of the consequences that can ensue when their paths collide. Over and again, the story is told in legends and myths, and in the worship of gods, and from the tragedies of Euripides to the operas of Wagner has continued to inspire our most enduring artistic creations. One of the masterpieces of world literature, Thomas Mann's *The Magic Mountain*, revolves around the unrelenting intellectual duel between the rational humanist, Lodovico Settembrini, and Leo Naphta, the Jesuit mystic, and the mental torments it inflicts upon Hans Carstorp, the novel's central character. It is a conflict that Mann never resolves, because as the story unfolds to its tragic end, it becomes evident that its narrator is persuaded that the defining characteristic of our species is the irreconcilability of reason and our passions. The poet Heinrich Heine came to the same conclusion.

Given the central role that love and reason play in our lives, it is hardly surprising that the two masters of the musical genre which more than any other, treats of the human condition, should explore our passions in their most sublime operas, Mozart in *The Magic Flute*, and Wagner in *Tristan and Isolde*. But the paths they follow lead to very different, even to a degree opposed conclusions. *The Magic Flute* is a strange mixture of low comedy, and Enlightenment philosophy, and it is the latter which is of relevance here. The main protagonists are the Queen of the Night, who represents the dark forces of the passions, especially revenge, and Sarastro, who rules over an order of light and reason. Sarastro's name is intended as an allusion to Zarothushtra, the founder of the ancient Persian faith of Zoroastrianism, which depicted all reality and all life as dominated by a perpetual struggle between the forces of good, represented by light, and evil, by darkness. The symbolism of the stage settings also hints at Freemasonry, which in Mozart's time (he was himself a committed Freemason) advocated the principles and pursued the goals of the Enlightenment. The temple is inscribed with the pantheist motto, 'Nature, Beauty, Wisdom', but a slight variation on Freemasonry's 'Beauty, Strength, Wisdom'.

Central to Zoroastrianism was the belief that that wisdom and the passions, including love, are naturally in harmony with each other, a conviction it shared with its analogue, the religion of the contemporaneous ancient Greeks. Both sons of Zeus, Apollo, the god of light, reason and order, and Dionysus, the god of passion and instinct, are depicted as being entwined, each playing their part in the act of creation. As one of its leading present-day devotees has it, the symbolic fire that Zoroastrians worship 'is the light of reason in every mind, the glow of the pure emotion of love'. And so it is with Sarastro's temple of enlightenment. There too, 'when a man has fallen, love shows him his duty', as if love cannot but work in accord with dictates of reason. The final triumph of reason over unbridled female passion is confirmed and celebrated by the enrolment of the Queen of the Night's daughter into the order when with her betrothed, she passes the three trials of induction.

Mozart was every inch the child of the Enlightenment, just as Beethoven was of the French Revolution. His operas exude optimism, and the conviction that good will in the end triumph over evil, and that together reason and love will find a way. The good guys always win in the end, and the merely foolish see the errors of their ways, while even when we cannot help admiring his audacity and seductive powers, Don Giovanni is at the end consigned to hell for his many sins. Anger, jealously, infidelity, fickleness…in fact, all the human frailties, yes, but no grief, no lasting anguish, no darkness of the soul. Good eventually triumphs when the emotions and sound common sense learn to mesh as smoothly as the cogs in a well-oiled watch. We know that life is not like that, never has been and never will be. So surely did Mozart. His was an ideal world that should be, and perhaps could be, if only we let reason do its work.

Wagner comes with a different message, one that is truer I believe to the stuff of the human condition, to the unresolvable conflict between love and duty, passion and reason, logic and feeling; one which can be seen as an anticipation of Freud's unending tug of war between the subterranean urges of the id and the socialised moral norms of the super ego. In the *Ring of the Nibelungen,* Brunnhilde's revolt against her father, the god Wotan is one of her valuing love and compassion above obedience to the law and family honour, for which she pays the ultimate price of death in the *Ring's* closing scene. Wagner is a child of a time when the Enlightenment and the French Revolution were but fading memories, and of the disillusioned aftermath of the failed revolutions of 1848. For him, the search for answers to the riddles of the human condition is to be conducted not in society, as with Marx, but in the darkest reaches of the individual human psyche, and what he finds there gives little grounds for hope. Whereas Mozart is the supreme optimist, with love and reason in harmony eventually conquering all, Wagner is the supreme Schopenhauerian pessimist. Only in and through death is the love of Tristan and Isolde truly consummated, where night triumphs over day.

The plot, as in the *Ring*, is essentially the same, and it is a simple one. Tristan is charged by King Marke of Cornwall to bring his bride to be, Isolde, from Ireland. But Tristan and Isolde are already in love, though out of loyalty to King Marke, they suppress and deny their feelings for each other.

Just before they arrive in Cornwall, they mistakenly drink a love potion, which sets their passions ablaze. Nothing but their love now matters. All notions of duty, loyalty, honesty, honour, politics, reason, count for nothing.

They are the concerns of the day. Love commands the night. While the royal party are out hunting, the lovers have arranged an assignation to consummate their passion. Tristan no longer cares for the world of court politics, or what might be the consequences of his infidelity to his king. Possessed by passion, his only thought is of Isolde. Unlike the one portrayed by Mozart, this is surely a love we can recognise and, if we have experienced it, as I have, it is a love we can understand.

> Oh how we were dedicated to night!
> Spiteful day with ready envy could part us with its tricks but no longer mislead us with guile. Its vain glory, its flaunting display are mocked by those to whom Night has granted sight.
> The fleeting flashes of its flickering light No longer dazzle us.
> The lies, the renown and Honour of Day, power and advantage, shining and glorious as the paltry dust caught in the sunbeams! Amid the vain fancy of Day
> He still harbours one desire – The yearning for sacred Night where, all-eternal true alone Love's bliss smiles on him!

Caught in the very act of their love by a jealous Melot, Tristan is severely wounded, and is taken by his friend Kurwenal to Kareol in Brittany (near to where Maureen and I spent a holiday), there to await the arrival of his Isolde. She does come, together with King Marke, who has realised that Isolde is no longer his but Tristan's. In another fit of jealousy, Melot again attacks Tristan, this time killing him.

Over his dead body, Isolde sings the most erotic, searing and soul-rending aria all music, and then dies herself of grief, as I wanted to die too at Maureen's side.

> How softly and gently he smiles, how sweetly his eyes open - can you not see it my friends, do you not see it?
> How he glows ever brighter

raising himself high amidst the stars? Do you not see it?
How his heart swells with courage gushing full and majestic
In his breast?
How in tender bliss sweet breath gently wafts from his lips – Friends! Look!
Do you not feel and see it? Do I alone hear this melody?
so wondrously and gently sounding from within him
in bliss lamenting, all expressing gently reconciling, piercing me, soaring aloft its sweet echoes resounding about me?
Are they gentle arial waves
Ringing out clearly surging around me? Are they billows of blissful fragrance? As they seethe and roar about me
Shall I breathe, shall I give ear!
Shall I drink of them, plunge beneath them? Breathe my life away in sweet scents?
In the having swell,
In the resounding echoes,
In the universal stream
Of the world-breath rapture.

XIX

Unlike birth, death is a great leveller. It awaits us all, rich and poor alike, even those who believe it is but the threshold to a life eternal spent in a 'better place', but are even so in no particular hurry to arrive there, and also grieve for those who have. And yet in all the seventeen years I spent with Maureen, I never once gave a thought to what life would be like if she died before me. Having lost her once and then, almost miraculously, found her, perhaps subconsciously I was unable to contemplate the prospect of losing her yet again. For nearly sixty years, she had been an overpowering presence in my life, and for the last seventeen, also a physical one. Consequently, I was mentally and emotionally incapable of conceiving my life without her. Maureen *was* my life. We sometimes talked about death, but in general terms, that it was a necessary part of the cycle of life.

We agreed that the religious idea of eternal life was not only absurd, but that if it was proved to be true, to quote James Joyce, like history, it would in time inevitably become a nightmare from which there could be no escape. Yes, I did warn her repeatedly that smoking would shorten her life, but that was more an argument to persuade her to give it up rather than a reality that one day I would have to contend with. Maureen brought to me the shared joys of life, lived day by day, with nothing but glowing memories of our past, yet no thought for what had to lay ahead for one of us. But Maureen had, because some years before she died, without telling me, she made an agreement with her daughter that as her mother's only next of kin, if Maureen died before me, Andrea would allow me to live at 169 for as long as I wished. I believe that Maureen had assumed this would be the most likely outcome because by this time, partly through her own lifestyle and self-neglect, her health was in steady, if only at first gradual decline.

When I found Maureen again, she described herself as 'having worn well', and that was certainly true. She not only looked a good ten or more younger than her sixty years, she was no less physically fit. She had a problem with her eyesight, but that was rectified by two retina operations. Her hearing was not so good either, and in later years, she acquired a hearing aid, but rarely used it, saying that while it amplified sound, it also distorted it. As with her smoking, all my attempts to persuade her to either have her hearing aid adjusted, or failing that, replace it with a better one, fell, literally, on partially deaf wars. It was another case of Maureen's misplaced stoicism.

More serious health problems began to afflict Maureen when she contacted polymyalgia. One of the side effects of the prescribed medication she took for the condition was the thinning of her skin, which in turn led to easy bruising. This meant she could not wear skirts, and always had to wear tops that covered her arms, which like her still shapely legs, were constantly being bruised at the slightest contact. And Maureen had such beautifully rounded arms too. The onset of the coughing, which I was sure even at the time, was the result of nearly half a century of smoking, was followed some years later by a worsening irritation of the right nipple, which on examination, proved to be the first stages of breast cancer. Fortunately, I was with Maureen at the hospital cancer unit when she was given the news, because if she had had her way, she would have put off her hysterectomy until after Christmas.

Despite all these accumulating ailments, Maureen's incredible mental resilience enabled her to maintain her normal routine until the last year of her life, when aching joints began to curtail her mobility. She would now ask me for a lift to the do the local shopping, just a short walk away. The weekly visit to town left her with a backache that could last for days. It must have around Christmas time that because they came out of the blue, she made two remarks that after her death, I realised she was aware her time was running out. As I have said, Maureen was parsimonious in the extreme when it came to giving me compliments. Yet now, after 17 years she said, 'you are a brilliant trumpeter'..

That and no more. A few days later came another five words, spoken in her typically matter of fact way: 'I know you love me'. I was so taken aback, I could say nothing. And anyway, what was there to say? Perhaps I should have understood that these were both things she needed to say before it was too late. But the prospect of Maureen being on the verge of death, which she indeed was, was beyond my comprehension. Even when early in January of 2017 her breathing suddenly became worse, and she had to be admitted to hospital, I was in a way glad, because at last, she would receive the treatment she had been evading for so long. It was not to be. At first it seemed that she would make a full recovery. But after about a week, complications set in, she contracted pneumonia, her kidneys began to fail, and I was told the prognosis was not good. Her body was too frail to resist its multiple infections. It was then, only then, that I realised that I would lose the light of my life, my beloved Maureen, whom I worshipped as devoutly and with a fervour to match that of any true believer in their God. I sat by her side, gazing at her for what I feared could probably be the last time. My beautiful, precious Maureen was dying, and there was nothing I or anyone else could do to save her. Even now, as I always did, I wanted to possess her body. Maureen's hair had long since turned white, her face was a little wrinkled, but her eyes and lips were as seductive as ever.

After I kissed Maureen before I left her on the evening before her death, although neither she nor I could have known it then, we each said 'I love you' for the last time. Then later that same night, after being called back to the hospital with Andrea and Jess, as she slipped away, she grasped my hand and said my name, the last word she ever spoke. In the terrible passion of that moment, as I kissed her and cried 'I love you' over and over again between my sobbing, the grief that engulfed and overwhelmed me then was, I now understand, but the inverse measure of a love that had endured undiminished since I first beheld her darkly glowing beauty so long ago. Hours later, as her breathing faded and then ceased, I kissed her now cold lips and looked for the last time on the face whose memory I had preserved through all our years apart, wishing as at moments I still do, that I could have died there, by her side, holding her tenderly, as if to make love. Now I know why elderly couples who rather than be separated by death, choose to die together. I wish to place on record here that for all our differences, the no less bereaved and grieving Andrea still found the strength to give me the emotional support that I so desperately needed, for which kindness I was and will always be grateful, just as I am similarly indebted to Andrew and Katharine, who together with Andrea and Jess, helped me to cope with the ordeal of Maureen's funeral, and who, now that I alone, have always made me welcome in their homes.

Neither Maureen nor I believed in an afterlife. But we will meet again, because I have arranged that when my turn comes, my ashes will be mingled with hers and returned to the nature from where we came, scattered where we found the most sublime joy, beauty and contentment, by Lake Thun in the midst of the tranquil majesty of the Swiss Alps. And for as long as the human race values and preserves the printed word, what I have written here will stand as monument to my beautiful, glorious Maureen, the light, the joy, the grief and the love of my life.

Returning home after Maureen's death, I wrote this poem dedicated to her life and memory, which was read at Maureen's humanist funeral by my daughter Katharine.

> Shallow gain brings clamour And fleeting joy for fools,
> An easy pleasure soon forgotten. But loss, the price we pay for love, Cuts deep
> And leaves us sobbing as it should. This is love's gauge And I marvel at its measure, While all else comes easy And so, it also goes.
>
> Your fire burned And burns in me yet On memory's fuel Too bright to fade.

I will remember all
And curse the time apart. Consumed by your love
Mine while I live will never die Nor yet fade.
I will remember all.
You were and are my joy, my grief, my passion, My all
My Maureen.

2 February 2017

XX

At Maureen's funeral, two tributes were made to her life and her memory. The first was by her daughter Andrea, whose kindness and understanding has done so much to help me survive and endure my grief. The second was made by me, though because I feared I could not deliver it without breaking down, it was rendered most movingly by the celebrant.

'Maureen Joyce Stewart, or Muvver as I often called her, was born on the 4 January 1939 in the North Middlesex Hospital. Her parents Freddy and Alice took her home to Eastfield Road, their family complete, but within a year she was struck down with peritonitis following a burst appendix. It very nearly killed her but thankfully, in a characteristic show of resilience, she survived. However, it left her severely weakened and she was sent to convalesce with family friends, Rose and John, who owned a smallholding in Buckingham, where she spent the next few years enjoying rural life and regaining her strength. There were, of course, regular visits from her parents.

Upon her return to the family home in Enfield she attended Eastfield Road Primary School. There, despite the setbacks with her health, she proved to be an exceptional student and went on to win a much sought-after scholarship to the prestigious Tottenham High School for Girls. Again, she excelled both as a student and in sport, playing both hockey and netball for her school. That's not to say she was always a model pupil. I can recall one anecdote in particular involving mum, a teacher and an airborne classroom chair...

She always talked of her childhood with great nostalgia. She loved school and had many friends, in particular her next-door neighbours the Mintons, with whom she maintained a life-long friendship. She also loved being part of the Griggs clan, an extensive but very close family.

From Tottenham High, she went on to Brunel University, where she gained a degree in micro biology, and to be a cosmetic chemist in the laboratories of the parfumier Lentheric. Her time at Lentheric was to shape the course of her life as it was there that she met both her future husband, my father Terry, and, as she would later come to realise, the love of her life, Robin.

After my parent's separation, mum and I moved in with Alice and we became a family unit. By this time, her adored father, Freddy, had passed away. She was a kind and loving mother but quite strict in comparison to my friends' parents. I vividly remember having to finish my reading was practice before being allowed out to play, something resented at the time, but which resulted in my starting school already being able to read. Nanny was always more laid back and I can recall as a nine-year-old having to enlist her, my dad and other assorted friends and family members in a war of attrition, the object being to persuade mum to let me have my ears pierced. She gave in, finally, and of course I can't remember the last time I wore earrings, but it felt like a significant victory at the time. But those perceived injustices now seem so trivial as I realise that mum just wanted what was best for me. She always had my best interests at heart, putting my needs before her own and sacrificing some long-held aspirations in the process; one example being her career in cosmetic science, which gave way to office work because she felt the latter was more compatible with raising a child, and while there was never a hint of resentment, there must at times have been the odd pang of regret.

Just as I was approaching adulthood, sadly Nanny became unwell and so mum became both parent and carer. Nanny had long wanted to return to her home town of Swansea and so mum decided to take the plunge and relocate there, although I wasn't ready to make the move until some years later. While the decision was born out of her unfailing sense of duty and a desire to fulfil her mother's wishes, mum would later say that it was one of the best she ever made. She spent many happy childhood summers in Swansea, staying with her grandparents and getting into scrapes with her cousins John, Francis and Bernard. We, in turn, would spend my summer school holidays here staying with the Jones family and, in later years, Aunt Mary. Mum was intensely proud of her Welsh roots. She regarded the Gower Peninsular and the Brecon Beacons as among the most awe-inspiring places on earth. She loved nothing more than driving around the Gower with Robin and marvelling at this area of outstanding beauty. She often said that when the sun was shining, she'd take the Bay of Swansea over the Bay of Naples any day. She loved Welsh culture, the poetry of Dylan Thomas and the otherworldly sound of a Welsh male voice choir. She was also an avid fan of the Welsh rugby team, although whenever things got too tense she'd hide in the kitchen and Robin would have to relay the score to her through the kitchen door.

Her love of nature extended to animals of all kinds. She had boundless compassion for waifs and strays as evidenced by the seemingly endless procession of cats that passed through 169 Pentregethin Road. She would never forgive me if I didn't give honourable mention to Bilbo Baggins, Mitch, Richard, Pippin, Sophie and Frankie. I'm convinced there's a stray cat version of Trip Advisor where mum consistently received five-star revues. She also fed the foxes and hedgehogs at the bottom of the garden, animals many would dismiss as vermin, but which she saw as beautiful creatures with of care and consideration. I know that Robin will continue to look after them in her memory.

There is so much I could tell you about mum. There's her great love of books from the literary classics of Shakespeare, Dickens and Austen to the epic fantasies of Stephen Lawhead and J.R.R. Tolkien. Her eclectic taste which spanned classical, jazz, folk, pop, and even, when a friend of mine once asked, "ambient with a touch of trance", the friend laughed. Muvver was not impressed.

Having devoted so many years to caring for others, her time finally came when Robin re-entered her life. They enjoyed numerous shared interests including art, music, the theatre, nature and science. They became part of the live music scene in Swansea, with Robin playing in various pubs and jazz clubs in the area and mum always in the audience, his most devoted fan. They enjoyed lively debate on a wide variety of topics and mum relished the opportunity to stretch her intellectual muscles. They travelled Europe extensively, and on the occasions when Jess and I would join them on one of their epic tours, mum was as relaxed and happy as I had ever seen her. Through her reconnection with Robin the last seventeen years of her life were filled with love, adventure and fulfilment she so deserved.

I hope I haven't portrayed mum as a tragic figure, all noble self-sacrifice and thwarted ambition, rescued in the final chapter by her knight in shining armour. She certainly didn't see herself that way and nor should she be. She was so much more than that. She was a highly intelligent, kind and beautiful woman. She was knowledgeable on a wide variety of subjects and had an opinion on everything. She was also incredibly self-possessed and could, on first acquaintance, seem aloof, but once she'd stepped back and taken the measure of you she was engaging and interesting, with a great sense of humour.

Having shared with you my memories of the woman who brought me into this world, I can honestly say that at a time of great sorrow, it brings me great comfort to know that the final chapter of her life was also among the happiest.'

****

'First, I want to give my heartfelt thanks to all those who come together here to pay their tributes to the life and memory of Maureen. I also want to thank those who have given myself and Andrea their support and kindness. There are here today those who themselves have experienced the terrible feeling of loss when a loved one dies, and their understanding has helped me through the last three weeks.

Now I must speak of Maureen. I first came to know and

fall in love with Maureen nearly sixty years ago. I was overwhelmed, when I first saw her, by her beauty. She was, and has remained, the most beautiful woman I have ever seen. Some say beauty is in the eyes of the beholder. I disagree. We find beauty in what we behold, and in Maureen, hers was truly a beauty to behold. There are no stronger forces that we can experience than love and beauty. We do not choose whom to love, or what we find beautiful. It is in our DNA.

Maureen not only had beauty in abundance. As I came to know her better, I found Maureen to be the most intelligent woman I have known, and had the times been different, she could have excelled at the highest academic level. All her interests were of serious things. As a highly-qualified scientist and lover of nature, she was an avid viewer of all the BBC science and wild life programmes. She would hold forth on her own views about the origins of the universe and the nature of time, subjects we used to debate for hours, without ever managing to fully agree. Yet for all intelligence and beauty, Maureen was supremely modest and very reserved.

As all those who know her will agree, Maureen was above a giver, and never a taker. Sadly, the sacrifices that she made for others ingrained her a self-denial that went beyond the call of duty, and it was this that made me determined, when we came together gain seventeen years ago, to do all I could to convince that receiving is not the same as taking. In this I believe I succeeded.

I have loved Maureen for nearly sixty years, and to my wonder, I discovered when we met again more than thirty years after we parted, that she retained her memories and feelings for me. She told me that she always believed that one day, we would meet again. Because we did, our lives now share a wonderful symmetry, for we were each the other's first lover, and now, the last.

Grief is the debt we must honour for lost love, but I am sustained by the certain knowledge that my love for Maureen was returned in full measure. Over these seventeen joyous years, Maureen and I made a new life together. We were inseparable, best of all when we were exploring the natural beauties and cities of Europe, seventeen countries in all, from Iceland and Poland to Sweden and Italy. Above all, Maureen and I found the greatest pleasure in returning, year on year, to the Swiss Alps, which she first visited with her school, and to the Loire Valley, where we spent one of first holidays abroad. And it was these two pilgrimages that we made again for the last, in the months before her death. I know that these adventures brought her great happiness, and enriched her life in ways that otherwise would have been denied to her.

Maureen was not only beautiful, she savoured and respected, the beauty of nature, of music, of art. If one can capture the essence of a person in a few words, Maureen was, and for will remain, loving, compassionate and beautiful beyond measure. She was the light, the passion the joy and love of my life. To the end of my days, I will honour and preserve her memory.

And so my story is told. One day maybe, science will explain why we love the way we do, but though reason and logic can persuade us not to act upon love, they will always be powerless either to create love or to deny it. And so it is with grief, which equally with love, has given mankind its highest artistic expressions, whether it be the tragedies of the Greeks, the operas of Wagner, or the Passions of Bach. It cannot be conjured away any more than can love by rational argument, or 'strategies' that have as their goal 'moving on' 'coming to terms' 'processing', and 'closure'. Those who offer as consolation the memories we have of our lost love simply do not comprehend that is these undying memories which are the cause of the grief. Even the sympathies of friends and relatives, however welcome and sincere, bring only a partial and temporary relief. All these supposed remedies fail because grief cannot be conquered by reason or kindness. Seated in different parts of our brains, love, grief and reason obey their own distinct imperatives, and when they intersect, reason not only meets its match but, as it did when I began my search for Maureen, can so easily become love's servant. And if it did not, life would not be worth the living. Beethoven once said that 'only art and science can raise men to the level of the gods'. And while so often at odds in life, it is in music that inspiration and reason find themselves most in harmony in the quest for the sublime. It was music that first brought Maureen and I together, and remained to the end our most profound and enriching shared passion. The debt I owe Maureen is beyond measure because not only did she bring me joy, she was in all my endeavours my inspiration. I am sure it was not by chance that I made and played my best music in the years we spent together. She was my lover and my muse.

Tragedy, the exploration of the power and meaning of loss and grief, alone has the capacity to make us weep and move us to our very cores, because it speaks to the human condition, of the infinite preciousness of human life and of the certainty of its end, while comedy simply makes us laugh, and what it is that made us laugh is easily forgotten. Grief, together with love, its obverse, acts with a force unlike any other, and again like love, leaves upon us an imprint that only death can erase. If I were to live to be a thousand, I am sure that I would remember just as clearly Maureen's face as she took her last breath as I remember her now when I first glimpsed her bewitching beauty, and when I found her again as I saw her through a pane of frosted glass. This is the grief, but also no less the glory of love. Maureen, you were, are and will be until I die, my Spiritus Sanctus.

> I so miss you in the car seat next to mine Your nagging when I drop some crumbs Being there when I come home
> The meals you cook for me Your sneezing fits Shopping with you at Lidl
> Your body next to mine in bed In your armchair next to

mine Arguing about this and that Your crooked teeth and tiny feet Feeding the cats
The foxes
And the hedgehogs Potting your plants Doing your crossword Your rumbling tummy Loving you
You loving me Kissing you You kissing me Caressing you
You caressing me
But most of all Maureen I miss you.

20 April 2017

These images help to tell the story of the life of Maureen, from her childhood to the last seventeen years we spent together. They are also a tribute to her beauty, which for me endured undiminished with the passing of the seasons.

My thanks to Colliers Photo Imaging of Swansea, for their superb reproductions.

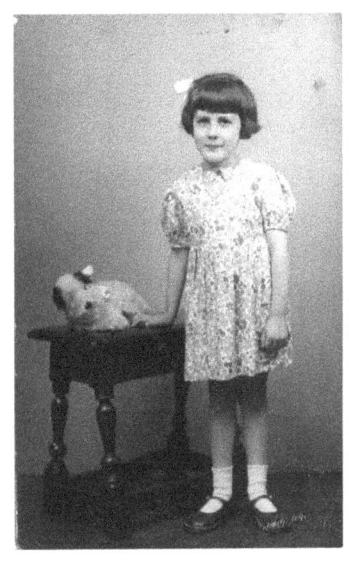

Back home from Buckingham

Schooldays

School excursion to the Swiss Alps

The budding beauty

And those legs

The bridesmaid I wanted to marry

Maureen as I first saw her

Father Freddie, daughter Andrea and mother Alice

Together again, Tenby, 2000

By the Loire, 2000

Her wartime home
in Buckingham,
2000

Coffee on the
Champs Elysees,
2000

Bruges, 2000

Aix-les-Bains, 2003

Besieged by pigeons, Venice

Florence, 2003

At her cousin John's wedding, 2010

Back in the Alps… with me

Venice

Marseilles

What's going on there?

Age cannot wither her

'nor custom stale her infinite variety

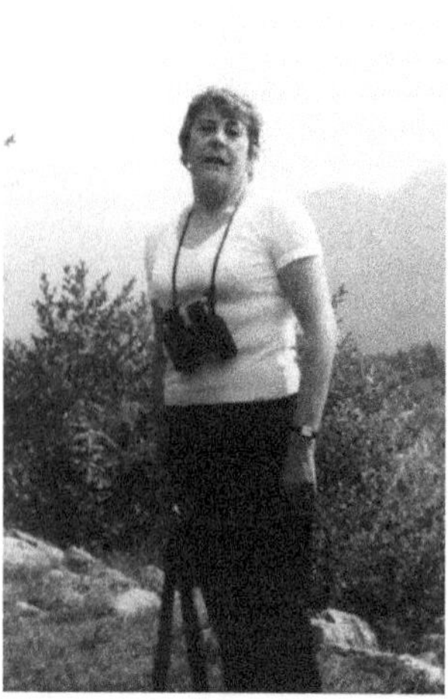

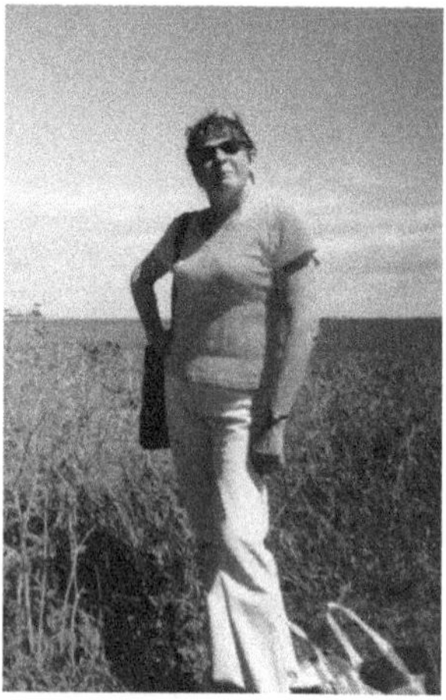

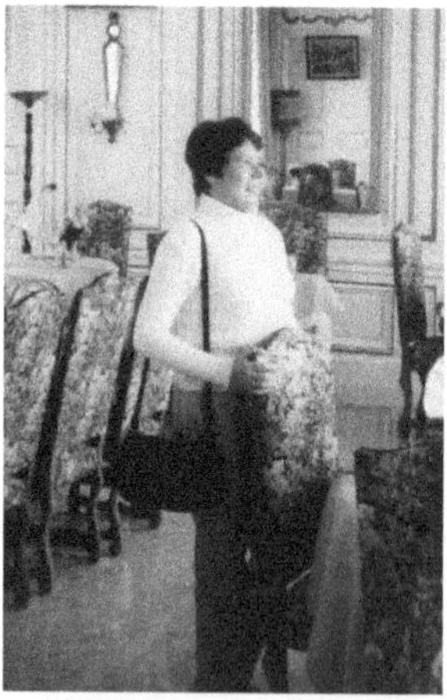

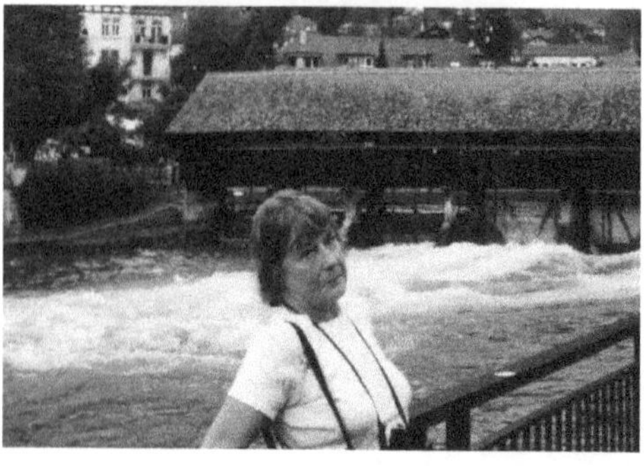

Blowpipe: left, my son Andrew, right, Patrick Mosely

Gyratory System: Centre, Andrew Blick, right, James Weaver

Horsepower: far left, my confessor Ian Bishop

The Medieval Baebes: far right, my daughter Katharine

Blowpipe: the Blicks at Ronnie Scotts, 1999

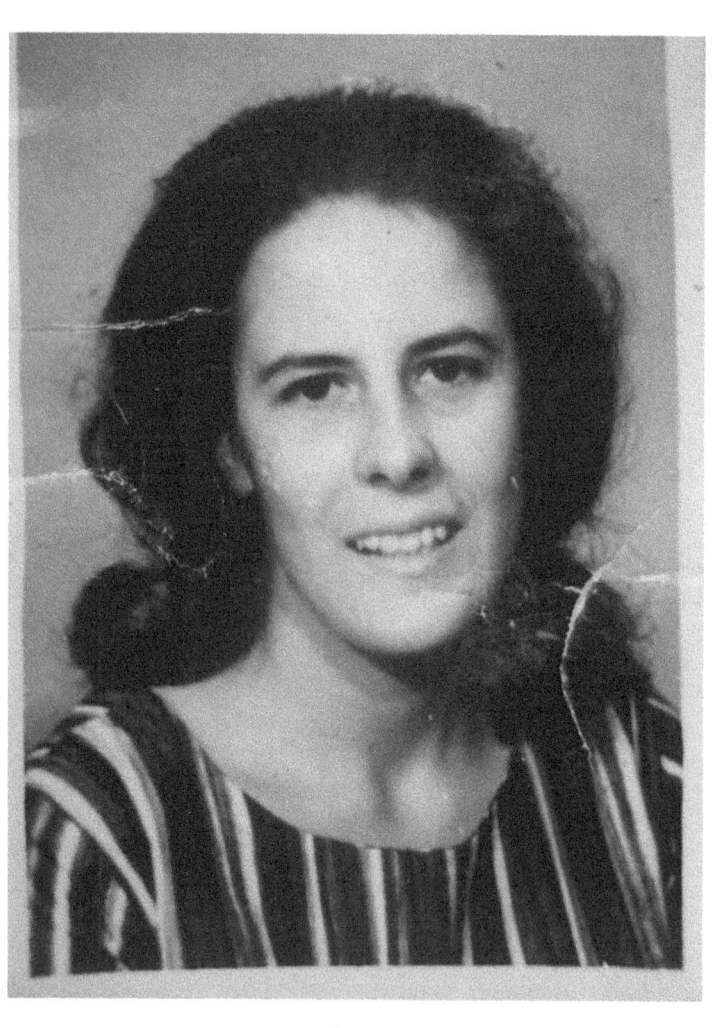

Goodbye my beauty

I Will Remember

Lake Thun...our last resting place